THE HEART OF AMERICAN POETRY

Also by Edward Hirsch

POETRY
Stranger by Night (2020)
Gabriel: A Poem (2014)
The Living Fire: New and Selected Poems (2010)
Special Orders (2008)
Lay Back the Darkness (2003)
On Love (1998)
Earthly Measures (1994)
The Night Parade (1989)
Wild Gratitude (1986)
For the Sleepwalkers (1981)

PROSE
100 Poems to Break Your Heart (2021)
A Poet's Glossary (2014)
Poet's Choice (2006)
The Demon and the Angel: Searching for the Source of Artistic Inspiration (2002)
Responsive Reading (1999)
How to Read a Poem and Fall in Love with Poetry (1999)

EDITOR
The Best American Poetry 2016 (2016), with David Lehman
The Making of a Sonnet: A Norton Anthology (2008), with Eavan Boland
To a Nightingale: Poems from Sappho to Borges (2007)
Theodore Roethke: Selected Poems (2005)
A William Maxwell Portrait: Memories and Appreciations (2004), with Charles Baxter and Michael Collier
Transforming Vision: Writers on Art (1994)

THE HEART OF
AMERICAN
POETRY
Edward Hirsch

A LIBRARY OF AMERICA
Special Publication

The Heart of American Poetry by Edward Hirsch
Introduction and volume compilation and previously unpublished material
copyright © 2022 by Edward Hirsch. All rights reserved.

Published in the United States by Library of America.
Visit our website at www.loa.org.

Book design and composition by Gopa & Ted2, Inc.

Distributed to the trade in the United States by Penguin Random House Inc.
and in Canada by Penguin Random House Canada Ltd.

Library of Congress Control Number: 2021946932
ISBN 978–1–59853–726–0

1 3 5 7 9 10 8 6 4 2

Printed in the United States of America

The Heart of American Poetry
is published with support from

ALAN M. KLEIN

and other friends of Library of America

CONTENTS

INTRODUCTION: THE EDUCATION OF A POET

JUNE 1970. I had just started working extra-board as a brakeman for the railroad, which meant that they could call me anytime, for any one of three shifts, and send me to one of six Chicago yards. I had finished my sophomore year in college, and I had set my sights on becoming a poet, much to the dismay of my family, and I needed something to read that would carry me through the summer, something that would catch me up on American poetry, and propel me forward. I didn't know much about our national literature, though I had taken heart from Saul Bellow's breakthrough novel, *The Adventures of Augie March*, which begins: "I am an American, Chicago born—Chicago, that somber city—and go at things as I have taught myself, free-style, and will make the record in my own way." I knew that I had to make my own entrance—"first to knock, first admitted," as Bellow put it, slyly echoing Matthew 7:7–8 (Ask, Seek, Knock)—but I was also seeking encouragement, something that would help me to envisage a life. I was on a quest. We invent ourselves as American writers—it's not a clerisy we're born into—and we each have to figure out how to create a path to our work.

I was roaming through a bookstore in a local mall trying to find something, anything, that would help me out and further my education—it was one of those suburban chain bookstores that don't carry many books—and that's how I stumbled on Hayden Carruth's paperback anthology of modern American poetry, *The Voice That Is Great Within Us*. It was the title that stunned me, and the epigraph, from Wallace Stevens's poem "Evening Without Angels," two lines that have stayed with me for fifty years:

> Where the voice that is in us makes a true response,
> Where the voice that is great within us rises up

I loved the confidence in these lines, the repetitive lilt and litany, almost like a chant, and all through that summer, as I rode on the engine from one gritty railyard to another, coupling and uncoupling cars, scrambling up and down the ladder on the side of moving trains, gazing out on the city as if it belonged to me, these lines kept coming back and inspiriting me with the sound of the voice that is great within us. That voice cannot be contained or repressed. Stevens suggests that it belongs to all of us, that we all have access to it, that it is a divinity that lives within ourselves. That summer I threw myself into Carruth's anthology—I treated it more as a rite of passage than a gathering of poems—and it enjoined me to the larger project of our poetry, the greater music.

This is a personal book about American poetry, but I hope it is more than a personal selection. I have chosen forty poems from our extensive archive and songbook that have been meaningful to me, part of my affective life, my critical consideration, but I have also tried to be cognizant of the changing playbook in American poetry, which is not fixed but fluctuating, ever in flow, and to pay attention to the wider consideration, the appreciable reach of our literature. This is a book of encounters and realizations. It is not meant to be definitive. Some pieces reexamine poems at the heart of the modern canon ("The Love Song of J. Alfred Prufrock," "Sunday Morning"), but others stretch further and open the gallery, such as Robert Johnson's "Cross Road Blues," and the Puerto Rican *independentista* Julia de Burgos's goodbye lyric, "Farewell in Welfare Island." The essays are organized chronologically, by the birth year of the poets. They can be sampled and read independently—each one stands alone—but the book is conceived as a whole. I have tried to respond to the sweep of American subjects, the eccentric encounter and the historical placement, the love poem and the anti–love poem, the song of doomed marriage, the environmental corrective, the rural work song and the urban ode, the surprised elegy and the ancestral lament, the poem of individuation and dawning self-consciousness, and the poem of plurality, political intervention, common suffering, the confessional lyric, and what Gertrude Stein calls "everybody's autobiography."

I was deeply absorbed in this book during the quarantine of 2020, and I know it is weighted by the experience of writing at a time when an unsuspected virus had virtually shut down the entire world—an unprecedented strangeness. I was safely ensconced, but the worry was everywhere, the anxiety, the mounting deaths. Another virus also rematerialized—the virus of racism, individual and institutional, a sickness unleashed. I am conscious, too, of writing at a time when a sustained authoritarian threat to democracy is bedeviling American life. This constellation of three intertwined viruses, three powerful threats to the republic, led me to reappraise the place of poetry in our culture, the work that it does, and how poetry contributes to the American experiment, what it means to American experience and life.

I wrote this book without benefit of my poetry library, which was sequestered in a high-rise building in New York City, and that stirred me, perhaps it even forced me, to think more thoroughly for myself. I was on my own, but I had these poems to companion and elate me. I have recurred often to memory, my first reading of a poem, my initial understanding of a poet, and my recalibrations over time. *The Heart of American Poetry* is in this way a partial autobiography, a story of education and induction, the history of my enthrallments and understandings, the schooling of my own heart. As a young poet, I was open to instruction, an ephebe and pilgrim eager to be tutored by poems and taught by books, which lessoned me in ways that my teachers often did not. I suppose I was purposing myself for the fuller immersion, the deeper initiation. "For poems are not, as people think, simply emotions (one has emotions early enough)—they are experiences," Rainer Maria Rilke declared, and I have tried to attend to the nature of these experiences in literature and life. I have endeavored to place them as precisely as possible. This has also led me to consider how each poet ties into their time period, and ours, the bulkier tapestry, the weave of American poetry itself. I have also tried to underscore the way that our national poetry participates in an international interchange with other poetries, other languages. There may be self-enclosed or island poetries, but ours is not one of them.

American poetry is both very old and very new. It stretches back tens of thousands of years to the oral songs and stories of Native nations, Indigenous peoples, aboriginal tribal cultures. And it is as up-to-date as protest poems posted on social media one hasty character at a time. There is no doubt that a central strand of our poetry traces to Puritanism and the Puritan code, the import of classical and English metaphysical forms applied to the New World. The New England Puritan poetic was a newfangled combination of theology and farming, a struggle not to get lost in the wilderness, hymns in small churches and meetinghouses, Virgilian songs roaming over rough landscapes. Puritan poetry is pious—of course, it is *puritanical*—but it also has an unexpected oddity, surrealistic moments like this one in Edward Taylor's *Preparatory Meditations*:

> Should Gold Wed Dung, should Stars Wooe Lobster Claws,
> It would no wonder, like this Wonder, cause.

To me, this rhyming couplet sounds like something that the Comte de Lautréamont might have written if he were guiding a small parsonage from a frontier outpost in western Massachusetts, and it suggests that Puritan religious poetry is also punning and deceptive, and secretly literary. Colonial poetry is not quite so disapproving as it might seem—the first poet featured in this book is a woman, Anne Bradstreet—and it mixes with other strains in our culture of religious difference.

White European slavers did not give credence to the fact that they would be changing American history and life when they treated African people as chattel and transported them to the New World, but that's precisely what happened, and a new people, now African Americans, gave rise to a new syncretic culture and poetry, too. That's why three bedrocks of our poetry are Indigenous chants and stories, white Protestant hymns, and African American field calls and songs—field hollers, ring shouts, work songs, and arhoolies, all of which establish a call-and-response pattern that later would be transformed into spirituals and blues. Ralph Waldo Emerson keyed American literature to what he called "the optative mood" ("The Transcendentalist," 1842), but that hopefulness had always already been shadowed by a deeper protest and lament, something older and darker, a legacy of trauma, a steeper and more sorrowful song.

I am not writing a history of American poetry, but I've tried to remain conscious of our diversiform ancestry and heritage. As an American poet and critic, I tend to be on the upbeat, but it's important to remember that we've always had domestic torture—we just carried it out under the disguise of an encompassing doctrine, like Manifest Destiny, which justified a murderous agenda and nationalist landgrab. It's part of our historical DNA, our barbarous racist history, our legacies of genocide and slavery. That consciousness also gives American poetry a conscience. I've tried to keep this historical backdrop in mind as I concentrate on the relatively recent poetry of the

New World, a refreshing new possibility in world literature, the poetry of democracy. Walt Whitman called it "Democratic Vistas." Intrinsic to this poetry, these vistas, are a premise and a promise of freedom and equality. The abiding ideal of the republic—"We hold these truths to be self-evident, that all men are created equal, that they are endowed by their Creator with certain unalienable Rights, that among these are Life, Liberty and the pursuit of Happiness"—keeps resurfacing in our poetry, our poetries, because we keep letting ourselves down. American poetry springs forward, keeping account, reminding us of our core values and commitments—that underlying promise, that true destiny.

We are by definition a plurality, one and many, a culture of individualism—"*Individualism* is a novel expression to which a novel idea has given birth," Alexis de Tocqueville explained in *Democracy in America* (1840)—that is also a collective, a complicated combine, a Commons. We are ever balancing an Emersonian ideal of self-reliance with a binding sense of the equality of souls. Many of the poets I consider in this book are struggling with identity, how and where and with whom they fit in. They devise themselves and create their own versions of a tradition. There is a way to honor difference while recognizing the expanse. If "Life is an ecstasy," as Emerson posits in *The Conduct of Life* (1860), then it should be an ecstasy for all.

There is a conversation in American poetry that is also a colloquial about American life. Each individual poet, wittingly or unwittingly, consciously or unconsciously, contributes to this exchange and discussion. The second poet I take up is Phillis Wheatley, who was enslaved as a small girl and takes her place with Lucy Terry and Jupiter Hammon as the first African American poets of record. This young woman, who wrote like Alexander Pope, adds a crucial early voice to the chorus. Is there another literature in which it would be possible to follow a poet like Phillis Wheatley with one like Henry Wadsworth Longfellow, who was the most popular American poet in the nineteenth century, perhaps rivaled only by Alfred, Lord Tennyson in world literature? My reading of Longfellow focuses on his visit to a Jewish cemetery in Rhode Island, which brings Jewish people into the historical equation and adds a Hebraic element to our poetry. When Emma Lazarus responded to Longfellow's poem, she also changed the dynamic and spoke from within a culture rather than from outside it. This sets the pattern of the American canon. It took us a long time to move from Longfellow's entirely fictitious

"Song of Hiawatha" (1855) to the Native nations songs and legends of the actual Ayenwathaaa, the cofounder of the Iroquois Confederacy.

After I returned for my junior year of college, I decided to take a deeper dive into the river of American poetry, to get a stronger sense of the current, and that's when I discovered F. O. Matthiessen's revelatory study, *American Renaissance* (1941), which clued me to the fact that in one five-year span between 1850 and 1855, five writers, four of whom considered themselves poets—Ralph Waldo Emerson, Henry David Thoreau, Nathaniel Hawthorne, Herman Melville, and Walt Whitman—created the foundation stones for an unprecedented American literature. It started with Emerson. When I was in high school, I had picked up the mistaken idea that Emerson was some sort of plaster sage, an avatar that I could dismiss in the ignorance of youth, but Matthiessen pointed me to a writer whose passionate nature has consistently been underestimated. "I never was on a coach that went fast enough for me," Emerson once confessed, and his wild, nervy, nearly out-of-control journals and essays are touchstones of mine. Always he argued against the conformity of the sect. "But do your thing, and I shall know you," he asserted. "Do your work, and you shall reinforce yourself." Emerson's weird fantasy of the Adamic is one of the clues to his American dream life:

> I dreamed that I floated at will in the great Ether, and I saw this world floating also not far off, but diminished to the size of an apple. Then an angel took it in his hand & brought it to me and said, "This must thou eat." And I ate the world.

George Santayana condescended to Emerson as a "champion of cheerfulness," though Emerson himself sometimes declined his own positivity: "I like the sayers of No better than the sayers of Yes," he confided to his journals. But from the podium Emerson made a point of stimulating an American originality. In his first book, *Nature* (1836), he asked: "Why should not we also enjoy an original relation to the universe? Why should not we have a poetry and philosophy of insight and not of tradition, and a religion by revelation to us, and not the history of theirs?" I'm struck by how often Emerson, someone who always praises the self-reliant self, resorts to the word *we*, the pull of the polis, *us*: *our* poetry and philosophy, *our* revelation. Emerson's inclination to the affirmative is well-balanced by Melville's counterexample

("Nay, I do not oscillate in Emerson's rainbow," he declared), his sustained way of confronting evil, his disappointment in our country to live up to its Edenic promise. The Civil War turned Melville from prose to poetry—it enabled him to become the poet he was meant to become—and his Civil War disenchantments are a crucial part of the chronicle.

There is a dialogue that is carried on within American poetry itself. This back-and-forth is part of a history of statement and counterstatement, a process of addition and revision, a reclamation central to the life of our poetry. It is a family quarrel, or argument, that sometimes gets extremely heated, voices rising, ill-tempered relatives storming off in different directions. At times, it seems closer to warring literary factions—manifestos drawn up like charters, anthologies launched—and the battle gets nasty, blood spilled on the page. I have not shied away from describing the conflicts and considering the stakes—this, too, is part of the overall pattern of our poetry, our culture—but I have tried to approach them with passionate engagement and intellectual agnosticism. To me, the questions of the most significant import are defined on two axes—one horizontal (the nature of democracy and society), the other vertical (the nature of the self, the soul, and God). I am attentive to the debate about language, form, and spiritual transport—what register to use, what vehicle to ride—and find these questions especially engrossing when they are blooded by experience and dramatized in poems.

Some of our poets work by stealth while others knock down walls and storm into the open. In American poetry, we make way for the singular refusal and revision, the idiosyncratic viewpoint, the unexpected revelation. Emily Dickinson placed herself at the center of our poetry by radically undermining the communal values of the Protestant hymn and repurposing it to a poetry of individual salvation. She reconfigures a devotional language and personalizes the sacred: "Life is a spell so exquisite that everything conspires to break it." Walt Whitman took the religious cadences of the King James Version of the Hebrew Bible—the model for English prose—and redeployed them for a democratic aesthetic. I am mindful of these two lines that open "One's-Self I Sing":

> One's-Self I sing, a simple separate person,
> Yet utter the word Democratic, the word En-Masse.

As is often the case with Whitman, the linguistic of this doctrinaire couplet is stranger than it might initially appear. For example, when you say the first line aloud, it sizzles with insistence, like a tongue twister, "One's-self I sing, a simple separate person." The line divides neatly in half. Whitman begins by emphasizing each of the first four one-syllable words, objectifying and dividing himself, "*One's-Self I sing*," even as he asserts that he is a simple, separated individual, though he immediately qualifies this point and pivots on the word *Yet*. He then foregrounds this isolate self as a speaker, someone who doesn't just sing but *utters* two words in particular, both of which he derives from French: "the word *Democratic*" (*démocratique*), "the word *En-Masse*" (literally, "in a mass"). He posits this adjective and this adverb without a supporting noun or verb so that they stand alone, together: *Democratic, En-Masse*. Here, the singular person joins himself to the mass through language, and the Whitmanian ideal, a Song of Myself, seeks to become a Song of Ourselves.

Whitman articulates an American dream that is ever in peril. He felt endangered himself, and a dark cloud overhangs some of his poems, like "Out of the Cradle Endlessly Rocking," which is the lyric that I treat in this book. The downward depressive side of poets, especially our founding figures, is often downplayed or even suppressed in our official narratives. Their idiosyncrasies are ironed out. Much has been made of our national bard's native idealism, his democratic ethos and optimistic faith in our country. He was like a cannon whose fuse was lit by Emerson's match of American individualism. Whitman wanted to sing the republic—"The United States themselves are essentially the greatest poem," he proclaimed in the preface to the 1855 edition of *Leaves of Grass*—but his cosmos was also troubled by something in his psyche, some inner feeling of abandonment and loss. Sometimes he worked hard to override that feeling, other times he reveled in it, but he was always driven by involuted internal forces. There is no doubt that "Walt Whitman" was the hero of his own poems, but I nonetheless feel that his bravado was something of a mask, a fabulous creation of persona. He was a tenderhearted solitary who posed as one of the roughs.

The need to treat Walt Whitman or Ralph Waldo Emerson or Robert Frost, for that matter, as overly optimistic poets speaks to our desire to see America as a shining example of democracy when, in fact, it has often fallen—and continues to fall—woefully short of the ideals that we profess to believe in. When Whitman himself sticks to the affirmative, other poets also step in to respond. He sings of the American adventure, the freedom of going wherever he likes, "Song of the Open Road" ("Afoot and light-hearted I take to the open road"), but there's an ideology hidden in his freewheeling push: westward expansion. That's why later poets started associating him with a vehicle driving heedlessly west. Writing from California in the early 1960s, Louis Simpson wryly declared, "The Open Road goes to the used-car lot" ("Walt Whitman at Bear Mountain"), and titled a book *At the End of the Open Road* (1964).

In *Studies in Classic American Literature* (1923), D. H. Lawrence caustically exposed the underlying Whitmanian premise:

> ONE DIRECTION! toots Walt in the car, whizzing along it.
>
> Whereas there are myriads of ways in the dark, not to mention trackless wildernesses. As anyone will know who cares to come off the road, even the Open Road.
>
> ONE DIRECTION! whoops America, and sets off also in an automobile.
>
> ALLNESS! shrieks Walt at a cross-road, going whizz over an unwary Red Indian.
>
> ONE IDENTITY! chants democratic En Masse, pelting behind in motorcars, oblivious of the corpses under the wheels.

Lawrence was more responsive to the creative originality of American literature than other English poets; in fact, he understood it better than many of the American moderns, like T. S. Eliot and Ezra Pound, but he was historically conscientious enough to unearth the forgotten body count, "the corpses under the wheels."

Where is the Whitmanian experience found in American life? Whitman moved easily among the multiplicity, listened hard to the plural American song—he was present to the moment—and presented what he heard. Randall Jarrell called him "the poet of parallel present participles." His verse is free. No one else had ever stood at street level and listened to commoners like this before:

I Hear America Singing

I hear America singing, the varied carols I hear,
Those of mechanics, each one singing his as it should be blithe
    and strong,
The carpenter singing his as he measures his plank or beam,
The mason singing his as he makes ready for work, or leaves off work,
The boatman singing what belongs to him in his boat, the deckhand
    singing on the steamboat deck,
The shoemaker singing as he sits on his bench, the hatter singing
    as he stands,
The wood-cutter's song, the ploughboy's on his way in the morning,
    or at noon intermission or at sundown,
The delicious singing of the mother, or of the young wife at work,
    or of the girl sewing or washing,
Each singing what belongs to him or her and to none else,
The day what belongs to the day—at night the party of young fellows,
    robust, friendly,
Singing with open mouths their strong melodious songs.

There is a strong working-class ethic that operates in this catalogue of indi-
vidual singing and songsters, a sort of anthemic masculine work song, which
does finally remember to include women, too, laborers of all kinds, the indi-
vidual who stands for the whole. The people are not named but identified by
their jobs, each one contributing to a new type of chorus coming together
in a healthy democratic harmonic: "America Singing."

But does this praise poem of the industrious variety, the robust working-
class melody, also incorporate Black people, who after slavery continued to
suffer from segregation and exclusion? Where is the nation that Whitman
promised? Langston Hughes felt strongly that Whitman's poem needed a
twentieth-century update, and as a young poet, down and out in Genoa,
Italy, he penned a flamboyant rejoinder, which he called "I, Too" and pub-
lished in his first book, *The Weary Blues* (1926):

I, Too

I, too, sing America.

I am the darker brother.
They send me to eat in the kitchen
When company comes,
But I laugh,
And eat well,
And grow strong.

Tomorrow,
I'll be at the table
When company comes.
Nobody'll dare
Say to me,
"Eat in the kitchen,"
Then.

Besides,
They'll see how beautiful I am
And be ashamed—

I, too, am America.

Hughes clips the Whitmanian long line and progresses from song to being, from "I, too, *sing* America" to "I, too, *am* America." He puns the word *too* (*two*) and refuses secondary or subservient status. He also nods to W.E.B. Du Bois, who had observed in *The Souls of Black Folk* (1903) that African Americans always existed in two places or realities at once:

One ever feels his two-ness,—an American, a Negro; two souls, two thoughts, two unreconciled strivings; two warring ideals in one dark body, whose dogged strength alone keeps it from being torn asunder.

As a young poet, Hughes was highly alert to what Du Bois termed the "double consciousness" of African Americans and inscribed it into his early lyrics.

At the beginning of "I, Too," Hughes identifies himself as "the darker brother," who is sent to eat in the kitchen. But he laughs off the insult, getting stronger, gathering his resources, and promises that soon he will come out of that kitchen, that quarantine, and clear a space for himself at the table. Company is coming to the house, too, non-family members, people from other places who will understand the present-day reality. He anticipates the later slogan "Black is beautiful." And he recognizes that white America will someday be ashamed of its conduct. The house is America, and everyone should be welcomed in as equals. I hear the reverberations of Abraham Lincoln's 1858 speech against a country that is furiously split between slavery and freedom: "A house divided against itself cannot stand." That's why I would say that Whitman's song about America singing inspires and even necessitates Hughes's confident and insistent response. This revisionary argument for the larger inclusion circulates in the bloodstream of American poetry. It is part of the undertaking of American culture. The line "I, too, am America" has become so representative that it is now engraved in large letters on the wall of the National Museum of African American History and Culture on the National Mall in Washington, D.C.

Emma Lazarus's patriotic poem for the pedestal of the Statue of Liberty, "The New Colossus," has an implicit antagonist—the old Colossus, of Rhodes, a European colossal of imperial glory and power. Lazarus's poem declares itself on the side of Lady Liberty, a welcoming female presence, and agitates for immigrants flooding into the United States to escape oppression abroad. She sings of opening the border, and thereby extends the democratic imperative and claim, the revolutionary purpose: "'Give me your tired, your poor, / Your huddled masses yearning to breathe free.'" But there are always reactionary nativists gathering on the other side. Not everyone wants to extend democracy. When I was twenty-five, I read a book by Robert Penn Warren called *Democracy & Poetry*, and one of the things he observed has stayed with me through the years:

> In other words, our poetry, in fulfilling its function of bringing us face to face with our nature and our fate, has told us, directly or indirectly, consciously or unconsciously, that we are driving toward the destruction of the very assumption on which our nation is presumably founded.

Warren is explaining the diagnostic side of our poetry, the scathing social cri-
tique of our condition that inheres in different ways in such epochal poems
as T. S. Eliot's *The Waste Land* and Robert Hayden's "Middle Passage" and
Allen Ginsberg's "America" and Adrienne Rich's "An Atlas of the Difficult
World," which broods over the difficulty of loving our country in a time
of unjust war. I hear it, too, in Lou Reed's sardonically frank song "Dirty
Blvd.," about the hard streets of New York in the 1970s and '80s, the treat-
ment of immigrants as second-class citizens, and the yawning gap between
rich and poor. Reed rhythmically talks and sings through a three-chord pro-
gression—it's the spoken-word poetry of glam rock—and there's an electric
shock in his bitter revision of the most exemplary lines in American culture:

> Give me your hungry, your tired, your poor, I'll piss on 'em
> That's what the Statue of Bigotry says
> Your poor huddled masses—let's club 'em to death
> And get it over with and just dump 'em on the boulevard

Dion DiMucci comes in with backup vocals to sing a chorus that riffs off
the sentence "I want to fly, fly away" and gives a gospel dimension and back-
drop to the lyric. Reed was mining his own experience of a squalid urban
street, which he treated as a microcosm of America, and as a rock-and-roll
songster he filtered it through the lens of a late nineteenth-century poem
dedicated to the American ideal. He was thus participating in a conversa-
tion about the meaning of the American dream. Like his mentor Delmore
Schwartz, who captioned a phrase by W. B. Yeats for his most enduring
achievement, *In Dreams Begin Responsibilities*, Reed believed in the literary
trust, the personal obligation.

I admire the open interchange in American poetry, the fervency of con-
sideration and reconsideration, the frightening downward pull of Eliot's
The Waste Land and Pound's "Hugh Selwyn Mauberley" and the difficult
upward swing of William Carlos Williams's *Spring and All* and Hart Crane's
The Bridge and Marianne Moore's "The Steeple-Jack." American poetry is an
adventurous hybrid. Eliot could not have anticipated that a late twentieth-
century Jewish American poet named C. K. Williams would someday recite
The Waste Land in a tearing whisper from the window of a *pensione* in Flor-
ence, Italy, and thereby find his own voice ("My Mother's Lips"). Pound

disapproved of how Amy Lowell colonized Imagism, and he could not have suspected that she would turn the Imagist method, which was partially borrowed from his concept of Chinese poetry, into passionate poems of same-sex love that have a statuesque beauty ("Two Speak Together"). So, too, Pound and Eliot created a modernist collage method that was forcefully redesigned in Hayden's "Middle Passage" and Hughes's *Montage of a Dream Deferred.* Eliot's grand idea of spiritual death in "The Hollow Men" is followed by Theodore Roethke's small-scale struggle for earthly regeneration and spiritual rebirth in his Greenhouse poems, principally "Cuttings" and "Cuttings (*later*)." The mystical grandeur of Eliot's *Four Quartets* is relocated in Roethke's "North American Sequence."

The heart-to-heart and head-to-head in American poetry is filled with adjustments and correctives. In the 1920s, a talented and diverse group of Black writers engineered an awakening in consciousness, an exciting urban movement centered in New York, the Harlem Renaissance, which changed American literature, and in the 1930s Sterling A. Brown reminded everybody of the rural backdrop to this movement, the starting point of the Great Migration, the forms of southern Black life. He also reclaimed the Black vernacular as a language of uncommon dignity. I take up the colloquy about this vernacular in my essay on Brown's "Southern Road." Writers like Hughes and Brown heard the continuity and recognized the difference between the oral and written records. They inscribed it.

I have tried to pinpoint in this volume some of the ways that our poetry moves fluently between speech and song, the casual comment and the determined prophecy; it rises almost imperceptibly from the sometimes expressive, sometimes blighted colloquial to something loftier, a higher rhetoric—"Should Gold Wed Dung"—and this unheeded eloquence is part of the unsung wonderment of our poetry. I am trying to tune it here, to trace its range so that you hear the undersong in the inscription, which surfaces in unlikely and decidedly "unpoetic" places, like the waiting room of a dentist's office in Worcester, Massachusetts (Elizabeth Bishop), or a high school football stadium in Martins Ferry, Ohio (James Wright), or a jail cell in Washington, D.C. (Muriel Rukeyser), or an overheated dry cleaners in Detroit, Michigan (Philip Levine). I hear a distinctly American vocality in the ruptured and reinvented forms, the broken ballad (Gwendolyn Brooks) and the devastated nursery rhyme (Sylvia Plath), the jazz elegiac (Frank O'Hara,

Michael S. Harper) and the "one-size-fits-all" confessional (John Ashbery), the slippery trickster tale (Joy Harjo) and the lament of lost lineage (Garrett Hongo), the reimagined Holocaust lyric (Anthony Hecht) and the lyric of survival (Lucille Clifton), the enduring dream of freedom (Robert Hayden). I take pride in the elasticity of American poems, the complex of our registers, and I return to them with a gratifying sense of enlargement and legacy.

It may sound strange to say so, but I have found it heartening to write this book about American poetry at a disheartening time in our republic, a time of broken promises. These poems hold us to a standard and remind us of the sacredness of the individual life, the single testamentary. I believe they offer us a healthy antidote, or perhaps forty fiery antidotes, to the moment of our malaise. We have a Library *of* America and a library *in* America, a documentary of achievement. American poetry is one of the underutilized resources of American culture, and these lyrics are an incitement to our better selves, a gift to the republic. Our poets have not abandoned their posts. We are still here, roaming the country, "Where the voice that is in us makes a true response, / Where the voice that is great within us rises up."

THE HEART OF AMERICAN POETRY

ANNE BRADSTREET (1612–1672)

The Author to Her Book

Thou ill-formed offspring of my feeble brain,
Who after birth didst by my side remain,
Till snatched from thence by friends, less wise than true,
Who thee abroad, exposed to public view,
Made thee in rags, halting to th' press to trudge,
Where errors were not lessened (all may judge).
At thy return my blushing was not small,
My rambling brat (in print) should mother call,
I cast thee by as one unfit for light,
Thy visage was so irksome in my sight;
Yet being mine own, at length affection would
Thy blemishes amend, if so I could:
I washed thy face, but more defects I saw,
And rubbing off a spot still made a flaw.
I stretched thy joints to make thee even feet,
Yet still thou run'st more hobbling than is meet;
In better dress to trim thee was my mind,
But nought save homespun cloth i' th' house I find.
In this array 'mongst vulgars may'st thou roam.
In critic's hands beware thou dost not come,
And take thy way where yet thou art not known;
If for thy father asked, say thou hadst none;
And for thy mother, she alas is poor,
Which caused her thus to send thee out of door.

Composed c. 1666

I GREATLY ADMIRE John Berryman's long poem "Homage to Mistress Bradstreet" (1956). It's a bravura performance, the first time Berryman figured out how to mix and match dictions, fusing high and low, gracefully veering from his own mid-twentieth-century vernacular to a seventeenth-century poetic diction, and turning back again. He invented an eight-line stanza, modelled on W. B. Yeats's ottava rima, that is remarkably flexible, sometimes jittery, sometimes dignified, and used it to dramatize Anne Bradstreet's life story. In a daring high-wire act that stretches across fifty-seven stanzas, he intermingles viewpoints and converses with her across the centuries.

It wasn't until I began teaching the poem in my late twenties that I realized just how strange it is from a psychological point of view. There is something off-kilter in Berryman's insatiable need to seduce Bradstreet, a high-minded Puritan woman happily married to Simon Bradstreet, with whom she had eight children. Berryman was living in Princeton and having an affair at the time, which he chronicled in *Sonnets to Chris* (written 1947, published 1966), and he projected his own adulterous experience onto the early American poet. I suppose this dubious sexual fantasy could be viewed most charitably as a complicated episode in Berryman's own psychobiography, which fastens on Bradstreet as the first American poet, a maternal figure.

Berryman's poem helped bring Anne Bradstreet into the conversation about American poetry, but what I find inexcusable is how dismissive he is about her work, how badly he underestimates her achievement. He relied too heavily on the judgments of his principal source, Helen Campbell's biography, *Anne Bradstreet and Her Time* (1891), and treated her exclusively as the writer of quaternions ("all this bald / abstract didactic rime I read appalled")—her four long poems on the four elements, humors, ages of man, and seasons, which are the primary work of her apprenticeship—and ignored the dynamic personal poems of her maturity. He was on the cusp of a dramatic confessional change in his own work ("I am a man of griefs & fits / trying to be my friend") and so, of all poets, he should have been able to recognize the difference in Bradstreet's practice between her well-proportioned public poems, which are wonderfully bookish but also stiff and conventional, and her private ones, which are surprising, intimate, and formally various. Bradstreet's breakthrough verse may not have had the literary qualities Berryman was seeking ("mistress neither of fiery nor velvet verse"), but it was cunning and well crafted, highly self-aware, even self-divided, biting, anxious, humorous, and insightful. It is sometimes grievous, sometimes exuberant, and has a shrewd, deceptive, sparkling wit.

Anne Bradstreet wasn't born to be an American poet—she turned herself into one. She would have been a different sort of writer, a coterie English poet, if her family had never crossed the Atlantic. Her sensibility was formed in England, where she was born in 1612. Her mother, Dorothy Yorke, was, in Hannah Winthrop's description, "a gentlewoman of good estate and good extraction"; her father, Thomas Dudley, was a rigid Nonconformist, or Dissenter, which meant that as an English Protestant he did not conform to the doctrines of the Church of England. He was a literal-minded and religiously intolerant Puritan thinker, but he was also a reader—Cotton Mather called him a "devourer of books"—and, as the estate manager for the Earl of Lincoln, he oversaw his daughter's classical education in geography, history, science, literature, and, principally, religion. The family often compared the translation of passages in the Geneva and King James versions of the Bible.

In the Earl's substantial library, Anne Dudley, who was a sickly child, read the Greek and Latin classics, and the English poets who would mean the most to her: Edmund Spenser, Sir Philip Sidney, and Francis Quarles. She called her father "a magazine of history," and they both loved Sir Walter Raleigh's *The History of the World, in Five Books* (1614). The Puritans were vehemently opposed to the theater, but passages in her work suggest that she knew Shakespeare's poems and plays. She schooled herself on Joshua Sylvester's translation of Guillaume de Salluste Du Bartas's *Divine Weekes and Workes* (1605). Berryman considered her love of Du Bartas "unfortunate," and the French poet's Protestant epic isn't read much anymore, but he was also John Milton's earliest literary model, a key source for *Paradise Lost*, and Bradstreet learned from him the courtier's stance. Here is stanza two from her poem "The Prologue":

> But when my wond'ring eyes and envious heart
> Great Bartas' sugared lines do but read o'er,
> Fool I do grudge the Muses did not part
> 'Twixt him and me that overfluent store;

A Bartas can do what a Bartas will,
But simple I according to my skill.

Anne Bradstreet had a self-concealing modesty, which she employed as a way of masking her enormous literary ambition. Her early poems are obviously studious, even ponderous, but they are also filled with wide-ranging observations and references. Her scriptural formalities can feel prescriptive, but she was fevered with inner turmoil, spiritual doubt. She was soulfully troubled. On her deathbed, she left an extraordinary retrospective letter to her children, which begins: "This book by any yet unread, / I leave for you when I am dead, / That being gone, here you may find / What was your living mother's mind." Giving vivid texture to her experience, Bradstreet recounts her struggles as a teenager:

> But as I grew up to be about 14 or 15, I found my heart more carnal, and sitting loose from God, vanity and the follies of youth take hold of me.
>
> About 16, the Lord laid His hand sore upon me and smote me with the smallpox. When I was in my affliction, I besought the Lord and confessed my pride and vanity, and He was entreated of me and again restored me. But I rendered not to Him according to the benefit received.

At sixteen, she married Simon Bradstreet, who was nine years older and assisted her father on the estate. He was the great love of her life. Two years later the whole family set out for the New World. Before they sailed with a Puritan group on the *Arabella*, John Winthrop warned them in a sermon that their new community would be "as a city upon a hill. The eyes of all people are upon us." This was the cornerstone of American exceptionalism, and Anne Bradstreet, a young woman who would someday become the first American poet, was sitting in a pew when it was laid down.

The mission was high, but the three-month crossing was difficult, and the new country seemed barbarous. Here is how she explained it to her children:

> After a short time I changed my condition and was married, and came into this country, where I found a new world and new man-

ners, at which my heart rose. But after I was convinced it was the
way of God, I submitted to it and joined to the church at Boston.

The Puritan world was a forbidding one, particularly for women, who
were considered helpmates and subordinates to their husbands. The Scrip-
tures were always near at hand, ready to be wielded. Patriarchal law was not
an abstraction. It can be challenging to figure out how Bradstreet navigated
it. Often she protested, as she did when she first set foot in the New World,
and then eventually submitted, or appeared to submit. This pattern follows
her through her work: an insurgent heart and an intellectual stricture, a
sarcastic tongue and a self-correcting effacement, a secret disobedience that
is then covered over by an external conformity. I detect a deep, ongoing,
unresolved tension in her poetry between wildness and control, rebellious-
ness and submission, her feeling and her faith.

The New World was a hard, inhospitable place to settle, and the Brad-
street family lived variously in frontier towns, Salem, Boston, Cambridge,
Ipswich, finally settling on a farm at North Andover, Massachusetts. The
places were remote, and she lived in the shadow of powerful men. Her father
served thirteen times as deputy governor and four times as governor of the
Massachusetts Bay Colony. Her husband, a businessman, diplomat, and
colonial magistrate, was more moderate than her father, and her poems to
him are filled with tenderhearted affection and sexual desire ("To My Dear
and Loving Husband," "A Letter to Her Husband, Absent Upon Public
Employment").

Anne Bradstreet was not a robust person—her health was precarious. She
initially had trouble conceiving a child, which seemed to her a judgment,
but then succeeded dramatically. Her childbearing years stretched across a
nearly twenty-year span from 1633 to 1652. As she cleverly summarized it, in
"In Reference to her Children, 23 June, 1659":

> I had eight birds hatched in one nest,
> Four cocks were there, and hens the rest.
> I nursed them up with pain and care,
> Nor cost, nor labour did I spare,
> Till at the last they felt their wing,
> Mounted the trees, and learned to sing;

A devoted wife and mother, Bradstreet somehow found the wherewithal to write her poems, which she first created out of a religious errand into the wilderness, a conflict between privilege and privation, a nostalgic look backward at an English world and an ambivalent step forward into a frontier society. She was not a firebrand, like her close friend Anne Hutchinson, who was tried twice for her heretical beliefs, excommunicated, and then banished from the colony. Bradstreet's stratagem was more outwardly conventional; she was willing to play the Puritan female roles, but as a poet she was also ferociously determined and should not be underestimated. As Adrienne Rich puts it: "To have written poems, the first good poems in America, while rearing eight children, lying frequently sick, keeping house at the edge of wilderness, was to have managed a poet's range and extension within confines as severe as any American poet has confronted."

During her lifetime, Bradstreet's handwritten poems were read, copied, and circulated in manuscript among a small circle. There was no model of a professional poet in her day, and there was no significant book trade in the colony. *The Bay Psalm Book*, which was printed in Cambridge in 1640, was the first book published in England's North American colonies, and the only local book she could have had at hand. Her brother-in-law, the pastor John Woodbridge, arranged to have her book of poems published in London under the title *The Tenth Muse, lately Sprung Up in America* (1650). It was written "By a Gentlewoman in those parts." It is impossible to verify his claim that he published it abroad without her prior knowledge or approval. It is plausible that it was pirated from her and published by her family against her will, but it seems equally feasible that she considered publishing a little "vulgar," as did Donne and Sidney, who oversaw the publication of their manuscripts and then disclaimed responsibility. For Bradstreet, this might also have been the necessary subterfuge of a female poet protecting herself from censorship. John Winthrop, for example, believed that authorship was not among "such things as belong to women." *The Tenth Muse* appeared with a subtitle—*Or, Several Poems, Compiled with Great Variety of Wit and Learning, Full of Delight*—and a reassurance that it "is the work of a woman, honored, and esteemed where she lives." Woodbridge made it clear that the book was written by a woman who did not neglect her duties and wrote poetry only in her idle hours.

Within her collection, Bradstreet's poem "The Prologue" makes the case for her work a little differently. She anticipated and treated her antagonists, men who believed that women shouldn't write books, with unconcealed sarcasm, and headed off the critique that her imitations were thefts or accidents.

> I am obnoxious to each carping tongue
> Who says my hand a needle better fits,
> A poet's pen all scorn I should thus wrong,
> For such despite they cast on female wits:
> If what I do prove well, it won't advance,
> They'll say it's stol'n, or else by chance.

> But sure the antique Greeks were far more mild
> Else of our sex, why feigned they those nine
> And poesy made Calliope's own child;
> So, 'mongst the rest they placed the arts divine:

In the seventeenth century, the word *obnoxious* meant "exposed to harm," and Bradstreet fights back by needling her enemies with a pen. This is feminism before there was a word for it and insubordination by female wit.

Bradstreet's strategy was often to make a more aggressive statement and then pull back. She concedes or appears to:

> Let Greeks be Greeks, and women what they are
> Men have precedency and still excel,
> It is but vain unjustly to wage war;
> Men can do best, and women know it well.
> Preeminence in all and each is yours;
> Yet grant some small acknowledgement of ours.

> And oh ye high flown quills that soar the skies,
> And ever with your prey still catch your praise,
> If e'er you deign these lowly lines your eyes,
> Give thyme or parsley wreath, I ask no bays;
> This mean and unrefined ore of mine
> Will make your glist'ring gold but more to shine.

Having yielded "preeminence," she reframes the argument and creates the space for a woman's voice, a different poetic. She takes the traditional laurel, which was used to form a wreath of honor for male poets and athletes, and refashions it as something more homespun, a crown made from various kitchen or cooking herbs. She is taking the heroic stance down a notch, making herself less threatening. This mode of self-depreciation is a type of literary masking. She gets a male readership to listen to her by lowering her voice even as she widens the space for an outsider who is working indoors.

Whatever complex of responses that Bradstreet had to the publication of her poetry, the only book published in her lifetime, it seemed to free her to write more personally. She did not spring full-blown from the rocky skull of New England, like Athena leaping from the head of Zeus. Rather, she carefully honed her craft on what her brother-in-law deemed "pleasant and serious" forms, and then turned to other subjects. Her father died in 1653 and this, too, seems to have released her from the more public deferential mode. Now she fastened on more ordinary actions, everyday feelings and experiences. She wrote love poems to her husband and epitaphs for her parents, elegies for two of her grandchildren, reflections on her illnesses, verses on the burning of her house in 1666 ("I wakened was with thund'ring noise / And piteous shrieks of dreadful voice"). She reached her spiritual peak with the reflective poems "Contemplations" and "As Weary Pilgrim." Bradstreet's later poems were added to a second carefully crafted and enlarged edition of *The Tenth Muse*, now called by its subtitle, *Several Poems . . .* , and published in America in 1678, six years after her death. Reading through this book, you can trace a developing democratic ethos, how an English woman confronted the New World and became an American poet.

One of Bradstreet's most skillful later poems was the piece "The Author to Her Book." It is a pivot point in her work. It was clearly a response to the publication of her book in 1650 and seems written as she prepared her second revised manuscript in the 1660s. There is no exact way to date it since it was found among her papers after her death. I suspect that Bradstreet's preamble, which is quirky and funny, shows genuine ambivalence about her publication, which was badly printed and filled with errors. It's hard to tell, though, because she was expert at feigned modesty. She had already internalized the formulas of humility that Renaissance poets picked up from their Greek and Latin models. Think of Spenser's apostrophe "To His Book," which opens

The Shepheardes Calendar (1579): "Go, little Book; thy self present / As Child whose Parent is unkent." Here, Spenser uses a now obsolete word, *unkent*, which meant strange or unrecognizable, to suggest the weird way in which a book leaves a writer's hand, like a child estranged from its parent. Or consider the first sonnet in Sidney's sequence, *Astrophil and Stella* (1591), which concludes with the exhortation: "Thus great with child to speak and helpless in my throes, / Biting my truant pen, beating myself for spite, / 'Fool,' said my Muse to me, 'look in thy heart, and write.'" Bradstreet's modesty may have been authentic, as was befitting a Puritan woman, but she was also relying on a Renaissance trope of the reluctant author.

Bradstreet begins with a title that names her role ("*The Author*") and characterizes herself in the third person ("to *Her* Book"). The poem is an apostrophe, a poetic mode of direct address, and so she immediately changes course and addresses her book directly, in the first person, as a poor child. She uses the consonant *f* to thread together the words: "Thou ill-*f*ormed *o*ffspring *of* my *f*eeble brain." In this poem, Bradstreet gives a new spin, an actual gender, to a long-standing male poetic idea: the poem as the child of its author. For her, as a woman who has had the experience of giving birth, the notion takes on new realism. She then goes on to develop the metaphor of the poem as deformed child over the course of twelve perfectly metrical, exactly rhymed, iambic pentameter couplets. She proves her skill even as she insists that her text is flawed. T. S. Eliot defined the seventeenth-century metaphysical conceit as "the elaboration . . . of a figure of speech to the furthest stage to which ingenuity can carry it." I wish Eliot had used Bradstreet instead of Donne as an example, because it might have changed the received idea that "The Author to Her Book" was, as Helen Campbell put it, "a deprecating little poem." On the contrary, it is a tricky, virtuoso performance. It makes a good strategic move: declare your insufficiency while displaying your craft.

Eliot also revived the concept of "wit," which he described in an essay on Andrew Marvell as "a tough reasonableness beneath the slight lyric grace." As an author and a mother, Bradstreet shows just such a tough reasonableness and takes her metaphor to surprising length. The sickly, poorly formed infant-book first stayed at its mother's side but then was "snatched" or stolen by friends, taken against her will, and exposed in public, forced to run abroad "in rags." The child, whose gender is never specified, comes home again older now, embarrassing its mother. The metaphor has taken on so much life that Bradstreet parenthetically reminds the reader that she is still talking about a written book—"My rambling brat (in print) should mother call"—before casting it out again: "I cast thee by as one unfit for light, / Thy visage was so irksome in my sight."

There is also a tough maternal logic operating here. The poem turns on the argumentative words "*Yet* being mine own, at length affection would / Thy blemishes amend, *if so* I could." She now further extends the metaphor by applying it to the process of poetic revision. She cleans up the child, as one would cleanse a text of its imperfections: "I washed thy face, but more defects I saw, / And rubbing off a spot still made a flaw." I'm fond of the pun on the word *feet* here, which is both a bodily reference and a metrical unit—"I stretched thy joints to make thee even feet, / Yet still thou run'st more hobbling than is meet." She now changes the term to refer to home-spun rather than silk clothes: "In better dress to trim thee was my mind, / But nought save homespun cloth i' th' house I find." It's noticeable how **Bradstreet suggests that the author is the one who makes the child's clothes** by hand. She is also the one responsible for dressing it. The poet in the house is a woman creating a homemade world.

I'm amused by the way that Bradstreet tells her kid to stay in the neigh-borhood ("In this array 'mongst vulgars may'st thou roam") and not venture into different parts where there are critics ("In critic's hands beware thou does not come, / And take thy way where thou art not known"). It's not far-fetched to suggest that in instructing her manuscript not to go abroad she is also making a statement about American poetry now finding its place in the New rather than the Old World. The last three lines have a decisive punch:

> If for thy father asked, say thou hadst none;
> And for thy mother, she alas is poor,
> Which caused her thus to send thee out of door.

Bradstreet is suggesting here that her child is scandalously illegitimate. It's a bastard whose poor mother gave birth to it alone. This isn't just a joke; it was an extremely disruptive and even dangerous way for a Puritan woman to describe motherhood and authorship. As an unwed mother, she also now takes responsibility for her malformed child. It was initially snatched from her, but she now actively sends it out the door. It is ready to go out into the world, ready to be published in a new edition. The poem ends with this leave-taking. The metaphor has been completed; the book has gone off to make its own way in the world.

Anne Bradstreet was an unlikely pioneer. Her early poems, which were homesick for England, sailed abroad and then returned to the New World, where they belonged. She was no longer an English subject. So, too, she turned for her subject matter to an unwritten world, the domestic realm, the life lived. She was not just writing a displaced English poetry—there was also something refreshingly American in her work. American poetry has almost always spoken from the margins. It has been a poetry of impurity and plurality, a "mean and unrefined ore," that began on the peripheries, the verge of wilderness. It has taken perverse pride and pleasure in escaping the confines of a colonial literature, in sounding what Whitman called a "barbaric yawp." But American poetry didn't begin with Whitman or Dickinson. Anne Bradstreet deserves her true acknowledgment. I continue to marvel at the cunning and courageous poetic of this singular Puritan woman, who internalized a harsh religious creed and observed the strict proprieties of her society, and yet opened the pantry door for others to barge in, for the wild, divergent, emerging poetry of the New World.

PHILLIS WHEATLEY (1753–1784)

To S. M. a Young African Painter, on seeing his Works

To show the lab'ring bosom's deep intent,
And thought in living characters to paint,
When first thy pencil did those beauties give,
And breathing figures learnt from thee to live,
How did those prospects give my soul delight,
A new creation rushing on my sight?
Still, wond'rous youth! each noble path pursue,
On deathless glories fix thine ardent view:
Still may the painter's and the poet's fire
To aid thy pencil, and thy verse conspire!
And may the charms of each seraphic theme
Conduct thy footsteps to immortal fame!
High to the blissful wonders of the skies
Elate thy soul, and raise thy wishful eyes.
Thrice happy, when exalted to survey
That splendid city, crown'd with endless day,
Whose twice six gates on radiant hinges ring:
Celestial *Salem* blooms in endless spring.

    Calm and serene thy moments glide along,
And may the muse inspire each future song!
Still, with the sweets of contemplation bless'd,
May peace with balmy wings your soul invest!
But when these shades of time are chas'd away,
And darkness ends in everlasting day,
On what seraphic pinions shall we move,
And view the landscapes in the realms above?
There shall thy tongue in heav'nly murmurs flow,

And there my muse with heav'nly transport glow:
No more to tell of *Damon's* tender sighs,
Or rising radiance of *Aurora's* eyes,
For nobler themes demand a nobler strain,
And purer language on th' ethereal plain.
Cease, gentle muse! the solemn gloom of night
Now seals the fair creation from my sight.

                                        1773

WHEN I was coming up in the early seventies, there was an idea floating around literary circles that Phillis Wheatley was too accommodating, too much of a neoclassicist, to be an important poet. She was sometimes honored as a precursor—the first African American poet to publish a book in the United States, the second woman writer to publish a book in the colonies—but her work itself was condescended to as too well mannered and formal. Heroic couplets no longer seemed heroic to most American poets. The Black Arts Movement was in full swing, and poetry was viewed primarily as a tool for social change. Wheatley started getting treated as an Uncle Tom and the condescension tipped over into disdain. A lot of poets and critics accepted Amiri Baraka's view that Wheatley's "pleasant imitations of eighteenth-century English poetry are far and, finally, ludicrous departures from the huge black voices that splintered southern nights with their *hollers, chants, arwhoolies,* and *ballits.*"

I wish I had the wherewithal in those days to recognize that Wheatley's eighteenth-century diction and formal eloquence, which was a requirement for written verse at the time, in no way disallows the tremendous folk art that was being created by enslaved African Americans forced to work in the fields. She was forced to work indoors. She wasn't free to speak her mind, and so her work is outwardly decorous, inwardly subversive. It is filled with stratagem and subterfuge; it has elements of literary masking. It didn't occur to many people—it certainly didn't occur to me—that she had an independence of mind rare for her era, that she was one of the essential colonial poets, like Edward Taylor and Anne Bradstreet. There was a consensus among critics like Addison Gayle, Jr., who declared that Wheatley was the first Black writer "to accept the images and symbols of degradation passed down from the South's most intellectual lights and the first to speak from a sensibility finely tuned by close approximation to [her] oppressors."

It took another wave, maybe fifteen years or so, for poets, critics, and scholars to start reevaluating the first self-defining African American poet. I remember taking note of Henry Louis Gates, Jr.'s celebration of Wheatley's courage in his introduction to a special issue of *Critical Inquiry* (1985), and I was blown away by June Jordan's full-throated defense, "The Difficult Miracle of Black Poetry in America," which was subtitled "Something Like A Sonnet for Phillis Wheatley" (1985). I'm still moved by Jordan's lines: "A child without safety of mother or marriage // Chosen by whimsy but born to surprise / They taught you to read but you learned how to write / Begging the universe into your eyes."

It's hard to fathom what Wheatley had to go through to write her poems. As a seven- or eight-year-old child, she was kidnapped from the Muslim area of Senegambia, transported from West Africa on a slave ship to Boston, and sold on an auction block to John Wheatley as a domestic servant for his wife, Susanna Wheatley. She was so young that she was still missing her front teeth. She probably spoke Wolof. We don't even know her African name. Instead, she was given the first name of the slave ship that brought her, *Phillis*, and the last name of the slaver who bought her, *Wheatley*. Her health was fragile, her intellectual gifts prodigious. She amazed the Wheatley family, whose children tutored her, and she was soon fluent in English, steeped in the Scriptures, conversant with the Greek and Latin classics and the history of British literature.

Phillis Wheatley started publishing poetry when she was thirteen or so. She staked her claim with her first poems, such as "On Messrs. Hussey and Coffin," a story about a miraculous survival at sea, and "On the Death of the Rev. Mr. George Whitefield. 1770.," an elegiac homage that made her name, and "To the University of Cambridge, in New-England," where she takes the role of a teacher to his pupils or a pastor to his flock: "While an intrinsic ardor prompts to write, / The muses promise to assist my pen." She owed a debt to others, she found her necessary white patrons and supporters, but she created herself.

Wheatley's first and only book, *Poems on Various Subjects, Religious and Moral*, was published in England in 1773, but not in America until 1786, two years after her death. The title is akin to other books by poets she admired, such as Alexander Pope's *Poems on Several Occasions* (1717) and her acquaintance Mather Byles's *Poems on Several Occasions* (1744). The idea was to rise to assorted occasions, to display a range of poetic skills and forms. Occasional poems, which represent the social or public side of poetry, were held in high regard in the eighteenth century—Goethe called them "the first and most genuine of all kinds of poetry"—and Wheatley was determined to show her mastery. In her era, you did that through imitation, an idea that was downgraded by the Romantics, but held in high esteem by writers like John Dryden and Pope, both of whom believed that nothing recommended itself to modern production so much as imitation of the ancients. The pastoral was given pride of place, and thus became one of Wheatley's favored modes.

Wheatley's trip to England and the publication of her book brought her international acclaim. She also got her manumission, long-sought freedom. She wrote a poem in honor of George Washington, who graciously responded, "the style and manner exhibit a striking proof of your great poetical Talents," and offered to meet "a person so favoured by the Muses." In the subsequent years, she was often held up by abolitionists as a model for emancipation. But there was always a backlash, and it's hard to stomach the long history of negative responses to her work, some of them merely misguided, many of them outright racist. Thomas Jefferson's response can stand as typical, particularly since it comes from such an august source, the one book published in his lifetime, *Notes on the State of Virginia* (1787), Query XIV:

> Misery is often the parent of the most affecting touches in poetry —Among the blacks is misery enough, God knows, but no poetry. Love is the peculiar oestrum [inspiration] of the poet. Their love is ardent, but it kindles the senses only, not the imagination. Religion indeed has produced a Phyllis Whately [*sic*]; but it could not produce a poet. The compositions published under her name are below the dignity of criticism.

Jefferson's racist view of human capacity homes in on Wheatley as he misspells her name, hints that she may not have written her own poems, and finally judges her beneath criticism. He uses this cudgel to dismiss the very idea of Black poetry. It is worth recalling that he is denigrating a poet who was more skillful at verse-making than he was, who wrote perfectly balanced iambic pentameter couplets, who repeatedly referred with dead-on accuracy to the canonical writers Horace and Virgil, who wrote a beautiful adaptation of a story from Ovid's *Metamorphoses* ("Niobe in Distress for Her Children Slain by Apollo, from Ovid's *Metamorphoses*, book 6. And from a View of the Painting of Mr. Richard Wilson"), who began her book with a highly literary tribute to a contemporary Maecenas, the great patron of Augustan poets, and who in doing so established a link to the only other African writer she knew about, Terence, a product of what she calls "*Afric's* sable race," a poetic forefather who wrote his way to freedom. She also syncretized her African origins with Western Christianity and created an orderly poetic universe in a dangerous, disorderly world.

Wheatley was ferociously determined to write her way into literary culture, which is precisely why her reputation has been dogged by questions of authenticity. At first a white readership found it hard to believe that a young Black woman could write such learned poetry, and so her book was prefaced with an attestation by sixteen luminaries of Boston, including the governor and lieutenant governor of the Massachusetts Bay Colony. She needed white witnesses to vouch for her. Given this history, it seems extremely painful that in the twentieth century African American writers started to label her a museum piece, too pious and grateful, too dependent on western sources. They dismissed the entire neoclassical tradition. At first, she was considered too Black, then condemned as too white. As Gates noted in his 2002 lecture "Mister Jefferson and the Trials of Phillis Wheatley": "It's striking that Jefferson and Amiri Baraka, two figures in American letters who would agree on little else, could agree on the terms of their indictment of Phillis Wheatley."

Wheatley was a decidedly American poet who identified herself as African in her poems, and perhaps savored the shock of calling herself "An *Ethiop*" and the "*Afric* muse." She foregrounded her heritage as a Black woman, "*Afric's* damsel." Kidnapped and transported to the New World, she nonetheless praised the American Revolution and the work of the founders. She used Christianity to justify emancipation. Her most notorious poem, "On Being Brought from Africa to America," which she wrote when she was around fourteen, begins with a declaration that made her a reviled figure: "'Twas mercy brought me from my *Pagan* land, / Taught my benighted soul to understand / That there's a God, that there's a *Saviour* too." At the end of the poem, this conventional self-hating concession turns into something else entirely, a religious defense of the "sable race" and a direct admonition: "Remember, *Christians, Negros,* black as *Cain,* / May be refin'd, and join th' angelic train." There will be equality in heaven, she argues, which is a purer place than earth.

Wheatley found in Christianity a corrective to slavery, not a justification for it. Her later poem "To the Right Honourable William, Earl of Dartmouth, His Majesty's Principal Secretary of State for North-America, &c." contains this crucial memory and defense of freedom, a sum of experience she deploys for "the common good":

> Should you, my lord, while you peruse my song,
> Wonder from whence my love of *Freedom* sprung,
> Whence flow these wishes for the common good,
> By feeling hearts alone best understood,
> I, young in life, by seeming cruel fate
> Was snatch'd from *Afric's* fancy'd happy seat:
> What pangs excruciating must molest,
> What sorrows labour in my parent's breast?
> Steel'd was that soul and by no misery mov'd
> That from a father seiz'd his babe belov'd:
> Such, such my case. And can I then but pray
> Others may never feel tyrannic sway?

It was as if this young woman was feeling her way toward Protestant liberation theology.

We know what Phillis Wheatley looked like from the vivid, accurate engraving that served as a frontispiece to her only book. It shows her in profile, wearing a servant's clothes and seated at a desk with a book and an inkwell, looking up from a manuscript, presumably lost in thought and caught at an unguarded moment. Her left hand rests on her face, her right holds a quill pen. There is no doubt that she is a writer.

This portrait of Wheatley is the only surviving work of art by Scipio Moorhead, the gifted artist who is addressed in "To S. M. a Young *African* Painter, on seeing his Works." Wheatley knew Moorhead, also an enslaved African, because he was in service to John Moorhead, a friend of the Wheatley family and pastor of the Church of Presbyterian Strangers. Many of her poems are elegies and consolations, odes and hymns, but this one speaks to a younger contemporary artist and makes a statement about two different art forms, one shared pursuit. We don't know anything about Moorhead's art or artistic development, though he was probably tutored by Sarah Parsons Moorhead, an art teacher, and seems to have absorbed his models. The engraving of Phillis Wheatley, probably based on one of his paintings, seems kindred to the portrait paintings of John Singleton Copley, which are filled with preoccupied female sitters.

The first thing to notice in Wheatley's poem is the dignity that she accords Scipio Moorhead. She treats him as equal to the white Protestant divines that she writes about elsewhere in her book. She recognizes him as "a Young *African* Painter," which is to say that she doesn't assimilate him, or downgrade him to "boy," or treat him as an enslaved person. She identifies him by his origin, Africa, and his art form, painting. She sees him by seeing his work. The poem consists of seventeen well-balanced rhyming couplets in two long stanzas. The heroic couplet was sometimes called *riding rhyme* and here it has that kind of momentum. Most of the lines are end-stopped, intact units. In the first six lines, each unit has its own meaning within the larger sentence, which starts as a declaration and ends as a question.

> To show the lab'ring bosom's deep intent,
> And thought in living characters to paint,
> When first thy pencil did those beauties give,
> And breathing figures learnt from thee to live,
> How did those prospects give my soul delight,
> A new creation rushing on my sight?

Wheatley was an exact rhymer, and it's noticeable here that the first two lines have a slant or half rhyme (*intent / paint*) while the next lines have full rhymes (*give / live; delight / sight*). The opening lines are about the viewer's response to the process of painting. She is surprised by the magical artistry that makes a drawing a breathing figure. In this poem the heroic couplets, which pair lines, evoke the paired art forms, poetry and painting. There is a nice pun on the word *prospects*, which suggests the likelihood of something happening, but also refers to a subgenre in eighteenth-century topographical poetry, the prospect poem. In this type of poem, which borrows its strategy from painting, the poet takes the view from a height and re-creates a landscape, a generalized *prospect*. Both the poet and the painter are giving us a view from an elevated place, but also a view into the distance, the future.

The speaker is excited and excitable. She almost can't believe that she has found such a marvelous fellow artist and kindred spirit. The next two lines have a quick exclamation and a plethora of adjectives—*wond'rous, noble, deathless, ardent*—as she reaches to describe both the artist and his vocation. She takes a didactic pose and can't resist telling him what to do:

> Still, wond'rous youth! each noble path pursue,
> On deathless glories fix thine ardent view:

Wheatley here insists on the deep connection between art forms, the visual work of the painter and the verbal work of the poet. The next two lines, which culminate in another exclamation, are the heart of the poem:

> Still may the painter's and the poet's fire
> To aid thy pencil, and thy verse conspire!

Wheatley follows her model Horace, who coined the phrase *ut pictura poesis* ("as in painting, so in poetry") to suggest the parallel between painting and poetry. It is possible that she knew Charles-Alphonse Du Fresnoy's 1668 poem *De arte graphica* (The Art of Painting), which was translated from Latin into English in the mid-eighteenth century and had a great vogue, especially the lines: "Ut pictura poesis erit, similisque poesi / Sit pictura" ("A poem will be like a picture, and let a picture be similar to a poem"). She had access to Mather Byles's library and studied his laudatory poem "To Pictorio, on the Sight of His Pictures" ("Thy Fame, PICTORIO, shall the Muse rehearse, / And sing her Sister-Art in softer Verse") since she borrowed a phrase from it ("round the central sun") for her poem "On Recollection." But the ancient linkage between the visual and verbal arts was also beginning to fray in the eighteenth century (Edmund Burke vigorously attacked the connection in his 1757 treatise *A Philosophical Enquiry into the Origin of Our Ideas of the Sublime and Beautiful*), and so Wheatley is asserting a connection under intellectual assault. She doesn't back down, but she does change the terms of the argument:

> And may the charms of each seraphic theme
> Conduct thy footsteps to immortal fame!

Wheatley is trying to charm Moorhead toward a more religious subject matter, something a little more uplifting perhaps, more angelic topics, and uses the topos of *immortal fame*, a long-standing literary ideal, which she merges with a Christian idea of eternity. There is a slight, perhaps unconscious dissonance in the rhyming of *theme* and *fame*, but the poet overrides this hesitation with another exclamation. Thereafter, the poem turns from the horizontal to the vertical, from the earthly to the celestial sphere. I have no idea if Moorhead was a skeptic or a believer, but I feel a strong determination, even insistence, by the speaker that he turn his eye, and presumably the subject matter of his paintings, toward something more exalted: "High to the blissful wonders of the skies / Elate thy soul, and raise thy wishful eyes."

The speaker affirms art as a form of worship and the poem lifts off, headed for exalted solar realms:

> Thrice happy, when exalted to survey
> That splendid city, crown'd with endless day,
> Whose twice six gates on radiant hinges ring:
> Celestial *Salem* blooms in endless spring.

Wheatley fixes her gaze on a timeless sun-drenched radiance, a Heavenly Jerusalem that she imagines with serene detail. This raises the question of just whose soul she is trying to elate. She is supposedly talking to Moorhead as a painter, but instead ends up addressing herself as a poet.

Now she kicks off the second section of the poem:

> Calm and serene thy moments glide along,
> And may the muse inspire each future song!

The poet extends the *c*, *l*, and *s* pattern of "*Celestial Salem*" ("*Calm* and *serene*") and employs the letter *m* to thread together the words *moments*, *may*, and *muse*. The rhythm enacts the feeling by gliding smoothly along. Wheatley often borrowed the language of argumentation that drives the eighteenth-century meditative lyric; this becomes evident in the turns she now makes, as in "*Still*, with the sweets of contemplation," and "*May* peace with balmy wings," and "*But when* these shades of time." She marshals her rhetoric for a rhetorical question and makes use of a turn toward topographical painting: "On what seraphic pinions shall we move, / And view the landscapes in the realms above?" What is striking throughout is how she mingles the terms of painting and poetry, sight and sound.

The references in the next sentence, which flows across six lines, the penultimate move in the poem, suggest that Wheatley has been writing earthly pastorals:

> There shall thy tongue in heav'nly murmurs flow,
> And there my muse with heav'nly transport glow:
> No more to tell of *Damon's* tender sighs,
> Or rising radiance of *Aurora's* eyes,
> For nobler themes demand a nobler strain,
> And purer language on th' ethereal plain.

Damon was a common name for shepherds in pastoral poems, such as Virgil's eighth "Eclogue," where he appears as a disappointed lover, and Pope's "Spring. The First Pastoral, or Damon," where he becomes the arbiter of a singing contest ("Then sing by turns, by turns the Muses sing"). Wheatley often referred in her poems to Aurora, the goddess of dawn in Latin poetry and Roman mythology. Fond of classical allusion, she also referred to the sun as Sol, the Roman sun god, and Phoebus (Apollo), the Olympian deity of poetry as well as the sun. The image of the sun consistently rises in her poems. According to Wheatley family legend, Phillis Wheatley had just one memory of Africa, the recollection of her mother pouring water at sunrise. This seems likely because it recalls a common ritual of Senegambian women who greet the rising of the sun with a religious ritual gesture. It is credible, then, as scholars have conjectured, that Wheatley syncretized three sources for her solar imagery: an African belief in a sun god, which she recalled from childhood, a Roman or pagan idea of sacred dawn, which she read about— Aurora was the sister of Helios, the sun god—and a Christian ideal of the eternal or heavenly day, which she took from Calvinistic Methodism. Like John Donne and George Herbert, she punned on *Sun* and *Son*, the physical sun in the sky and the Christian savior.

Wheatley defines her sun-drenched hymns as pastorals and thus self-consciously places her work in a classical tradition. The Greek poet Theocritus invented the genre, but Virgil created the enduring model of the pastoral: a conventional poem that expresses an urban poet's nostalgic image of the simple, peaceful life of shepherds living in an idealized natural setting. But there is always a politics attached to the pastoral. For the early African American poet, it takes on a special valence because it posits an alternative world, an escape from her actual circumstances, the oppressive reality of slavery. Perhaps it involves a memory of Africa. Her experiences in America chain her down. Now she takes an uplifting view—"For nobler themes *demand* a nobler strain"—and endorses a purer world, some otherworldly paradise beyond. What she is leaving behind, and what she is asking Moorhead to leave behind, too, is a chained world. After death, they will understand the purer language of God.

But the speaker can't sustain this higher vision for long, and so she comes crashing back to earth. Wheatley liked to close a poem with a sign-off to the muse. Pope's pastoral competition concludes with Damon commanding: "Cease to contend." Midway through "To Pictorio," Byles also asked the muse to depart: "But cease, fond Muse, nor the rude Lays prolong." Wheatley amends this in her final couplet and exclaims:

> Cease, gentle muse! the solemn gloom of night
> Now seals the fair creation from my sight.

The sun has gone down and the poem, like the day, has come to an end. She is addressing a painter, and so she also uses a visual metaphor. The "fair creation" refers to both the painter's art and God's eternal creation. It is now too dark to see. There is firm closure in the final rhyming couplet, in ending the lyric on the word *sight*. The poem has been a statement of solidarity between a young poet and a young painter, but it also ends on a strange note of "solemn gloom." Now that the two artists can no longer see each other, the speaker has been brought back to the reality of their world. For all their Christian uplift, Wheatley's poems often close on a sorrowful or dispirited note. I believe they are a dam holding off a flood of racial grief.

In 1978, some two hundred years into the American experiment, Robert Hayden published a book, *American Journal*, which includes his poem

"A Letter from Phillis Wheatley: London, 1773." Hayden's understated epistolary poem, which he called a "psychogram," purports to be a letter that Wheatley wrote home to her friend Obour Tanner, another enslaved woman. Here, the uneventful sailing across the Atlantic reminds Wheatley of her first "Destined" voyage during the Middle Passage ("I yet / have some remembrance of its Horrors"), the nightmarish trace of her journey to slavery in America. Hayden imitates Wheatley's restrained diction and quiet formality, the nearly unbearable irony of her situation, which she faced with stoic faith. He also understood something about her ostracism from the African American literary canon and implicitly stood up for her inclusion.

It's necessary to hold American poetry to a democratic ideal. We may not have much sense of history in America, but poetry is a historical archive. It's a way of leaving a verbal trace. There are barriers to entry and there are contending forces operating at any one time that make it easier to enter for some people and nearly impossible for others. There are systems at work in the making of a canon. And yet no one is born into poetry. It's a family you need to inscribe yourself into; you have to write or sing your way onto the record. Other people need to care about your work. I don't consider it a deficit that a young Black woman in prerevolutionary America, who was given the name Phillis Wheatley, was influenced by the Western classics and used them to forge an unlikely new African American poetry. I think it's a miracle.

HENRY WADSWORTH LONGFELLOW (1807–1882)

The Jewish Cemetery at Newport

How strange it seems! These Hebrews in their graves,
  Close by the street of this fair seaport town,
Silent beside the never-silent waves,
  At rest in all this moving up and down!

The trees are white with dust, that o'er their sleep
  Wave their broad curtains in the south-wind's breath,
While underneath these leafy tents they keep
  The long, mysterious Exodus of Death.

And these sepulchral stones, so old and brown,
  That pave with level flags their burial-place,
Seem like the tablets of the Law, thrown down
  And broken by Moses at the mountain's base.

The very names recorded here are strange,
  Of foreign accent, and of different climes;
Alvares and Rivera interchange
  With Abraham and Jacob of old times.

"Blessed be God! for he created Death!"
  The mourners said, "and Death is rest and peace;"
Then added, in the certainty of faith,
  "And giveth Life that nevermore shall cease."

Closed are the portals of their Synagogue,
  No Psalms of David now the silence break,
No Rabbi reads the ancient Decalogue
  In the grand dialect the Prophets spake.

Gone are the living, but the dead remain,
    And not neglected; for a hand unseen,
Scattering its bounty, like a summer rain,
    Still keeps their graves and their remembrance green.

How came they here? What burst of Christian hate,
    What persecution, merciless and blind,
Drove o'er the sea—that desert desolate—
    These Ishmaels and Hagars of mankind?

They lived in narrow streets and lanes obscure,
    Ghetto and Judenstrass, in mirk and mire;
Taught in the school of patience to endure
    The life of anguish and the death of fire.

All their lives long, with the unleavened bread
    And bitter herbs of exile and its fears,
The wasting famine of the heart they fed,
    And slaked its thirst with marah of their tears.

Anathema maranatha! was the cry
    That rang from town to town, from street to street;
At every gate the accursed Mordecai
    Was mocked and jeered, and spurned by Christian feet.

Pride and humiliation hand in hand
    Walked with them through the world where'er they went;
Trampled and beaten were they as the sand,
    And yet unshaken as the continent.

For in the background figures vague and vast
    Of patriarchs and of prophets rose sublime,
And all the great traditions of the Past
    They saw reflected in the coming time.

And thus forever with reverted look
    The mystic volume of the world they read,

Spelling it backward, like a Hebrew book,
  Till life became a Legend of the Dead.

But ah! what once has been shall be no more!
  The groaning earth in travail and in pain
Brings forth its races, but does not restore,
  And the dead nations never rise again.

1854

I DON'T OWN many books from my grandfather's bookcase—he died when I was eight years old, and my grandmother gave most of his books away to a Jewish charity—but as a teenager I found his brown leather-bound copy of Longfellow's *Collected Poems* in our family basement. He had turned down a corner of the page at "The Jewish Cemetery at Newport," which suggests that it piqued his interest, probably because there are so few poems about Jewish life in nineteenth- and early twentieth-century American poetry, which is overwhelmingly Christian. I read the poem and found it bizarre ("How strange it seems! These Hebrews in their graves"), not just because of the dated language, but because it seemed to me that Longfellow must not have known many actual Jewish people. The individuals buried in the cemetery were not very real to him. He was interested in them only collectively. It took me years to return to the poem and realize how remarkable it is, not just because it is a philosemitic poem, which is a rare enough thing in canonical American poetry, but also because it is so learned about Jewish learning. It also takes us back to the foundations of American Jewish life.

There were more than twenty-five Sephardic families living in Newport, Rhode Island, by the time of the American Revolution, which made it one of the largest Jewish communities in the colonies. The founders of the town had offered it "as a haven of refuge." It's heartening to recall George Washington's visit to Newport in August 1790 (Moses Seixas, the leader of the Jewish community, welcomed him with the words "Permit the children of the Stock of Abraham to approach you with the most cordial affection and esteem for your person & merits") because it resulted in his brief letter to the Jews of Newport, one of the great early pronouncements about religious freedom under the new United States Constitution. "The Government of the United States . . . gives to bigotry no sanction, to persecution no assistance," Washington wrote, making abundantly clear that our government would oppose any type of religious intolerance. I suspect that my grandfather would not have been surprised to discover that there is a trapdoor near the bimah just in case Washington's promise didn't hold up and the Jews had to hide—that would have been a holdover strategy from the Inquisition.

The Jewish community in Newport had a distinguished history, but there were no more Jews living in the seaside city by the time that Longfellow took his family there for a summer vacation in 1852. He was forty-five years old at the time and had published six books of poems—*Voices of the Night* (1839), *Ballads and Other Poems* (1842), *Poems on Slavery* (1842), *The Belfry of Bruges and Other Poems* (1845), *Evangeline* (1847), and *The Seaside and the Fireside* (1849)—that were beginning to establish him as the most beloved American poet of the nineteenth century. Such poems as "Hymn to the Night," "A Psalm of Life," "The Light of Stars," "The Wreck of the Hesperus," and "The Village Blacksmith" were instantly popular, memorized, and recited in homes and schools. During a period when America was undergoing a vast urban and industrial change, his poems created a reassuring space where the mesmerizing storyteller and his rapt listeners seemed to meet in the soft glow of the hearth: "Around the fireside at their ease / There sat a group of friends, entranced / With the delicious melodies" (*Tales of a Wayside Inn*, 1863).

Longfellow had a superb gift for languages. I wish he were better known as a translator, our first true internationalist. For example, in 1845 he published a weighty anthology of his various linguistic adventures, *The Poets and Poetry of Europe*, which begins with a reference to the troubadours: "'The art of poetry,' says the old Spanish Jew, Alfonso de Baena, 'the gay science, is a most subtle and most delightful sort of writing or composition.'" Longfellow was interested in the Sephardic Jews as a conduit of Spanish literature and culture because they linked the Hebraic tradition to the origin of European poetry, which in turn informed his own burgeoning idea of the American romance. That's one reason he was so well poised to respond to an unsuspected Jewish burial ground in a New England resort town.

Wandering around the streets on Friday, July 9, Longfellow came across the old Touro Synagogue and cemetery and convinced the gatekeeper to let him enter. He recounted the experience in a diary entry:

July 9, 1852. [Newport, R. I.] Went this morning into the Jewish burying-ground, with a polite old gentleman who keeps the key. There are few graves; nearly all are low tombstones of marble, with Hebrew inscriptions, and a few words added in English or Portuguese. At the foot of each, the letters S. A. G. D. G. [Su Alma Goce Divina Gloria. May his soul enjoy divine glory.] It is a shady nook, at the corner of two dusty, frequented streets, with an iron fence and a granite gateway.

Moved by the melancholy quiet and beauty of the setting, which contrasted so dramatically with the busy seaport town that surrounded it, Longfellow set out to write a commemorative poem. He labored over the piece—there are four manuscript drafts among his papers—and published it two years later in *Putnam's Monthly Magazine*.

Longfellow had long been fascinated by the Jews and their history, and his poem is replete with references to the Hebrew Bible. It is purposefully written in heroic quatrains—four iambic pentameter lines with an alternating rhyme scheme of *abab*—which is the same form that Thomas Gray utilized for "Elegy Written in a Country Churchyard." Longfellow retools Gray's elegiac stanza to speak of the heroic nature of the Jewish people, who have suffered persecution and exile. He doesn't pay attention to individuals but stands in the midst of the old burial grounds and sympathetically memorializes the Hebrews.

Cemeteries were often breeding grounds for poems in the nineteenth century. Here, you can feel the secret pleasure Longfellow takes in the paradoxical situation, the quiet graveyard by the street in a bustling seaport, "Silent beside the never-silent waves, / At rest in all this moving up and down!" In the second stanza, he cleverly turns the dusty white trees into an image of "leafy tents" and recalls a biblical people who have now suffered what he allegorically calls "The long, mysterious Exodus of Death." In the third stanza, he extends the reference to the book of Exodus, and compares the old brown "sepulchral stones" to "tablets of the Law, thrown down / And broken by Moses at the mountain's base." There is bravura in the way that Longfellow keeps finding and extending the analogies, linking what he sees in the cemetery to the history he recalls, the people of the Book.

Longfellow seems struck by the foreignness of Jews, the wide gap between bygone Jewish culture and mid-nineteenth-century American life. The Spanish and Portuguese family names, like Alvares and Rivera, which now are common, feel unfamiliar and even un-American to him, which is why he compares them to the biblical Abraham and Jacob. In the fifth stanza, he takes the Jewish funeral service, which he seems to know ("'Blessed be God! for he created Death!'"), and Christianizes it by focusing on the afterlife, something understated in the Jewish funerary ("And giveth Life that never-more shall cease"). To give him credit, though, later in the poem he recognizes the mystical Kabbalistic current in nineteenth-century Jewish thinking, which speculates about the fate of the soul after death.

Longfellow has a homiletic streak and a tendency to sentimentalize death, but he is also following a close associative logic here. The speaker of his poem is struck by the fact that the oldest temple in the United States is now closed and thus there is no rabbi to conduct the service, to read from the Decalogue, or Ten Commandments. His elegy—"Gone are the living, but the dead remain"—turns to Jewish history as he asks, somewhat rhetorically, "How came they here?" European Jews escaped to America just as the ancient Israelites fled from Egypt. He views them as archetypal figures: "These Ishmaels and Hagars of mankind."

In the 1830s, Longfellow had travelled widely and studied in France, Spain, Italy, and Germany, and thus had become acquainted with the historical situation of Jews in Europe, the ghetto where they were so often forced to live and the *Jüdenstrasse*, the so-called street of the Jews, which he misspells. Hence, "They lived in narrow streets and lanes obscure, / Ghetto and Judenstrass, in mirk and mire." He savors the humming sound ("*mirk and mire*") and lingers over the well-balanced and contrasting line, the allegorical enlargement: "Taught in the school of patience to endure / *The life of anguish* and *the death of fire*."

In the first draft of the poem, Longfellow even more emphatically foregrounded the contemporary harassment of Jews in Europe. Here is a stanza in which he marshaled the biblical litany and recalled that Cain's sentence was to wander ceaselessly:

> *A sword still bars* the gate of rest and peace;
>   *A foot still breaks* and grinds them like the grain!
> *A voice still speaks* the doom, that ne'er shall cease;
>   *A hand still points* to the deep mark of Cain!

Here is another revealing stanza that he cut from the final version. Now he introduces a rhetorical pattern of negation:

> Is there *no hope*? *no end* of all their wrongs?
> *No rest*—*no Truce* of God to intervene,
> For those who gave the world its noblest songs,
> The only perfect man this world hath seen?

Longfellow makes a case for giving the Jews a break from suffering and suggests that, after all, they gave the world both the Psalms and the Savior, a cache of songs and a means of salvation.

Longfellow was well versed in the book of Exodus and the Passover service. In the tenth stanza, he refers to the unleavened bread, or matzoh, that the Israelites are commanded to make as they leave Egypt in haste during the Exodus. He refers to the bitter herbs that are commanded for the Passover seder (Exodus 12:8). And he recognizes that the water at Marah slakes their thirst after Moses transforms it (Exodus 15). Yet in the next stanza, Longfellow uses a liturgical curse—"Anathema maranatha!"—that comes from 1 Corinthians 16:22: "If any man love not the Lord Jesus Christ, let him be Anathema Maranatha" (King James Bible), which suggests that the heretic would be excommunicated. He is so thoroughly steeped in Christian scripture that he can't help reading the Israelite experience through the lens of the New Testament. As a poet of the learned biblical reference, he also keeps the parallel going between the olden and the contemporary by referring to "the accursed Mordecai," who, according to the book of Esther, was persecuted by Haman with the rest of the Jewish people.

Longfellow views Jewish history through a double lens—the pride of a tribe who have a sublime Past (he capitalizes the word for emphasis), the humiliation of a people who have suffered persecution through the ages. He seems to know the mystic or religious idea of *olam haba* (the world to come), or hereafter, and cleverly utilizes the fact that Hebrew is read from right to left, or "backward," like the past. But he also suggests that Jews cannot adapt to contemporary life; they are so directed toward the past that they are doomed to extinction.

Longfellow stumbles badly in the last stanza and concludes that the Jewish people cannot survive, that Jewish history has come to grim conclusion. It's as if he has been carried away by the melancholy sadness of the cemetery.

So, too, he uses the words *races* and *nations* as if their death is some inevitable fact of nature.

> But ah! what once has been shall be no more!
>   The groaning earth in travail and in pain
> Brings forth its races, but does not restore,
>   And the dead nations never rise again.

Longfellow accepted an idea that would become commonplace among the Fireside poets, a group that held wide sway in the second part of the nineteenth century. These five highly respected figures (Longfellow, William Cullen Bryant, John Greenleaf Whittier, Oliver Wendell Holmes, and James Russell Lowell) believed that the Jewish people symbolized a great religious tradition but that they were culturally unable and unfit to survive in the modern world. Judaism had no language or feeling for the present tense. At the age of eighteen, Emma Lazarus was so infuriated by the conclusion of Longfellow's poem that in rebuttal she penned her first poem on a Jewish theme, "In the Jewish Synagogue at Newport" (composed in 1867). The young poet purposefully mimics Longfellow's meter and form—one could say that she Judaizes it—and responds to the original in stanza after stanza. To begin, she borrows the template of a quiet, abandoned religious place surrounded by a bustling town.

> Here, where the noises of the busy town,
>   The ocean's plunge and roar can enter not,
> We stand and gaze around with tearful awe,
>   And muse upon the consecrated spot.

Lazarus faces Jewish history from a living present: "How as we gaze, in this new world of light, / Upon this relic of the days of old, / The present vanishes." She feels mournful and even uncomfortable in the empty synagogue ("Our footsteps have a strange unnatural sound"), but she also recognizes a continuity of suffering between the Old and New Worlds, the Jewish people in the past and the ones in the present:

> Nathless the sacred shrine is holy yet,
>   With its lone floors where reverent feet once trod.

> Take off your shoes as by the burning bush,
> Before the mystery of death and God.

Lazarus understands that the Jews left Newport during and after the Revolutionary War, but that did not mean that they had died out as a people. On the contrary, they had simply scattered elsewhere in the United States. She, too, mourns the past, but in her last stanza she purposefully declares that "the sacred shrine is holy yet." Whereas Longfellow eulogizes an entire people in a little cemetery in Rhode Island, Lazarus reverently stands in an empty synagogue and speaks to the ongoing continuity of Judaism in American life.

Emma Lazarus wrote a warm appreciation of Longfellow after his death. She pointedly praised "The Jewish Cemetery at Newport" for its "tender humanity," but she also crisply stated that "Jewish readers will not be so willing to accept the concluding stanzas of the poem." If I could send an encrypted message in a bottle, I would take a copy of that essay, which appeared in *The American Hebrew* (1882), and place it in Longfellow's *Collected Poems* for my grandfather to read. I would underline this passage:

> The rapidly increasing influence of the Jews in Europe, the present universal agitation of the Jewish question, hotly discussed in almost every pamplet, periodical and newspaper of the day, the frightful wave of persecution directed against the race, sweeping over the whole civilized world and reaching its height in Russia, the furious zeal with which they are defended and attacked, the suffering, privation and martyrdom which our brethren still consent to undergo in the name of Judaism, prove them to be very warmly and thoroughly alive, and not at all in need of miraculous resuscitation to establish their nationality.

WALT WHITMAN (1819–1892)

Out of the Cradle Endlessly Rocking

Out of the cradle endlessly rocking,
Out of the mocking-bird's throat, the musical shuttle,
Out of the Ninth-month midnight,
Over the sterile sands and the fields beyond, where the child leaving
    his bed wander'd alone, bareheaded, barefoot,
Down from the shower'd halo,
Up from the mystic play of shadows twining and twisting as if they
    were alive,
Out from the patches of briers and blackberries,
From the memories of the bird that chanted to me,
From your memories sad brother, from the fitful risings and fallings I
    heard,
From under that yellow half-moon late-risen and swollen as if with tears,
From those beginning notes of yearning and love there in the mist,
From the thousand responses of my heart never to cease,
From the myriad thence-arous'd words,
From the word stronger and more delicious than any,
From such as now they start the scene revisiting,
As a flock, twittering, rising, or overhead passing,
Borne hither, ere all eludes me, hurriedly,
A man, yet by these tears a little boy again,
Throwing myself on the sand, confronting the waves,
I, chanter of pains and joys, uniter of here and hereafter,
Taking all hints to use them, but swiftly leaping beyond them,
A reminiscence sing.

Once Paumanok,
When the lilac-scent was in the air and Fifth-month grass was growing,

Up this seashore in some briers,
Two feather'd guests from Alabama, two together,
And their nest, and four light-green eggs spotted with brown,
And every day the he-bird to and fro near at hand,
And every day the she-bird crouch'd on her nest, silent, with bright
    eyes,
And every day I, a curious boy, never too close, never disturbing them,
Cautiously peering, absorbing, translating.

Shine! shine! shine!
Pour down your warmth, great sun!
While we bask, we two together.

Two together!
Winds blow south, or winds blow north,
Day come white, or night come black,
Home, or rivers and mountains from home,
Singing all time, minding no time,
While we two keep together.

Till of a sudden,
May-be kill'd, unknown to her mate,
One forenoon the she-bird crouch'd not on the nest,
Nor return'd that afternoon, nor the next,
Nor ever appear'd again.

And thenceforward all summer in the sound of the sea,
And at night under the full of the moon in calmer weather,
Over the hoarse surging of the sea,
Or flitting from brier to brier by day,
I saw, I heard at intervals the remaining one, the he-bird,
The solitary guest from Alabama.

Blow! blow! blow!
Blow up sea-winds along Paumanok's shore;
I wait and I wait till you blow my mate to me.

Yes, when the stars glisten'd,
All night long on the prong of a moss-scallop'd stake,
Down almost amid the slapping waves,
Sat the lone singer wonderful causing tears.

He call'd on his mate,
He pour'd forth the meanings which I of all men know.

Yes my brother I know,
The rest might not, but I have treasur'd every note,
For more than once dimly down to the beach gliding,
Silent, avoiding the moonbeams, blending myself with the shadows,
Recalling now the obscure shapes, the echoes, the sounds and sights after
     their sorts,
The white arms out in the breakers tirelessly tossing,
I, with bare feet, a child, the wind wafting my hair,
Listen'd long and long.

Listen'd to keep, to sing, now translating the notes,
Following you my brother.

Soothe! soothe! soothe!
Close on its wave soothes the wave behind,
And again another behind embracing and lapping, every one close,
But my love soothes not me, not me.

Low hangs the moon, it rose late,
It is lagging—O I think it is heavy with love, with love.

O madly the sea pushes upon the land,
With love, with love.

O night! do I not see my love fluttering out among the breakers?
What is that little black thing I see there in the white?

Loud! loud! loud!
Loud I call to you, my love!

High and clear I shoot my voice over the waves,
Surely you must know who is here, is here,
You must know who I am, my love.

Low-hanging moon!
What is that dusky spot in your brown yellow?
O it is the shape, the shape of my mate!
O moon do not keep her from me any longer.

Land! land! O land!
Whichever way I turn, O I think you could give me my mate back again
*   if you only would,*
For I am almost sure I see her dimly whichever way I look.

O rising stars!
Perhaps the one I want so much will rise, will rise with some of you.

O throat! O trembling throat!
Sound clearer through the atmosphere!
Pierce the woods, the earth,
Somewhere listening to catch you must be the one I want.

Shake out carols!
Solitary here, the night's carols!
Carols of lonesome love! death's carols!
Carols under that lagging, yellow, waning moon!
O under that moon where she droops almost down into the sea!
O reckless despairing carols.

But soft! sink low!
Soft! let me just murmur,
And do you wait a moment you husky-nois'd sea,
For somewhere I believe I heard my mate responding to me,
So faint, I must be still, be still to listen,
But not altogether still, for then she might not come immediately to me.

Hither my love!
Here I am! here!
With this just-sustain'd note I announce myself to you,
This gentle call is for you my love, for you.

Do not be decoy'd elsewhere,
That is the whistle of the wind, it is not my voice,
That is the fluttering, the fluttering of the spray,
Those are the shadows of leaves.

O darkness! O in vain!
O I am very sick and sorrowful.

O brown halo in the sky near the moon, drooping upon the sea!
O troubled reflection in the sea!
O throat! O throbbing heart!
And I singing uselessly, uselessly all the night.

O past! O happy life! O songs of joy!
In the air, in the woods, over fields,
Loved! loved! loved! loved! loved!
But my mate no more, no more with me!
We two together no more.

The aria sinking,
All else continuing, the stars shining,
The winds blowing, the notes of the bird continuous echoing,
With angry moans the fierce old mother incessantly moaning,
On the sands of Paumanok's shore gray and rustling,
The yellow half-moon enlarged, sagging down, drooping, the face of the
    sea almost touching,
The boy ecstatic, with his bare feet the waves, with his hair the atmosphere
    dallying,
The love in the heart long pent, now loose, now at last tumultuously
    bursting,
The aria's meaning, the ears, the soul, swiftly depositing,

The strange tears down the cheeks coursing,
The colloquy there, the trio, each uttering,
The undertone, the savage old mother incessantly crying,
To the boy's soul's questions sullenly timing, some drown'd secret hissing,
To the outsetting bard.

Demon or bird! (said the boy's soul,)
Is it indeed toward your mate you sing? or is it really to me?
For I, that was a child, my tongue's use sleeping, now I have heard you,
Now in a moment I know what I am for, I awake,
And already a thousand singers, a thousand songs, clearer, louder and more
    sorrowful than yours,
A thousand warbling echoes have started to life within me, never to die.

O you singer solitary, singing by yourself, projecting me,
O solitary me listening, never more shall I cease perpetuating you,
Never more shall I escape, never more the reverberations,
Never more the cries of unsatisfied love be absent from me,
Never again leave me to be the peaceful child I was before what there in
    the night,
By the sea under the yellow and sagging moon,
The messenger there arous'd, the fire, the sweet hell within,
The unknown want, the destiny of me.

O give me the clew! (it lurks in the night here somewhere,)
O if I am to have so much, let me have more!

A word then, (for I will conquer it,)
The word final, superior to all,
Subtle, sent up—what is it?—I listen;
Are you whispering it, and have been all the time, you sea-waves?
Is that it from your liquid rims and wet sands?

Whereto answering, the sea,
Delaying not, hurrying not,
Whisper'd me through the night, and very plainly before daybreak,

Lisp'd to me the low and delicious word death,
And again death, death, death, death,
Hissing melodious, neither like the bird nor like my arous'd child's heart,
But edging near as privately for me rustling at my feet,
Creeping thence steadily up to my ears and laving me softly all over,
Death, death, death, death, death.

Which I do not forget,
But fuse the song of my dusky demon and brother,
That he sang to me in the moonlight on Paumanok's gray beach,
With the thousand responsive songs at random,
My own songs awaked from that hour,
And with them the key, the word up from the waves,
The word of the sweetest song and all songs,
That strong and delicious word which, creeping to my feet,
(Or like some old crone rocking the cradle, swathed in sweet garments,
    bending aside,)
The sea whisper'd me.

                                        1859, 1860, 1871

As a fledgling poet, I felt that all true poetry came from the dark night of the soul. I was starting out and didn't know much about St. John of the Cross, but I gravitated to his experience of the "dark night" (*noche oscura*). To me, poetry was a voice desperately crying out in the wilderness. I still love this idea of poetry—after all, St. John's crisis of faith points backward to Dionysius the Areopagite and forward to Federico García Lorca and César Vallejo—but at first it blinded me to other forms of thought. I had some received ideas, like the cliché that Walt Whitman was too optimistic, too cheerful, and even serene about the future. Somewhere I picked up Yeats's notion that he lacked a vision of evil—this was a charge that was also leveled against Emerson—and I parroted the idea floating around various English departments that he was some sort of preadolescent, prototypical American Adam who was ignorant about history. One time I was bandying these ideas about with my teacher Charles Cleaver, a gentle soul who taught American Studies at Grinnell College, and he suggested that maybe I was underestimating Whitman, who had greater depths than I realized. He shared Kenneth Burke's suspicion that Whitman's strategy was a way of "whistling in the dark," which had never occurred to me, and he thought that I should turn to some of Whitman's darker, more upsetting poems, like "Out of the Cradle Endlessly Rocking."

That afternoon I discovered one of Whitman's darkest nights, his song of origins, the story of an initiation rite. "Out of the Cradle Endlessly Rocking" has a deep, grief-stricken, incantatory music, which reveals something crucial I had overlooked about the nature of Whitman's practice. He famously listened to America singing, but, less famously, he also heard the desolated song of a bereft mockingbird trilling of lost love. Most great poems tend to be stranger than their reputations—they often seem normalized by the canonical status of anthologies—and this one seems to me deeply weird, instructive, and beautiful.

As soon as it appeared, Whitman's poem had its detractors and defenders, but I wonder what ordinary nineteenth-century readers might have made of it. It's curious to think of the subscribers to the *New-York Saturday Press* peering at the front page of the weekly on the morning of December 25, 1859, and thereby finding what the editor called a Christmas or New Year's present, "the curious warble of Walt Whitman." It had a reassuring title, "A Child's Reminiscence," though it is a far from reassuring gift. Whitman changed the title to something less explanatory, more mysterious, and subterranean, "A Word Out of the Sea," for the third (1860) edition of *Leaves of Grass*, and then settled on the final title, "Out of the Cradle Endlessly Rocking," for the fifth (1871) edition of his endlessly evolving collection. It was fitting for him to give it pride of place at the head of the "Sea-Drift" section in the deathbed edition of *Leaves of Grass* (1892), a self-defining poem for the defining book of American poetry. It was followed by the poems "As I Ebb'd with the Ocean of Life," where the poet hears "the fierce old mother" crying for all her castaway children, and "Tears" ("Tears! tears! tears! / In the night, in solitude, tears").

In 1859, Whitman read Dante's *Inferno* and compared it to the Bible. He could relate to the idea of lost souls rendered in epic proportion. Over the years I have come to feel that he was crying not just for himself but also for his country, which he feared was descending into hell. His personal lament was shadowed by the fact that America was rushing headlong toward a Civil

War that would break his heart. If, as Whitman wrote in the 1855 preface to *Leaves of Grass*, "a bard is to be commensurate with a people" because "his spirit responds to his country's spirit," then what happens when the country betrays its ideals? Whitman's outsider dream of an egalitarian society, the high hope of the first edition of *Leaves of Grass*, was being shattered and shipwrecked because of national self-divisions, because of racism and slavery. He revised "Out of the Cradle Endlessly Rocking" during what he called his "quicksand years," and every time he turned back to it, he understood it more and more as a representative poem. He was devastated by the suffering of so many wounded soldiers, the boys he cared for as a volunteer nurse in a Washington hospital, and was gravely dispirited by the assassination of Abraham Lincoln, which led to one of his deepest elegies, "When Lilacs Last in the Dooryard Bloom'd." His grieving for lost love took on greater and greater dimensions.

Despite his sympathies, Whitman was not immune to the racist virus. Later in life he made insulting comments about Black people and was seduced by racist pseudoscientific ideas that continued to circulate through post–Civil War America. These prejudices are inexcusable and tarnish his legacy, but he kept them out of *Leaves of Grass*, where he consistently celebrated the diversity and "aboriginal" heritage of America. He did not forget his uneducated roots, his queer, working-class, outsider status. Whitman was celebratory by nature and, determined to negate the negative, he embraced our unlimited potential, but he whistled in the dark because he was afraid, trying to keep the darkness at bay. He put on a brave front, but he felt that something dangerous was out there, lurking in the shadows, waiting to engulf him. Whitman knew our better nature, but that darkness, the shadow side of American history, has always hovered over American poetry.

"Out of the Cradle Endlessly Rocking" shoots out of the gate with a prodigious liturgical cadence that carries you away. It loosens the mind for reverie. Whitman times his anaphoric line here, as he does in almost all of his poems, to a repetitive pattern of his own making, not to the ten-syllable or blank-verse line that was the norm for English poetry, but to something more accentual and irregular, something dreamlike and associative, something oracular. I like to feel the sea drift of the first stanza, which consists of one sentence stretched across twenty-two lines. Everything is held in a kind of suspension as the main subject of the sentence, *I*, is held back until the twentieth line, and the main verb, *sing*, only emerges as the last word of the stanza. This section is an overture to the poem, as in an opera. The images rapidly accrue without clear connection. Whitman creates here the very rhythm of a singular reminiscence emerging out of the depths of mind, out of the sea waves and the rocking cradle, out of all the undifferentiated sensations of infancy, out of the myriad memories of childhood, out of all possible experiences the formative event of a boy leaving the safety of his bed and walking the seashore alone, moving "Out," "Over," "Down," "Up," "From," exchanging the safety of the indoors for the peril of the outdoors, facing his own vague yearnings and the misty void, mixing his own tears and the salt spray of the ocean, listening to the birds, understanding the call, the very language, of one bird in particular. He walks the Long Island shore on the edge of the world, the edge of the unknown, the boundary line between life and death. He has entered the space that Emerson calls "*I and the Abyss*," the space of the American sublime.

There is an element of lullaby in this lyric, which carries in its body the lulling motion of the waves, the consoling sound of the sea, the memory of the cradle's first unity. But this is a lullaby that wounds (as Lorca said about Spanish lullabies), a lullaby of sadness that permeates the universe itself. In this region: out of all potential words, these words alone; out of all potential memories, this memory alone. It is the emerging rhythm itself that creates the Proustian sensation of being in two places at once, "A man, yet by these tears a little boy again, / Throwing myself on the sand, confronting the waves." Whitman creates through the rhetorical rhythm of these lines the urgency of fundamental memory triggered and issuing forth. He splits himself off and moves seamlessly between the third person and the first person. As the bird enchanted him ("From the memories of the bird that chanted to me"), so he will enchant us ("I, chanter of pains and joys, uniter of here and hereafter").

The speaker closes the first stanza with a self-command, "A reminiscence sing." Whitman takes a memory, or possibly the germ of a memory, and constructs a story of his beginnings as a poet. He sounds like a storyteller or a balladeer settling into a yarn: "Once Paumanok, / When the lilac-scent was in the air and Fifth-month grass was growing." He knows how to tell a story, secure a narrative, and the second stanza, which consists of one sentence stretched across nine lines, seems pitched slightly closer to speech than to song. The storyteller remembers discovering two nesting mocking-birds. He points out that the "Two feather'd guests from Alabama" were "two together," a *he-bird* and a *she-bird*, and that every day he watched them from a safe distance, "Cautiously peering, absorbing, translating." The word *translating* is apt here because the speaker now proceeds to translate the song of the birds.

In the history of poetry, both oral and written, birds have often been viewed as messengers from the beyond. The singers or shamans who put on a bird's head are showing that they can communicate with the spirit world. Like other Romantic poets, Whitman viewed the bird as a symbol of imaginative freedom, but he was also tapping something more archaic or tribal. For example, the Kaluli people of Papua New Guinea, in the southwest Pacific, who speak Bosavi, treat poetry as what they call *bird sound words*. For them, "poetic language is bird language," the ethnomusicologist Steven Feld points out in *Sound and Sentiment: Birds, Weeping, Poetics, and Song in Kaluli Expression*. Whereas talk is pragmatic and serves utilitarian ends, song, Feld says, "is a communication from the point of view of a person in the form of a bird." Like the tribal poet, the American writer also recognizes the song of the birds as the prototype for poetry and music.

Formally, Whitman figures the act of translation, a move into birdsong, by switching to italics and elevating the pitch of the diction. When I reread it, I pay closer attention to the flurry of exclamations that heighten the tension and signal that he is operating in another register now: "*Shine! shine! Shine! / Pour down your warmth, great sun! / While we bask, we two together.*" Whitman loved Tennyson's grief-stricken lyric "Break, Break, Break," and the birds sound positively Tennysonian. Over the course of two short stanzas, the birds insist that they always travel together, day and night, over rivers and mountains, "*singing all the time, minding no time.*" The poem then turns back from the atemporal song of the birds to the narrative or chronological time of the human storyteller: "Till of a sudden." The speaker then explains how the female bird simply vanishes one day, possibly killed—neither the boy nor the male bird knows what happened to her—and thenceforward he hears, though no longer all the time now, only at intervals, the male mockingbird singing alone. Once more, the speaker translates the bird's song, but now it is a solitary song of longing: "*Blow! blow! blow! / Blow up sea-winds along Paumanok's shore; / I wait and I wait till you blow my mate to me.*" The bird sings to the sky, to the winds, to whatever unknown force blew away his lover. He hits a plaintive, beseeching note.

The human speaker nods in agreement with him: "*Yes*, when the stars glisten'd." What is striking here is the affirmation, the solidarity the boy feels with the bird, "the lone singer," who brings him to tears. And this solidarity is a presumptive recognition: "He call'd on his mate, / He pour'd forth the meanings of which I of all men know." There is a change from the past to the present tense: "Yes my brother I know, / The rest might not, but I have treasur'd every note." He returns as a man to the beach he once haunted as a boy. He clings to the shadows, as if he is ashamed of his own feelings. Biographers have speculated that the trigger for this poem was some personal crisis in Whitman's life at the end of the 1850s, possibly a feeling of abandonment because his closest brother had just gotten married, more likely "a devastating amorous defeat" in his relationship with Fred Vaughan, who almost certainly inspired the "Calamus" poems in *Leaves of Grass*. Whitman doesn't specify, but whatever he has lost now touches a primal hurt, the separation of the child from its mother's body, and his identification with the lovelorn bird is entire.

The language here is intentionally vague. The poet uses adjectives like *dimly* and *obscure* as he struggles to describe a vision of something he intuits out in the sea waves, something that once more propels him into the darkness of his boyhood feelings: "For more than once dimly down to the beach gliding, / Silent, avoiding the moonbeams, blending myself with the shadows, / Recalling now the obscure shapes, the echoes, the sounds and sights after their sorts, / The white arms out in the breakers tirelessly tossing, / I, with bare feet, a child, the wind wafting my hair, / Listen'd long and long." Whitman is describing an epiphanic experience that is very much like Wordsworth's formulations of "spots of time" in *The Prelude*. Everything about the atemporal experience is transitory and difficult to pin down. To cite an example from the section "School-Time" in book 2:

> and I would stand
> If the night blackened with a coming storm,
> Beneath some rock, listening to notes that are
> The ghostly language of the ancient earth,
> Or make their dim abode in distant winds.

The language is "ghostly" and comes from a long way off, from "the *ancient earth*"; it makes its "*dim* abode in *distant* winds." Whitman, too, is drinking what Wordsworth calls "the visionary power," a dark ecstasy, and finding profit from "*fleeting* moods / Of *shadowy* exultation"; he, too, "retains an *obscure* sense / Of *possible* sublimity."

Whitman's diction is stranger than Wordsworth's, and it elevates whenever he translates the bird's song, which is formally signaled as italics. Paul Valéry called the passage from prose to verse, from speech to song, from walking to dancing, "a moment that is at once action and dream." Whitman creates such a moment here as he moves from chanting to singing. For the next eighteen short stanzas he re-creates the desperate song of the lovelorn mockingbird. He is not ornithologically oriented—for that one should turn to the nineteenth-century rural English poet and tramper John Clare—but linguistically evocative. He loved Italian opera, and the poem takes on a high operatic quality as it channels the bird's expressive song of tragic passion, which follows the slow pattern of an aria. He may have been influenced by Septimus Winner's popular song "Listen to the Mockingbird" (1855). Some opera buffs think that Marietta Alboni, a great contralto who sang in New York in the 1852–53 opera season, is the "progenitor" of his truest vocalist, the mockingbird. This isn't far-fetched. Whitman claimed to have seen all of her New York performances and later noted that "her singing, her method, gave the foundation, the start . . . to all my poetic literary effort."

Whitman's basic strategy is to imitate the way a mockingbird typically creates a long series of phrases, each phrase repeating two to six times. He translates this mode of birdsong by repeatedly echoing the sound of the words with the intensity of refrain, whether it is "*But my love soothes not me, not me*," or "*O madly the sea pushes upon the land, / With love, with love*," or "*Loud! loud! loud! / Loud I call to you, my love!*" He fuses this mockingbird music with the boy's separate, downstage, companionable response. Listen to how insistently he hits the word *Carols*, which he repeats six times. I don't see how anyone listening to this can hold on to a naïve idea of Whitman's optimistic song:

> *Shake out carols!*
> *Solitary here, the night's carols!*
> *Carols of lonesome love! death's carols!*

Carols under that lagging, yellow, waning moon!
O under that moon where she droops almost down into the sea!
O reckless despairing carols.

By now, Whitman identifies so closely with the reckless despair of the carol that he can't quite separate himself from the bird. This identification reaches a fever pitch at the end of the bird's song, which has nine exclamation points in five lines. Whitman claimed to have no use for John Keats's poetry, but to me he imitates a mockingbird in much the way that Keats imitates a nightingale. But whereas Keats imitates the nightingale's range of whistles and trills, Whitman hits upon the mockingbird's repetitive phrasing.

O past! O happy life! O songs of joy!
In the air, in the woods, over fields,
Loved! loved! loved! loved! loved!
But my mate no more, no more with me!
We two together no more.

This is the melodramatic end of the bird's song. It is also the end of a certain level of music in the poem, "The aria sinking." The song is over but everything else seems to continue, the boy is alone with his own feelings, with the stars, the wind, and the sea, "the fierce old mother incessantly moaning," with a natural world that seems completely in tune with his own loss, with an emotion so intense that his grief becomes a kind of ecstasy: "The boy ecstatic, with his bare feet the waves, with his hair the atmosphere dallying, / The love in the heart long pent, now loose." The boy is sobbing now as he begins to interpret the meaning of the aria. The ocean is explicitly a grieving mother "incessantly crying," and the boy recognizes his own originary isolation, his terrible separateness. He starts to hear his soul's own questions. Most crucially, he refers to himself as "the outsetting bard."

The boy has been so responsive to the bird's caroling despair that he now begins to wonder if the bird had been singing just so that it could instigate the boy's own song, like some knowing, sinister voice rising unseen from the sea. The anxious young bard even begins to wonder whether the mocking-bird ever really had a lover. Every stanza in roman type in this poem is one sentence long, except for this one, which interrupts itself with an exclamation, a parenthesis, and two questions:

> Demon or bird! (said the boy's soul,)
> Is it indeed toward your mate you sing? or is it really to me?

Whitman is trying to pinpoint his vocation ("Now in a moment I know what I am for, I awake"), the exact moment in time when a "thousand warbling echoes" stirred him into song.

I feel Percy Bysshe Shelley's poem "To a Skylark" casting its shadow. Whitman considered Shelley's poetry too "lush" and ethereal, lacking in sensuality, but he read it more closely than he pretended. It's as if his doubt is pulling him down and away from, even inverting, Shelley's invisible skylark ("Teach us, Sprite or Bird, / What sweet thoughts are thine"), who sings with such pure rapture, such glad celestial spirit, and projects so much dynamic uplift and "unbodied joy." The skylark is all lightness and air, the very embodiment of Shelley's "harmonious madness." By contrast, Whitman's anguished figure stands as a kind of natural genius emanating from the unknown waters, from the darkly mysterious universe. He is a vibrating songbird, a Virgil to the outsetting Dante ("O you singer solitary, singing by yourself, projecting me, / O solitary me listening"). He seems to provide the necessary demonic song—the word out of the sea—that formulates the boy's still unformulated desire, his future vocation. Whitman is signaling how much this experience changed and transformed him, how he can never turn back to a more innocent time. Listen to how hard he hits the phrase *never more*, which mimics Edgar Allan Poe's "The Raven" (1845), and then *never again*: "*Never more* shall I escape, *never more* the reverberations, / *Never more* the cries of unsatisfied love be absent from me, / *Never again* leave me to be the peaceful child I was before what there in the night." He is making a pledge to a fire that has been awakened inside of him ("the sweet hell within") and turning this desire ("The unknown want") into a prophetic path ("the destiny of me").

Whitman is explicit that he is searching for a word, a clue, as he stands on the shore, listening, trying to figure out his mission. He is equally explicit that the sea provides an answer. It neither delays nor hurries, but it does speak to him in a low whisper that lasts the course of a night. It singles him out. It does not hold back, but

Lisp'd to me the low and delicious word death,
And again death, death, death, death,
Hissing melodious, neither like the bird nor like my arous'd child's heart,
But edging near as privately for me rustling at my feet,
Creeping thence steadily up to my ears and laving me softly all over,
Death, death, death, death, death.

I don't think Whitman could be much more explicit as he repeats the word *death* ten times. This move mirrors and doubles the number of times the mockingbird called out the word *loved*. The word *death* comes to him not from the mockingbird or from his child heart, but from the sea itself, the mother laving him all over, luring him in, calling him back.

At the climax of the poem, Whitman carefully goes on to link his initiation into death with his initiation into art—his burgeoning creativity, his bardic calling and craft. It takes him one sentence that snakes across ten lines to describe how everything came together. The rhythm recurs to the beginning of the poem, and thus closes a circle:

Which I do not forget,
But fuse the song of my dusky demon and brother,
That he sang to me in the moonlight on Paumanok's gray beach,
With the thousand responsive songs at random,
My own songs awaked from that hour,
And with them the key, the word up from the waves,
The word of the sweetest song and all songs,
That strong and delicious word which, creeping to my feet,
(Or like some old crone rocking the cradle, swathed in sweet
    garments, bending aside,)
The sea whisper'd me.

Whitman's seashore lyric is wide open to death, the mortal foe of memory, and his childhood memory is awakened in the presence of death, because his initiation into art is an arm-to-arm combat with a delicious forgetfulness, with oblivion itself. He has been chosen to remember, which is to say that he has become an Orphic vehicle. He will sing the music of the spheres. A thousand warbling echoes reverberate through him and refuse to die.

"It is not upon you alone the dark patches fall," Whitman declares in "Crossing Brooklyn Ferry." "The dark threw its patches down upon me also." "Out of the Cradle Endlessly Rocking" is a child's reminiscence, an operatic parable, that considerably darkens the source of Whitman's song, his fabled starting point. The egalitarian poet who embraced humanity also tells us that he entered poetry on his own initiative by sneaking down to the shore and listening to birdsong. He began as a vulnerable solitary, a lonely singer by the night sea. The word emanating out of that sea was *death*, and Walt Whitman's poetry originated in its mysterious presence.

Shiloh.
A Requiem.

(April, 1862.)

Skimming lightly, wheeling still,
  The swallows fly low
Over the field in clouded days,
  The forest-field of Shiloh—
Over the field where April rain
Solaced the parched ones stretched in pain
Through the pause of night
That followed the Sunday fight
  Around the church of Shiloh—
The church so lone, the log-built one,
That echoed to many a parting groan
    And natural prayer
  Of dying foemen mingled there—
Foemen at morn, but friends at eve—
  Fame or country least their care:
(What like a bullet can undeceive!)
  But now they lie low,
While over them the swallows skim,
  And all is hushed at Shiloh.

1866

THE CIVIL War transformed Herman Melville into a poet. He was so shocked by the carnage of our self-division that he pivoted from prose to verse and responded with a sequence of lyrics that documented the unbearable fact of war. He was in his mid-forties and had written poetry before—he had a full unpublished collection of Mediterranean travel pieces—but nothing of this magnitude. He was disheartened by his lack of success and undergoing a personal crisis, but he did not renounce prose because of the failure of *Moby-Dick* (1851) or because he had lost confidence in *The Confidence-Man* (1857), as is sometimes thought. Melville changed modes and genres because he was galled and inspired to respond as a citizen-poet to the American catastrophe. He wanted to combine the intensity of the singular lyric with the grander sweep of the sequence. He was coolheaded, but he did not shy away from the national trouble.

"Shiloh" is one of the centerpieces of Melville's first and strongest collection of poems, *Battle-Pieces and Aspects of the War* (1866). He considered the Civil War an ethical rupture, a definitive break, with the founding ideals of the republic, and he responded with his own edgy intervention, a book of stinging ballads and fierce elegies with its own Romantic poetic. He presents "the strife as a memory," as he puts it in the preface, and thus echoes William Wordsworth's idea that "Poetry is the spontaneous overflow of powerful feelings; it takes its origins from emotion recollected in tranquillity." So, too, he borrows the Coleridgean image of the Aeolian harp ("I seem, in most of these verses, to have but placed a harp in the window, and noted the contrasted airs which wayward winds have played upon the strings") to suggest that he is an inconsistent but inspired voice of nature, a human intermediary who is not imposing his opinions but nonetheless refuses to naturalize the violence of war.

In an episodic sequence of seventy-two poems, Melville dramatically chronicles the trauma of the war years from the hanging of the abolitionist John Brown in 1859 ("The Portent") to the assassination of Abraham Lincoln in 1865 ("The Martyr"). Each lyric finds its own nonce form. The poems are written in what he calls "moods variable," a multivoiced and polyphonic collection of conflicting viewpoints, often disappointed, often struggling to make sense of a foundering democratic promise, a collective tragedy. Individually, many of the lyrics stalk single battles, horrifying battle pieces, tableaus of war, but the sequence as a whole has a novelist's sense of time. It has epic ambitions.

I want to pause a moment over Melville's rough poetic style. He could write polished verses when he chose—listen to the opening of "Dupont's Round Fight":

In time and measure perfect moves
All Art whose air is sure;
Evolving rhyme and stars divine
Have rules, and they endure.

But Melville mostly eschews smooth verses, regular meters, and well-timed rhymes, pleasing airs, "measure perfect." Rather, he made a conscious decision to roughen his rhythm to meet his subject matter. Unlike most of his contemporaries, he was not writing an uplifting, heroic, or patriotic poetry. He was not trying to encourage sacrifice but to represent suffering. That's why he needed a harsher and more discordant music, something more unruly and battle-scarred. He lays out the aesthetic in "A Utilitarian View of the Monitor's Flight":

Plain be the phrase, yet apt the verse,
More ponderous than nimble;
For since grimed War here laid aside
His Orient pomp, 'twould ill befit
Overmuch to ply
The rhyme's barbaric cymbal.

Melville alludes to the preface of *Paradise Lost*, where Milton declares his freedom from what he calls "the bondage of rhyming" and insists that "true musical delight . . . consists only in apt numbers, fit quantity of syllables, and the sense variously drawn out from one verse into another." That's precisely the model for Melville's metrical irregularities and sometimes roughshod enjambed lines, his warring meters.

Melville penned *Battle-Pieces*—the title evokes Dutch genre paintings—while he was living in New York, reading Northern newspaper accounts, and studying the first volumes of Frank Moore's *The Rebellion Record: A Diary of American Events, with Documents, Narratives, Illustrative Incidents, Poetry, Etc.*, which eventually came to eleven volumes. Melville had many relatives involved in the war effort, and he was in Washington to observe the Senate debate about secession in 1861. Three years later he went to visit his cousin, Henry Gansevoort, at a cavalry camp in Virginia—Melville's brother said that he was on a literary mission "so that he should have opportunities" to see the army that he was trying to describe—but his cousin was absent, and Melville accompanied the troops on a scouting mission to the Virginia front, which he fictionalized in "The Scout toward Aldie," the longest poem in *Battle-Pieces*. After that he travelled to the headquarters of the Army of the Potomac and interviewed General Grant. Melville wrote almost the entirety of the book in the eighteen months after the fall of Richmond in April 1865, which instigated his response. He wasn't writing poems as a reporter, a Northern apologist for the war, or a moral crusader. Rather, he presents a series of bitter, granular poems that rail against death on such mass scale. At times, he sounds like one of the disillusioned poets of World War I.

Melville's focus on the war was unwavering. "Shiloh" refers to the Battle of Shiloh, which was fought around the Shiloh Baptist Church in southwestern Tennessee on April 6–7, 1862. The irony was not lost on Melville that Shiloh was named after a village in ancient Israel (Genesis 49:10). Secluded and peaceful, it was the site of the tabernacle during the period described in Judges. Christians associated the name, which means "the peaceful one," with the coming of the Messiah. But the figure of peace was notably missing from what is sometimes known as the battle of Pittsburg Landing, an obscure hamlet in Hardin County, Tennessee. The carnage was tremendous—most of the troops were inexperienced—and the combined Union and Confederate casualties were more than twenty-three thousand men killed, missing, or wounded. It was up to that point the bloodiest battle in American history and set a new standard for slaughter, though it would soon be surpassed by the battles of Antietam and Gettysburg.

Melville subtitles his poem "A Requiem," which he pinpoints to a precise historical moment in time: April 1862. He recognizes that the requiem in poetry, a lamentation or threnody, has its roots in religious practice, the Requiem Mass, a musical service for the repose of the dead, and thus creates a sacred aura around a secular event. As Ishmael explains in *Moby-Dick*: "The Romish mass for the dead begins with 'Requiem eternam' (eternal rest), whence Requiem denominating the mass itself, and any other funereal music." Melville forges a dirge for the troops on both sides, a group memorial for all those who died on two spring days in a blood-soaked year.

It was highly unusual to write such an encompassing lamentation, and there were few models in the long history of war poetry. One such precursor is James Shirley's seventeenth-century poem "The Glories of Our Blood and State," which takes up the leveling power of death:

> The garlands wither on your brow;
>> Then boast no more your mighty deeds!
> Upon Death's purple altar now
>> See where the victor-victim bleeds.

One practically has to turn back to the *Elegies* of the Roman poet Propertius (book 4, 6) for a poem of comparable stature that mourns for soldiers on both sides of a battle. Melville's poem brings to mind the cold-eyed way that Aeschylus describes soldiers and death in *The Persians*, especially the passage where the ghost of Darius speaks about the Battle of Plataea and describes the corpses "piled up like sand," which shall bear mute witness for generations to come (lines 813ff.). Melville, too, sees a tasseled field of doom and a deadly harvest watered and reaped by tears.

"Shiloh" consists of nineteen lines, sometimes sinuous, sometimes stately, that comprise one solid block, a single solemn chant. It has dashes and commas but no full stops, no periods until the final punctuation mark. This one-sentence poem is as quietly unnerving as a poem by Emily Dickinson or Thomas Hardy. When you read it aloud and follow it on the page, you especially notice the instability of the meter, which is echoed in the irregular pattern of indentation, and the unpredictability of the rhymes. This creates a feeling of the chancy, erratic nature of warfare. The poem is set in the aftermath of battle. It begins as a pastoral with an image of low-flying swallows, skimming and wheeling over the "forest-field of Shiloh." But the pastoral soon darkens—these are "*clouded* days"—and we recognize that the rain over the field is the same rain that came to parch the wounded and dying soldiers that were strewn across this very field not so long ago.

If you slow the poem down, you observe how it is structured through a series of rhetorical and associative repetitions. It begins by mimicking the movement of birds. The swallows fly low—

> *Over the field* in clouded days,
>> *The forest-field* of Shiloh—
> *Over the field*

and the Sunday fight took place around—

> *the church* of Shiloh—
> *The church* so lone.

The wording "*That followed* the Sunday fight" is echoed in "*That echoed* to many a parting groan." Every one of these repetitions constitutes a turn in the poem, a movement from something peaceful to something war-torn.

The speaker emphasizes the bitterness of the fact that this horrific battle took place on a Sunday night around a place of worship. The church creates a context and frame. It is solitary, empty, still. This heightens the fact that war is sacrilegious and unnatural. The meter is jagged, the rhyming insistent but erratic. The first and third lines do not rhyme; the second and fourth do, as in a ballad or hymn (*low* / *Shiloh*). But the reassuring ballad or narrative form soon changes momentum. The 4/3 common meter blows open in the lengthening fifth and sixth lines, and the sixth line breaks the meter:

> Óver the field where Ápril ráin
> Sólaced the párched ónes strétched in páin

Suddenly, a series of full rhymes, which are purposefully plain, even crude, emphatically clench the lines into couplets, not just *rain* and *pain*, but also

> Through the pause of *night*
> That followed the Sunday *fight*

Melville tactically enjambs the line here so that "the Sunday fight" hesitates and then falls into a line that stands alone, unrhymed: "Around the church of Shiloh."

Melville is working the changes quickly, like a jazz musician, and now there is a single discordant or slant rhyme:

> The church so lone, the log-built *one*,
> That echoed to many a parting *groan*

You can particularly hear the dissonance when you match the phrases, *the log-built one* and *a parting groan*. There is simultaneously an interior rhyme that clenches *lone* to *groan*, the solitary church to the dying men. These rhyming lines intensify and elongate the feeling of wounded soldiers lying in agony through the natural adjournment and discontinuity, "the pause of night." Then he returns to the full couplet rhyme:

> And natural *prayer*
> Of dying foemen mingled *there*—

All this is meant to amplify the truth that a solitary home-built church intended for prayer has become a field rotting with young men who had attacked and killed one another.

The most radical move in the poem is inaugurated with the repetition of the word *foemen*. Melville intentionally uses an archaic word, which derives from the Middle English *foman* (an enemy, devil, demon) to make his case. The rhythm becomes catchy and the lines end-stopped, almost homiletic. There is also an echo chamber of sounds that becomes operational now. It started with the words *rain* and *pain*:

> The church so *lone*, the log-built *one*,
> That echoed to many a parting *groan*
> And natural prayer
> Of dying *foemen* mingled there—
> *Foemen* at *morn*, but friends at eve—
> Fame or country least their care:
> (What like a bullet can undeceive!)

Here, Melville hits upon his most crucial and even didactic point in a beautifully balanced and memorable formulation: *Foemen at morn, but friends at eve.* He presses the *f* sound as he converts *foemen* into *friends*. Think of the righteous and patriotic militarism of "The Battle-Hymn of the Republic," which was published in 1862, the year of the Battle of Shiloh, and you'll understand the sentiment that Melville was trying to counter. Like Julia Ward Howe, Melville was a Unionist, a Northern abolitionist who despised racism and slavery, but he is not writing to rally the troops with a Christian message ("Mine eyes have seen the glory"). On the contrary, he argues for the fraternity of the dying, whose abstract ideals, "Fame or country," suddenly pale before the existential fact of dying. He rhymes *eve* and *undeceive* and uses parenthesis to seal off the next statement, which brings home the sharp, acerbic truth: ("What like a bullet can undeceive!)." This isn't framed as a question but as an exclamatory statement. It might well be the most significant tagline from the poetry of the Civil War period.

Melville was one of the undeceived. The poem turns like the end of a Shakespearean sonnet—"*But now* they lie low"—and closes with a dual sense of the ongoing nature and final silence of death. It circles back and returns to the pastoral image of swallows flying low and skimming lightly over the field, "wheeling still," but there is no other sound present. It also circles back to the original rhyme of the ballad or hymn (*low / Shiloh*). The final line has a ceremonial or ritual feeling—"And all is hushed at Shiloh." There is no redemption here, no victory or triumphalism, just a hushed silence. Shiloh has now become a place for the hallowed dead. And the poem itself stands as a dark instruction to the future. Or as Melville puts it in the Supplement to *Battle-Pieces*: "Let us pray that the terrible historic tragedy of our time may not have been enacted without instructing our whole beloved country through pity and fear."

Along with Walt Whitman's book of vigils, *Drum-Taps* (1865), *Battle-Pieces* stands as one of the two most fearless and shattering books of Civil War poems. It is gutsy and unremitting. Whitman and Melville were the only two American poets who tried to describe what Wilfred Owen would later call "the pity of War," the horror of war on a monstrous scale. Whitman's contribution to our poetry is now a bedrock, but Melville's *Battle-Pieces* is still underacknowledged. By writing requiems for "dying foemen" and linking art to war, by recognizing that war was a necessary and perhaps even inescapable subject for our poetry, Melville was also creating a documentary archive for poets to come, poets who self-consciously looked for American precedents.

Melville's conscientiousness ("I muse upon my country's ills"), his poetic contribution, came to me through the Melville revival of the 1920s, from F. O. Matthiessen's *American Renaissance* and a group of poet-scholars who recognized Melville's misgivings and confrontations, such as Charles Olson, Robert Penn Warren, and Daniel Hoffman, who found Melville's legacy ("All wars are boyish, and are fought by boys") in the bitter lyrics of Stephen Crane ("Do not weep, maiden, for war is kind"). Think of Muriel

Rukeyser's groundbreaking long poem, "The Book of the Dead" (1938), about mine workers in West Virginia in the late 1920s and early '30s, and Charles Reznikoff's *Holocaust* (1975), which compresses twenty-six volumes of courtroom testimony from the trials of Nazi war criminals at Nuremberg and Jerusalem. These books were emotionally costly and even harrowing to write and thus challenging to read. Personally, I am grateful for these courageous testaments to what Melville called the "visible truth," which he defined as "the apprehension of the absolute condition of present things as they strike the eye of the man who fears them not, though they do their worst to him."

EMILY DICKINSON (1830–1886)

#479

Because I could not stop for Death -
He kindly stopped for me -
The Carriage held but just Ourselves -
And Immortality.

We slowly drove - He knew no haste
And I had put away
My labor and my leisure too,
For His Civility -

We passed the School, where Children strove
At Recess - in the Ring -
We passed the Fields of Gazing Grain -
We passed the Setting Sun -

Or rather - He passed Us -
The Dews drew quivering and Chill -
For only Gossamer, my Gown -
My Tippet - only Tulle -

We paused before a House that seemed
A Swelling of the Ground -
The Roof was scarcely visible -
The Cornice - in the Ground -

Since then - 'tis Centuries - and yet
Feels shorter than the Day
I first surmised the Horses' Heads
Were toward Eternity -

Composed c. 1862

I HAD NO concept of the radicality of Emily Dickinson's work. I did not understand her passionate intellectual ferocity. Like all poets setting out and making their way through high school, I felt like an oddball and should have liked her most popular piece—"I'm Nobody! Who are you? / Are you - Nobody - too?"—which is about being an outsider, but I thought it was cutesy and mixed it up with the poems of E. E. Cummings, which I condescended to as an adolescent. My teacher liked a verse that would later go on a postage stamp, "If I can stop one heart from breaking, / I shall not live in vain," but I thought it sounded treacly, like something from the Girl Scouts. I practically gagged over a poem called "The Railway Train" ("I like to see it lap the Miles - / And lick the Valleys up"). Dickinson's poems were given fake titles and regularized in textbooks in those days, and their mysterious splendors evaded me.

My senior year I met an art student who wore a faded leather jacket and smoked cigarettes and loved Emily Dickinson's poems. She said that Dickinson was so far out of the box that we were still trying to put her back inside. She said that Dickinson was a spiritual force to be reckoned with, like Emily Brontë or St. John of the Cross. I should stop comparing her to Longfellow and start thinking about Arthur Rimbaud or Sylvia Plath, who were Loaded Guns. Listen to this, she said, fixing me with a stare: "I like a look of Agony, / Because I know it's true." One day she noticed I wasn't wearing a belt and said, "He put the Belt around my life - / I heard the Buckle snap." She said that I was deceived because Dickinson wore a brooch and an old-fashioned dress; in fact, her poems were volcanoes ready to erupt, they were fractured and filled with calamity, I should take the test:

> If I read a book [and] it makes my whole body so cold no fire can warm me, I know *that* is poetry. If I feel physically as if the top of my head were taken off, I know *that* is poetry. These are the only way I know it. Is there any other way.

Dickinson's idea of poetry changed me. Unlike my high school teachers, she didn't say that she knew poetry by any intrinsic qualities of poetry itself, like rhyme and meter. Rather, she recognized true poetry by the extremity, the actual physical intensity, of her response to it. She knew it by contact, what it did to her, and she trusted her response. She had a voracious appetite for reading poetry. She read it with hunger and thirst—it was sustenance to her. I vowed to be more like that. I wanted to catch up, and so I bought a copy of her *Selected Poems*, which baffled and intrigued me, like Rimbaud's prose poems, which I gobbled up in bad translations. I decided that if I memorized some of her poems then I would understand them better. I still recall the night I rifled through the pages and came to "Because I could not stop for Death," which stopped me in my tracks. I didn't know it was famous. "If I feel physically as if the top of my head were taken off, I know *that* is poetry."

I have been reciting this poem for fifty years and I'm still not certain that I can encompass it. Emily Dickinson seems to have written this untitled lyric sometime in 1862, in the midst of the Civil War. One of the odd lusters of American poetry is that the early 1860s were the years of her greatest productivity as a poet. She wrote roughly half of her nearly eighteen hundred poems while a war raged obliquely in the background. It seems meaningful that Dickinson, who was a shocking poet and an American original, found it necessary to write poems of self-division at such a decisive moment of self-division for the country.

No one poem can enclose Dickinson's work. She pointed a wide compass. In the best single essay written about her work, "Vesuvius at Home," Adrienne Rich catalogues some of her subjects: "volcanoes, deserts, eternity, suicide, physical passion, wild beasts, rape, power, madness, separation, the daemon, the grave." I would add crucifixion, pain, and the afterlife, among others. Many of Dickinson's poems are surgically probing, skeptical, deathward-leaning, concerned with deliverance, obsessed with endings. She satirized the hypocrisy of organized religion, the outdated Puritanism of her day, but she was interested in the metaphysical concerns of Christianity and created her own idiosyncratic theology. Her poems seem written in the aftermath of some extraordinary unnamed personal trauma. One after the other, her adorations come to grief. Most of them do not address a collective suffering directly, though they are shaded by the Civil War much more than has been previously thought. They have a martial backdrop. Writing to *Poetry* magazine in 1932, Marianne Moore, a figure also lauded for her "purity," noticed something that has been repeatedly overlooked: "Emily Dickinson cared about events that mattered to the nation."

In 1864, Dickinson wrote to her first cousins, Louise and Frances Norcross, "Sorrow seems more general than it did, and not the estate of a few persons, since the war began; and if the anguish of others helped one with one's own, now would be many medicines." She was not a didactic poet like, say, Julia Ward Howe, who justified the American conflict with biblical righteousness, but she followed the political and social issues, the cataclysm that convulsed the nation, and registered the overriding anguish. She told her cousins, "I noticed that Robert Browning had made another poem, and was astonished—till I remembered that I, myself, in my smaller way, sang off charnel steps." In her most explicit Civil War poem, she confessed: "It feels a shame to be Alive - / When Men so brave - / Are dead - / One envies the Distinguished Dust - / Permitted - such a Head -" (#524). Many of Dickinson's poems address mortality, the war outside matched only by the one within. During these years, Dickinson often wavers or argues or even wars with herself about the concept of death as grievous end point. Sometimes she suggests we are doomed to oblivion, other times she posits a form of ongoing or eternal life. "The Risks of Immortality are perhaps its' charm," she speculated to Thomas Wentworth Higginson, "A secure Delight suffers in enchantment."

It was initially possible to overlook the historical timeline of "Because I could not stop for Death" because it wasn't published until some three decades later in her first posthumous collection, *Poems of Emily Dickinson* (1890), which was edited by two of her friends and advocates, Higginson and Mabel Loomis Todd. They were more sensitive to the merits of her work than has been allowed, though they also bowdlerized her texts. They regularized the punctuation, changing dashes to commas, semicolons, and periods. In this poem, they altered the wording in four of the lines and deleted the crucial fourth stanza, which they viewed as contradictory. They also added a sentimental title, "The Chariot." It wasn't until Thomas Johnson's 1955 edition of Dickinson's poems that the original was partially restored, and it wasn't until R. W. Franklin's facsimile edition of *The Manuscript Books of Emily Dickinson* (1981) that readers could see for themselves Dickinson's handwritten final version of what Allen Tate called "one of the perfect poems in English."

"Because I could not stop for Death" has an eerie fatalism. It pairs with "I heard a Fly buzz - when I died" (#591). In these two poems the speaker is already dead and addresses us from the other side of the grave. This estranges the ritual or processional feeling. We don't usually think of a dead person consciously attending her own funeral. Dickinson's poems are almost always spoken from the first-person point of view and feel confessional, but her characteristic speaker is fictive or provisional. She throws her voice. I consider her as much a poet of persona as, say, Robert Browning and Elizabeth Barrett Browning, two of her favorite poets. As she cautioned Higginson in a letter in July 1862: "When I state myself, as the Representative of the Verse—it does not mean—me—but a supposed person."

Dickinson's poems are also suppositions, many of them about time and timelessness. Her innate skepticism keeps undermining her faith, and she can't hold fast to one belief. As she wrote to her cousin Perez Dickinson Cowan, "You speak with so much trust of that which only trust can prove, it makes me feel away, as if my English mates spoke sudden in Italian." She often seems panicky and terrified of death, somewhat at sea, frightened of the literal moment of dying, and determined to find something in its aftermath. She chastised Cowan and confided in him: "It grieves me that you speak of Death with so much expectation. I know there is no pang like that for those we love, nor any leisure like the one they leave so closed behind them, but Dying is a wild Night and a new Road. I suppose we are all thinking of Immortality, at times so stimulated that we cannot sleep." Dickinson's nervous excitement is often palpable in her poems. She kept working variations on her core subjects, death and immortality, and testing their consequences. That's why it's so hard to get a single fix on her belief system. For example, in "Because I could not stop for Death" the speaker is accompanied by Immortality, which suggests something deathless, and headed toward Eternity, which suggests something endless, an indefinite length of time. In a later poem, #743, she reverses the terms and proposes just the opposite:

> Behind Me - dips Eternity -
> Before Me - Immortality -
> Myself - the Term between -

Dickinson treats the self here as small and liminal: it exists between hyphens, two endless expanses. The word *Term* is abidingly clever. It suggests that the self is a word with a precise meaning, like a figure in a poem, but it also connotes a fixed period of time. We are not made to last. Dickinson's wit was a shield against fear. She was a recluse, a stay-at-home, but poetry was her means of transport and she used it as a vehicle to journey beyond time.

Dickinson's poems are simultaneously compressed and expansive—she has a way of stretching out or contracting time—and here it takes her six stanzas, just twenty-four lines, to dramatize a personal encounter with death, who is personified as a gentle, courteous male figure who takes her on a mysterious carriage ride and journey. A. R. Ammons said that "a poem is a walk," but this one is paced as a carriage ride, like the ones that the Dickinson girls, Emily and Lavinia, often took with their father. In New England towns, it was common for young men to take young women for outings in a horse-drawn carriage. Dickinson's biographers have speculated that this poem was specifically instigated by the death of her distant cousin Olivia Coleman, a beautiful twenty-year-old, much sought after in Amherst, who was sick with "galloping consumption" and suddenly suffered a hemorrhage while she was out riding in a carriage. It seems likely that Dickinson took a biographical incident and fused it with her literary influences. For example, I hear an echo of Keats's "Ode to a Nightingale" ("for many a time / I have been half in love with easeful Death") and Robert Browning's poem "The Last Ride Together":

> What if we still ride on, we two
> With life for ever old yet new,
> Changed not in kind but in degree,
> The instant made eternity,—
> And heaven just prove that I and she
>   Ride, ride together, for ever ride?

Dickinson might have felt the relevance of the medieval story of Death and the Maiden, though her maiden has a speaking role, and I feel the backdrop of the classical myth of Persephone, who was violently abducted by Hades and carried off to the underworld. But unlike the Greek mythicist, Dickinson adds an element of genteel courtesy to the terrifying operation.

One of the more startling things about "Because I could not stop for Death" is that the speaker doesn't take herself to be a victim or rail against her fate. She goes off willingly, almost without affect. There is a quiet, cordial formality to the trip, which is echoed in the form of the poem. Dickinson employs here one of her favorite metrical forms, common meter, which consists of alternating four-beat and three-beat lines. This traditional form— think of "Amazing Grace"—is one of the three standard variations of the hymn form, and she uses it here to create the steady, rocking motion of a final ride in a horse-drawn carriage.

Dickinson was outwardly quiet but inwardly subversive, a secret revolutionary, and she typically used the hymn form to undermine its inherent communitarian values. David T. Porter and other scholars have argued that by its very nature the hymn form carries an attitude "of faith, humility, and inspiration," a baseline of orthodoxy that Dickinson artfully refracts in her poems. Think of her quirky punctuation. It was not unusual to capitalize nouns for emphasis in the mid-nineteenth century, and letter writers commonly used dashes, and yet Dickinson marshaled these devices with so much force that it seems almost as if she invented them, capitalizing nouns for special emphasis, and punctuating her poems liberally with dashes, creating extra intensities, isolating phrases. So, too, she uses a traditional rhyme scheme of *abcb* but fulfills it with a series of loose, surprising, and unorthodox rhymes. For her, the rebellion is personal, the feeling distinct, and scandalously individualistic.

"Because I could not stop for Death" is conceived in the past tense. At the beginning, the speaker remembers being immersed in life itself, too busy to pay attention to death, but then death comes calling at her door. This is a witty comment on normal human experience because we are all always too busy to die, though death is never too busy to stop by for us. We don't ordinarily think of death as "kindly"—it is more often figured as a "grim reaper"—but here it is personified as a well-mannered caller who takes the speaker on a formal outing. It's the two of them and one other unexpected companion, a sort of chaperone, Immortality. There are dashes at the end point of each of the first three lines, as if to isolate each stage of the departure. This creates an additional surprise at the end of the third line, where there is no grammatical purpose to the extra dash. The reader pauses at the end of the line—"just Ourselves"—and then breathes out, "And Immortality." Note the end rhyme in the first stanza, how a small, one-syllable word, *me*, rhymes with a grand five-syllable word, *Immortality*, capitalized for emphasis. In a letter to Higginson, Dickinson called Immortality "the

Flood Subject," which suggests that it's totally uncontainable. Now that very immensity, something or someone completely overwhelming, is accompanying her speaker. Present and accounted for, it is inside the carriage with her.

There is calm stateliness to the procession—"We slowly drove - He knew no haste"—since death doesn't need to hurry, He exists outside of time. The speaker acknowledges that she had now "put away" or given up her earthly days, which the poet ties together with the alliterative words *labor* and *leisure*. She has traded them in for his comity. There is an eye rhyme in the words *away* and *Civility*. Death is characterized as a courtly suitor.

There is a precise process of maturation encapsulated in the third stanza, which progresses through the course of a day from noon to dusk. Dickinson purposefully capitalizes and alliterates *Recess* and *Ring*, *Gazing Grain*, and *Setting Sun*. This helps to slow and ritualize the movement of the carriage in time. The children at play, the only other people in the poem, still have a future in front of them. The gazing grain is ripe and has reached maturity, the sun is going down or dying. There is a slight dissonance in the supposed rhyme of *Ring* and *Sun*, which sets up the jarring turn in the fourth stanza: "Or rather - He passed Us."

Dickinson corrects herself here. This move troubled her editors, but now seems a sign of her intellectual trustworthiness. The galloping motion of the horses, the iambic meter and steady rhythm, are suddenly ruptured. The poem takes on a different time signature. She now understands that the sun will continue revolving day after day, but her journey is ending. She captures the texture of time passing—the word *passed* is repeated four times in the third and fourth stanzas, the middle of the poem—and a warm day inevitably turning into a chilly night. The speaker is dressed for an evening out—she is wearing a gossamer, or very thin, light gown and a tippet, a narrow piece of clothing worn over the shoulders, that is made of tulle, a lightweight, extremely fine, even dreamy fabric, often used to embellish wedding gowns. The implication is inevitable that she is dressed for some grand outing, probably a ball, possibly a wedding. But she has forgotten her coat and now seems exposed to the cold. Dickinson's tight alliterations—"*D*ews / *d*rew"; "*G*ossamer / *G*own"; "*T*ippet / *T*ulle"—suggest how the shivery cold is pressing down on the speaker. There is a purposeful slant rhyme in *Chill* and *Tulle*.

Everything has been leading to the next quatrain, which might have concluded the poem. The journey should have ended, but the speaker uses the word *paused* to indicate how the carriage has come to a halt outside what is presumably a cemetery. She describes a stone vault—seemingly her own grave—as a house buried in the ground. So this is where her body will be permanently housed. She emphasizes the finality by doubling the word *Ground* and using it as an identical rhyme. But this house only *seems* to be her final resting place.

The last stanza still comes as a shock:

> Since then - 'tis Centuries - and yet
> Feels shorter than the Day
> I first surmised the Horses' Heads
> Were toward Eternity -

The speaker is addressing us from beyond the grave now in some altered, ever-present moment. Time has been skewed. Centuries have passed and yet feel shorter than the momentous single day that death stopped and carried her away. The lyric changes from past to present tense with the verb *Feels*. The word *surmised* is noteworthy because it indicates that the speaker initially presumed something to be true based on scanty evidence. She recalls that it was during her carriage ride that she first guessed that the horses in front of her were continuing past the graveside, their heads angled "toward Eternity." What she first conjectured now seems even more likely, though she still can't quite see beyond the heads of the horses. Just as the tiny word *me* rhymes with the enormous word *Immortality* at the beginning of the poem, so now does the small word *Day*, which suggests something temporal, pair with the larger word *Eternity*, which is beyond time. So, too, the poem closes with a dash and not a period. It halts but doesn't conclude. The speaker is left in a state of suspended animation, always traveling, never arriving.

Emily Dickinson was an extremist of the imagination, a visionary thinker, a spiritual revisionist, like Emily Brontë and St. John of the Cross, like Sor Juana and Arthur Rimbaud. She stated, "Forever - is composed of Nows" (#690), and proposed, "Forever might be short" (#618). At the conclusion of "Because I could not stop for Death," she posits the soul of a speaker who is still alive centuries after her mortal death, someone who is forever in transit and never stops, never lands, never reaches a final fixed or stable destination. She now exists in a state of timelessness. To read Emily Dickinson's work is to travel from one state of time to another, to accompany her on a stately, original, and terrifying journey.

The New Colossus

Not like the brazen giant of Greek fame,
With conquering limbs astride from land to land;
Here at our sea-washed, sunset gates shall stand
A mighty woman with a torch, whose flame
Is the imprisoned lightning, and her name
Mother of Exiles. From her beacon-hand
Glows world-wide welcome; her mild eyes command
The air-bridged harbor that twin cities frame.
"Keep, ancient lands, your storied pomp!" cries she
With silent lips. "Give me your tired, your poor,
Your huddled masses yearning to breathe free,
The wretched refuse of your teeming shore.
Send these, the homeless, tempest-tost to me,
I lift my lamp beside the golden door!"

1883

EMMA LAZARUS came from a prominent family with an unusually long American history; her great-grandparents were early settlers in the colonies, her grandparents lived in New York City as far back as the American Revolution. As a fourth-generation Sephardic American Jew, she felt part of the country, the American entitlement, which was rare for most Jews of her time period, the second half of the nineteenth century. That's why she was so well positioned to write a rejoinder to Longfellow's eloquent elegy, his premature funeral oratory for a people, "The Jewish Cemetery at Newport." She admired him greatly—he was already established in the firmament, she was virtually unknown—and yet that did not impede her from using his own poetic weapon, i.e., the heroic quatrain, to refute his conclusion that Jewish civilization was sadly doomed to extinction. She didn't feel that she was part of a dying breed; on the contrary, she affirmed that she was part of a continuity, an ancient civilization reformed and re-created in the New World.

Lazarus published three books of poems in her short life: *Poems and Translations* (1866), which came out when she was only seventeen years old, *Admetus and Other Poems* (1871), and *Songs of a Semite: The Dance to Death and Other Poems* (1882). In her day, she was a well-known translator and person of letters—I am especially taken with her book *Poems and Ballads of Heinrich Heine* (1881) and her translations of Hebrew poets from medieval Spain: Judah ha-Levi, Solomon Ibn Gabirol, and Moses Ibn Ezra. "In her lifelong devotion to verse in other languages and the importance of translation for her own poetry," John Hollander points out, "Lazarus belongs in the line of American poets running from Longfellow to Pound, Robert Lowell, and W. S. Merwin." Lazarus was also a literary exotic in Victorian America, something the popular Fireside poets, who cherished the image of the cozy homestead hearth and the Christian schoolroom, found hard to fathom, a postbiblical American Jew. Lazarus was only thirty-eight when she died of cancer in 1887, and now her posthumous fame rests on her authorship of a single poem, which contains the two most famous lines of poetry in American culture: "Give me your tired, your poor, / Your huddled masses yearning to breathe free."

My grandmother was not a literary person, but she told me about Emma Lazarus, who, like her, was born in the United States but stood up for refugees, like my grandfather, who had emigrated from Eastern Europe, one of "the huddled masses." My father, whose family fled Germany in the 1920s, recalled that "The New Colossus," which he noticed on the pedestal of the Statue of Liberty, was the first poem that he ever saw in English, a language he couldn't understand. He wondered what it was all about. That is how I learned about Emma Lazarus's quintessential American poem.

Lazarus wrote her poem at a time when European immigrants were arriving in large numbers in the United States. There was a rabid nativist backlash against foreigners, enacted through racist policies like the Chinese Exclusion Act of 1882. Determined to do something for people on the lower rung, Lazarus was inspired by Henry George's book *Progress and Poverty* (1879), which proposed to solve the problem of income inequality by taxing

landowners and using the money for the public good. George's political eco-
nomics and democratic vision, "Georgism," spoke to her deepening social
consciousness, and she titled a sonnet "Progress and Poverty" (1881), whose
opening lines prefigure "The New Colossus": "Oh splendid age when Sci-
ence lights her lamp / At the brief lightning's momentary flame, / Fixing
it steadfast as a star." Two years later she would reconfigure Science as "A
mighty woman with a torch, whose flame / Is the imprisoned lightning." She
linked the situation of workers to the plight of impoverished Russian Jewish
refugees, who were fleeing pogroms and antisemitic violence at home. The
fact that not everyone was on board only fevered her project. She was poised
to write a public poem and stand up on behalf of the exiled.

"The New Colossus" was commissioned for an auction to raise the cash
needed to build a pedestal for the French sculptor Frédéric-Auguste Barthol-
di's statue *La Liberté éclairant le monde* (Liberty Enlightening the World).
The statue, whose subject was the Roman goddess Libertas, was braced from
within by a structure designed by Gustave Eiffel. The poem was read at
the opening of a fundraising exhibit on November 2, 1883—James Russell
Lowell told Lazarus that her sonnet "gives its subject a raison d'être"—and
subsequently recited three years later at the statue's dedication. It was printed
as part of a group of sonnets in her posthumous two-volume collection, *The
Poems of Emma Lazarus* (1889). It wasn't actually embossed on the pedestal
until 1903 when it was republished in the *New York World* and *The New York
Times*. It was timely then and it is timely now.

Lazarus's vision of America as a haven for people fleeing ungodly historical
circumstances—poverty, tyranny—has always had its entrenched antago-
nists, and so I was only partly surprised that "The New Colossus" came
back into the news in the summer of 2019 when the Trump administration
was promoting its reactionary anti-immigration policy. That's when Ken
Cuccinelli, the acting director of U.S. Citizenship and Immigration Services,
appeared on NPR's *Morning Edition*. The moderator, Rachel Martin, asked
him an apt question: "Would you also agree that Emma Lazarus's words
etched on the Statue of Liberty, 'Give me your tired, your poor,' are also part
of the American ethos?" Cuccinelli's response had so much gall that it was
almost exciting: "They certainly are: 'Give me your tired and your poor who
can stand on their own two feet and who will not become a public charge,'"
he answered, and added, "That plaque was put on the Statue of Liberty at

almost the same time as the first public charge law was passed—very interesting timing." This revision of the wording and intent of Lazarus's poem would be funny if it weren't so ignorant and infuriating.

To be clear: Lazarus believed in spreading the wealth. She embraced George's moral idea of "a wider, loftier, truer public spirit," and supported his argument that it was time to empower "the men and women who are at the very bottom of the social scale. In securing the equal rights of these we shall secure the equal rights of all." This pact did not mean inviting into the country only the wealthy or credentialed, "those who can stand on their own two feet," but those who could not walk by themselves and needed help, the oppressed. The ignorant attempt by a right-wing government operative to repurpose "The New Colossus" also speaks to the poem's continuing power of authority, its inherent idealism and cherished place in the American canon, on the American conscience.

Lazarus initially balked at the idea of writing a poem "to order" but found herself absorbed by the subject, and unable to resist the challenge. According to Constance Cary Harrison, who approached her on behalf of the fundraising committee, Lazarus changed her mind when Harrison linked the statue to the immigration of Russian Jews: "'Think of that Goddess standing on her pedestal down yonder in the bay, and holding her torch out to those Russian refugees of yours you are so fond of visiting at Ward's Island,' I suggested. The shaft sped home—her dark eyes deepened—her cheeks flushed—the time for merriment was passed—she said not a word more, then." There is some self-aggrandizement and mythologizing here and yet the linkage gave Lazarus her stimulus and motive to art.

It may take a couple of readings to realize that "The New Colossus" never actually names the Statue of Liberty. In point of fact, the statue is given a new name, "Mother of Exiles." So, too, Lazarus ignores the French origin of the giant female figure. At the time, she was also making the case for an Indigenous, self-consciously American literature. In 1883, the idea was still being bandied about that "the extremely adverse conditions" of America explained the absence of a great national poet, and Lazarus responded vehemently: "I have never believed in *the want of a theme*—wherever there is humanity, there is a theme for a great poem—& I think it is the poet's fault if he does not know how to utilize the materials & accessories which surround him." Lazarus had an Emersonian confidence in American originality, and she realized that she was being presented with an opportunity, a statue for the New World, "the materials & accessories" for a poetic response. She was struck by lightning when she wrote the lines that everyone knows, but these memorable lines are invariably lifted out of context and the odd result is that the poem as a totality is often neglected and underread.

The title of Lazarus's poem, "The New Colossus," immediately confronts the enormous scale of the statue. It is colossal—larger than life. This also indicates that the Statue of Liberty is a replacement for a gigantic precursor, the Colossus of Rhodes, the great bronze monument to the sun god Helios, "the brazen giant of Greek fame." The word *brazen* means "made of brass," but it also means "brash, presumptuous, arrogant," the traits of a conqueror. Lazarus was well aware that the Old Colossus was constructed to celebrate a military victory, which at the time was believed to straddle the entrance to the Mandrákion harbor in Rhodes, Greece. It was a beacon that operated as a warning: "Beware all those who enter here." It may have been considered one of the Seven Wonders of the World—it reportedly stood about 110 feet tall atop a 50-foot platform—but she was eager to topple and replace it with Bartholdi's torch-bearing *Liberté*, a strong, embracing female alternative to Old World male military power. The poem stages a conflict between patriarchal and maternal values, and it is not much of a stretch to think that Lazarus was self-consciously writing as a woman talking back to male power and dominion.

"The New Colossus" is a firmly constructed Petrarchan sonnet, which is a bipartite invention, a two-part argument. Lazarus understood it as an asymmetrical form that invites a two-part division of thought. The octave, the first eight lines, consists of two quatrains, which tightly rhyme: *abbaabba*. She purposefully links *fame* and *flame*, *name* and *frame*. She joins together *land* and *stand*, *hand* and *command*. She signals the turn, or *volta*, by having the statue itself speak in the sestet, the last six lines.

Lazarus was influenced by Whitman's poem "Crossing Brooklyn Ferry," which is also situated in the waters around New York City. More pertinently, Shelley's sonnet "Ozymandias," an allegorical poem about a statue, trails somewhere in the background. She is in some way responding to Shelley's meditation on the transient, vainglorious nature of power, and might well have recalled Ozymandias's words, which were purportedly inscribed on the pedestal of a ruined sculpture: "Look on my Works, ye Mighty, and despair!"

As Austin Allen puts it, "Though the allusion is never explicit, it's tempting to contrast Lady Liberty's mild-eyed 'command' with Ozymandias's 'sneer of cold command'; her democratic compassion with his autocratic cruelty; her message of hope with his call to 'despair'; her triumphant wholeness with his brokenness."

There is a decisive argument in the first sentence of "The New Colossus," which moves in stately procession across five lines and then comes to an upright standstill. As I've reread the poem over the years, my admiration for it has increased—I've found it bolder, stranger, more insistent. For example, it's a brazen act to begin a patriotic poem with a negative comparison, a simile in reverse, an outright refutation:

> *Not like* the brazen giant of Greek fame,
> With conquering limbs astride from land to land;
> Here at our sea-washed, sunset gates shall stand
> A mighty woman with a torch, whose flame
> Is the imprisoned lightning, and her name
> Mother of Exiles.

At a metrical level, Lazarus begins somewhat impudently by rupturing the iambic pattern—she starts the line with a trochee and ends it with a spondee: "Nót like the brázen giant of Gréek fáme." She echoes the Greek dactylic hexameter, the meter of epic, and thus gives the line an epic weight. She captures a sense of the annihilative power of the giant in the second line, which is more metrically regular—it strides forward. There is an avowal in the third line: "*Here . . . shall stand.*" The future tense—*shall stand*—reminds us that this replacement was still a prophecy, though you can hear her verbal savor in the prospect, the phrasing of sibilants, "Here at our *sea-washed, sunset gates shall stand.*" It all has the feeling of statuesque command.

Ekphrasis is the rhetorical description of a work of art, and the first eight lines encapsulate an ekphrastic description of the statue. It breaches a divide. Some ekphrastic poems are notional—they represent imaginary works—but Lazarus takes on the task of describing an actual work of art, a living statue. But the ekphrastic mode invariably does more than merely describe a silent work; it also ventures to address it. In Lazarus's case, she throws her voice and speaks on the statue's behalf. She is so adept at describing Lady Liberty that it's possible to miss how carefully she sneaks in and insinuates her own editorial intention. For example, she is accurately illustrating the statue when she calls her "A mighty woman with a torch," but she is projecting something onto her when she names her "Mother of Exiles."

As the poet continues, she does more than describe the statue's physical gesture, she also interprets it:

> From her beacon-hand
> Glows world-wide welcome; her mild eyes command
> The air-bridged harbor that twin cities frame.

As a reader, the stutter-step of *w* sounds—"Glows *w*orld-*w*ide *w*elcome"—forces you to loiter over the fact that the statue is welcoming people to the island. By the way she positions her phrase at the end of the line, Lazarus emphasizes her claim that the female eyes are "mild" but assertively "command" the harbor with as much authority as the Old Colossus.

There is a specific reality here, too, being metaphorically described. In the first stanza, those lovely "sea-washed, sunset gates" refer to the entrance-ways to the Hudson and East Rivers. The "imprisoned lightning," which illuminates but doesn't destroy, refers to Liberty's electrically lit torch. "The air-bridged harbor that twin cities frame," a sentence that sounds like Hart Crane, cites the harbor that stands between Manhattan and Brooklyn, which were still separate cities in the 1880s.

I want to linger over the now-familiar image of the mother holding up a torch, a lamp. As a reader of the Hebrew Bible, Lazarus lit a flame from the book of Judges, which especially appealed to nineteenth-century women poets. The scholar Shira Wolosky has perceptively pointed out the significance of the recurrent lamp imagery in Lazarus's work, which is associated with the Jewish Enlightenment (Haskalah) and the Chanukah lamp, "the sign of freedom from Hellenist oppression," and the subtle recasting of the statue so that it resembles the figure of Deborah, who is also called a "woman of torches" (Judges 4:4) and designated "a mother in Israel" (Judges 5:7). She is a prophet who empowers the army of Barak, whose Hebrew name means "lightning." Without explicitly saying so, Lazarus treats the statue as a biblical prophet. Like the Puritans, she brings the Hebrew Bible to the American mission.

Lazarus's strategic method becomes evident in "1492," the lesser-known sonnet that she wrote to accompany "The New Colossus." The year 1492 is characterized as "Thou two-faced year," because it marks the expulsion of Jews from Spain, the height of the Spanish Inquisition, and the year of Columbus's arrival in the Americas. Here, Lazarus purposefully joins American life to the stream of Jewish history, her own family history, which informs *Songs of a Semite*:

> Thou two-faced year, Mother of Change and Fate,
> Didst weep when Spain cast forth with flaming sword,
> The children of the prophets of the Lord,
> Prince, priest, and people, spurned by zealot hate.
> Hounded from sea to sea, from state to state,
> The West refused them, and the East abhorred.
> No anchorage the known world could afford,
> Close-locked was every port, barred every gate.
> Then smiling, thou unveil'dst, O two-faced year,
> A virgin world where doors of sunset part,
> Saying, "Ho, all who weary, enter here!
> There falls each ancient barrier that the art
> Of race or creed or rank devised, to rear
> Grim bulwarked hatred between heart and heart!"

"The sunset gates" of one poem rhyme with the "doors of sunset" of the other, and the harbor finds a true anchorage. The clumsy formulation of the virgin world—"'Ho, all who weary, enter here!'"—pointedly reverses the Dantean inscription over the gate of Hell: "Abandon all hope, you who enter here." It isn't nearly as memorable or elegant as the statuesque Deborah, who asserts, "Give me your tired, your poor," but it carries the same underlying message and spiritual import. The New World may not have been quite so virginal as Lazarus supposed—there were already people living here for thousands of years—but she does break down an "ancient barrier" and hold up a democracy of reception, regardless of race, creed, or rank, as a foundational premise of the republic. That's why the prophetess holds a torch over her head with her right hand and in her left hand carries a tablet inscribed with the date of the Declaration of Independence, July 4, 1776.

Lazarus carefully generalizes the ethnic and biblical references in "The New Colossus," which everywhere shadow and deepen it. This informs my rereading of the last six lines of the poem. Here, the poet treats the statue as a golem, an image of liberty created from stone and magically endowed with life. She lets us know that she is putting words into the statue's mouth since it speaks with "silent lips." In fact, the language is pegged higher than speech, closer to a cry or even an outcry. Keeping the figure of Deborah in mind, you hear it pitched differently, more akin to prophecy, someone taking up the mantle of prophet, judge, and deliverer:

> "Keep, ancient lands, your storied pomp!" cries she
> With silent lips. "Give me your tired, your poor,
> Your huddled masses yearning to breathe free,
> The wretched refuse of your teeming shore.
> Send these, the homeless, tempest-tost to me,
> I lift my lamp beside the golden door!"

The rhyming is purposeful in these six lines: The word *poor* washes up on *shore*, a slant rhyme, and closes with *door*, a full rhyme. The word *she* rhymes exactly with the words *free* and *me*. There is a subtle change in the vocabulary and diction, which starts out like Shelley, "Keep, ancient lands," and ends up closer to Whitman: "Give me your tired, your poor." "Defying the 'storied pomp' of antiquity, precedent, and ceremony," the scholar Esther Schor argues, "the statue speaks not in the new language of reason and light but in in the divine language of lovingkindness."

The poet interpolates what the statue silently cries and gives us a pronouncement that is still controversial, still provocative: "Give me your tired, your poor, / Your huddled masses yearning to breathe free, / The wretched refuse of your teeming shore." Part of the formulaic power of this is how Lazarus takes words that are usually adjectives, *tired* and *poor*, and gives them the authority of nouns, of people: "your tired, your poor." She builds an incantatory power into the triple repetition so that the three words operate as adjectives, "*your tired, your poor, / your huddled* masses." We have waited all this time, almost the entire poem, for the word *free* to appear, and when it finally arrives it is linked to breathing ("breathe free") and placed in a woman's voice. Some critics hear a kind of aristocratic condescension in the tag "wretched refuse," a term that is certainly weighted—perhaps this is how the Europeans view these people. Lazarus's sympathy for the outcast is clear and undeterred. Formally, the adjectives create a kind of subject rhyme: "*huddled* masses," "*wretched* refuse," "*teeming* shore." The language seems almost desperate as the poet struggles to capture the suffering of the wandering homeless.

There is a compelling migration of pronouns in this section of the poem, an interweaving between the second person ("*your* storied pomp"), the third person ("cries *she*"), and the first person ("Give *me*"). The ventriloquist behind the statue is making an American claim on those who have been summarily discharged from their countries of origin. The final charge of the poem has become utterly crucial in our troubled, xenophobic times: "Send these, the homeless, tempest-tost to me, / I lift my lamp beside the golden door." Lazarus has been retooling a rhetoric of high command, moving from "*Keep*, ancient lands" to "*Give me* your tired" to "*Send these*, the homeless." She savors the coined consonantal "*t*empest-*t*ost," repurposes the letter *l*—"I *l*ift my *l*amp beside the go*l*den door"—and clinches the sound with the letter *d*, "gol*d*en *d*oor." The lifting of the lamp is the speaker's last prophetic gesture.

What Lazarus calls "the golden door" is literally the entranceway to the United States through Ellis Island. It is "golden" because it stands for new opportunity, a promise of freedom for people like my grandfather, who came from Latvia, or my father, who sought refuge from the Nazis. Lazarus believed that the doorway to America should be opened to the despised poor, the otherwise refused. She stood in solidarity with them, with us. She uses the Statue of Liberty to make a powerful statement about what America represents. "The New Colossus" is a constant reminder of America's pledge to embrace immigrants, its commitment to relieve the suffering of others.

EDWIN ARLINGTON ROBINSON (1869–1935)

Eros Turannos

She fears him, and will always ask
  What fated her to choose him;
She meets in his engaging mask
  All reasons to refuse him;
But what she meets and what she fears
Are less than are the downward years,
Drawn slowly to the foamless weirs
  Of age, were she to lose him.

Between a blurred sagacity
  That once had power to sound him,
And Love, that will not let him be
  The Judas that she found him,
Her pride assuages her almost,
As if it were alone the cost.—
He sees that he will not be lost,
  And waits and looks around him.

A sense of ocean and old trees
  Envelops and allures him;
Tradition, touching all he sees
  Beguiles and reassures him;
And all her doubts of what he says
Are dimmed with what she knows of days—
Till even prejudice delays
  And fades, and she secures him.

The falling leaf inaugurates
  The reign of her confusion;

The pounding wave reverberates
   The dirge of her illusion;
And home, where passion lived and died,
Becomes a place where she can hide,
While all the town and harbor side
   Vibrate with her seclusion.

We tell you, tapping on our brows,
   The story as it should be,—
As if the story of a house
   Were told, or ever could be;
We'll have no kindly veil between
Her visions and those we have seen,—
As if we guessed what hers have been,
   Or what they are or would be.

Meanwhile we do no harm; for they
   That with a god have striven,
Not hearing much of what we say,
   Take what the god has given;
Though like waves breaking it may be,
Or like a changed familiar tree,
Or like a stairway to the sea
   Where down the blind are driven.

1914

I LOVED THE Montana poems of J. V. Cunningham, and so I decided to crash his office hours at Brandeis University to tell him so. I was twenty-one years old then and thought it was a good idea. I saw him coming down the hall and almost lost my nerve—he was gaunt and lined, slightly bent over, wearing a string tie—but a friend of mine pushed me forward. I remember three questions from our conversation. I asked him how he felt about undergraduate verse and he said that he would be glad to read my poems. I asked him about Yvor Winters, his teacher at Stanford, and he said that Winters was a great man with great faults, like Dr. Johnson. I asked him what modern poet he returned to most often—I half expected him to say Wallace Stevens or Robert Frost—and he said: Edwin Arlington Robinson. Everything else is a blur, but his unlikely first choice of the moderns has stayed with me.

Afterwards, I went home and discovered that Cunningham had written a brief biography of Robinson, a primary model for the bare, plain style of his western poems. I was soon immersed in Tilbury Town, the New England village that Robinson based on his hometown of Gardiner, Maine. I leaned into Morton Dauwen Zabel's edition of Robinson's *Selected Poems* (1965), with its introduction by James Dickey, in which I met John Evereldown and Luke Havergal, Richard Cory and Reuben Bright, Annandale and Flammonde, Miniver Cheevy, Mr. Flood, and, most notably, the unnamed couple in "Eros Turannos." I was moved to see how his fictive characters, quirky figures who seemed to have stepped out of a realistic novel by Honoré de Balzac or Émile Zola, acted at their crucial, defining moments. There was such an enormous gap between the way they felt on the inside and how they presented themselves on the outside. I did not yet understand how exceedingly rare it is for American poets to place other human beings at the center of their work. It's still uncommon. "Robinson has been perhaps the only American poet," Dickey speculated, "interested *exclusively* in human beings as subject matter for poetry." Robinson knew the people he was writing about, the sad characters he was creating, the introverts and recluses, the gloomy oddballs, and alcoholics, like his brothers and himself, and a genuine understanding flows out of his work for all the marginal and doomed people who live in any small American town.

Robinson crossed the nineteenth and twentieth centuries. He came of age in the era of Longfellow and Tennyson, and it took quiet determination for him to lower the diction of lyric poetry and bring it into the range of common speech. Edgar Lee Masters, his near contemporary, was doing something similar, though Robinson's sensibility is probably closer to Sherwood Anderson in *Winesburg, Ohio*. It can be hard to recall how progressive it once was to pressurize ordinary language in poems. He was tuned in to the way that people talk, primarily in small northeastern towns, and called himself "an incorrigible fisher of words." Formally, he was an unobtrusive traditionalist, a poet who skillfully adapted and maneuvered the common tongue into prescribed forms. He looked back to the Victorian poems of Coventry Patmore, especially the long narrative *The Angel in the House*, and to the literary ballads of William Wordsworth, who worked "to bring [the poet's] language near to the language of men," to the narrative forms of George Crabbe, who crossed the eighteenth and nineteenth centuries (see his sonnet of praise, "George Crabbe"), and to the plain-style lyrics of Ben Jonson, hence his long poem "Ben Jonson Entertains a Man from Stratford."

Robinson's tragic sensibility seems close to A. E. Housman and Thomas Hardy, and he created a model for Robert Frost, who called him "the prince of heartachers." Frost forged his own dialogue poems of household crisis, such as "Home Burial" and "West-Running Brook," which show a husband and wife at tragic cross-purposes and operate in the same vicinity as "Eros Turannos." Robinson's strongest influence may have been on Randall Jarrell, who followed up on his domestic dramas, especially of lonely women, those key agents of his sensibility, and James Wright, who knew his poems by heart and took his example to the Ohio Valley. As a young modernist, Conrad Aiken praised Robinson for being "the first American thing, the old oak, the first with a classical firmness, that we could, like young mistletoe, live upon." It may seem like a stretch but it's really just a short leap in sensibility to a singer like Paul Simon, who in some ways got his emotional education from reading Robinson's work. He famously set Robinson's "Richard Cory" to music, his own song with that title, and you can also hear the influence in other Simon & Garfunkel songs like "The Sound of Silence," "Save the Life of My Child," and "America."

"Eros Turannos," which appeared in *The Man Against the Sky* (1916), shows Robinson's psychological acuity and classical firmness. The poem's title is Greek for "Love, the Tyrant." The ancient Greeks took a political idea, an unconstitutional leader who has usurped and seized power, and yoked it to erotic love. For years, Robinson tried to become a playwright, and he brought the sensibility of Greek tragedy, the fatefulness of Sophocles's play *Oedipus Tyrannus* (Oedipus the King), to this short narrative about a failed marriage, a couple who created a home "where passion lived and died."

The story is told dispassionately. The first four stanzas narrate the tale in the third person, seemingly without a narrator, but the community enter in the fifth stanza, like a Greek chorus: "We tell you, tapping on our brows, / The story as it should be." The entrance of the chorus—"As if the story of a house / Were told, or ever could be"—creates an enlarged, heroic feeling of inevitability.

"Eros Turannos" is a lyric poem, not a short story or a drama, and I've always suspected that it is powered by personal experience, something unspoken, which gives it an extra electrical charge. I don't mean to reduce the interpretation of the poem to mere biography, but the fact that Robinson's biographers believe that the couple in the poem are his brother and sister-in-law, Emma and Herman Robinson, may indicate something of the investment of the speaker, who disguises himself as a communal "we," a collective voice.

Cunningham noted that Robinson was "a man almost without biography who became a legend to his friends." What didn't happen to Robinson haunted him all his life. He had one great unrequited love, Emma Shepherd, who married his charismatic older brother, who had swooped in and won her away from him. Robinson never quite recovered his equilibrium. The marriage was a disaster. Herman lost the family fortune in the panic of 1893 and started to drink himself to death. After Herman died and left Emma destitute with three daughters—she believed that her husband was the real "Richard Cory," a man who "glittered when he walked" and one day killed himself—Robinson tried to woo her back. He helped to support her family and proposed to her twice but was rebuffed both times. That's how he became a lifelong bachelor, a person lacking a romantic biography, who understood the tyrannical power of love.

"Eros Turannos" has a narrative drive, a ballad music. It consists of six eight-line stanzas with an ingenious rhyme scheme: *ababcccb*. Robinson doubles the ballad stanza and closes its rhymes from something that alternates (*abab*) to something even more relentlessly compressed (*cccb*). From the beginning, the lilting rhythm, a mixture of lines with four and three accents, creates a feeling of the ineluctable. The poem commences by creating the portrait of a sensitive person paralyzed by dual fears: the unnamed woman knows that she made a terrible choice for a husband, but also fears old age without him. There are three verb tenses in the first two lines, which swiftly condense her agonizing history:

> She *fears* him, and *will* always *ask*
> What *fated* her to choose him;

Robinson's rhyming is both insinuating and skillful. When I reread the poem, I become increasingly aware of the doleful drumbeat of the word *him*, which repeats ten times in the first three stanzas. The feminine rhymes almost tell the story in themselves: *choose him, refuse him, lose him, sound him, let him, found him, around him, allures him, reassures him, secures him.* The first rhyme—*ask* / *mask*—suggests a communication denied. The heavy tread of the triple rhyme—*fears* / *years* / *weirs*—creates a feeling of entrapment. She is drifting through time and slowly getting drawn into "the foamless weirs," which is to say the fences in a waterway, "Of age." It doesn't take long for Robinson to suggest the downward spiral of the years.

Each stanza in this poem reads like a short chapter in a novella. The poem unfolds in a continuous present tense through the first three stanzas: her fear of being alone leads her to delude herself about her husband, who betrays her. She pays for her pride with a wounded loneliness. The tyrannical force of love has "blurred" her "sagacity." In the third stanza, the viewpoint also blurs from her to him. It happens so unobtrusively that you almost miss the quiet change and slippage:

> A sense of ocean and old trees
>   Envelops and allures him;
> Tradition, touching all he sees
>   Beguiles and reassures him;
> And all her doubts of what he says
> Are dimmed with what she knows of days—
> Till even prejudice delays
>   And fades, and she secures him.

Now, he is the one who seems taken in and fooled by nature, "a sense of ocean and old trees," lured by tradition, falsely reassured. As in a short nineteenth-century novel, say, Henry James's *Washington Square*, we come away with a portrait of two people who are inextricably bound together even as they are existentially isolated. The word *secures* is hauntingly ironic. She gives him safety, but one can almost hear the turning of the lock behind them.

I have always loved the conclusive fourth stanza, which reaches a lyric pitch. Listen to the pounding sound of the word *pounding* and the reverberation of the word *reverberates*, how the word *dirge* tolls like a bell, and *confusion* rhymes with *illusion* and concludes with *seclusion*, while *died* interlocks with *hide* and *side*:

> The falling leaf inaugurates
>   The reign of her *confusion*;
> The *pounding* wave *reverberates*
>   The *dirge* of her *illusion*;
> And home, where passion lived and *died*,
> Becomes a place where she can *hide*,
> While all the town and harbor *side*
>   Vibrate with her *seclusion*.

The woman's isolation reaches a fever pitch. She is left alone with her feelings, with the sure knowledge that everyone in her harbor town is talking about her. As in a line of music, the word *vibrate* creates a kind of electrical current running through her body, which quivers with so much loneliness that we almost need to turn away.

And we do turn away, as the speaker steps in and serves as the deputy of a public or communal voice, as in a traditional ballad: "*We tell you.*" The camera pulls back. Robinson's delicate skepticism tells us that we can never know the full story ("*As if the story of a house / Were told, or ever could be*"), that we can never be certain about someone else's sufferings, and that we have to guess "what hers have been, / Or what they are or would be." The interior lives of other people can only ever partly be understood. He is modest and over-forgiving about the townspeople, for whom he is a spokesman: "Meanwhile we do no harm." Of course, the gossip of the townspeople does cause harm even as it elevates the story and gives it a more extensive import and status:

> Meanwhile we do no harm; for they
>   That with a god have striven,
> Not hearing much of what we say,
>   Take what the god has given;
> Though like waves breaking it may be,
> Or like a changed familiar tree,
> Or like a stairway to the sea
>   Where down the blind are driven.

Robinson takes the language up to a higher pitch here. The first four lines reaffirm the title, "Love, the Divine Tyrant," and give the tale a legendary,

EDWIN ARLINGTON ROBINSON   87

perhaps even mythic quality. It is this heroic or mythical feature that radiates a kind of timeless fatality, as if everything that had happened was somehow ordained. The poem closes with the charged rhetoric of three consecutive similes. It is as if the poet is searching to get the comparison right—it is either "*like* waves" or "*like* a changed familiar tree" or "*like* a stairway." And yet the analogies are also additive, "what the god has given." The days and years pitch forward with a kind of relentless pressure "like waves breaking." The old tree, an ancestral marker of a family, has been irreparably changed, degraded. The final comparison signals a final fatefulness, a stairway that leads to the sea. The inverted syntax turns the usual noun-verb progression of regular speech into something closer to Greek tragedy: "Where down the blind are driven."

Yvor Winters called "Eros Turannos" "a universal tragedy in a Maine setting." Robinson worked hard to create that fiction, an allegorical feeling of universality. Projecting outward, he took a local situation and tale, something fateful that he probably experienced in his own life and family, and turned it into an archetypal story, the narrative of a fall. He gave it a heightened speech, a serious dignity, and a classical magnitude. No wonder we respond to it with tragic pathos, pity, and fear.

AMY LOWELL (1874–1925)

Madonna of the Evening Flowers

All day long I have been working,
Now I am tired.
I call: "Where are you?"
But there is only the oak-tree rustling in the wind.
The house is very quiet,
The sun shines in on your books,
On your scissors and thimble just put down,
But you are not there.
Suddenly I am lonely:
Where are you?
I go about searching.

Then I see you,
Standing under a spire of pale blue larkspur,
With a basket of roses on your arm.
You are cool, like silver,
And you smile.
I think the Canterbury bells are playing little tunes.

You tell me that the peonies need spraying,
That the columbines have overrun all bounds,
That the pyrus japonica should be cut back and rounded.
You tell me these things.
But I look at you, heart of silver,
White heart-flame of polished silver,
Burning beneath the blue steeples of the larkspur,
And I long to kneel instantly at your feet,
While all about us peal the loud, sweet *Te Deums* of the Canterbury bells.

1919

A MY LOWELL was one of the two or three most famous poets in America when she died of a stroke in 1925. She was just fifty-one years old. But literary history can be cruel, and Lowell was no longer a canonical presence by the early 1970s. She was forgotten by the literary establishment, the poets, critics, and anthologists who tended the flames of modernism. A free-verse poet who had advanced the modernist cause, she was now relegated to the margins, like the skillful female lyricists who wrote romantic formal poems and were once well known for their racy subject matter: Edna St. Vincent Millay, Sara Teasdale, Elinor Wylie, and others. There seemed to be room in the modernist canon only for women poets who presented themselves dispassionately, like Marianne Moore and Louise Bogan.

Ezra Pound's comments inadvertently got me interested in Amy Lowell's work. I was galvanized by Pound's curriculum, especially his love of the troubadours and his curiosity about Chinese poetry, but I was put off by his biases, like his sneers at Wordsworth and his condescension to Whitman. I recall being irritated by reading a letter that he sent to Margaret Anderson, the editor of *The Little Review*: "Do you honestly think that a serious writer OUGHT to be reminded of the United States??" Pound wondered. "Ought one to be distracted, ought one to be asked to address that perpetual mother's meeting, that chaste Chitaqua [*sic*], that cradle of on-coming Amys???" I was not charmed by Pound's deriding of "Amygism," his denigration of "Amy-just-selling-the-goods," his patronizing attitude toward Lowell and other poets—his former classmate William Carlos Williams comes to mind—who wanted to re-create poetry in what he coyly misspelled as "the Eunited, Eunuchated States of America."

I was surprised by what I found when I finally got around to Lowell's work. It's not just that it's much more compelling than we were led to believe, but also that there is an enormous gap between Lowell's poetry and her reputation, between the sensitivity of her love poems, which are written in a thinly disguised sexual code—it takes a willful cluelessness to miss it—and her public persona as a bellicose advocate for modern poetry, a sort of barker for a new aesthetic credo. I was reading Gertrude Stein at the same time, too, who put up a greater barrier, a more insurmountable fortress, and thereby even more fully protected her privacy, her tender passions and sentimental education. She was a pragmatist, like her teacher William James. I was excited by my discoveries and learned a crucial lesson, too, which was not to take the evaluations of the canon for granted—it is filled with prejudices and blind spots, inherited ideas, received opinions, trendy thinking. It's better to read widely and figure things out for yourself.

Amy Lowell's poetry was underestimated for much of the twentieth century. Instead of contending with her work, we encountered stories about her outsize figure and personality. She called herself "one of the last barons" and comported herself as an androgyne—part diva, part Roman emperor. She was large and smoked cigars, like Wallace Stevens; she was rich and came from the upper class, like James Merrill. She was a Boston Brahmin who looked backward to James Russell Lowell and forward to Robert Lowell— her brother was president of Harvard College ("And this is good old Boston, / The home of the bean and the cod, / Where the Lowells talk to the Cabots, / And the Cabots talk only to God")—but that didn't stop her from being as pugnacious as Norman Mailer. Eliot called her a "demon saleswoman," Van Wyck Brooks wrote that "she whizzed and she whirred, and she rustled and rumbled, and she glistened and sparkled and blazed and blared." In his poem "Dinner Call," her friend John Brooks Wheelwright teased that she was "the Biggest Traveling One-Man Show since Buffalo Bill caught the Midnight Flyer to Contact Mark Twain."

In *A Homemade World: The American Modernist Writers*, the literary critic Hugh Kenner compared Lowell to "some Peoria craftsman" trying "to confect a palazzo." He intended it as an insult, but I like this local, homemade aspect of her work. "The poet must learn his trade in the same manner, and with the same painstaking care, as the cabinet-maker," she said in the preface to her second book, and added that poetry is "a created beauty, even if sometimes the beauty of a gothic grotesque." Lowell was an autodidact who started writing poetry in her late twenties—a performance by the Italian actress Eleonora Duse inspired her calling. "The effect on me was tremendous," she recalled. "What really happened was that it revealed me to myself." Lowell began with traditional forms—she was a Romantic poet by temperament and wrote a two-volume biography of Keats, whom she adored—and her path seemed set with her first book, *A Dome of Many-Coloured Glass* (1912). But everything changed when she read the poems of "H.D., Imagiste" in *Poetry* magazine the next year. She responded to the precision and clarity of H.D.'s poems and decided to become an Imagist, too. She travelled to London twice, met Pound and everyone else associated with the movement, especially Richard Aldington and Hilda Doolittle (H.D.), F. S. Flint and D. H. Lawrence—her sensuality seems closer to Lawrence than to any of the other poets—and carried the banner home. When Pound turned to Vorticism, Lowell wrested Imagism away from him and edited two annuals called *Some Imagist Poets* (1916, 1917). She barnstormed the country on behalf of the new movement, or her version of it.

The study of the single-image lyric clarified Lowell's thinking and cleaned out the clutter from her writing. Her lyrics are written in a rhythmical free verse, or what she called "unrhymed cadence" or "cadenced verse." "Cadence is rhythm," Lowell wrote. "Modern *vers libre*, far from being non-rhythmical as some people have supposed, is entirely based upon rhythm. Its rhythms differ from those of metre by being less obvious and more subtle, but rhythm is, nevertheless, the very ground and root of its structure." Lowell also experimented with a kind of writing that her friend John Gould Fletcher termed *polyphonic prose*, which intercuts lyric with narrative passages, rhymed metric with cadenced verse, and brings historical events into the equation. If you're looking for the spread, the wider canvas, I'd recommend the four long poems in *Can Grande's Castle* (1918), especially the first two, "Sea-Blue and Blood-Red" and "Guns as Keys: And the Great Gate Swings," which were self-consciously written against the backdrop of World War I.

Lowell is most moving as an Imagistic poet of erotic love. It's disheartening to read the critical studies, memoirs, and biographies that started coming out soon after her death. Beginning with Clement Wood's openly homophobic study, *Amy Lowell* (1926), the criticism is not just beside the point, it's downright aggressive. It can be difficult to tell Lowell's friends from her enemies. There's a surprising amount of fat-shaming (she suffered from an untreated glandular condition) and a lot of potshots at her as a deviant spinster, pathetically lonely, intellectually isolated. Sometimes she's criticized for having too much feeling, sometimes for being cold. Lesbianism is treated as an untreatable condition that she covered over with aggressive bravado. It was often insinuated, sometimes stated outright, that she bought her way into American poetry. Some of these criticisms landed; all of them distracted people from her work, which began to languish in the shadows and then disappeared altogether.

Until recently, most anthologies of American poetry either excluded Lowell entirely or selected one of her poems, usually "Patterns," and left it at that. Unfortunately, this method of reduction leaves out the history of her formal understandings, her contribution to the long history of the love poem. But things have shifted over the past twenty years, and Lowell's work has been given a second chance, mostly through the efforts of feminist poets (Alicia Ostriker, Honor Moore) and scholars (Lillian Faderman, Adrienne Munich, Melissa Bradshaw) intent on reevaluating the canon of women's poetry. Looking back at Lowell's work through the lens of a later poet like Adrienne Rich, it has become possible to see Lowell in a fresh light as a poet of passionate same-sex love. Like many love poets, male and female, she addresses her poems to an unnamed Beloved, but unlike them she is not exclusively a poet of longing and loss, but also one of celebration and attainment.

Lowell was in love with the actress Ada Dwyer Russell, whom she met in 1909. They were reintroduced in 1912 at a meeting of the Lunch Club, a group of "accomplished women." Russell was playing the lead role in a drama called *The Deep Purple*, and she so successfully won over the group that they changed their name to the Purple Lunch Club. That's why the hue of "purple" is part of Lowell's code for Russell. Lowell had always been in love with the theater and now she found it incarnated in a person—Russell, her muse. She courted Russell for two years; there's a refracted record in her second book, *Sword Blades and Poppy Seed* (1914), that moves from the blunder of "Stupidity" ("Dearest, forgive that with my clumsy touch / I broke and bruised your rose") to the bewilderment of "The Taxi" ("When I go away from you / The world beats dead / Like a slackened drum") to the declarative of "Aubade," a sexy love song of the early-morning watch:

> As I would free the white almond from the green husk
> So I would strip your trappings off,
> Beloved.
> And fingering the smooth and polished kernel
> I should see that in my hands glittered a gem beyond counting.

In the end, Lowell convinced Russell to come and live with her at Sevenels, her mansion in Brookline, Massachusetts. They became lifelong partners. Russell forbade Lowell from dedicating her books to her, but that was a mere formality, a practical cover. They were all dedicated to her in body and spirit.

Lowell's most sustained achievement as a love poet is the sequence of forty-three poems, "Two Speak Together," in her fifth book, *Pictures of the Floating World* (1919). She borrowed the title of the book from Japanese woodblock prints and paintings (*Ukiyo-e*) that evoked a various, stylish, and fleeting urban world. These artistically rendered urbane settings provided her with a model for how she wanted to present her life and work. Lowell was especially fascinated by Japanese and Chinese poetry—she was also competitive with Pound and read *Cathay* (1915) with scarcely concealed envy—and this interest surfaces in the first part of the book, which consists of a sequence called "Lacquer Prints" and another termed "Chinoiseries." She would go on to collaborate with Florence Ayscough on an anthology of Chinese translations, *Fir-Flower Tablets* (1921). I admire the Imagistic impulse in Lowell's original haiku-like poems, but they don't survive their lacquered air of Orientalism. They mimic a mannerism and explore a zone of imagery, but they lack an emotional imperative. As a result, they miss the piercing insight, the sudden illumination that marks the short work of a great Japanese poet like Bashō or a Chinese one like Du Fu. Something of what Lowell was seeking was later fulfilled by Charles Wright in his book *China Trace* (1977), which could have been called, as he suggested, *The Book of Yearning*. What's interesting for Lowell is that some of these impulses are carried over into the love poems of "Two Speak Together," which, she claimed, derive "from everywhere and nowhere." This is not quite accurate. In 1928, the critic William Leonard Schwartz stumbled into an unintentional truth when speaking of the "latent queerness" of Lowell's Asian figures.

"Madonna of the Evening Flowers" is the fifth poem in the sequence. When John Livingston Lowe complimented Lowell on her portrait of Russell in this poem, she responded by saying, "How could so exact a portrait remain unrecognized?" She seems to have meant this as a rhetorical question, but one comes away from the poem with no idea, for example, of what Russell looked like. But what the poem does give us is the portrait of a relationship, what she calls "planes of personality," an impractical poetic lover and her more practical-minded beloved. The drama plays out through the floral imagery of the garden. It covers a terrific amount of ground in a short space and accelerates from a plain domestic lyric into a romantic devotional.

The speaker in Lowell's sequence comes across as tenderhearted, some-times insecure, and sick with longing, even crazed by passion. "Why are you not here to overpower me with your tense and urgent love?" she asks at the end of the first poem, "Vernal Equinox." There is a moment in the second poem, "The Letter," when Lowell hits a note of intense longing, what she calls "The want of you," that invokes Sappho: "And I scald alone, here, under the fire / Of the great moon." The third poem, "Mise en Scène," connects the companion to the green estate ("When I think of you, Beloved, / I see a smooth and stately garden") and describes her shawl flaring out "in great curves / Like the swirling draperies of a painted Madonna." In the fourth poem, "Venus Transiens," she tries to outdo Botticelli in his description of Venus on a plaited shell, but recognizes that her portrait of Venus is transient, not permanent. The subtle accumulation of overlapping images in "Two Speak Together" creates a sense of sustained natural, artistic, and religious devotion.

"Madonna of the Evening Flowers" conjoins a Christian icon with a gar-den setting and turns the natural world into a church. But the poem itself lowers the volume and begins indoors on a quotidian note. Lowell doesn't specify the gender of her speaker, but she also makes little attempt to disguise it. She is speaking as a version of herself, a writer who has been working indoors for the entire day. The poem is carefully structured in three parts of unequal length. The method is Imagistic, the scene visual—it could eas-ily be filmed—but, as you reread it, you become increasingly aware of the underlying logic, as in an Elizabethan sonnet. This is a typical domestic situation—one person has been working at a desk, another has gone out to the garden—but it is infused with a quiet uneasiness:

All day long I have been working,
Now I am tired.
I call: "Where are you?"
But there is only the oak-tree rustling in the wind.
The house is very quiet,
The sun shines in on your books,
On your scissors and thimble just put down,
But you are not there.
Suddenly I am lonely:

Where are you?
I go about searching.

Lowell has learned how to marshal her Imagist weaponry here through the simple declarative sentence. There is a quick, studied progression from sound to silence. The sun illuminates the books, scissors, and thimble, so that they still vibrate with the beloved's presence, like a still life by the Italian painter Giorgio Morandi. This play on absence and presence prepares us for the sudden feeling of loneliness that overcomes the speaker: "Where are you? / I go about searching."

The lyric structurally turns in the second stanza: "*Then* I see you." For the rest of the poem, the speaker addresses her companion directly. The next line hits the first churchly note and links it to the image of flowers: "Then I see you, / Standing under a *spire* of pale blue larkspur." There is an implicit contrast between the insecurity of the speaker and the calm of her companion: "You are cool, like silver / And you smile." Lowell relies here on the long-standing association of the color silver with feminine energy, a link to the moon, which she often uses to evoke Russell, and the ebb and flow of tides, a metallic sparkle with a feeling of mystery. The reassuring smile radiates with beatitude. Pound said that "the natural object is always the *adequate* symbol," and here Lowell ingeniously invokes the Canterbury bells, a flowering plant that in floriography represents constancy and gratitude. She uses the annual to sound a defining note—you can hear her catching it: "I think the Canterbury bells are playing little tunes."

The last section toggles between two people, one pragmatic, the other idealizing. The speaker is impatient with the difference between them, but the poet takes pleasure in the metaphorical possibility, seizing on the distinction between a real garden and an imaginary one:

You tell me that the peonies need spraying,
That the columbines have overrun all bounds,
That the pyrus japonica should be cut back and rounded.
You tell me these things.
But I look at you, heart of silver,
White heart-flame of polished silver,
Burning beneath the blue steeples of the larkspur,

> And I long to kneel instantly at your feet,
> While all about us peal the loud, sweet *Te Deums* of the
>   Canterbury bells.

Somewhat amusingly, Russell speaks here as a gardener—"You tell me these things"—while Lowell is so overpowered by feeling that she can scarcely hear what her muse is saying. She sees the passion reflected under the silver surface, the heat underneath. "Repetition itself creates bliss," Roland Barthes declares in *The Pleasure of the Text*, and you can hear the speaker working herself into a state of passionate regard through the precise repetition and accrual of phrasing: "heart of silver, / White heart-flame of polished silver, / Burning." The floral imagery takes on a religious aura, and the sound burns through the letter *b*: "*Burning beneath* the *blue steeples* of the larkspur." The poem reverberates with the Song of Songs, where we read: "I am come into my garden, my sister, my spouse: I have gathered my myrrh with my spice; I have eaten my honeycomb with my honey; I have drunk my wine with my milk: eat, O friends; drink, yea, drink abundantly, O beloved" (5:1, King James Bible).

In the end, the speaker in Lowell's poem longs to take up the posture of the supplicant, the kneeling lover of troubadour poetry who masochistically prostrates himself before the beloved. By changing the gender of the speaker, she reconfigures and enlarges the tradition. Nature has become a cathedral and the "little tunes" of the Canterbury bells now peal out a music that is loud and sweet. Here, the euphoric singer of the *Te Deums* ("Thee, O God, we praise") harnesses a sacred vocabulary for erotic love, and Amy Lowell takes her rightful place among the poets of romantic pleading, the Provençal troubadours and the Italian Petrarchans.

It is always transgressive to call the words of passion holy, but desire testifies, joy declares itself. Time and again, Lowell praises her lover's "ice and fire" ("Opal"), her brilliant nakedness, a sun-drenched brightness that pains and blinds her, a shining moonlight. "Without you," she declares in a poem called "Left Behind," "there is no garden." Amy Lowell was writing passionate lesbian love poems in an era that prized the cold sculpture of a detached ironic sensibility. She was careful and protected herself, but at heart she is a poet of erotic anxiety and rapture, excitement and vulnerability, vertiginous bliss.

ROBERT FROST (1874–1963)

The Most of It

He thought he kept the universe alone;
For all the voice in answer he could wake
Was but the mocking echo of his own
From some tree-hidden cliff across the lake.
Some morning from the boulder-broken beach
He would cry out on life, that what it wants
Is not its own love back in copy speech,
But counter-love, original response.
And nothing ever came of what he cried
Unless it was the embodiment that crashed
In the cliff's talus on the other side,
And then in the far distant water splashed,
But after a time allowed for it to swim,
Instead of proving human when it neared
And someone else additional to him,
As a great buck it powerfully appeared,
Pushing the crumpled water up ahead,
And landed pouring like a waterfall,
And stumbled through the rocks with horny tread,
And forced the underbrush—and that was all.

1942

THERE IS an oddly persistent popular image of Robert Frost as a homespun Yankee farmer, a weathered sage who kept his feet on the ground and his head out of the clouds. It was a good role and Frost played it well. On my eleventh birthday, my family watched him on television reciting a poem at John F. Kennedy's inauguration. He couldn't see the page in the sunlight and seemed befuddled, but then he recovered and recited "The Gift Outright" from memory, which cemented my parents' idea of a poet. It was a moment of dignity that I missed. My junior high and high school English teachers loved his adages and wise sayings, such as "Good fences make good neighbors"—did we really need to hear that twice? Even my mother got in on the act when I had a decision to make and declaimed "Two roads diverged in a yellow wood," though she diverged from the poem and always plunked for the safer, more well-trodden path. I got the impression that Frost used poetry to give folksy advice. The stance irritated me, and I couldn't wait to escape to college ("College is a refuge from hasty judgment," my guidance counsellor opined), where I could lose myself in something profound, like *The Waste Land.*

It took me a few years to realize just how badly I had underestimated Frost's work. I wish I could say that I read his poems and suddenly understood, like Paul on the road to Damascus, but I was busy catching up with the high moderns—Yeats, Stevens, Pound, Eliot—and ignored the locals, like Robinson and Frost. I first gleaned the magnitude of my mistake when I discovered how Lionel Trilling had caused an uproar with some unsettling praise at Frost's eighty-fifth, or "Sophoclean," birthday celebration. Someone named J. Donald Adams pounced on Trilling in *The New Times Book Review*: "Professor Trilling confessed that he thinks of Frost as a 'terrifying' poet, and that 'the universe he conceives is a terrifying universe.' Holy mackerel! Frost simply sees the universe as it is and accepts it. He isn't terrified by what he sees, and neither should we be." I realized then that there must be dangerous undertows in Frost's poetry that I had missed. I threw myself into his work, and that's when I encountered what Randall Jarrell called "The Other Frost" (1953), the darker, lonelier one, a terrifying realist whose vision of things can keep you awake long into the night.

It would be gratifying to follow Robert Frost through his various moods and modes, to linger over the poems that have been with me since college, some of them on the main road, such as the short poem "Nothing Gold Can Stay" ("So Eden sank to grief") and the long one "Home Burial," which dramatizes an internal scene between a couple that is so painful and claustrophobic one can barely stand to stay inside the house with them, and others a little off the beaten track, like "A Brook in the City," a proto-ecological city poem, and "To E. T.," a mournful poem for Edward Thomas, whom he loved without reservation, and "Desert Places," a desolating lyric of vacancy that faces an inner darkness even greater than the external void.

Frost was akin to Thomas Hardy in the way he faced the world without any supernatural warrant or guarantee, how he stared down the abyss, but his locale, his language, and his sensibility were American, and so he often tried to present himself as a regular guy, a swinger of birches, a tough, cracker-barrel optimist. But his poems keep coming back to the edge of the woods, to deserted farmhouses and diminished towns, disappointed people, lost worlds, the lure of oblivion, "that other fall we name the fall" ("The Oven Bird"). His work is deft and playful, but it is also unsparing, frightening, and brave.

Frost's nature poems can be deceptive. The prefatory poem "The Pasture," in his first book, *A Boy's Will* (1913), is a warm invitation to join him in the pasture spring: "I sha'n't be gone long.—You come too." This friendly style lures you in and doesn't prepare you for the rude shock of his later nature poems, like "Neither Out Far Nor In Deep," "Design," and "The Most of It," which are more likely to appall. That's how they are designed. Frost was primarily a poet of dark pastorals, like his model, the Roman poet Virgil. He noted that he "first heard the voice from a printed page in a Virgilian eclogue and from Hamlet." Like Virgil, Frost was "versed in country things" and created his rural poems in troubled times. He had a flair for the dramatic lyric and an ear well tuned to the American vernacular, to what he called "sentence sounds."

For Frost, Virgil's influence is refracted through Emerson and Wordsworth, poets he first learned about from his mother, who loved them. He took to heart Emerson's credo of self-reliance and unwavering commitment to freedom, and said:

> I think some of my first thinking about my own language, the language I wanted to express myself in, was with Emerson. He says of Montaigne somewhere "Cut these sentences and they bleed."

By slightly misremembering Emerson, who said, "Cut these words and they would bleed," Frost demonstrates his focus on the rhythmic movement and sound of sentences. He also responded to Wordsworth's democratic individualism and Virgilian ethos, a commitment to what the Romantic poet called "humble and rustic life." Frost vied with his predecessor and claimed with some accuracy: "I dropped to an everyday level of diction that even Wordsworth kept above."

Frost had a skeptical, empirical temperament, like his favorite philosopher, William James, and thought of every poem as "a figure of the will braving alien entanglements." He was a competitive person and placed high premium in poetry on technical prowess, unobtrusive virtuosity, feats of association, and lyric performance. He said that whenever he read a rhyming poem, he scanned the right-hand margin to see who had won, the poet or the rhyme scheme. His own rhyming was so skillful and unassuming that he usually won the match. He also said that writing free verse is like playing tennis without a net, which is clever but inaccurate. Frost's idea that there are virtually but two meters in English, "strict iambic and loose iambic," points to his own metrical resourcefulness and reveals something crucial about his own literary practice. But it misreads and underestimates the Whitmanian or prophetic tradition in American poetry.

Frost wrote "The Most of It" in the late twenties and published it in *A Witness Tree* (1942). The poem was first called "Making the Most of It," which suggests trying to use or enjoy something as much as possible. Tonally, the phrase can be either cheerful or resigned. The phrasing seemed to align the speaker and the poet, who is a "maker," which is probably why Frost dropped the word *making*, thereby clipping the idiom, opening up and unsettling the title. The literary critic Anne Ferry points out that the wordage is akin to other proverbial statements, such as *that's the least of it*, which indicates an understatement, or *getting the worst of it*, which means that you lost an argument or fight, or even *making the best of it*, which means dealing with a bad situation in a positive way. Frost typically leaves the reader to determine the meaning of his cutoff motto as it reverberates through the poem.

"The Most of It" unfolds as an adroit twenty-line iambic pentameter poem. It consists of five heroic quatrains, which rhyme alternately *abab*, comprising a single stanza. It's possible that Frost was ironizing the very idea of a "heroic" stanza, since the speaker is talking about someone who is decidedly unheroic: "He thought he kept the universe alone." Frost reiterates the third-person vantage point three times in the first nine lines, but then drops it from the poem, somehow leaping beyond that limited consciousness.

I had been reading and thinking about "The Most of It" for years before

I discovered from the first volume of Lawrance Thompson's biography of Frost—a distorted, even vengeful book, which is nonetheless filled with useful information—that the poem was nudged into being by Frost's ironic response to the work of a young poet named Wade Van Dore, whom he had taken under his wing. Frost helped Van Dore with the manuscript for his first book, *Far Lake* (1930). The text included two poems, "The Echo" and "Man Alone," based on a camping experience in the Canadian wilderness. In Van Dore's "The Echo," which was cut from the finished book, the speaker complains about the indifference of nature. Van Dore calls out to the birds and birches but hears only his own voice rebounding:

> Made mellow by a wall of trees
> My call came swiftly back to me.
> My word the forest would not take
> Came bounding back across the lake.

Van Dore's "Man Alone" returns to the same subject and adds a deer to the equation:

> If he should loudly call, then stand and wait
> Until the sound had traveled far and made
> A voice reply, he'd know the forest held
> No mate for him. An echo would reply,
> Giving him back his lonely call and word.
> A deer might start.

The disappointment of the speaker in these poems seems to have triggered Frost's imagination to take up a situation that had long fascinated him, to make the most of it.

Frost may initially have had Van Dore in mind when he started the poem, but he ended up creating an Adamic figure, someone who sings alone and thinks that he alone possesses or controls the natural world. As I reread the poem, I become more aware of the steady iambic drumbeat of the first eight lines, which consist of two evenly balanced sentences. The rhyming here is so perfect that one hears the final rhyme (*wants / response*) as something slightly off, even wanting.

> He thought he kept the universe alone;
> For all the voice in answer he could wake
> Was but the mocking echo of his own
> From some tree-hidden cliff across the lake.
> Some morning from the boulder-broken beach
> He would cry out on life, that what it wants
> Is not its own love back in copy speech,
> But counter-love, original response.

Frost had a gift for taking a specific situation and enlarging its scope. He begins by juxtaposing a tiny individual with a large universe. He signals his own distance from the unnamed person he is speaking about—"He *thought*"—and places him in a natural scene, calling out and hearing an echo reverberating from a hidden cliff on the other side of a lake. There's a nice play on the freshness of the world, the movement from "he could wake" to "Some morning." Reading aloud, it's hard not to trip over "the *b*oulder-*b*roken *b*each." The scene is amplified and takes on a sort of allegorical significance when the speaker proclaims, "He would cry out on life, that what it wants / Is not its own love back." There is another stutter of sound from *what it wants*—the word hangs on the edge of the line—which topples over into a negation, *Is not its own*. The word *love* looks back with some disappointment to the word *life*. Frost's watchwords here take on a life of their own: *copy speech, counter-love, original response*. These coinages speak beautifully to a deep human longing to get a response from the inhuman world, to feel some feeling coming back to us from nature.

Part of Frost's counter-love is the way that he places himself in dialogue with the poets who have meant the most to him. Here, as the critic Richard Poirier and others have pointed out, he responds directly to an episode in Wordsworth's autobiographical poem *The Prelude*. In this memorable passage, Wordsworth recalls "the Boy of Winander," who died before the age of twelve: "There was a Boy; ye knew him well, ye cliffs / And islands of Winander!" The boy often stood alone at evening, under the trees or near the lake, Wordsworth writes,

> And there, with fingers interwoven, both hands
> Pressed closely palm to palm and to his mouth

Uplifted, he, as through an instrument,
Blew mimic hootings to the silent owls
That they might answer him.—And they would shout
Across the watery vale, and shout again,
Responsive to his call,—with quivering peals,
And long halloos, and screams, and echoes loud
Redoubled and redoubled.

The boy provides an early model for the poet Wordsworth, who would carry "far into his heart the voice / Of mountain-torrents." But Frost rewrites this confident passage so that the world does not respond to the man alone. It does not recognize his human cry, those "mimic hootings." On the contrary, it is totally unresponsive to any human intervention or presence.

The final movement of "The Most of It" consists of a single sentence stretched across twelve lines. As I reread it, I hear the more irregular meter, which begins with the tenth line, and notice the logical terminology, as in a Shakespearean sonnet—*And nothing*; *Unless*; *And then*; *But after*; *Instead of*—which the speaker deploys to try to understand an illogical, incomprehensible experience. The multisyllabic word *embodiment* unnerves the diction. Everything is unsettled by what happens next:

And nothing ever came of what he cried
Unless it was the embodiment that crashed
In the cliff's talus on the other side,
And then in the far distant water splashed,
But after a time allowed for it to swim,
Instead of proving human when it neared
And someone else additional to him,
As a great buck it powerfully appeared,
Pushing the crumpled water up ahead,
And landed pouring like a waterfall,
And stumbled through the rocks with horny tread,
And forced the underbrush—and that was all.

The speaker is trying to describe an uncanny experience. Something unexpected comes violently crashing through the world—it is heard before it's seen—and impinges on consciousness. The movement of the lines enacts the way the buck arrives, how it first *crashed* and then *splashed*, how it initially *neared*, and finally *appeared*. We normally think of an embodiment as a tangible form of something intangible, the manifestation of a feeling or idea, but what is being embodied here? The poem never says. Frost's cunning logic of disappointment is evident in the phrase "Instead of *proving human.*" The buck has enormous presence, is a fleeting irrefutable being, but what does it represent? It seems like a figure of the sublime—after all, it pushed the water aside "And landed pouring like a waterfall"—but then it "*stumbled* through the rocks with *horny tread*, / And *forced* the underbrush." The buck has a savage grandeur, but it mocks our longing for "counter-love" with its brute masculine force. It's certainly not the embodiment of a large, unexpected grace, like its obvious descendent, Elizabeth Bishop's female moose, who suddenly looms up in the middle of the road on a bus ride through Nova Scotia ("The Moose").

The end of "The Most of It" is eerie and powerful. It circles back to the beginning and concludes with an ironic shrug. Finally, this is the most that we can make of it, whatever that *it* includes—the poem, the experience, the universe. The final phrasing, *and that was all,* is both marvelously off the cuff—it signs off the lyric, there's nothing more to say—and rife with significance. It suggests that there really is no one else recognizable out there in the natural world, which does not recognize or return human feeling. And yet there also might be a note of wonder in it, too. The expression *and that was all* also means "and that was everything." The world is something we can never fully comprehend; it is beyond us. It is all and nothing.

Robert Frost is an endlessly surprising poet, a tricky, devastating moralist. Look deeply into his *Collected Poems* and you discover that anything you might say against him was something that he had already leveled against himself. One of the words that keeps cropping up in his work is *confusion,* such as his notion that a poem is "a momentary stay against confusion" ("The Figure a Poem Makes") and his declaration "Drink and be whole again beyond confusion" ("Directive"). He was stalked by grief, a deep bewilderment and uncertainty, which he tried to hold off with witty maxims and clever proclamations that fooled a lot of people. But the way that he owned up to the darkest truths about nature, human and otherwise, is an education unto itself, and I now think of him as an American pragmatist, a poet of steely nerve who took the hard road and reckoned with the hard realities of existence. He didn't avert his gaze. He may have treated poetry as a game, but it was a game that he played for mortal stakes. The other Frost is the truthful one. He is a terrifying poet and the universe he conceives is a terrifying universe.

WALLACE STEVENS (1879–1955)

Sunday Morning

I

Complacencies of the peignoir, and late
Coffee and oranges in a sunny chair,
And the green freedom of a cockatoo
Upon a rug mingle to dissipate
The holy hush of ancient sacrifice.
She dreams a little, and she feels the dark
Encroachment of that old catastrophe,
As a calm darkens among water-lights.
The pungent oranges and bright, green wings
Seem things in some procession of the dead,
Winding across wide water, without sound.
The day is like wide water, without sound,
Stilled for the passing of her dreaming feet
Over the seas, to silent Palestine,
Dominion of the blood and sepulchre.

II

Why should she give her bounty to the dead?
What is divinity if it can come
Only in silent shadows and in dreams?
Shall she not find in comforts of the sun,
In pungent fruit and bright, green wings, or else
In any balm or beauty of the earth,
Things to be cherished like the thought of heaven?
Divinity must live within herself:
Passions of rain, or moods in falling snow;
Grievings in loneliness, or unsubdued

Elations when the forest blooms; gusty
Emotions on wet roads on autumn nights;
All pleasures and all pains, remembering
The bough of summer and the winter branch.
These are the measures destined for her soul.

III

Jove in the clouds had his inhuman birth.
No mother suckled him, no sweet land gave
Large-mannered motions to his mythy mind.
He moved among us, as a muttering king,
Magnificent, would move among his hinds,
Until our blood, commingling, virginal,
With heaven, brought such requital to desire
The very hinds discerned it, in a star.
Shall our blood fail? Or shall it come to be
The blood of paradise? And shall the earth
Seem all of paradise that we shall know?
The sky will be much friendlier then than now,
A part of labor and a part of pain,
And next in glory to enduring love,
Not this dividing and indifferent blue.

IV

She says, "I am content when wakened birds,
Before they fly, test the reality
Of misty fields, by their sweet questionings;
But when the birds are gone, and their warm fields
Return no more, where, then, is paradise?"
There is not any haunt of prophecy,
Nor any old chimera of the grave,
Neither the golden underground, nor isle
Melodious, where spirits gat them home,
Nor visionary south, nor cloudy palm
Remote on heaven's hill, that has endured

As April's green endures; or will endure
Like her remembrance of awakened birds,
Or her desire for June and evening, tipped
By the consummation of the swallow's wings.

V

She says, "But in contentment I still feel
The need of some imperishable bliss."
Death is the mother of beauty; hence from her,
Alone, shall come fulfilment to our dreams
And our desires. Although she strews the leaves
Of sure obliteration on our paths,
The path sick sorrow took, the many paths
Where triumph rang its brassy phrase, or love
Whispered a little out of tenderness,
She makes the willow shiver in the sun
For maidens who were wont to sit and gaze
Upon the grass, relinquished to their feet.
She causes boys to pile new plums and pears
On disregarded plate. The maidens taste
And stray impassioned in the littering leaves.

VI

Is there no change of death in paradise?
Does ripe fruit never fall? Or do the boughs
Hang always heavy in that perfect sky,
Unchanging, yet so like our perishing earth,
With rivers like our own that seek for seas
They never find, the same receding shores
That never touch with inarticulate pang?
Why set the pear upon those river-banks
Or spice the shores with odors of the plum?
Alas, that they should wear our colors there,
The silken weavings of our afternoons,

And pick the strings of our insipid lutes!
Death is the mother of beauty, mystical,
Within whose burning bosom we devise
Our earthly mothers waiting, sleeplessly.

VII

Supple and turbulent, a ring of men
Shall chant in orgy on a summer morn
Their boisterous devotion to the sun,
Not as a god, but as a god might be,
Naked among them, like a savage source.
Their chant shall be a chant of paradise,
Out of their blood, returning to the sky;
And in their chant shall enter, voice by voice,
The windy lake wherein their lord delights,
The trees, like serafin, and echoing hills,
That choir among themselves long afterward.
They shall know well the heavenly fellowship
Of men that perish and of summer morn.
And whence they came and whither they shall go
The dew upon their feet shall manifest.

VIII

She hears, upon that water without sound,
A voice that cries, "The tomb in Palestine
Is not the porch of spirits lingering.
It is the grave of Jesus, where he lay."
We live in an old chaos of the sun,
Or old dependency of day and night,
Or island solitude, unsponsored, free,
Of that wide water, inescapable.
Deer walk upon our mountains, and the quail
Whistle about us their spontaneous cries;
Sweet berries ripen in the wilderness;

And, in the isolation of the sky,
At evening, casual flocks of pigeons make
Ambiguous undulations as they sink,
Downward to darkness, on extended wings.

                                    1915

WHAT DO you do on Sunday morning, in particular Easter Sunday morning, if you do not go to church or believe in God? I remember precisely where I was standing, on the corner of High Street and First Avenue in Grinnell, Iowa, when I first read Wallace Stevens's poem "Sunday Morning." I was waiting for a girl—I was always waiting for a girl in those days—and thought it would be clever to surprise her with a poem about Sunday morning on Easter Sunday. I was wrong—she slept in and never showed—and it wasn't clever, it was a mistake. I had no idea what sort of consolation I was seeking, but I was so absorbed by the poem that I forgot about everything else. There was no one around, no traffic, no other college students, not even any churchgoers. And yet I did not feel alone, I felt befriended by something that I didn't understand. I loved the high language of the poem, and I think I intuited how much Wallace Stevens loved poetry, how much he cherished the Anglo-American tradition, the way that language had been phrased and inspirited over the centuries. "After one has abandoned a belief in God," Stevens wrote, "poetry is that essence which takes its place as life's redemption."

What did Wallace Stevens do with himself on Sunday morning? As an atheist who had grown up in Pennsylvania in the Dutch Reformed Church, as a former student and disciple of the philosopher George Santayana at Harvard who had mused over his teacher's 1900 book, *Interpretations of Poetry and Religion*, as a secular poet with a religious sensibility ("God is in me or else is not at all," he said), Stevens was acutely conscious of an acute spiritual loss. He recognized the power of Christianity—the lyrical beauty of hymns, the soaring grandeur of cathedrals—and felt the diminishment of disbelief. For some people, the loss of faith feels like the loss of innocence—it can never be recovered. To fill the void of what, like Nietzsche, Stevens took to be the death of God, he looked to poetry. He made a prodigious effort of consciousness to create something beautiful as an alternative to what he could no longer believe. "Sunday Morning" was his first extraordinary bid to write a miraculous poem not of heaven but of earth.

Wallace Stevens was a mature thirty-six years old when he published "Sunday Morning" in *Poetry* magazine in November 1915. World War I hovered in the background. The poem was not only missing three of its eight stanzas, which the editor Harriet Monroe asked him to cut, but it was also reordered (I, VIII, IV, V, and VII). Stevens consented to and even suggested the new structure, which was feasible because each stanza is a numbered, self-contained unit with a single underlying proposition, but he carefully restored the stanzas and the original order when he printed the poem in his debut volume, *Harmonium* (1923). Twenty years later Yvor Winters, one of the strictest modern critics, was already declaring that "'Sunday Morning' is probably the greatest American poem of the twentieth century and is certainly one of the greatest contemplative poems in English."

"Sunday Morning" is a crisis poem, like Wordsworth's "Ode: Intimations of Immortality" and Samuel Taylor Coleridge's "Dejection: An Ode," which stand behind it like instruction manuals on how to mourn a lost celestial light. Milton's "Lycidas" closely shadows it, too. In some ways, Stevens is writing an anti-Lycidas, a poem that posits earthly practice, and earthly pleasure, as an alternative to God's grace. So, too, his poem is steeped in Keats's luxuriant language—in one stanza, he responds directly to "Ode on a Grecian Urn"; in another, to "To Autumn." He paces his poem in a flexible blank verse, a noble-sounding five-beat, ten-syllable line, which places him in the Miltonic lineage of the English Romantic elegy. Stevens's poem seems grander than common speech, a meditative monologue about how one poetic idea, God, has been replaced by another poetic idea, the cycle of four seasons.

In "Sunday Morning," Stevens carries on a dialogue with other poets, even with poetry itself, as he faced a hard truth, what called the death "of the gods, both ancient and modern, both foreign and domestic." Stevens faces this death without affect. It is a melancholy truth that mut be accepted and transformed. But he understands what he has given up—a Christian God hangs invisibly in the wings of the poem like a guilty conscience. The death of Stevens's mother also looms somewhere in the background. Margaretha Catharine Zeller was a devout Christian all her life, and her wayward son grieved for her as well as for her rickety but comforting belief system.

Throughout "Sunday Morning," Stevens keeps insisting that the divinity dwelling within us, within himself especially, can match the divinity no longer dwelling above us, but he may be overinsistent, trying to convince himself. He is mourning for our mortality. He divides his consciousness and splits himself off into two entities in the poem. He addresses himself as if he is talking to a woman to whom he can explain things. His early letters show that he thought of poetry as somewhat embarrassingly feminine, a bit "ladylike," and was conscious of protecting his own sensitivities. He idealizes the woman as a muse figure. There's a moving moment when he declares, "Divinity *must* live within herself." Perhaps it is a surmise, perhaps an imperative, maybe both. Stevens staked his life's work on the idea. It's as if he is taking Pascal's wager about the existence of God and betting the other side. There's a lot riding on the gamble over the vacant spaces between stars.

Stevens begins the poem by projecting himself into an unnamed woman's point of view, though the woman is more a cipher than a person, a figure of reverie. By presenting the poem in a close third person—what fiction writers call a third-person center of consciousness—Stevens evokes the woman's meditative outlook, re-creating the way he would like her to think and feel. There is no "I" in the poem, but the poet does sometimes pull away from the character's vantage point to provide a corrective point of view. He is arguing with his own anima, some version of himself. What is the argument about? As Stevens formulated it in a journal entry as early as 1902: "An old argument with me is that the true religious force in the world is not the church but the world itself: the mysterious calling of Nature and our responses."

"Sunday Morning" commences with the figure of a woman lounging in a light dressing gown over a late breakfast and enjoying the colorful pageant of nature outside her window. The scene is lush, painterly, Matissean. She's in a state that Keats called "ardent listlessness." The first sentence, which creates the leisurely feeling of someone taking coffee, concludes in the fifth line with the woman's drowsy awareness that she is not in church. Stevens has a gift for defining silence, as in the locution *holy hush* or the way he slows the rhythm in two repetitive six-beat lines that echo with the letter *w*: "*W*inding across *w*ide *w*ater *w*ithout sound, / The day is like *w*ide *w*ater, *w*ithout sound." The alliteration that is sometimes gaudily displayed in his other poems works here to create a feeling of quasi-religious awe. Even the pungent oranges and the bright green bird seem like "things in some procession of the dead." This is the heart of the matter, of the music. Stevens's gorgeous catalogues, which recur throughout the poem, create their own quasi-religious processionals. In the meantime, there is a Great War going on overseas and the woman becomes all too aware of an "ancient sacrifice," of that "old catastrophe," of the "blood and sepulchre" of the crucifixion of Jesus Christ.

"Sunday Morning" operates by alternations of repose and movement. The woman is fully awake in the second stanza and poses three questions to herself. One feels the poet closely shadowing her thoughts as the poem restates its crisis of belief. The woman wonders why she should sacrifice her only life, her body and spirit, to an outmoded belief system, a supposedly "dead" God, a divinity that hides in mysteries. She wonders whether she can find in "comforts of the sun" or any earthly beauty "Things to be cherished like the thought of heaven?" This passage leads the poet-narrator to merge viewpoints with the next declaration about divinity. Nothing seems more Stevensian than the sensuous catalogue that pairs frames of mind with nature: "*Passions* of rain, or *moods* in falling snow, / *Grievings in loneliness*, or *unsubdued* / *Elations* when the forest blooms." This gusty list stands for "all pleasures and all pains" in the cycle of the seasons that now seems "destined" for the soul. The fact that Stevens uses such an old-fashioned religious word, *soul*, suggests that he hasn't exactly rid himself of a Christian vocabulary, though he transforms it into a language of secular beauty.

Stevens turns to Roman mythology in the third stanza—"Jove in the clouds had his inhuman birth"—and, somewhat sacrilegiously, parallels the story of the king of the gods to the Christian nativity. The mythologies progress from a completely inhuman Jove to a partly human Jesus to the human god that the poem projects. There is a moment when Stevens asks a question—"And shall the earth / Seem all of paradise that we shall know?"— that precisely echoes and questions a moment in *Paradise Lost* when Michael describes to Adam how Christ will return: "Whether in Heaven or Earth; for then the Earth / Shall all be Paradise" (book 12, 463–64). Stevens rewrites Milton and replaces his mythic creation with a palpably physical world. Linking the Roman and Christian stories, which he implicitly treats as equally mythological, Stevens wonders whether one can give up their gods and reconnect, even reunite with the natural world. If so, he posits, "The sky will be much friendlier then than now."

The fourth stanza commences with the unnamed woman asking a question about transience: "where, then, is Paradise?" She does not sound like a woman talking—Stevens didn't have Robert Frost's or William Carlos Williams's feeling for the vernacular—but the question defines a theme and enables him to shift viewpoints, to respond with a catalogue of fantastical other worlds, eternal afterlives. One feels the poet's rhetorical excitement in negatively naming these mystic imaginaries: "*There is not* any haunt of prophecy, / *Nor* any old chimera of the grave, / *Neither* the golden underground, *nor* isle / Melodious, where spirits gat them home, / *Nor* visionary south, *nor* cloudy palm / Remote on heaven's hill, that has endured / As April's green endures." This is reminiscent of Milton's dismissals in *Paradise Lost*, the rhetoric he summons to describe the seven deadly sins. Stevens's language of false belief is so enraptured that it seems infused with the Miltonic spirit it denies.

The opening declarations of the fifth stanza have an aphoristic element: "She says, 'But in contentment I still feel / The need of some imperishable bliss'" and "Death is the mother of beauty." Stevens revises Keats's confident motto, "A thing of beauty is a joy for ever" ("Endymion"), to articulate a later Keatsian aesthetic creed under the sign of mortality. He repeats the statement in the next stanza, where it becomes a litany to death and the maternity of earth: "Death is the mother of beauty, mystical, / Within whose burning bosom we devise / Our earthly mothers waiting, sleeplessly." Whereas Keats writes about gradual increase and diminishment, Stevens celebrates the mournful majesty of the cresting moment, which is poignant precisely because it cannot last, because it perishes, like us. Stevens's diction becomes slightly archaic and harkens back to the eighteenth and nineteenth centuries—"For maidens who were wont to sit and gaze"—as he seeks a language to describe a radiant world that shines forth under the presiding spirit of death. One feels the giddy linguistic poet—"She causes boys to pile new plums and pears / On disregarded plate"—harmonizing with the old-fashioned Romantic: "The maidens taste / And stray impassioned in the littering leaves." This is another way of saying that he moves fluently between lightheartedness and a feeling of lament or dirge.

Stevens creates an extra aphoristic emphasis whenever the line and the sentence coincide, as in "Is there no change of death in paradise?" This rhetorical question serves as a topic sentence for the stanza. As the poet fantasizes about some sterile, unchanging other world—the woman has momentarily disappeared from the poem—the language seems nostalgic and spellbound. He is responding directly to "Ode on a Grecian Urn" and the hell of an unchanging permanence, a "Cold Pastoral." Even the language of Stevens's poem becomes Keatsian, hence: "Alas, that they should wear our colors there, / The silken weavings of our afternoons, / And pick the strings of our insipid lutes!"

Moving forward, Stevens contrasts this vision of dull immortality with the orgiastic pagan dance of a naked ring of men who come turbulently bursting into the next stanza. The rhythm is excited, the feeling wild, a boisterous prayer to a human god. In a 1928 letter, Stevens said that "Sunday Morning" is "an expression of paganism," which is probably why he felt comfortable letting stanza VII stand as the conclusion of the version in *Poetry* magazine. Stevens is celebrating a paleolithic view of the world, "the heavenly fellowship / Of men that perish and of summer morn." He was very much a poet of thought, of abstraction, but at times he showed a fervent longing to stand with the archaic poets who greeted the world as alive in all its parts. To fill the body of the sun and moon, to speak not just to the Other but also from its vantage point is to harness something of its primitive power. Stevens's longing seems apparent, but he was ultimately excluded from this Dionysian male revelry, like the woman in the poem.

The poem regains its composure when the sensibility of that woman returns in the final stanza. Stevens was attuned to a Christianity he rejected, and thus his spiritual amanuensis hears a voice that cries out to her, "The tomb in Palestine / Is not the porch of spirits lingering. / It is the grave of Jesus, where he lay." For the rest of the poem, Stevens speaks as a plurality, a "we," and sets out different interpretive possibilities for how we live without the comfort of divinity. Helen Vendler and other critics have noted the exact way that the last stanza rewrites Keats's ode "To Autumn." Stevens's revisions of Keats also point to the way that he was both an American and a modern poet. For example, the succession of tiny and domestic animals in Keats (small gnats, full-grown lambs, hedge crickets) is transformed into something wilder and more unruly in Stevens (mountainous deer, quail, pigeons), who takes a Whitmanian pride in the landscape ("Deer walk upon *our* mountains, and the quail / Whistle about *us*"). The softly whistling, red-breasted bird in Keats is changed by Stevens into whistling quail who fill us with their "spontaneous cries." The word *spontaneous* makes the point that there is no spiritual warrant for the birds' cries, which spring up naturally from their mortal bodies. Stevens takes celebratory pride in the sweet berries that "ripen in the wilderness," and he seems especially American in the way he prizes the values of spontaneity, freedom, and wilderness. But, most crucially, the gathering swallows who "twitter in the skies" in Keats are transfigured by Stevens into a final ambiguous and complex image of birds flying downward:

> And, in the isolation of the sky,
> At evening, casual flocks of pigeons make
> Ambiguous undulations as they sink,
> Downward to darkness, on extended wings.

I find these lines so beautiful, phrase by phrase, that it requires an effort of concentration to comprehend their meaning. Almost imperceptibly, Sunday morning has turned into Sunday evening. Stevens begins with the "isolation of the sky," a figure for the emptiness of the heavens. *Isola* is Latin for "island," and so the sky is not merely empty but a separate, far-off region. Stevens follows this with an image of "casual" flocks of pigeons, meaning gatherings that are pointedly relaxed, even accidental, unexpected, and impermanent. Birds have consistently been used as signifiers of transcendence in the history of poetry, especially in Romantic poetry, where they so often figure as signs of imaginative freedom, but Stevens's birds are making "ambiguous undulations" and sinking rather than rising. The final phrasing is so memorable—"Downward to darkness, on extended wings"—that it creates a transcendent feeling in a line pointedly against transcendence. The extension of the wings makes one feel that the birds are meant to soar, but instead they are heading toward a darker mortal ending.

Wallace Stevens was a radiant poet seeking to compensate for a loss of permanence. Like Keats, he longed for "a Life of Sensations rather than of Thoughts." He took the idea of heaven and replaced it with something sensuous, intellectual, and abstract. He famously worked for an insurance company, but he otherwise lived in an island solitude. Isolated, lonely, and free, he would spend much of the rest of his poetic life trying to figure out how to make the most of our perishable earthly paradise, how to create his own supreme fiction.

WILLIAM CARLOS WILLIAMS (1883–1963)

from Spring and All

I

By the road to the contagious hospital
under the surge of the blue
mottled clouds driven from the
northeast—a cold wind. Beyond, the
waste of broad, muddy fields
brown with dried weeds, standing and fallen

patches of standing water
the scattering of tall trees

All along the road the reddish
purplish, forked, upstanding, twiggy
stuff of bushes and small trees
with dead, brown leaves under them
leafless vines—

Lifeless in appearance, sluggish
dazed spring approaches—

They enter the new world naked,
cold, uncertain of all
save that they enter. All about them
the cold, familiar wind—

Now the grass, tomorrow
the stiff curl of wildcarrot leaf

One by one objects are defined—
It quickens: clarity, outline of leaf

But now the stark dignity of
entrance—Still, the profound change
has come upon them: rooted, they
grip down and begin to awaken

1923

THERE ARE moments in your reading life that rock you, like a hard hit in football, the sort of tackle that you still feel as you stumble to your feet and stagger back to the huddle. There's a passage in William Carlos Williams's *Autobiography* that struck me like that. I loved the jaunty way that Williams recounted the story of his life, and I was expressly interested in his mixed ancestry. Like most of us, he started out as a literary outsider. There was something that seemed quintessentially American about his childhood in New Jersey, his multicultural perspective, the way he grew up listening to different languages. He had French, Spanish, Dutch, and Jewish ancestors. His father was British and had spent much of his life in the Virgin Islands. His mother was from Puerto Rico, which helps to explain why his idea of America was hemispheric, the Americas. "Mother could talk very little English when I was born, and Pop spoke Spanish better, in fact, than most Spaniards." Williams loved our mongrel version of English. He was intent on "defining our right as Americans to our own language," and declared that his idiom came to him directly from immigrants, i.e., "from the mouths of Polish mothers."

The passage that surprised me had to do with T. S. Eliot. At the time, I was under the impress of *The Waste Land* as an open structure of fragments, a poem without a fixed center that contains scenes and vignettes from a wide variety of times and places: agitated scraps of conversations, parodies, intertextual allusions, unattributed, often broken quotations, a medley of radically shifting languages, a cacophony of voices. It's a poem with the feeling of a nightmare. As a piece about modern life, I thought it pointed the way forward. But in November 1922 Williams understood it the opposite way:

Then out of the blue *The Dial* brought out *The Waste Land* and all our hilarity ended. It wiped out our world as if an atom bomb had been dropped upon it and our brave sallies into the unknown were turned to dust.

To me especially it struck like a sardonic bullet. I felt at once that it had set me back twenty years, and I'm sure it did. Critically Eliot returned us to the classroom just at the moment when I felt we were on the point of an escape to matters much closer to the essence of a new art form itself—rooted in the locality which should give it fruit. I knew at once that in certain ways I was most defeated.

Eliot had turned his back on the possibility of reviving my world. And being an accomplished craftsman, better skilled in some ways than I could ever hope to be, I had to watch him carry my world off with him, the fool, to the enemy.

I was shocked by the extremity of Williams's response and needed to look again—did he really compare the publication of the greatest poem of the twentieth century to an atom bomb? Less globally, Williams also acted as if he had been gunned down by a "sardonic bullet." He felt defeated, even vanquished. He was a credible witness—it couldn't have been easy to admit that Eliot had superior literary skills—and it took me a moment to register that one poet's revolutionary advance can be another's rearguard action. But who precisely was the enemy and why did Williams think that Eliot was destroying a vanguard American poetry?

I learned that to figure this out, you have to dial back the calendar to an era when critics were questioning not only the value but even the existence of American literature itself, let alone American poetry. In "The Literary Life," his contribution to an important cultural book, *Civilization in the United States* (1922), Van Wyck Brooks surveyed the history of American literature as a "very weak and sickly plant" that couldn't be expected to flourish in the decaying soil of American civilization. Critics were eager to echo Brooks's opinion that, in comparison to European literature, American literature "is indeed one long list of spiritual casualties. For it is not that the talent is wanting, but that somehow this talent fails to fulfill itself." D. H. Lawrence offered a counterview in *Studies in Classic American Literature* (1923), which assumed that there was such a thing as an "American classic," and Williams followed this with his own act of cultural reclamation, *In the American Grain* (1925). But there was a literary and cultural battle going on in the teens and twenties, which was bloodier than it might seem to us, and it included a fight for the heart and mind of American poetry.

I appreciate Williams's well-timed word *hilarity* to describe the project that he shared—or thought he shared—with his contemporaries. There *is* something hilarious and socially disruptive about early modernism, its rebellious spirit and giddy humor, its determination to thumb its nose at the old guard. Williams liked to invoke the 1913 New York Armory Show, the International Exhibition of Modern Art, as a starting point for artistic revolution. The show, which introduced Cubism, Futurism, and other styles of modern art to the American public, provoked tremendous civic outrage and consternation, but Williams felt liberated by it. He said that seeing Marcel Duchamp's *Nude Descending a Staircase, No. 2* made him "burst out laughing from the relief it brought me!" He felt that a sizable weight, the burden of tradition, had been lifted from his shoulders. He also liked Duchamp's urinal, which he called "magnificent," and thought the committee was "silly" for rejecting it.

Williams was unabashedly excited and upbeat about American literature. He searched for fresh forms and declared, "Language is in its January" (*January: A Novelette*, 1932), embracing the idea of a new language for a New World. He believed in democratic individualism, the American possibility, and so, like Emerson, he could seem gullible, overly optimistic. He was vulnerable to cynical criticism because there was something purposefully naïve and even nativist about his project. But, in fact, his philosophy was pragmatic. What he wanted from poetry was contact, physicality, something concrete and seen in a flash, art for the present moment, gritty and homegrown. He was determined to get American poetry to dig in and take root in American soil.

Williams was a doctor by profession—I like to think of him opening his practice at the kitchen pantry in his family home in Rutherford, New Jersey—and many of his lyrics have a rushed feeling, something jotted down between appointments, in the hospital parking lot, at the office. His poems are spontaneous, immediate, urgent; they are also humane. Williams was both a general practitioner and a pediatrician—for more than a decade he was the school physician for the Rutherford Public Schools—and his daily, intimate connection to ordinary people gives his work a different valence than the poetry of his contemporaries. What he called his "medical badge" enabled him "to follow the poor defeated body into those gulfs and grottos . . . to be present at deaths and births."

Williams didn't start out as an up-to-date modern poet; he had Romantic underpinnings. As a young poet, he veered between Walt Whitman and John Keats—his first book, *Poems* (1909), sounds like something from *Palgrave's Golden Treasury*—but he quickly learned to sign in to the twentieth century. He was enabled by his close friendships with Ezra Pound and Hilda Doolittle, whom he knew from his medical school days at the University of Pennsylvania. He said, "Before meeting Ezra Pound is like B.C. and A.D.," and it would be fair to say that Pound carried him along into the Imagist movement. Williams found his footing when he grounded his poetry in perception and locale, in "direct treatment of the 'thing.'" It was if he had suddenly cleared away the detritus and spotted the objects in the world. He became a poet of immanence, an anti-symbolist, who accorded objects a life of their own. So, too, for him words were fundamentally things in themselves, solid objects that match the things they name. They are marked by "the shapes of men's lives in places." That's one reason he was so frustrated by America's cultural dependence on the European past.

Williams did not forge ahead alone. He coedited the little magazine *Contact* with Robert McAlmon (its aim was "to emphasize the local phase of the game of writing"), and he was part of a group that gathered around Alfred Kreymborg's journal of new verse, *Others*, which was financed by Walter Conrad Arensberg, and included Marianne Moore, Mina Loy, and Man Ray. He envied the sensuous immediacy of painting—"I've attempted to fuse the poetry and painting to make it the same thing," he once said—and he was nurtured by hanging out with painters and looking at pictures. He was part of the cluster around the photographer Alfred Stieglitz's gallery, 291, and made friendships with painters John Marin, Marsden Hartley, Charles Sheeler, and others. Along with cultural journalists, like Waldo Frank (*Our America*, 1919) and Paul Rosenfeld (*Port of New York*, 1924), these artists emphasized swift visual experience and the need for establishing American values in art.

It was this optimistic milieu—a fresh voicing, a set of artworks stamped

Made in America—that Williams felt was exploded by *The Waste Land*. He explained further in *I Wanted to Write a Poem* (1958):

> I felt [Eliot] had rejected America and I refused to be rejected and so my reaction was violent. I realized the responsibility I must accept. I knew he would influence all subsequent American poets and take them out of my sphere. I had envisaged a new form of poetic composition, a form for the future. It was a shock to me that he was so tremendously successful; my contemporaries flocked to him—away from what I wanted.

Williams had cause for thinking that Eliot had won the day and blown up the future, relegating American poetry to the classroom for another few decades. Personally, I still love *The Waste Land*, but he wasn't entirely wrong about this; think of New Criticism and its idolatry of closed forms, which devalued Williams's type of formal improvisation and innovation. "[Williams's work] is not only *about* the failure of language," one critic opined, "it *is* a failure of language." It would take another generation of American poets to start flocking to his work in the 1950s. If you had been in Williams's situation in the winter of 1922, if you suddenly realized that your version of American poetry was now a lost cause, then you, too, might start referring to Eliot's depressive masterpiece as a sardonic bullet and an atom bomb.

Williams struck back immediately with his book *Spring and All* (1923), his first shot at *The Waste Land*. The title itself, which has a kind of slangy offhandedness, is a response to Eliot's heralded opening, "April is the cruelest month." Williams was trying to escape his own barren wasteland. In the title to his book of prose poems, *Kora in Hell* (1920), he referred to the legend of Spring captured and taken to Hades. "I thought of myself as Springtime and I felt I was on my way to Hell," he said. Now, three years later, he was trying to climb back with an experimental weaving together of poems and prose manifestos about poetry.

Williams later referred to *Spring and All* as a book of "philosophy and nonsense," and the hilarity returns as a "travesty on the idea" of typographical form. He commences with chapter 19. Chapter titles are subsequently numbered in the wrong order, some of them have roman numerals, a few are printed upside down. Williams intentionally misspells *rhythm* as *rhthm* and *writer* as *writter*. Question marks are left floating with an extra space on either side. He uses both French-style angular quotation marks and Central European–style quotation marks (in which the open quote faces outward and runs down at the comma line); in fact, he uses one of each in the very first quotation in the book, pages 1–2! Williams later gave titles to the twenty-seven individual poems, but here they were still untitled.

Williams was on the defensive—he was afraid of not being taken seriously—and his playfulness is a form of masking and foolery. His underlying intention was deadly serious and he was determined to find a way to break down "a constant barrier between the reader and his consciousness of immediate contact with the world." The fragmentary, often Dada-like mini-essays combine violent indictments of contemporary civilization with impassioned pleas on behalf of the imagination. These two modes come together in one of the decisive poems of the volume, XVIII, which notoriously declares, "The pure products of America / go crazy." The anthropologist James Clifford rightfully calls this a moment of "ethnographic modernity."

What is most exciting in *Spring and All* is how Williams finds his voice with poems of visual accuracy and precision, lyrics in which familiar objects are clarified and presented in a fresh context, such as the now famous red wheelbarrow upon which "so much depends" (XXII). The book is dedicated to Williams's lifelong friend, the painter Charles Demuth, whom he first met over a bowl of prunes at Mrs. Chain's boardinghouse on Locust Street in Philadelphia, and one poem (II) references Demuth's painting *Tuberoses*, which Williams owned. Demuth responded with a canvas version of Williams's poem "The Great Figure," and thereby created one of the most dynamic paintings of American modernism: *I Saw the Figure 5 in Gold* (1928).

The first poem in *Spring and All* hits a brand-new note in American poetry. It is an antipastoral or perhaps even a subpastoral, since it speaks to what is underground and trying to spring up. It is an urban poem about a neglected landscape—Williams shows us that city people have nature, too. In "To Autumn," Keats inquired, "Where are the songs of spring? Ay, where are they?" and immediately responded, "Think not of them." But Williams now was prepared with a diverging answer—not just to Keats but also to Romanticism. He does think of them; the songs of spring are right here, he suggests, in March in New Jersey. These are not going to be easy songs, he knows; this birth will be painfully difficult. But the physician is present.

Williams refers in the first stanza to "the contagious hospital," which in his day was a literal place, a nickname for a wing or building for patients with infectious diseases. This dangerous location would have been part of his regular rounds. It makes sense that in our time readers found a metaphor in the phrase "contagious hospital" for the quarantine of people sick with COVID-19. As a family doctor, Williams was on the front lines of the influenza epidemic of 1918–19, a losing battle that eventually claimed some 675,000 American lives. In his *Autobiography*, he recalled, "We doctors were making up to sixty calls a day. Several of us were knocked out, one of the younger of us died, others caught the thing, and we hadn't a thing that was effective in checking the potent poison that was sweeping the world." Williams lost two young female patients and was shocked by the rapidity of the disease: "They'd be sick one day and gone the next, just like that, fill up and die."

This backdrop of disease and suffering informs the poem "Spring and All," as it came to be known, and the sense of contagion from the hospital spills over or leaks into the surrounding landscape. The unnamed speaker, a stand-in for the doctor-poet, pauses outdoors to observe the natural world. What he sees is a brutally barren landscape, one of the waste places of nature, a sterile winter scene. It's as if a doctor has gotten in his car and discovered that Whitman's Open Road has led to the contagious hospital.

> By the road to the contagious hospital
> under the surge of the blue
> mottled clouds driven from the
> northeast—a cold wind. Beyond, the
> waste of broad, muddy fields
> brown with dried weeds, standing and fallen

Formally, this isn't a poem to be scanned: a traditional metric doesn't apply. The music is harsh, the rhythm off-balance. The first line is a recognizable unit—"By the road to the contagious hospital"—but thereafter the beat is choppy, the lines irregular. It's worth pausing over the technique because Williams is striving for a new effect, a different rhythmic push. He is a poet of jagged turns, terse enjambments, and suspended moments. The sentence structure purposefully buries the lead, the driving agent from the northeast, the cold wind. The second line initially seems to be an intact unit—"under the surge of the blue"—but then the word *blue* turns from a noun into an adjective ("the blue / mottled clouds") and the line spills forward. Williams consistently breaks the line on an unemphatic word, a conjunction or article ("driven from *the*"; "Beyond, *the*"), and thus also breaks an unspoken rule of lineation in traditional poetry. But this enables him to create a downbeat on the new line, emphasizing the first word: *mottled, northeast, waste, brown*. These unexpected line breaks create an uneventful event.

Williams's poem moves forward by a series of starts and stops. The second stanza hits pause and stands alone, a set of unpunctuated parallel phrases, a couplet of stasis. It captures a moment when spring waits in a state of suspension:

> patches of standing water
> the scattering of tall trees

There is a piling up of adjectives in the third stanza, a stutter-step of gritty particulars. I recall the first time I read it and how I kept waiting for the noun, which gets postponed five times:

> All along the road the *reddish*
> *purplish, forked, upstanding, twiggy*
> stuff of bushes and small trees
> with dead, brown leaves under them
> leafless vines—

I still think it's funny how this series of precise adjectives leads to the very American and generalized word *stuff*. But there is method in the patterning of "stuff . . . and small trees" and the combination of "dead, brown leaves" and "leafless vines." This is also meant to capture a locale that on the surface seems lifeless.

Williams's poem is everywhere ghosted by *The Waste Land*. Whereas Eliot describes a dead landscape, Williams describes one coming to life. He is determined to prove that life comes after "the burial of the dead." Even the weather patterns are misaligned, European versus American. When Eliot asks, "What are the roots that clutch, what branches grow / Out of this stony rubbish?" Williams answers, "under the surge of the blue / mottled clouds." When Eliot writes, "Winter kept us warm, covering / Earth in forgetful snow," Williams replies,

> Lifeless in appearance, sluggish
> dazed spring approaches—

Williams is talking about the resurrection of the natural world, but the next stanza suggests that he is also referring to the creation of a new American culture, which is why Paul Mariani adopted the maxim *A New World Naked* for his expansive biography of Williams:

> They enter the new world naked,
> cold, uncertain of all
> save that they enter. All about them
> the cold, familiar wind—

The pronoun *They* is intentionally vague. It refers to the bushes and small trees, but also encompasses some other unnamed entity, not just things but people. One thinks of Dante and his reference to souls in purgatory. Williams twice repeats the word *cold*, first pairing it with *uncertain*, and thus emphasizing the tentative nature of birth. But the cold wind of the first stanza now recurs as the "cold, familiar wind," and the word *familiar* seems notable. This icy wind is not reassuring, but it is recognizable.

I have always loved the way things are clarified in the final three stanzas, which have their own stature and dignity. Williams creates this effect through eight beautifully balanced lines, a pair of couplets and a quatrain. There is a final underlying argument here—"*But now . . . Still*"—that shows a driving intelligence, a poet making a point even as he describes an exact natural phenomenon and even achievement. The phrasing is precise, the timing perfect:

> Now the grass, tomorrow
> the stiff curl of wildcarrot leaf

One by one objects are defined—
It quickens: clarity, outline of leaf

But now the stark dignity of
entrance—Still, the profound change
has come upon them: rooted, they
grip down and begin to awaken

Williams reenacts here the difficult struggle to be reborn, to grab down and reach up. He was not a symbolist, but the word *rooted* carries overtones of a new American poetic. It is as if the natural world models "the stark dignity of / entrance," "the profound change" and awakening.

William Carlos Williams wrote his own declaration of independence. He had what Robert Coles called "the knack of survival in America." He took the American colloquial, the language that people speak, and used it as an instrument of precision and eloquence. He was trying to fuse words and experience. He could go into paroxysms of rage against T. S. Eliot, but it turns out that he just needed to bide his time, to wait for American poets and poetry to catch up to him. Williams's reputation is secure, he is one of the heroes of our consciousness, but the American imagination is still a contested battlefield, a work in progress. We need models, examples, and counterexamples. It's a hard winter and it takes time for us to "grip down and begin to awaken."

The River-Merchant's Wife: a Letter

While my hair was still cut straight across my forehead
I played about the front gate, pulling flowers.
You came by on bamboo stilts, playing horse,
You walked about my seat, playing with blue plums.
And we went on living in the village of Chokan:
Two small people, without dislike or suspicion.

At fourteen I married My Lord you.
I never laughed, being bashful.
Lowering my head, I looked at the wall.
Called to, a thousand times, I never looked back.

At fifteen I stopped scowling,
I desired my dust to be mingled with yours
Forever and forever, and forever.
Why should I climb the look out?

At sixteen you departed,
You went into far Ku-to-Yen, by the river of swirling eddies,
And you have been gone five months.
The monkeys make sorrowful noise overhead.
You dragged your feet when you went out.
By the gate now, the moss is grown, the different mosses,
Too deep to clear them away!
The leaves fall early this autumn, in wind.
The paired butterflies are already yellow with August
Over the grass in the West garden,
They hurt me, I grow older,

If you are coming down through the narrows of the river Kiang,
Please let me know beforehand,
And I will come out to meet you,
                    As far as Cho-fu-Sa.

                              By Rihaku

                                        1915

I WAS IN London! I had a room in a flat somewhere or other, a head full of ideas, and a reader's pass to the British Library, which was still part of the British Museum. I was on my own and diligently studied all day in the grandeur of the central Reading Room. But I didn't know anyone in England, and at night I was unexpectedly lonely, soul-crushingly homesick. I put a pot of tea on the hot plate, opened a copy of Ezra Pound's *Translations*, and soaked up the poems, the Anglo-Saxon lament *The Seafarer* ("May I for my own self song's truth reckon"), and the Provençal poets, especially Arnaut Daniel ("Aye, life's a high thing"), and the Florentine Guido Cavalcanti ("I am reduced at last to self compassion, / For the sore anguish that I see me in"), and fantasized that I could become part of something.

Every reading has its own history. Above all else, I loved the fourteen Chinese poems in Pound's *Cathay* (1915). One night I reread "The River-Merchant's Wife: a Letter" and felt—I'm not sure how to phrase this—I felt that I had found a home for my homesickness. The time period was remote and the setting faraway, and yet I projected myself so far into the situation that I couldn't tell if I identified more with the female speaker or the male addressee, the trader's wife or the trader. I knew that the author, Rihaku, was the Japanese name for the Tang dynasty poet Li Po (Li Bai), though I had no idea of the original poem or how much Pound had transcribed, paraphrased, or invented. But I responded to the heartbreaking clarity of the lyric, its melancholy longing, and I realized that I had found a poem that would companion me.

Over the years, I've learned more about the great eighth-century poet Li Bai, who is often referred to as a "Banished Immortal," and his poem "Chang-gan xing" (Ballad of Changgan), which has inspired a countless number of other translations (Arthur Waley, Amy Lowell, Witter Bynner, William Carlos Williams, Arthur Cooper, Wai-lim Yip, David Hinton, Arthur Sze, and others), each with its own merits and corrections, none a better poem in English. Eliot famously called Pound "the inventor of Chinese poetry for our time," a designation that has stuck, though Eliot also hedged and recognized that what "*seem* to be . . . translucencies" were not accurate renderings of Chinese originals—they were not "Chinese poetry-in-itself."

Pound's inventions were not intended as copies. To borrow the terms that John Dryden outlined at the end of the seventeenth century: Pound had little or no interest in *metaphrase*, word-for-word, interlinear translation, and he moved beyond *paraphrase* or "Translation with Latitude," into *imitation*, which frees the writer to create a new work in the style of the original. As an imitator, Pound rebelled against what he called "Wardour Street English," the diction of Victorian translators, like William Morris, and turned traditional meters into *vers libre*. His translations were new poems, contemporary reenactments.

To be clear: Pound did not speak or read Chinese. He was working from the voluminous notes of Ernest Fenollosa, an American art historian, who specialized in Japanese art and taught philosophy and economics at Tokyo Imperial University. Pound's imitations, which have sparked acrimonious debates about authenticity and appropriation, the nature of translation, and the Orientalism of modernist poetry, turn out to be much more mediated than most of us ever realized. Thanks to a groundbreaking critical edition of *Cathay*, edited by Timothy Billings, it's now possible to see that "The River-Merchant's Wife" is part of an elaborate process of cultural transmission, which relies on an eighth-century poem, itself built on a long history of folk songs from different dynasties, that was reprinted in a popular Japanese anthology of Chinese poetry. Fenollosa didn't know Chinese either—he was rapidly taking notes from a Japanese interpreter, Ariga Nagao, who was translating the comments of a Japanese poet, Mori Kainan, who wrote in *kanshi*, or the classical Chinese manner. Mori relied on a Japanese method of reading Chinese texts called *kundoku*, "gloss readings." This hybrid way of reading, a sort of creolization that is part annotation and part translation, enabled Japanese poets and scholars who did not speak Chinese to interpret Chinese language and literature.

All this clarifies the subtitle to *Cathay*: "Translations by Ezra Pound for the most part from the Chinese of Rihaku, from the notes of the late Ernest Fenollosa, and the decipherings of the professors Mori and Ariga." It makes evident why Fenollosa called Chinese poets by their Japanese names and used Japanese terms to designate Chinese places. As a result, Pound also blurred the distinction between the Japanese and Chinese languages. Fenollosa's essay "The Chinese Written Character as a Medium for Poetry," a key modernist text that Pound edited and published in 1919, suggests that they both misunderstood the Chinese writing system as pictorially transparent. We now know why they over-visualized Chinese characters. But cultural transmission is complicated, and this mistaken notion also enabled Pound to employ what he deemed "the ideogrammic method," a way of connecting and juxtaposing abstract ideas through concrete images. I would also point out that Fenollosa was arguing for the importance of intercultural transmission and knowledge at a moment when the racist Chinese Exclusion Act was still operating in the United States.

Pound had a splendid ear for poetry, but he was not much of a Sinologist, and he overlaid his idea of Chinese poetry with the three main tenets of Imagism:

1. Direct treatment of the "thing" whether subjective or objective.
2. To use absolutely no word that does not contribute to the presentation.
3. As regarding rhythm: to compose in sequence of the musical phrase, not in sequence of a metronome.

There is a parallel here with John Locke's opposition between simple ideas and complex ideas in *An Essay Concerning Human Understanding* (1689). Pound's Imagist credo demonstrated his eagerness to syncretize ancient Chinese and modern English language poetry. I wouldn't underestimate his keen interest or overestimate his sketchy knowledge of Chinese poetry and art, most of which he had gleaned from Herbert Giles's *A History of Chinese Literature* (1901) and Laurence Binyon's lectures and books, such as *Painting in the Far East* (1908) and *The Flight of the Dragon* (1911). He had only a partial grasp of Li Bai's range and achievement. And yet he was triggered by Fenollosa's detailed crib into creating one of the foundational poems of modernism. As a young poet, I marveled at the naturalness of Pound's version, and I wondered how he managed it.

I like to recall the exuberance with which a twenty-three-old American aspirant rolled into London in 1908. He covered up his shyness with bohemian swagger. He had a suitcase filled with sixty copies of his first book, *A Lume Spento* (With Tapers Quenched), which he had self-published in Venice, and a salesman's charm, and he soon convinced the bookseller Elkin Mathews first to display the collection and then to publish his books in quick succession: *Personae* (1909), *Exultations* (1909), *Canzoni* (1911), and others. He was educating himself in public, trying on and casting off different masks for the self. Indeed, he called his long series of translations "more elaborate masks."

Pound set up shop in a flat in Kensington, where he made tea and pronouncements for his guests. He had a Westerner's bravado—he hailed from Idaho—and a wild confidence in his own taste. The young poet viewed himself as an unerring scout for the avant-garde, the advance troops, and took aim at the genteel Georgian poets, such as Lascelles Abercrombie, who had the temerity to suggest that modern poets should model themselves on Wordsworth. Pound dashed off a note and challenged him to a duel on the grounds that "stupidity carried beyond a certain point becomes a public menace." Pound was a dangerously skilled fencer, but Abercrombie saved himself (and won the day) by suggesting that they should attack each other with unsold copies of their own books.

Ford Madox Hueffer (later Ford) gives a striking portrait of Pound's appearance:

> Ezra . . . would approach with the step of a dancer, making passes
> with a cane at an imaginary opponent. He would wear trousers
> made of green billiard cloth, a pink coat, a blue shirt, a tie hand-
> painted by a Japanese friend, an immense sombrero, a flaming
> beard cut to a point, and a single, large blue earring.

Pound tried hard to cut a figure, make an impression. He kept his saber close, intellectually speaking—he loved a good sword fight with the old guard—and would soon start issuing proclamations and manifestos. He was eager to tell everyone what to read (the medieval troubadours) and what not to read (the Edwardians), what to do ("Make It New") and what not to do ("A Few Don'ts"). He sought out W. B. Yeats, whom he considered the greatest living poet, and acted as Yeats's secretary for three winters (1913–16) at Stone Cottage in Sussex, where he corrected the grand master's poems and steered him away from abstraction. He had a remarkable ear for the new thing and championed his former classmates Hilda Doolittle, whom he dubbed "H.D., Imagiste," and William Carlos Williams, and bet hard on acquaintances, such as Robert Frost and T. S. Eliot. He tirelessly advocated for prose writers he admired, such as Henry James, James Joyce, Ford Madox Ford, and Ernest Hemingway. He bullied Harriet Monroe at *Poetry* and did more than any other writer to impose Continental modernism on American literature, which is why Hugh Kenner deemed it, with loyal exaggeration, *The Pound Era*.

Pound's literary criticism raced ahead of his poetic practice. He was a rapid learner, but he needed to extricate himself from the symbolist method and antique diction of the late nineteenth century. His archaic lexicon and medievalism sounded a lot like Algernon Charles Swinburne or Dante Gabriel Rossetti (when it came to Tuscan poetry, he said, Rossetti was "my father and my mother"). The beginning of "Canzon: The Vision" is typical: "When first I saw thee 'neath the silver mist / Ruling thy bark of painted sandal-wood / Did any know thee?" On a visit to Germany, Pound was propelled into the modern era when he brought his *Canzoni* to Ford, who reacted to his overwrought language by rolling around on the floor in mock torment. Pound later said that Ford's ridiculous, didactic roll saved him at least two years, perhaps more. He took Ford's laughter to heart and declared, "Poetry must be *as well written as prose.*"

Late in 1913, Pound met Fenollosa's widow, Mary McNeil Fenollosa, who took a shine to him and sent him her husband's unpublished notes on some 150 Chinese poems and Japanese Noh plays. All through 1914 Pound homed in on the texts, which he considered "terse, polished, emotionally suggestive." The timing matters because the slaughterous reality of World War I shadows the translations, many of which are war poems. In one sense, Pound used Chinese poetry as a foil against official English verse, the patriotic work of a popular poet like Rupert Brooke. At this moment, too, he was moving away from the single-image poem, which stripped the lyric to its bare bones, and searching for something more dynamic, Imagism in action or Vorticism. Chinese poetry gave him the material to practice what he called "the method of Luminous Detail." It does not comment or generalize, it presents.

Li Bai's poem "Ballad of Changgan" is a literary ballad. Pound did not know that it was the first of a pair of poems with the same voice and theme.

It is styled as the sort of ancient folk song that was popular among women in the southern area around the Chang Jiang, or Yangtze River, hundreds of years earlier. The music of these songs was lost, but the words survived in a form of poetry called *yueh-fu* (Music Bureau). Li Bai admired the fluidity and immediacy of these song-poems derived from common people's lives. He came from a mercantile family, and here he takes the narrator of a traditional ballad, a boatwoman or fisherman's wife, and transforms her into the spouse of a merchant who lives near the banks of the Yangtze River. Li Bai was not a "compiler," as Pound thought—he built on these folk songs and imitations of folk songs in something of the same manner that Yeats imitated Irish folk poems and ballads, or Woody Guthrie reworked traditional American folk songs.

Whereas Li Bai's original hovers between a song and a letter, Pound lowers the diction from song to speech. Fenollosa's note explained the title:

> Chokan = place {name of town}   ko = uta = narrative song
> long—mt. side

Since Chokan was a port town filled with traders and their families, Pound changed the title to something more exciting, "The River-Merchant's Wife: a Letter." He invented a job description, "the river merchant," and added water to the stream of the poem's imagery, underscoring it as a piece of epistolary writing from a woman's perspective.

Li Bai's poem consists of thirty lines stretched across one stanza. The layout looks like couplets of five monosyllabic characters. The rhyme scheme is regular. Pound retained the feeling of parallelism, but divided the symmetrical structure into uneven stanzas, which operate as verse paragraphs, and changed the pattern to a rhythmic free verse. He revised the poem in small ways when he reprinted it in his essay "Chinese Poetry" (1918).

What has always struck me about Pound's adaptation is how he animates the character of the speaker as if he knew her personally. In more literal translations, she appears as a slightly more generic or representative figure, the sort of voice you find in a folk song, a person who stands in for the community. But in Pound's recasting she is individuated and filled with personality. He invokes the personal history, the intersubjectivity, of two people and represents them with poised dignity.

It turns out that I was on to something when I identified with both the woman and the man in Li Bai's poem, which has an element of disguise or masking. Arthur Cooper suggested that Li Bai's contemporary readers would have recognized that this was "a love-poem to his wife but written as if from her to him, which was a common Chinese practice at the time." Li Bai was not married when he wrote this poem, but the point holds—he might have been writing to a distant lover. Pound, too, is literary cross-dressing, self-consciously building on a tradition that derives from Theocritus's idyll of a woman spinning at her wheel and Ovid's *Heroides*. As a wartime non-combatant, Pound might well have felt like a woman left behind, and so he takes on the voice of a teenage wife who misses her childhood friend and husband.

Pound's verse is filled with nuance and indirection. Mori noted this about the poem: "The thought not logical or straight, but trailing / here and there like a woman's mind." The gradation of feeling that Pound tries to capture is something he partly learned from Robert Browning. A. R. Orage, who edited the influential magazine *The New Age*, noticed the similarity between "The River-Merchant's Wife" and "Bishop Blougram's Apology" in terms of their profound and "natural" simplicity. Pound himself noted that his poem could have been slipped into Browning's *Men and Women* (1855) without surprise. But I think Pound learned something even more important than plain utterance from Browning, who prefaced his *Sordello* (1863), one of Pound's favorite narrative poems, by stating, "my stress lay on the incidents in the development of a soul: little else is worth study."

Pound's dramatic lyric was dependent on a Chinese original, which was triply refracted, and therefore he made mistakes, sometimes because he took license, other times because of the notes. But there are fewer outright errors than one might expect, and the imitation works well as an organic whole. The opening stanza vibrates with an ambivalent sense of lost innocence, a girl pressed into marriage before she becomes a woman. Pound's working method becomes apparent in the first line, which Fenollosa transcribed as "mistress hair first cover brow" and he rendered as "While my hair was still cut straight across my forehead," a line that resonates with the lingering power of the past. Women grew their hair long, girls did not, and in one small stroke, just by adding the word *still*, Pound evokes a more innocent age when boys and girls both wore their hair in bangs.

I still marvel at the rhythmic opening of this poem, the natural cadence, the syntactic and rhythmic phrasing, the parallelism of the first four lines:

> While my hair was still cut straight across my forehead
> *I played about* the front gate, *pulling flowers.*
> *You came by* on bamboo stilts, *playing horse,*
> *You walked about* my seat, *playing with* blue plums.

The words *played* and *playing* are repeated three times, foregrounding the spatial distinction between the girl's experiences, which are imaged horizontally, and the boy's experiences, which are presented vertically. I've always been mildly baffled by the third line. It turns out that Fenollosa recognized the toy as a bamboo horse, but Mori and Ariga took the Japanese compound as bamboo stilts, and Pound combined them into what Billings terms a uniquely "Anglo-Sino-Japanese line." Pound couldn't quite catch Li Bai's image of "green plums and hobby horse," which was so culturally resonant that it became a saying for innocent children's games, childhood sweethearts, or a married couple who grew up as childhood friends. Pound captures the feeling of children who seem as natural together as colorful flowers. The boy circles the girl, elevated, almost in ceremony.

Pound's first four lines build to a summary statement that threads from "While my hair was still" to "And we went on":

> And we went on living in the village of Chokan:
> Two small people, without dislike or suspicion.

This locates the poem in a river town near Nanjing. Pound refers to them not as children but as "two small people," which sounds like a nursery rhyme, and creates a portrait of a woman already looking back to a presexual time when she and her husband were still carefree.

The next stanza develops the plot. The speaker presents herself as a timid girl looking up to her new husband, trying to resign herself to her fate. As an apprentice, I could tell that Pound was a tactician of line and sentence, and I noticed how each line operates as an intact unit. The phrasing is exact.

> At fourteen *I married* My Lord you.
> *I never laughed*, being bashful.

Lowering my head, *I looked* at the wall.
Called to, a thousand times, *I never looked* back.

Pound took the set phrase "My Lord" and interjected it between "I married" and "you," and by this short move implied a hierarchy of gendered relationship. He moved from "being bashful" to "Lowering my head," and created a quietly surreal feeling of a girl sitting in a dark corner, ashamed. He seems to have ignored or missed the sexual overtones, the shyness she might feel after her first night of marriage. What he did insert was an Orphic reference. The American poet faintly invokes Eurydice as a teenage girl, who has left her girlhood behind.

Pound treats the stanzas as temporal marking places, leaps in time. He uses the crossover from one stanza to the next to move the young marrieds into an incipient adulthood.

At fifteen I stopped scowling,
I desired my dust to be mingled with yours
Forever and forever, and forever.
Why should I climb the look out?

Li Bai created an amazing leap in consciousness here, depicting an enormous change in a girl who accepts married life and begins to understand love. Pound placed his own special emphasis on the tense of the verb *desired*, which has a certain ambiguity. Is this desire over or ongoing? Pound must have been puzzled by the literal transcription of a line in this section—"eternally preserve embrace pillar faith," which Fenollosa copied and mistranslated as "I always had in me the faith of holding to pillars." That might explain why Pound sidestepped Li Bai's reference to a legendary story recounted by the classical Daoist philosopher Zhuangzi:

Wei Sheng made a date with a girl beneath a bridge. The girl did not come, and the water rose. But Wei Sheng would not leave. He grasped a pillar and died.

Ignoring this story of tragic love, which reverses the position of husband and wife, but seeking greater expanse in English, Pound interposed a line that gives a sense of endlessness: "I desired my dust to be mingled with yours

/ Forever and forever, and forever." By borrowing a triple repetition in phrasing from Shakespeare, "Tomorrow, and tomorrow, and tomorrow" (*Macbeth*), he created a feeling of timelessness and juxtaposed it with the young wife's puzzling question: "Why should I climb the look out?" Fenollosa's note identifies "the husband / looking out terrace," and refers to the story of a woman who died waiting for her lover to return. Pound decontextualizes the image of what was known in eighth-century China as the "Husband-watching Mountain," which symbolizes the longing and loyalty of a forlorn wife. The speaker sees no reason for this farseeing platform. Or does she? She could never have imagined that someday she would need to be on the watch.

The fourth stanza moves the poem forward to another station in time. The young marrieds are suddenly adults. The husband has become a traveling businessman.

> At sixteen you departed,
> You went into far Ku-to-Yen, by the river of swirling eddies,
> And you have been gone five months.
> The monkeys make sorrowful noise overhead.

Here, Pound combined and inadvertently foreshortened two names of a place in Sichuan Province—you couldn't find it on a map. He doesn't quite capture the reality of a towering stone in the Qutang Gorge, one of three gorges in the Yangtze, which looks like an island in the dry season but is entirely submerged in the rainy season and thus is extremely dangerous for boats to pass. But he delicately brings the river imagery into play; the river merchant is far off, and his wife feels "the swirling eddies," the undercurrents of worry and confusion. He has placed himself in one kind of danger, her in another. Pound enacts one of his basic Imagist principles, the natural object as the adequate symbol, and follows the simple declaration "And you have been gone five months" with an image freighted with meaning: "The monkeys make sorrowful noise overhead." In Li Bai's poem, the wife empathically imagines the melancholy cries of the monkeys that her husband listens to as he journeys through the Three Gorges, but in Pound's reimagining the sadness of the river merchant's wife also finds a corollary in the "sorrowful noise" of the monkeys that she hears above her at home.

This brings us to the conclusive turn in the poem, the long final stanza.

In just a few strokes, Pound re-creates the reluctance of the husband to leave—"You dragged your feet when you went out"—and the sense of time passing. The gate, where the speaker played as a child, is reinvoked, but now it is no longer a gateway. The wilderness of the great world has impinged on the domestic realm. The natural object here creates an inner feeling of inertia: "By the gate now, the moss is grown, the different mosses, / Too deep to clear them away!" No one is visiting and the isolation seems too much for her to bear.

There is a poignant succession of early autumnal images in the penultimate movement of the poem. The greenness of youth is turning into the premature yellowness of aging.

> The leaves fall early this autumn, in wind.
> The paired butterflies are already yellow with August
> Over the grass in the West garden,
> They hurt me, I grow older

The speaker invokes the early falling leaves and the two butterflies as an external correlative for her own feeling of lostness and isolation. I've always loved the directness of the juxtaposition, the contrast between "the paired butterflies" and the lone speaker, who longs for her other half. The two declarative sentences in succession are so simple and direct that they sting: "They hurt me, I grow older." Pound combined two lines here. This is a move beyond Imagism because it follows an image with two short statements, which are separated by commas, not periods. The line vibrates with barely concealed feeling, a complex of confusion and the pain of vanishing youth.

These declarations lead to the final winding movement and sentence of the poem, which begins with the line: "If you are coming down through the narrows of the river Kiang." I liked the drift of this thought when I first read it, the slightly pained emphasis on the word *If* and the light pressure on the word *narrows* that leads into the phrase "of the river Kiang." So apparently did Pound, who treated "the river Kiang" as the name of a river, which is like saying "the river Yangtze." But "Kiang" means river, and Pound unintentionally called it "the river River."

The sentence moves sinuously and ends with a dropped phrase that creates the sensation of separation and travel.

> If you are coming down through the narrows of the river Kiang,
> Please let me know beforehand,
> And I will come out to meet you,
>   As far as Cho-fu-Sa.

At the end of the poem, Pound refers to "Cho-fu-Sa." Wai-lim Yip and others have pointed out that Chang-feng-sha literally translates as "Long Wind Sand." Yet here Pound translates for sound and purposefully uses a proper name to designate a place, as in a document. The place is some two hundred miles away, but you don't need to find it on a map to know that the young wife is offering to venture a long way to someplace she has almost certainly never been in order to meet her husband.

Other translators hear a note of resentment here, suggesting that the speaker will go so far and no farther to meet her husband. Billings notes that Cho-fu-Sa was a notoriously dangerous passage. The young wife might well be hinting that her husband has a tragic fate ahead of him. I take this final statement as an offer of meeting and mutuality. It's a quietly formal request, as in a letter—"please let me know"—and contains a wealth of understated feeling for a lover and husband who has traveled too far away and may never return.

I love "The River-Merchant's Wife: a Letter," but I'd like to separate my response from Ezra Pound's most zealous defenders and equally zealous detractors. Pound made mistakes, he did not have magical powers, and he did not "divine" Li Bai's original. Yet he did create something unique. He worked from detailed and helpful interlinear notes, which have been historically undervalued, and he sourced them to create a fresh music in one of the great poems of *Cathay*. I learned something useful when Garrett Hongo called this "a new sound" and compared it to "the saxophone and trumpet of John Coltrane and Miles Davis in the sextet that recorded *Kind of Blue* in the late 1950s." Their musical reaction against the over-proliferation of rhythmic complexity has a parallel in the way modern poets reacted against older types of ornamentation. The comparison to jazz is apt because Pound's poem isn't a solely authored text. In truth, we don't really have a name for its intercultural dependencies, its complex of collaborators, many of them unknown to each other, the work of oral and written poets from different centuries, different cultures, passing on their work to translators and scholars of goodwill.

When I read "The River-Merchant's Wife: a Letter" I think of illiterate folksingers and the collectors who transcribed their songs, of an eighth-century Chinese poet taking on the voice of a young woman in one of those songs, perhaps writing a hidden letter to a lover, of three late nineteenth-century intellectuals putting their heads together and puzzling over classical Chinese texts, of the odd route that these hastily scrawled notes took to get to a displaced twenty-nine-year-old American poet in London during World War I, trying to reform modern poetry and make sense of his own feelings, disguising himself in a letter-poem. And I also think of a young American setting out for a new life, a twenty-two-year-old hopeful trying to make his way in a foreign city, leaning over a lonely poem in a lonely room, and finding solace in a voice that is almost unbearably moving and beautiful.

The Steeple-Jack

Dürer would have seen a reason for living
   in a town like this, with eight stranded whales
to look at; with the sweet sea air coming into your house
on a fine day, from water etched
   with waves as formal as the scales
on a fish.

One by one, in two's, and three's, the seagulls keep
   flying back and forth over the town clock,
or sailing around the lighthouse without moving their wings—
rising steadily with a slight
   quiver of the body—or flock
mewing where

a sea the purple of the peacock's neck is
   paled to greenish azure as Dürer changed
the pine green of the Tyrol to peacock blue and guinea
grey. You can see a twenty-five-
   pound lobster; and fishnets arranged
to dry. The

whirlwind fifeanddrum of the storm bends the salt
   marsh grass, disturbs stars in the sky and the
star on the steeple; it is a privilege to see so
much confusion. Disguised by what
   might seem austerity, the sea-
side flowers and

trees are favored by the fog so that you have
   the tropics at first hand: the trumpet-vine,
foxglove, giant snap-dragon, a salpaglossis that has
spots and stripes; morning-glories, gourds,
   or moon-vines trained on fishing-twine
at the back

door; cat-tails, flags, blueberries and spiderwort,
   striped grass, lichens, sunflowers, asters, daisies—
the yellow and the crab-claw blue ones with green bracts—toad-plant,
petunias, ferns; pink lilies, blue
   ones, tigers; poppies; black sweet-peas.
The climate

is not right for the banyan, frangipan, the
   jack-fruit tree; nor for exotic serpent
life. Ring lizard and snake-skin for the foot if you see fit,
but here they've cats, not cobras, to
   keep down the rats. The diffident
little newt

with white pin-dots on black horizontal spaced
   out bands lives here; yet there is nothing that
ambition can buy or take away. The college student
named Ambrose sits on the hill-side
   with his not-native books and hat
and sees boats

at sea progress white and rigid as if in
   a groove. Liking an elegance of which
the source is not bravado, he knows by heart the antique
sugar-bowl shaped summer-house of
   interlacing slats, and the pitch
of the church

spire, not true, from which a man in scarlet lets
    down a rope as a spider spins a thread;
he might be part of a novel, but on the sidewalk a
sign says C. J. Poole, Steeple-jack,
    in black and white; and one in red
and white says

Danger. The church portico has four fluted
    columns, each a single piece of stone, made
modester by white-wash. This would be a fit haven for
waifs, children, animals, prisoners,
    and presidents who have repaid
sin-driven

senators by not thinking about them. There
    are a school-house, a post-office in a
store, fish-houses, hen-houses, a three-masted schooner on
the stocks. The hero, the student,
    the steeple-jack, each in his way,
is at home.

It could not be dangerous to be living
    in a town like this, of simple people,
who have a steeple-jack placing danger signs by the church
while he is gilding the solid-
    pointed star, which on a steeple
stands for hope.

                                                    1932

MARIANNE MOORE was a quiet revolutionary working at the center of the convulsion that was modernism. Poets who disagreed about almost everything else, such as T. S. Eliot and William Carlos Williams or Ezra Pound and Wallace Stevens, agreed about the dazzling originality of her work, its startling precision and particularity. She had an acute visual sense—her first full-length collection was appropriately called

Observations (1924)—and treated poems as acts of attention. Reading her work, you sometimes feel as if you're looking afresh at the world, studying it with a painter's eye and a biologist's curious scrutiny. There is voracious determination in her inquiry, her laboratory studies, and thickened descriptions. She loved the Victorian English critic John Ruskin, who treated seeing as morality, and copied this passage from his *Modern Painters* into her notebook:

> —the greatest thing a human soul ever does in this world is to *see* something, and tell what it *saw* in a plain way. Hundreds of people can talk for one who can think, but thousands can think for one who can see. To see clearly is poetry, prophecy, and religion,—all in one.

Moore praised the virtue of clear sight, but the sense of transparency in her work can be deceptive. She may have been a realist, but only in the way that the painters of the Dutch Golden Age were realists—she, too, moved around waterfalls and changed the location of cliffsides. Her observations have a relentless accuracy, but it is a composed accuracy, and she looks at things so closely that they start to seem strange. She defamiliarizes the world. I think of her as a rapt, solitary observer describing the world in her own incremental and detailed way so that we see it differently, too.

Moore's reputation for scrupulous exactitude precedes her. Her work is so highly structured that it can seem decorous—it is not—and impersonal, though her sensibility was so strong that it's impossible to mistake her poetry for anyone else's. She was not a poet of persona, like Dickinson or Pound, but she prized disinterestedness, like a scientist, and tried not to reveal herself. Her use of individual words is so concrete and singular, her descriptions so vivid and precise, that it feels as if her language had been cleaned and held up to the light at a slight distance. Her habit of breaking down words into constituent parts and counting syllables, the smallest units of measurable sound, contributes to the effect. It gives her work a scapular feeling that Williams characterized as her linguistic mode:

> With Miss Moore a word is a word most when it is separated out by science, treated with acid to remove the smudges, washed,

dried, and placed right side up on a clean surface. Now one may say that this is a word. Now it may be used, and how?

Williams thought of Moore as an objectivist, like himself, who had freed her work from what he considered smudgy thinking, "the attachments of thought," but that seems closer to the way that he thought than the way she proceeded. She didn't really embrace his motto of "no ideas but in things." In fact, her poems are filled not just with facts but also with propositions and ideas, which are treated as things, as if they, too, had concrete reality. Her treatment of matter was mindful. Her mode was descriptive, but it was also self-conscious and discursive, pointedly critical, even argumentative. She schooled herself on Henry James's work, especially his late novel *The Golden Bowl*, and imitated his titanic effort of consciousness. Sometimes you can chart her serpentine sentences winding across lines and stanzas and feel as if James were looking over her shoulder.

Moore wrote two main kinds of verse—long free-verse collages, like "Marriage" and "The Octopus," and elaborate syllabically patterned pieces, which foreground the visual aspect of her work, like "The Fish" and "The Steeple-Jack." The collages point forward to the poetry of John Ashbery, who said he was tempted to crown her "our greatest Modern poet"; the descriptive pieces to the work of May Swenson and Elizabeth Bishop, who called her poems "miracles of language and construction." Moore's syllabic method is intrinsically counterintuitive, at least in English language poetry. Pure syllabic meter measures only the number of syllables in each line. It pays no attention to accentuation and thus goes against what the critic Paul Fussell termed "our own Anglo-Saxon lust for stress." Moore's compositions in verse—she was reluctant to call them "poems"—make the syllable a visible particle of language. This gives an edgy sharpness and slightly clinical feeling to her measures. She intermingles line lengths, and every stanza repeats the syllabic pattern exactly. Thus, each one of her poems feels like a game or puzzle with its own self-determined rules.

Moore's method is adventurous and disruptive. She often begins a poem as if she is speaking directly to the reader, initially going with the rhythmic swing of the lines, but then she deliberately breaks the syntactic flow, mis-aligning the syntax and the lineation, and thus makes it impossible to sustain that illusion. In her syllabically timed poems the stanza, as opposed to the line, is the operative unit, and each stanza is a formal replica of the previous one. Moore's geometrically shaped verses rely on the cadences of prose as well as the music of colloquial speech, but they shun traditional effects. They seem hammered out on a typewriter, like pattern poems. Hugh Kenner said that she read her poems badly on purpose because she sensed that they were not meant for the voice. This is witty but only partly true—the voicing is subtle, and the formal arrangement of her work gives the impression of something intentionally hard to read aloud, something *made* rather than *said*. The poems stand as a sturdy corrective to the shoddy in life and art.

Moore is particularly American in her belief in "accessibility to experience" ("New York") and her faith in locale, her aesthetic of the independent observer looking intently at the inhuman forces of nature. She loved animals of all sorts, especially armored animals, and once confessed, with unusual straightforwardness, that she wanted to be a dragon. I've always been taken by the ferocious American independence and lingo of her work, the way she looks acutely and knowledgeably at our "grassless, linksless, languageless country in which letters are written / not in Spanish, not in Greek, not in Latin, not in shorthand, / but in plain American which cats and dogs can read!" ("England"). It's typical of Moore's sly subversive temperament to add "shorthand," which was once a mandatory office skill for female secretaries, to the many languages we don't speak in America.

Moore stopped publishing poetry for a seven-year period during which she edited the innovative modernist journal *The Dial*, where she also contributed many incisive reviews and essays. "The Steeple-Jack" signals her return. It was published in *Poetry* magazine in June 1932 as the first section of a three-part sequence called "Part of a Novel, Part of a Poem, Part of a Play." She subsequently separated "The Steeple-Jack" from parts two and three, "The Student" and "The Hero," and published it as the lead poem in *Selected Poems* (1935) and in subsequent editions of her work. But the sense that the poem is part of a more extensive fictional world still clings to it, like a place you intended to visit or, perhaps more accurately, a book you'd once intended to read. The book doesn't exist, but three of its characters, the hero, the student, and the steeple-jack, have all survived.

"The Steeple-Jack" has elements of pastoral—the town is simplified and so are the people—but the rustic safety seems precarious. The mode is scenic, but the scene changes and complicates as we go along. It starts off as a travelogue, but you won't be able to find this town on a map. It is a fictitious composite. Moore lived with her mother in Fort Greene when she wrote it—her brother, a commander and chaplain in the navy, was stationed nearby at the Brooklyn Navy Yard—and she told a correspondent that she had in mind both Brooklyn and various New England seacoast towns she had visited over the years.

Moore fantasized about writing novels and plays. The first published version of "The Steeple-Jack" declared that it was "part of a novel," but that turns out to be a ruse. Moore revises the idea in the poem itself by clarifying that the title character "might be part of a novel, but on the sidewalk a / sign says C. J. Poole, Steeple-jack, / in black and white; and one in red / and white says // Danger." Here the line and stanza felicitously coincide so that the rhythm lands hard on the word *Danger*. Moore recalled:

> C. J. Poole was a Brooklyn steeple-jack who worked on the various high buildings and steeples and had his name on the sidewalk danger sign, warning passersby to keep clear of ropes and grapnels on the sidewalk. He was repairing the steeple of the Lafayette Avenue Presbyterian Church, the steeple was finally considered infirm and was replaced by 4 Gothic points.

Moore didn't invent C. J. Poole, she could see his sign from her window in Brooklyn, and he appears here in black and white, i.e., in print, a figure in a poem. The red and white danger sign also reminds me that Moore wrote this poem in the early 1930s. There is something civic in its sensibility; it has a backdrop of the Great Depression. The town seems safe, but it survives on a stormy seashore, and the times are dangerous.

"The Steeple-Jack" consists of thirteen six-line stanzas. The poem is numerical—*numbers* is an ancient word for poetry—and each stanza has lines of eleven, ten, fourteen, eight, eight, and three syllables. The second and fifth lines are indented and rhymed, thereby paired for emphasis. There is virtuosity in the natural way Moore navigates the arbitrary form, which keeps changing pace to accommodate and pressurize all sorts of information.

"The Steeple-Jack" is also singularly structured. The first and last stanzas parallel each other, each consisting of a lone sentence, but all eleven of the other stanzas are enjambed and hurry over from one to the next, never pausing for long, never stopping. It has been a formal commonplace that poets save the most significant word or phrase for the end of a line or stanza. Moore does this emphatically at the beginning and end of the poem, but over the course of it she does just the opposite, ending a line and stanza on a word like *and*. She seems bemused by some of her stanza breaks, such as "of the church // spire" and "sin-driven // senators." She starts a sentence at the end of the line and stanza, such as "The // whirlwind." She often enjambs lines on tiny words like *to*, *in*, and *a*. The result is that the next line gets an emphatic boost, as in *to / keep down* or *in / a groove* or *a / sign*. Something posed as a noun at the end of one line, *the sea*, turns into an adjective after the line break, *the sea- / side flowers*. In the penultimate stanza, Moore cleverly rhymes *a* and *way* to show how the three outsiders, all of whom are away, feel at home in the town.

I'm fond of the nonchalance with which Moore introduces Albrecht Dürer, one of the old masters. It's an American move. Hence the incisive first line, "Dürer would have seen a reason for living," which then tumbles over into "in a town like this." The phrasing suggests that Dürer would have *seen* a reason for living in this sort of town, i.e., a town *like* this, a place beside itself, but also that the perspective would have given him an existential *reason for living*. The sentence then unspools across the stanza to describe a seacoast village that is settling down after a storm (those eight stranded whales). It is placid and picturesque. This isn't a real town but one that has been artfully arranged and constructed. There is something fantastical and Dürer-like in the way the poet mixes the gigantic and the miniature, using an artistic term to note that the sea air comes into the house from water "etched / with waves as formal as the scales / on a fish."

Like Williams, Moore loved Stieglitz's gallery 291, which she called "an American acropolis," and was part of the movement for an independent American art, which is precisely why it seems noteworthy that in 1932 she begins by invoking a European artist, a German one no less, and thus asserts a kind of cultural continuity at a time when fascism was on the rise. The literary scholar Bonnie Costello, who observes that "almost every poem Moore wrote involved a picture or art object at some stage of composition," has pinpointed Moore's knowledge of Dürer's work. For example, Moore discovered from one of his journal entries, quoted in T. Sturge Moore's monograph on Dürer, just how much the artist from Nuremberg had wanted to see a stranded whale when he was visiting the Netherlands in 1520. She must have thought about him when she read a newspaper article about eight whales beached in Brooklyn Harbor or Sheepshead Bay. In a way, she gifts the whale back to him here and multiplies it eight times. She also throws in a twenty-five-pound lobster.

Moore begins with a nod to the art of engraving, but then turns to topographical watercolor. She starts with shape and moves to color. In doing so, she captures the rhythmic flight of the seagulls through ten lines, which crosses two stanzas and then stops. These are not smooth French-style syllabics, which require linear regularity. She finds and sustains an accentual rhythm until bringing it to an abrupt halt.

> One by one, in two's and three's, the seagulls keep
>   flying back and forth over the town clock,
> or sailing around the lighthouse without moving their wings—
> rising steadily with a slight
>   quiver of the body—or flock
> mewing where
>
> a sea the purple of the peacock's neck is
>   paled to greenish azure as Dürer changed
> the pine green of the Tyrol to peacock blue and guinea
> grey.

Moore is referring to Dürer's watercolor drawing of a rock formation topped by a citadel, *View of Val D'Arco in South Tyrol*, which he sketched on a spring morning in Italy in 1495. She picks up the grays, browns, and greens of Dürer's palette, and takes as a model the way he changed the color scheme. This is not an ekphrastic poem—it drops any explicit reference to Dürer after the third stanza—but something else entire. Dürer serves as a guide, an artist of mathematical precision and imaginative liberty. Writing about an exhibition of Dürer's prints at the New York Public Library, Moore said: "The conjunction of fantasy and calculation is unusual, but many sagacities seem in Dürer not to starve one another." There is a spiritual element operating as well. "The Steeple-Jack" is not an overtly religious poem, but Moore was a lifelong Presbyterian, and her Virgil here is the first Protestant artist, a humanist who brought the Renaissance home to Northern Europe. She evokes a Protestant ethos—a delight in creation tempered by an apprehension of human evil—at a moment of rising historical barbarism.

Crossing from the third to the fourth stanza, Moore presents "The // whirlwind fifeanddrum of the storm," which makes the weather sound like a small-town concert by Charles Ives, and notices how it "disturbs stars in the sky and the / star on the steeple; it is a privilege to see so / much confusion." Once more the emphasis on sight, "it is a privilege to *see*," celebrates the artistic gaze, while the flip to "so / much confusion" celebrates the disorderly world. Here the poem consciously turns or changes viewpoint. We realize that we have been observing the town from a bird's-eye view, from the steeple-jack's high vantage point, but now observe it from ground level. Everything grows here in unlikely, foggy, seaside conditions, which are chancy but fortuitous. Hence the Whitmanian catalogue of tropical flowers and plants, which gustily savors every detail, every name. It has something of what she described as the ornithologist John James Audubon's "observatory nerves." The New World Eden is followed by a negative catalogue of trees and animals ("The climate // is *not* right for"), things that can't thrive here, most notably "exotic serpent / life." This detailed catalogue of what's in, what's out, comes to a sudden conclusion: "yet there is nothing that / ambition can buy or take away." The word *ambition* arrives with a jolt. It is a sideswipe at consumerism.

The poem then introduces Ambrose, a foreign college student sitting on a hillside. It is not accidental that Ambrose shares the same name as the fourth-century ecclesiastical figure St. Ambrose. Moore has had some acidulous scholars, and Victoria Bazin has tracked down Kenneth Burke's essay "Psychology and Form," which appeared in *The Dial* in 1924 and refers to "St. Ambrose, detailing the habits of God's creatures, and drawing from them moral maxims for the good of mankind, St. Ambrose in his limping natural history rich in scientific inaccuracies that are at the very heart of emotional rightness." Burke locates in the "sure rightness" of St. Ambrose's program "the truth of art." Moore's incarnation of Ambrose with his "not-native books," which is a jibe against nationalism, is exemplary because of the way he observes, appreciates, and memorizes the view. He has taken what he sees to heart.

In her poem "The Student," Moore also deploys the student to make a Jamesian critique of the immaturity of American culture: "we are / as a nation perhaps, undergraduates not students. / But anyone who studies will advance." Then she asks: "Are we to grow up or not?" It's a good question, and we still haven't figured out the answer.

If Ambrose is an unlikely figure for the poet, then perhaps so is the steeple-jack, a person who climbs steeples, towers, and other high structures to build, paint, and repair them. It is from Ambrose's view that we are introduced to the title character, C. J. Poole, the Steeple-Jack, lowering his rope "as a spider spins a thread." After describing his two signs, the figures by which we know him—one an advertisement, the other a warning—Moore further complicates the view of the town. The steeple-jack has lowered his rope into a place of natural beauty and human corruption. He has placed his "Danger" sign next to the lovely church with its four fluted columns and modest whitewash. But there is a leap from the church, a place of salvation, to the rest of the town, a potential refuge—"This *would be* a fit haven"—for various outsiders and victims, waifs, children and animals, but also prisoners, presidents, and sin-driven senators, figures of crime, politics, and corruption. The town brings together in harmony this disparate group. Moore continues on to describe the charms of a small town with a schoolhouse, a post office located in a store, and even a grounded ship. This is the world where the three figures, the student, the hero, and the steeple-jack, feel "at home." They recognize it as sanctuary.

There is no other hero in this poem beside the steeple-jack, a person of service. He returns in the last stanza, which parallels the first one:

> It could not be dangerous to be living
>   in a town like this, of simple people,
> who have a steeple-jack placing danger signs by the church
> while he is gilding the solid-
>   pointed star, which on a steeple
> stands for hope.

This perfectly formed sentence seems slightly overinsistent. So much of "The Steeple-Jack" appears to be about danger; it feels as if the poet has been detailing the world in order to keep that danger at bay. One can take Moore at her word and also feel that in truth it could be dangerous to be living in a town like this, or, for that matter, any town. We are buoyed by the steeple-jack, who works in a highly dangerous profession. He is not merely modest or pragmatic, but a heroic daredevil who might fall at any moment. He is a craftsman who places a danger sign next to the church, on ground level, and then climbs up to the spire to gild something substantial, "the solid-pointed star," which is symbolic. We're at a spiritual peak now and the last word of the poem is *hope*. Think of the steeple-jack as a modest artisan who works for the community and restores the emblem of faith.

Marianne Moore was a poet of firm opinion, of scruples and exactitudes, of felt thought. Her work can seem outwardly chilly and objective, but it has a wellspring of feeling held in check. I read her poetry and think of someone posting a danger sign, climbing to the very top of a high church, precariously fastening a star onto a steeple, and letting down a rope.

T. S. ELIOT (1888–1965)

The Love Song of J. Alfred Prufrock

S'io credesse che mia risposta fosse
A persona che mai tornasse al mondo,
Questa fiamma staria senza piu scosse.
Ma perciocche giammai di questo fondo
Non torno vivo alcun, s'i'odo il vero,
Senza tema d'infamia ti rispondo.

Let us go then, you and I,
When the evening is spread out against the sky
Like a patient etherized upon a table;
Let us go, through certain half-deserted streets,
The muttering retreats
Of restless nights in one-night cheap hotels
And sawdust restaurants with oyster-shells:
Streets that follow like a tedious argument
Of insidious intent
To lead you to an overwhelming question. . . .
Oh, do not ask, "What is it?"
Let us go and make our visit.

In the room the women come and go
Talking of Michelangelo.

The yellow fog that rubs its back upon the window-panes,
The yellow smoke that rubs its muzzle on the window-panes,
Licked its tongue into the corners of the evening,
Lingered upon the pools that stand in drains,
Let fall upon its back the soot that falls from chimneys,

Slipped by the terrace, made a sudden leap,
And seeing that it was a soft October night,
Curled once about the house, and fell asleep.

And indeed there will be time
For the yellow smoke that slides along the street,
Rubbing its back upon the window-panes;
There will be time, there will be time
To prepare a face to meet the faces that you meet;
There will be time to murder and create,
And time for all the works and days of hands
That lift and drop a question on your plate;
Time for you and time for me,
And time yet for a hundred indecisions,
And for a hundred visions and revisions,
Before the taking of a toast and tea.

In the room the women come and go
Talking of Michelangelo.

And indeed there will be time
To wonder, "Do I dare?" and, "Do I dare?"
Time to turn back and descend the stair,
With a bald spot in the middle of my hair —
(They will say: "How his hair is growing thin!")
My morning coat, my collar mounting firmly to the chin,
My necktie rich and modest, but asserted by a simple pin —
(They will say: "But how his arms and legs are thin!")
Do I dare
Disturb the universe?
In a minute there is time
For decisions and revisions which a minute will reverse.

For I have known them all already, known them all:
Have known the evenings, mornings, afternoons,
I have measured out my life with coffee spoons;

I know the voices dying with a dying fall
Beneath the music from a farther room.
So how should I presume?

And I have known the eyes already, known them all—
The eyes that fix you in a formulated phrase,
And when I am formulated, sprawling on a pin,
When I am pinned and wriggling on the wall,
Then how should I begin
To spit out all the butt-ends of my days and ways?
And how should I presume?

And I have known the arms already, known them all—
Arms that are braceleted and white and bare
(But in the lamplight, downed with light brown hair!)
Is it perfume from a dress
That makes me so digress?
Arms that lie along a table, or wrap about a shawl.
And should I then presume?
And how should I begin?

*   *   *   *

Shall I say, I have gone at dusk through narrow streets
And watched the smoke that rises from the pipes
Of lonely men in shirt-sleeves, leaning out of windows? . . .

I should have been a pair of ragged claws
Scuttling across the floors of silent seas.

*   *   *   *

And the afternoon, the evening, sleeps so peacefully!
Smoothed by long fingers,
Asleep . . . tired . . . or it malingers,
Stretched on the floor, here beside you and me.

Should I, after tea and cakes and ices,
Have the strength to force the moment to its crisis?
But though I have wept and fasted, wept and prayed,
Though I have seen my head (grown slightly bald) brought in upon
    a platter,
I am no prophet—and here's no great matter;
I have seen the moment of my greatness flicker,
And I have seen the eternal Footman hold my coat, and snicker,
And in short, I was afraid.

And would it have been worth it, after all,
After the cups, the marmalade, the tea,
Among the porcelain, among some talk of you and me,
Would it have been worth while,
To have bitten off the matter with a smile,
To have squeezed the universe into a ball
To roll it toward some overwhelming question,
To say: "I am Lazarus, come from the dead,
Come back to tell you all, I shall tell you all"—
If one, settling a pillow by her head,
Should say: "That is not what I meant at all;
That is not it, at all."

And would it have been worth it, after all,
Would it have been worth while,
After the sunsets and the dooryards and the sprinkled streets,
After the novels, after the teacups, after the skirts that trail along
    the floor—
And this, and so much more?—
It is impossible to say just what I mean!
But as if a magic lantern threw the nerves in patterns on a screen:
Would it have been worth while
If one, settling a pillow or throwing off a shawl,
And turning toward the window, should say:
"That is not it at all,
That is not what I meant, at all."

*   *   *   *

No! I am not Prince Hamlet, nor was meant to be;
Am an attendant lord, one that will do
To swell a progress, start a scene or two,
Advise the prince; no doubt, an easy tool,
Deferential, glad to be of use,
Politic, cautious, and meticulous;
Full of high sentence, but a bit obtuse;
At times, indeed, almost ridiculous—
Almost, at times, the Fool.

I grow old . . . I grow old . . .
I shall wear the bottoms of my trousers rolled.

Shall I part my hair behind? Do I dare to eat a peach?
I shall wear white flannel trousers, and walk upon the beach.
I have heard the mermaids singing, each to each.

I do not think that they will sing to me.

I have seen them riding seaward on the waves
Combing the white hair of the waves blown back
When the wind blows the water white and black.
We have lingered in the chambers of the sea
By sea-girls wreathed with seaweed red and brown
Till human voices wake us, and we drown.

1915

T. S. ELIOT can seem like the Westminster Abbey of modern poetry. He is so elevated and monumental, so dauntingly grand, the first fixture of the modern canon, that it can be hard to recall the human presence underneath. Living in London, Eliot contributed to this feeling of distant formality by out-Englishing the English—Virginia Woolf joked that he wore "a four-piece suit" and Aldous Huxley called him "the most bankclerky of all bank clerks"—and kept people at a certain remove. As a literary figure, he was sheltered behind a series of what even he considered embarrassingly successful formulas and proclamations, such as the *objective correlative* and the *dissociation of sensibility*, which ended up surrounding his work, like a moat protecting a castle. In retrospect, he can appear so cold, serious, and conservative that it takes conscious effort to recall him as a young man from St. Louis, a student of philosophy at Harvard, shy, pedantic, hypersensitive, nervously overcivilized, well educated in the classics, steeped in French literature, a reserved revolutionary who invented modern poetry for himself.

T. S. Eliot began writing "The Love Song of J. Alfred Prufrock" in Cambridge, Massachusetts, in February 1910—the milieu of the poem is Boston—when he was still only twenty-one years old. He completed it in Paris and Munich on a year abroad the following year. After Eliot moved to London during the war, Ezra Pound got hold of the poem and determined to get it published in *Poetry* magazine. "He has actually trained himself AND modernized himself ON HIS OWN," Pound exclaimed to the editor, Harriet Monroe, and it appeared there in 1915. It subsequently led off Eliot's twelve-poem chapbook, *Prufrock and Other Observations* (1917). This was the first poem in the first book that Eliot ever published, and it changed the way people wrote poetry the way that Igor Stravinsky's *The Rite of Spring* changed the way that people wrote music. J. Alfred Prufrock, Eliot's stand-in, feels somehow adolescent, though he looks middle-aged—he seems to be about forty. The poet who created him was just starting out, lonely and displaced, but artistically self-assured, strangely attuned to a new feeling, a new time.

"The Love Song of J. Alfred Prufrock" is a dramatic monologue, but Prufrock himself is not a full-fledged character, as in, say, a dramatic monologue by Robert Browning. He is, as Hugh Kenner puts it, "a name plus a voice." It was inspired for Eliot to affix a memorable title to an otherwise autobiographical text and thus permanently separate the speaker from the author. To break down that title: "The Love Song" has a kind of upward lift that is deflated by the name, "J. Alfred Prufrock." Eliot got the idea for the title from Rudyard Kipling's "The Love Song of Har Dyal," a poem that stuck in his head over the two-year period that he was writing "Prufrock." At one point, Eliot used to sign his name "T. Stearns Eliot" and once said that Prufrock seemed like the sort of person who would have been ashamed of his first name, hence the initial in "J. Alfred." He recalled that Prufrock-Littau was the name on a furniture shop that he used to pass as a boy growing up in St. Louis, Missouri. It was mischievous for him to recycle the name, which seems slightly ridiculous, but then so do the names of many Browning characters.

The poem was initially subtitled "Prufrock among the Women," but Eliot later decided to drop the subtitle, though it points to the tormented subtext of the poem, which seems driven by an irrational, overburdening fear of women, who suddenly enter "the room" and fleetingly "come and go / Talking of Michelangelo." This bit of rhyming nonsense verse, which appears twice as a refrain, heightens the unreality of the people. The ghostly figures in Dante seem more real to Prufrock than the well-appointed women in drawing rooms in Boston.

The unattributed epigraph, which armors the poem, is lifted from Dante's *Inferno* (canto 27, 61–66). Embodied in a flame, Count Guido da Montefeltro, whom Dante condemns for giving false counsel, is the speaker: "If I believed my answer would be to someone who would ever return to the world, this flame would move no longer, but because no one ever returned alive from this abyss, if what I hear is true, then I can reply with no fear of infamy." This suggests that the speaker is somewhere in a lower rung of Hell, and so is the person being addressed. We can speak frankly, he says, because no one ever returns from these depths. This testimonial reverberates through the rest of the poem, though, as we know, Dante's pilgrim does return to tell the tale. The inference is inevitable that decorous New England society is a stale, present-day version of Hell.

"Prufrock" begins with an address, an invitation: "Let us go then, you and I." This might sound as if the speaker is inviting someone on a formal outing or date—it is, after all, "a love song"—but Eliot suggested that the "you" in the poem "is merely some friend or companion, presumably of the male sex, whom the speaker is at that moment addressing, and that it has no emotional content whatever." The one being addressed is not a romantic companion, not even really a person, but a cipher, a listener, who enables the speaker to confide his feelings, if that is what there are, and observations. John Berryman considered the first two lines "a come-on, designed merely to get the reader off guard, so that he could be knocked down." I was that reader and can still recall the first time I read the description of a sunset "spread out against the sky / Like a patient etherized upon a table." I had not yet read Wordsworth's Romantic sonnet "It is a beauteous evening, calm and free" (1807), but I had seen plenty of beautiful evenings. This subversive comparison changed the way I viewed the sky, it altered time, and gave me the feeling of a dusky night suddenly arrested in space. I loved the shock of the medical word *etherized*. I recognized the "half-deserted streets" and quasi-sordid city scenes. The first two lines rhymed, as in a singsong couplet; the word *table* only vaguely rhymed with *hotels* and *oyster-shells*; and the couplets unscrolled until I came to the word *question*, which doesn't rhyme with anything. I was instructed not to ask, "What is it?" but was led inside: "Let us go and make our visit." Eliot borrowed this free-verse form from the French poet Jules Laforgue. As he explained it, "This meant merely rhyming lines of irregular length, with the rhymes coming in irregular places." He also felt a certain kinship with Laforgue's sensibility—temperamentally romantic but externally ironic, dandyish, cynical, even self-parodic. Eliot was drawn to other writers who were inclined to degrade their own romantic tendencies.

There is an echo chamber of repetitions in the poem, and this heightens its musicality, its symbolic resonances. The monologue is not stream of consciousness, that misnomer of the classroom, but it is structured associatively. It keeps circling back and finding other ways to describe Prufrock's hesitancy, his inability to commit. The setting shifts repeatedly between the street and the drawing room, outside and inside, until it washes up on the seashore. Metrically, Eliot keeps reestablishing an iambic base that he subsequently ruptures, first elongating, then dramatically cutting the length of the lines. This is the music of free verse, or what Eliot and Pound preferred to call *vers libre*, giving it a French provenance, though Laforgue and other French symbolist poets clearly borrowed it from Whitman, a poet of soaring parallels. Like Whitman's, Eliot's repetitions come with slight but emphatic repetitions, as in "The yellow fog that rubs its back upon the window-panes, / The yellow smoke that rubs its muzzle on the window-panes." What is unusual about this is the metonymic way that Eliot's description of the fog invokes a cat who isn't there, never appearing, though everyone feels its presence.

Eliot takes a nineteenth-century anaphoric method and gives it a different sound chamber, an up-to-date enervated mood. The ritualistic repetitions sound as if Ecclesiastes has been transported to a contemporary metropolis:

> *There will be time, there will be time*
> To prepare a face to meet the faces that you meet;
> *There will be time* to murder and create,
> *And time* for all the works and days of hands
> That lift and drop a question on your plate;
> *Time* for you *and time* for me,
> *And time* yet for a hundred indecisions,
> And for a hundred visions and revisions,
> Before the taking of a toast and tea.

Eliot's buried reference to Hesiod's *Works and Days* doesn't tell us much about rural labor, but it does evoke the unworkmanlike atmosphere in which Prufrock finds himself. The critic Christopher Ricks cites Revelation 9:20–21: "yet repented not of the works of their hands . . . neither repented they of their murders" (King James Bible). The anticlimax here comes as a surprise, a trap. There is an almost comical feminine rhyme on *indecisions* and *revisions* and a precipitous letdown in the fact that all this comes to "*t*he *t*aking of a *t*oast and *t*ea."

Prufrock's rhetorical insistences—"And indeed there will be time"—only heighten his fear of other people and his paralyzing self-consciousness. There is really no plot to the poem, no other people, only his fear of taking a chance ("'Do I dare?' and, 'Do I dare?'"), his anxiety about his hair loss, his clothes, his skinniness, which brings him to an existential question, "Do I dare / Disturb the universe?" It's as if everything has already happened ("For I have known them all already, known them all"), an inference of endless awkward meetings and arrangements. The feeling is infernal, the settings Jamesian.

Eliot's poetry has a definite aphoristic quality, which is partly why it is so quotable. He was a socially fearful person, but a courageous inventor of phrases, and so he is able to find memorable formulations for Prufrock's situation, such as "I have measured out my life with coffee spoons," and "I know the voices dying with a dying fall," which echoes the opening of Shakespeare's *Twelfth Night* ("That strain again—it had a dying fall"), and "I should have been a pair of ragged claws / Scuttling across the floor of silent seas."

Eliot's mode of anxiety has permeated literary and popular culture. In 1937, the twenty-one-year-old Saul Bellow and the nineteen-year-old Isaac

Rosenfeld penned a spot-on Yiddish spoof, "Der shir hashirim fun Mendl Pumshtok" (The Song of Songs of Mendl Pumshtok). My favorite line is the question: "Meg ikh oyfesen a floym?" (May I eat a prune?). Henry Reed's cunning wartime parody of Eliot's mannerisms, "Chard Whitlow" (1941), which is primarily aimed at *Four Quartets*, begins by nodding at Prufrock: "As we get older we do not get any younger." So, too, Eliot's purported love song, which Marshall McLuhan interpreted as "a Chaplin-like comedy" (*Understanding Media*, 1964), has often attracted comedians and filmmakers, such as Woody Allen (*Love and Death*, 1975; *Midnight in Paris*, 2011), Peter Ormond (*Eat the Peach*, 1986), and Patricia Rozema (*I've Heard the Mermaids Singing*, 1987), who have a rollicking good time parodying Prufrock's hemming and hawing. In later life Eliot had an unlikely correspondence with Groucho Marx, who might well have tapped his cigar and said, "I grow old . . . I grow old . . . / I shall wear the bottoms of my trousers rolled." Eliot's moments of Lewis Carroll–like nonsense verse have a satiric tone, a comic despair, which at times seems to anticipate the dark humor in Franz Kafka's *The Metamorphosis*. That's how I read the moment when Prufrock views himself as a social specimen, a creature with a near-pathological fear of women, a bug "sprawling on a pin, / . . . pinned and wriggling on the wall." The comedy sours amidst a wellspring of self-contempt, hence the tobaccoey question, "Then how should I begin / To spit out all the butt-ends of my days and ways?" Eliot liked this phrasing so much that he repeated it in his poem "Preludes," where he refers to "The burnt-out ends of smoky days."

Eliot had a dry sense of humor. He once coined the phrase "The Prufrock Complex" to annotate the diagnosis of a palm reader: "when faced with a personal problem, any prolonged contemplation of probabilities merely produces hesitancy and indecision." One of the formal features of "Prufrock" is how quickly the poem changes moods. Several times Eliot punctures a romantic gesture with the phrase, "So how should I presume?" Prufrock sighs, "And I have known the arms already, known them all," and the description that follows has a secret yearning, as if Eliot were evoking the love-song tradition of the Renaissance: "Arms that are braceleted and white and bare / (But in the lamplight, downed with light brown hair!)." Eliot loved John Donne's metaphysical poetry—he almost single-handedly resurrected Donne's reputation in the first part of the twentieth century—

and here he summons up one of Donne's most beautiful lines, "A bracelet of bright hair around the bone" ("The Relic").

Prufrock gets distracted by his sexual desire ("Is it perfume from a dress / That makes me so digress?"). Whenever a genuine sense of longing arises in the poem, Eliot humiliates the desire and mocks the feeling. That's why Prufrock's longing turns into an image of lonely old men in shirtsleeves leaning out of windows and the violent self-contempt that makes him picture himself as some primitive, less-than-human form of life, "a pair of ragged claws." This stanza's five lines are all that survive of a thirty-eight-line divagation that Eliot planned called "Prufrock's Pervigilium" and eventually cut from the poem. Prufrock's mild insomnia, his unwilling wakefulness, nonetheless still factors into his consciousness.

Prufrock can't tolerate his own desires. He is repelled by his sexual paralysis, his inability to ask anyone to marry him or "force the moment to its crisis." He feels the need to repel the emotions that keep welling up and troubling him. One way that Eliot defends himself against too much unseemly feeling is by allusions to other texts, and you can sometimes feel him churning into high gear.

> But though I have wept and fasted, wept and prayed,
> Though I have seen my head (grown slightly bald) brought in upon
>   a platter,
> I am no prophet—and here's no great matter

In three lines, Prufrock views himself as a slightly balding St. John the Baptist, whose head was given by Herod to Salomé as a gift (Matthew 14:3–11), and the prophet Amos who was commanded not to prophesy: "I was no prophet, neither was I a prophet's son" (Amos 7:14, King James Bible). Eliot mines the gap between the politeness of the setting (teatime with its chatter) and the literary and biblical references. The pattern of romantic longing, which is then refuted and demeaned, is repeated in the next stanza when Eliot first alludes to Andrew Marvell's seduction poem "To His Coy Mistress" ("Let us roll all our strength and all / Our sweetness up into one ball"), and then mockingly refers to Prufrock as someone who is so emotionally dead that he needs to be resurrected, "I am Lazarus, come from the dead, / Come back to tell you all, I shall tell you all" (Luke 16:19–31).

Prufrock finds it difficult, even impossible, to explain what he means, and thereby longs for a magic lantern to project his nerves upon a screen for a potential lover to see. The magic lantern, so dear to Proust as a metaphor for vision, was a sort of early slide projector, and Eliot interjects it as a fantasy to visualize a man's inner workings, his nervous system. Eliot periodically suffered from "nervous attacks," and Prufrock seems to be having a prolonged one here. He is at cross-purposes with any possible female companion. Whatever he says, whatever he cannot say, always brings him to the same blind corridor: "That is not what I meant, at all."

This leads us to one of the culminating refusals in the poem, the nine-line sentence that begins "No! I am not Prince Hamlet, nor was meant to be." This stand-alone stanza reads almost as a set piece—you can feel the pleasure that the poet takes in his negative rhetoric, in the audacity of the extended conceit, which he later defined as the elaboration "of a figure of speech to the furthest stage to which ingenuity can carry it." Hence, this witty parody of Hamlet's most famous speech, "To be or not to be."

> No! I am not Prince Hamlet, nor was meant to be;
> Am an attendant lord, one that will do
> To swell a progress, start a scene or two,
> Advise the prince; no doubt, an easy tool,
> Deferential, glad to be of use,
> Politic, cautious, and meticulous;
> Full of high sentence, but a bit obtuse;
> At times, indeed, almost ridiculous—
> Almost, at times, the Fool.

The joke here is that Prufrock is very much like Hamlet, who is also indecisive and overwhelmed by "overwhelming questions." Prufrock does him one better by establishing that he was never meant to be a prince at all. Eliot mimics a comic Shakespearean monologue with a well-timed iambic pentameter and a quadruple feminine rhyme (*use, meticulous, obtuse, ridiculous*). He holds the word *tool* in abeyance for five lines and then clinches it with the capitalized word *Fool*, a Shakespearean figure if there ever was one. He also lifts a phrase from Chaucer's "General Prologue" to the *Canterbury Tales* ("ful of hy sentence") as he compares Prufrock to Polonius with a rhetorical flourish. A moment later he is back at it and compares Prufrock to Falstaff ("I am old, I am old") in *2 Henry IV*. Prufrock may be unbearably stifled, but the poet who created him is filled with creative excitement at the inventive, incautious ways he keeps finding to describe his own cautious inabilities.

"Prufrock" rides to its conclusion while making point after point about its own paralyzing self-reflexivity. There is precision and power in how the lines divide in this fully intact unit, a triple rhyming triplet:

> Shall I part my hair behind? || Do I dare to eat a peach?
> I shall wear white flannel trousers, || and walk upon the beach.
> I have heard the mermaids singing, || each to each.

The trochaic meter sounds like something out of Gilbert and Sullivan as Eliot deliberately moves from two overly scrupulous, even pathetically trivial questions to the high romance of hearing mermaids singing to each other in the sea. The next one-line stanza makes a definitive refusal: "I do not think that they will sing to me." Once more Eliot turns to Donne—"Teach me to hear mermaids singing" ("Song")—to pay homage to a chief precursor and rewrite metaphysical English poetry.

I have been returning to the last stanza for half a century, and I still find it elusive, riveting, musical, a beautifully doom-ridden scene. It consists of two perfectly balanced sentences that marvelously prefigure the mature mode of *Four Quartets*. The steady rhythm and consonantal sound pattern, the way that the waves turn into the sea, the four rhyming lines, including a final conclusive couplet, all contribute to the effect.

> I have seen them riding seaward on the waves
> Combing the white hair of the waves blown back
> When the wind blows the water white and black.
> We have lingered in the chambers of the sea
> By sea-girls wreathed with seaweed red and brown
> Till human voices wake us, and we drown.

Eliot was a disillusioned fantasist and sometimes he sounds more like a disciple of Walter Pater than a contemporary of Ezra Pound. To me, it's as if the poem takes an abrupt swerve toward the American seashore lyric and thus situates itself in a Romantic poetic tradition. I hear it suddenly stationed between Whitman's "Out of the Cradle Endlessly Rocking" and Stevens's "The Idea of Order at Key West" as well as Bishop's "The End of March."

Prufrock stands here on the edge of an abyss. He has had a vision of something beyond us, some otherworldly female creatures, "sea-girls," who have welled up out of the oceanic depths, a dreamlike beauty that is so fleeting it can scarcely be remembered, except perhaps in reveries and dreams, in visionary moments. In the last three lines, the speaker of the poem, an "I," morphs into a communal figure, a "we." Eliot takes on a plural voice, the "you" and "I" who set out at the beginning of the poem, but also something larger, some collective consciousness, presumably male, but not necessarily so, since it encompasses anyone who has glimpsed mermaids in the distance and fantasized another imaginative life. The high rhetoric, the utterly convincing rhythmic music, carries us into the dreamlike realm of enchantment, which has always been the country of romance, and then wakes us up to the reality of consciousness and human voices, what Prufrock views as the social nightmare, "and we drown."

Eliot's magic lantern was the poem. In "The Love Song of J. Alfred Prufrock" he showed a preternatural gift for projecting his own anxieties so that others could identify with them. He became a famed ironist—an entire school of criticism was built on his notion of irony—but he was also something even rarer, a poet who could enlarge his feelings into a state of cosmic despair, which other people recognized as their own. I like to remember him as a young poet transfiguring his nervous frustrations into a voice and a method, breaking free and fearlessly turning his fears into a new music, taking a defeatist persona and transforming it into a victorious poem.

To Brooklyn Bridge

How many dawns, chill from his rippling rest
The seagull's wings shall dip and pivot him,
Shedding white rings of tumult, building high
Over the chained bay waters Liberty—

Then, with inviolate curve, forsake our eyes
As apparitional as sails that cross
Some page of figures to be filed away;
—Till elevators drop us from our day . . .

I think of cinemas, panoramic sleights
With multitudes bent toward some flashing scene
Never disclosed, but hastened to again,
Foretold to other eyes on the same screen;

And Thee, across the harbor, silver-paced
As though the sun took step of thee, yet left
Some motion ever unspent in thy stride,—
Implicitly thy freedom staying thee!

Out of some subway scuttle, cell or loft
A bedlamite speeds to thy parapets,
Tilting there momently, shrill shirt ballooning,
A jest falls from the speechless caravan.

Down Wall, from girder into street noon leaks,
A rip-tooth of the sky's acetylene;

All afternoon the cloud-flown derricks turn . . .
Thy cables breathe the North Atlantic still.

And obscure as that heaven of the Jews,
Thy guerdon . . . Accolade thou dost bestow
Of anonymity time cannot raise:
Vibrant reprieve and pardon thou dost show.

O harp and altar, of the fury fused,
(How could mere toil align thy choiring strings!)
Terrific threshold of the prophet's pledge,
Prayer of pariah, and the lover's cry,—

Again the traffic lights that skim thy swift
Unfractioned idiom, immaculate sigh of stars,
Beading thy path—condense eternity:
And we have seen night lifted in thine arms.

Under thy shadow by the piers I waited;
Only in darkness is thy shadow clear.
The City's fiery parcels all undone,
Already snow submerges an iron year . . .

O Sleepless as the river under thee,
Vaulting the sea, the prairies' dreaming sod,
Unto us lowliest sometime sweep, descend
And of the curveship lend a myth to God.

                    1930

H ART CRANE was a dreamer. His dreams were difficult to sustain and crashed against the harshness of modern life, and yet he was determined to transcend the prevailing spirit of negation and become a poet of joy. I'm moved by his struggles, his stubborn determination to view Brooklyn Bridge as a version of the democratic sublime. I cross it often now, almost nonchalantly, but I still find it imposing and beautiful. There is a festive mood among the mingled commuters and tourists, too. As a young poet I fell in love with *The Waste Land*, which I took as a clinically accurate diagnosis of modern life, but reading Crane cracked a chip in the edifice. The first time I crossed Brooklyn Bridge I didn't feel at all as if death had undone so many. On the contrary: the place seemed filled with life. Now, looking up at the cables of the bridge, which soar over the water, I recall how Crane countered modern pessimism with a renewed hope in the American city. He held fast to the American story and celebrated our modernity. I believe that his work makes a promise to the future. I try to remember that promise when I feel disheartened about our country. All you need to do is to head over to Brooklyn Bridge to remember the grandeur.

Something about Crane's life always seemed close to the brink of disaster. He was self-schooled and disorderly; he drank too much and courted a visionary drunkenness (his poem "The Wine Menagerie" begins: "Invariably when wine redeems the sight"), what Rimbaud called "a long, boundless, and systematic derangement of all the senses." Out of a deeply troubled personal life—an unhappy childhood in Cleveland, a constant struggle to keep financially afloat, a series of thwarted gay love affairs—he imagined another type of modern world, another life really, a different kind of country, an American beyond. He deliberately punned on his name ("We can evade you, and all else but the heart: / What blame to us if the heart live on") and sought to outwit time. As he put it at the end of "For the Marriage of Faustus and Helen":

> Distinctly praise the years, whose volatile
> Blamed bleeding hands extend and thresh the height
> The imagination spans beyond despair,
> Outpacing bargain, vocable and prayer.

Crane published one book of lyrics in his short lifetime, *White Buildings* (1926), a thickly textured and radiant record of his desire to elevate the era and view it under the sign of eternity. He had the Romantic, slightly crazed notion of the poet as a seer testifying to the reality of the absolute. As he suggested in his manifesto, "General Aims and Theories" (1925), he emulated his precursors Arthur Rimbaud and William Blake and tried to see *through* and not *with* the eye, to use the real world as a springboard for what Blake called "innocence" and he called "absolute beauty," seeking a higher consciousness and transcendental realm, "moments of eternity." His poems often descend into a sulk of squalor out of which a grail of light radiates. If Neoplatonism hadn't already existed, then Crane would have invented it—he needed a compensatory philosophy, something to strive for as he tried to reconcile the rival claims of the actual and the ideal, the sensuous and spiritual worlds. The world he lived in never lived up to the one he envisioned.

Crane was lastingly influenced by the vocabulary and blank verse of the Elizabethans (in one of his letters he refers to his "Elizabethan fanaticism"), and his work often relies on a rhetoric derived from reading Christopher Marlowe, John Webster, and John Donne. He loved the way Eliot's poems encompassed contemporary life—he confessed that he read "Prufrock" and "Preludes" continually—but after the publication of *The Waste Land* he began to think of his work as a constructive alternative and direct counterstatement to Eliot's view of the world. Writing to the poet Allen Tate in June 1922, he declared: "In his own realm Eliot presents us with an absolute *impasse*, yet oddly enough, he can be utilized to lead us to, intelligently point to, other positions and 'pastures new.' Having absorbed him enough we can trust ourselves as never before, in the air or on the sea. I, for instance, would like to leave his 'negations' behind me, risk the realm of the obvious more, in quest of new sensations, *humeurs*." He relied on intuition, he said, to fill up the page. Writing to his friend Gorham Munson seven months later, he further clarified:

> There is no one writing in English who can command so much respect, to my mind, as Eliot. However, I take Eliot as a point of departure toward an almost complete reverse of direction. His pessimism is amply justified, in his own case. But I would apply as much of his erudition and technique as I can absorb and assemble toward a more positive, or (if [I] must put it so in a skeptical age) ecstatic goal. I should not think of this if a kind of rhythm and ecstasy were not (at odd moments and rare!) a very real thing to me. I feel that Eliot ignores certain spiritual events and possibilities as real and powerful now as, say, in the time of Blake. . . .

> After this perfection of death—nothing is possible in motion but
> a resurrection of some kind.

It still interested him, he said, to "affirm certain things."

Like William Carlos Williams, Crane took *The Waste Land* as a personal affront as well as a massive setback for our poetry, a nightmare of infernal proportion. They both felt as if American poetry itself had been dragged down into hell, like Persephone, and needed resurrection. They are both descendants of Whitman, but whereas Williams was an objective poet, a materialist, Crane was a subjective one, a supernaturalist. Williams looked down into the earth, Crane gazed upward toward the heavens. They had a shared purpose, but a variable aim. As readers, we are encountering two different aesthetic projects, homegrown modernisms. It shows in the language and the measure, too—Williams wrote in a variable foot, Crane in a mighty blank verse. It's the difference between a pragmatist in the American grain and an impractical reverent who "entered the broken world / To trace the visionary company of love ("The Broken Tower"). One doesn't need to choose between them. Their influences fuse in certain poets who loved them both, like Frank O'Hara, Allen Ginsberg, and Philip Levine.

Crane was not an innocent, he was a skilled tactician of verse, but there is always something naïve and vulnerable about wonderment, the positive embrace, which leaves one wide open to attack. He took his share of criticism—his work was always too much for the ironists, too sincere, too compressed, too elusive, too lyrical—and yet he was willing to risk the exposure. As he phrased it in "For the Marriage of Faustus and Helen":

> Greet naively—yet intrepidly
> New soothings, new amazements
> That cornets introduce at every turn—
> And you may fall downstairs with me
> With perfect grace and equanimity.

Crane used a sanctified vocabulary to describe sin and fantasized that he could absorb the influences of the modern era—jazz, electric light displays, advertising—and become a farsighted and even sacred poet of the Machine Age. He exclaimed to Tate, "Let us invent an idiom for the proper transposition of jazz into words! Something clean, sparkling, elusive!" This transposition became his method of trying to move beyond despair, showing what he called "One inconspicuous, glowing orb of praise."

This is the prospect that Crane brings to his wildly dense, verbally packed, explosive American epic, *The Bridge* (1930). Crane's verbal wizardry and intoxicated vision cannot overturn Eliot's nihilism—you never have to go very far in a city to find despondency—but it provides a counterweight of vision, a mythopoesis. That's why his poem "To Brooklyn Bridge" is a good place to start with his work, since it introduces the vision. Crane uses the Greek epic tradition of the proem, a singer's prelude, to set the stage and define the terms for what was to come, a loosely joined group of fifteen poems that he wrote from 1923 to 1929. Crane got the idea for this long poem when he was living in an apartment in Brooklyn Heights adjacent to the bridge. He wanted to dramatize and present what he called the "Myth of America," to create a "mystical synthesis" of the American past, present, and future. He longed to become "a suitable *Pindar* for the dawn of the machine age," and intended an "epic of the modern consciousness," a dynamic embrace of contemporary life.

Walt Whitman acts as the presiding spirit of *The Bridge*, and Crane asserts a spiritual alliance with Whitman's large, transcendental vision of America, especially in "Crossing Brooklyn Ferry," which overhangs his poem like a Virgilian shadow. But Whitman's encouraging word was hard for Crane to hold on to, and in the many years of writing his lyrical epic, he often suffered a wavering confidence about the spiritual worthiness of American life in an industrial and scientific era. Crane began his poem in the early years of the roaring twenties, but by the time he published it the stock market had crashed and the Great Depression was under way. One of the underlying dramas of *The Bridge* is Crane's struggle to maintain his initial optimistic faith in the spiritual possibilities of America during the 1920s.

The crucial fact and symbol of Crane's sequence is Brooklyn Bridge itself. To Crane, the bridge not only connected Brooklyn to Manhattan, but also linked the past to the present, earth to heaven. It was a product of modern technology and science as well as a work of labor and art, a symbol of America's "constructive future" and "unique identity." Beyond its commercial and practical purposes, Crane also read it as a "harp and altar," a magnificent span between time and eternity, "terrific threshold of the prophet's pledge," a sign of America's religious need to transcend the realm of ordinary experience in quest of some ideal purity and permanence.

Written in blank verse in a Romantic mode, Crane's proem is an invocation and a prayer. It's an ode, a celebratory poem in an elevated language, and follows the Pindaric model of the heroic Greek odes to victorious athletes and warriors. It turns away from the Latin model, the more intimate odes of Horace. Its direct antecedent is Whitman's poem "To a Locomotive in Winter," which begins, "Thee for my recitative." The idea is to praise something industrial and peculiarly American, something hopeful for our democracy:

Type of the modern—emblem of motion and power—pulse of the
    continent,
For once come serve the Muse and merge in verse, even as here I see thee

In just this way Crane called for a modern invention to serve the American Muse.

"To Brooklyn Bridge" begins with a view of New York harbor as it might be seen at dawn looking seaward from the bridge. The seagull has a fortunate freedom of movement. It starts with a sense of true renewal, of striking out and setting off for a refreshed world. The city in the early morning is unprofaned, unbroken, inviolate. It is beautiful and spectral. But then the working day begins. The perspective shifts from a view of the bay and the Statue of Liberty to the imagination of an office worker in a skyscraper in lower Manhattan, who is laboring over "Some page of figures" for filing. That's when "elevators drop us from our day." Crane includes himself in the quotidian grind ("*our day*").

In the third stanza, the speaker directly enters the poem—"I think of cinemas"—and the language changes and becomes more contemporary. The cuts and shifts in perspective—from the view of the bird to the vision of the office worker to the position of the moviegoer—seem cinematic. We've entered a darkened movie house. It's as if the movies have become our source of religious solace, our church. But Crane contrasts the secular feeling of looking at a giant screen in the dark to the true feeling of levitation that comes with the panoramic view of the bridge. Outdoors, the narrator looks up. It's as if the sun is following in the steps of the bridge, rather than the other way around:

> And Thee, across the harbor, silver-paced
> As though the sun took step of thee, yet left
> Some motion ever unspent in thy stride,—
> Implicitly thy freedom staying thee!

Crane addresses the bridge almost as a god of radiant splendor.

In the fifth stanza, the bedlamite enters the poem with pained suddenness. Reality hits, and Crane jump-cuts from the transcendent upward beauty of the bridge to a tormented contemporary emerging from the subway, or some other cramped urban space, like a cell or a loft, and climbing the rails of the bridge to commit suicide. Crane may have recalled the upsetting figure in an early untitled poem by Charles Reznikoff that begins, "On Brooklyn Bridge I saw a man drop dead. / It meant no more than if he were a sparrow" (*Rhythms*, 1918). Here, Crane purposely uses an archaic word to describe a mentally ill person overwhelmed by modern life. I suspect that he was personally terrified of becoming that bedlamite and tried to stave off his own fate—he committed suicide in 1932—by writing about someone else's derangement. Poetically, he recognizes that his ideal world has been profaned by the violence of city life, the materialism represented by Wall Street.

The poem progresses from a pristine dawn to the leaky light of noon, and the perspective changes to a position under the bridge, in its gigantic shadow. All afternoon the speaker seems to be looking up at the "sky's acetylene"—Crane uses an industrial image of hydrocarbon gas, which burns with a bright flame, to describe the vista—and watching the enormous oil derricks working in the distance. One feels the strain of him trying to praise the industrial view, to see heaven through the technological shape of the bridge. That's how he comes to assert, "Thy cables breathe the North Atlantic still." Crane was fascinated by Lola Ridge's short poem "Brooklyn Bridge"— he reviewed her first book, *The Ghetto and Other Poems* (1918)—and here he directly contradicts her:

> Pythoness body—arching
> Over the night like an ecstasy—
> I feel your coils tightening . . .
> And the world's lessening breath.

Ridge's sadomasochistic image of serpentine strangulation is countered by Crane's vision of an open structure breathing in the sea.

As a poet, Crane looks back to Plato and the Greeks, not to the Hebrew Bible and the Judeo-Christian tradition, but I've always liked his reference to the "obscure . . . heaven of the Jews," since the Jewish idea of the afterlife is vague and indeterminate. For him, though, the key is that the bridge is redemptive. Once more he reaches for an archaic word, *guerdon*, to name the recompense that the bridge offers us. "O harp and altar, of the fury fused," he cries out, which suggests that he is imaginatively viewing the cables of the bridge as a magical instrument and describing the granite towers as a hallowed place. The bridge is an Aeolian harp, a medium that transfigures the wind into music, which the Romantic poets (from Coleridge and Shelley to Emerson and Melville) often used as a metaphor for poetic inspiration. As a Romantic American modernist, Crane thus joins himself to a visionary company.

Crane repeatedly reaches for religious symbolism to describe his vision. He is a churchly spirit without a church, someone looking for a refreshed founding doctrine. For him, the welding action of the bridge, "the fury fused," is a kind of synthesis and affirmation, something that transcends "mere toil," the physical labor and construction that created it. Crane's fury is a poetic fury, a term of art—not anger but inspiration. One feels him striving to look beyond the daily traffic and quotidian quality of the bridge. He insists on seeing it as the embodiment of an ideal, some "Unfractured idiom." That's how he comes up with that sacred declaration, "condense eternity," and lovely observation, "And we have seen night lifted in thine arms," an image that evokes Michelangelo's marble sculpture of the Virgin Mary cradling the dead body of Jesus. Crane adapted a theme from Christian art so that the bridge could be transformed into a steel pietà.

By the end of "To Brooklyn Bridge," Crane has progressed through the course of a day from early in the morning to late at night. This is a strategy that he had picked up from Guillaume Apollinaire's "Zone" and Joyce's *Ulysses*:

> O Sleepless as the river under thee,
> Vaulting the sea, the prairies' dreaming sod,

Unto us lowliest sometime sweep, descend
And of the curveship lend a myth to God.

The bridge is sleepless, like the city itself, like the river beneath it and the sky above. So, too, the bridge is always in motion, like American history, which is radically compressed into this last stanza. The strange and bold final line suggests that the bridge, which he is looking up at, somehow descends "And of the curveship lend a myth to God." Crane coins the word *curveship*, which seems akin to lordship or kingship in an early modern drama (Your Lordship, Your Kingship), to suggest the royal nature of the sweeping curves of the bridge. In the end, he reaches back to the ancient idea of myth, a sacred or foundational story, to indicate that the very curves of the bridge incarnate a transcendental American spirit. The myth is borrowed from us, "on loan" to God. We've gone from the bedlamite jump cut to a spacious, arching conception.

According to Hart Crane, that mythic story is part of our inheritance, our democratic ideal, something that must repeatedly be reimagined over time. It calls for a walk across a bridge and an effort of imagination. I take that walk all the time now. Most of the time I'm rushed and distracted, but every now and then I come across someone reading "To Brooklyn Bridge" in the middle of the bridge itself, and I pause to listen. Loitering amidst the noisy crowd, looking up and spanning the view, I find myself wondering again at these two engineering marvels and lofty structures, one a poem, the other a bridge:

O harp and altar, of the fury fused,
(How could mere toil align thy choiring strings!)

Harlem

What happens to a dream deferred?

   Does it dry up
   like a raisin in the sun?
   Or fester like a sore—
   And then run?
   Does it stink like rotten meat?
   Or crust and sugar over—
   like a syrupy sweet?

   Maybe it just sags
   like a heavy load.

   Or does it explode?

               1951

A ONE-WORD TITLE, a simple place-name, "Harlem," and then a short poem in free verse, a mere eleven lines, fifty-one words. Six questions and one statement, a provisional one at that (*Maybe*). And yet this brief poem of protest and conviction has a long reach and vibrates through American culture in a way that few other poems have done. It has lodged itself in the American mind. The opening question, concise, direct— "What happens to a dream deferred?"—is significant because it addresses our dearest ideal, the American dream, and forces us to reevaluate it. I have to reach back to Emma Lazarus's inscription on the pedestal of the Statue of Liberty to come up with a lyric formulation that has meant as much to so many people, that has been invoked and reinvoked to help us think about the American situation, our terrible legacy of racism and injustice—our history, ourselves. But where Lazarus gives us a statement about immigration, and thereby holds us to a standard of acceptance and openness, Hughes offers up what might be *the* American question.

Hughes's phrasing of the African American dilemma helped Martin Luther King, Jr., to crystalize an ideal. The poem "Harlem" found its way to King through the playwright Lorraine Hansberry, who borrowed an image from Hughes's poem for her groundbreaking play, *A Raisin in the Sun* (1959), about a Black family on the south side of Chicago. The scholar W. Jason Miller points out that King saw the play on Broadway, read Hughes's poem in the playbill, and wrote to him about the countless number of times he had read Hughes's poems aloud to audiences: "My admiration for your works is not only expressed in my personal conversations, but I can no longer count the number of times and places, all over the nation, in my addresses and sermons in which I have read your poems." Soon afterwards, he quoted "Harlem" in his Easter sermon "Shattered Dreams." In his historic "I Have a Dream" speech at the Lincoln Memorial, King reconfigures Hughes's question and imagines a dream that is no longer deferred but realized. He also places it at the heart of the civil rights movement. More quietly, King later admitted in a sermon: "I am personally the victim of deferred dreams."

At the end of May 2020, I was reminded of the ongoing relevance of Hughes's poem, which he later retitled "Dream Deferred," when it appeared in an eloquent op-ed in the *Los Angeles Times* by Kareem Abdul-Jabbar that explained the necessity of Black protests in the wake of the murder of George Floyd by a Minneapolis police officer. Nearly seventy years after the poem was published, Abdul-Jabbar excerpted Hughes's lyric and linked it to Marvin Gaye's song "Inner City Blues": "Make me wanna holler / The way they do my life." Abdul-Jabbar cites these two texts because of their applicability to American society, because the institutional racism of America is still trying to silence the voices and steal the breath of African Americans, because we still need a movement to holler "Black Lives Matter." "What I want to see is not a rush to judgement," Abdul-Jabbar affirms, "but a rush to justice." And that's the underlying premise of Hughes's lyric, too.

Hughes was galvanized by the life and music of Harlem. He was born at the beginning of the twentieth century in Joplin, Missouri, and grew up as a lonely, unhappy, bookish kid in a series of midwestern cities. He came to

New York as a precocious, fresh-faced nineteen-year-old who had already written "The Negro Speaks of Rivers." He was disheartened by the racism he found at Columbia University and dropped out, but found what he was seeking farther uptown, in an activist haven and cultural emergence where he discovered a budding club scene and heard performers like Bessie Smith, Duke Ellington, and Fats Waller. "I was in love with Harlem long before I got there," he wrote in his autobiography, *The Big Sea*.

Hughes found a perch in the neighborhood, which he called "the great dark city," but I want to stress the range of his early working-class jobs and the extent of his travels. As a young man, Hughes visited his father in Mexico and worked as a delivery boy and a messman in New York; as a steward on the S. S. *Malone* and *McKeesport* freighters, on which he bopped around various West African and European port towns; as a cook and a doorman at the Grand Duc nightclub in Montmartre (see "Jazz Band in a Parisian Cabaret"); and as a busboy in a hotel in Washington, D.C., where he dropped three of his poems next to the plate of Vachel Lindsay, who began to proclaim his merits from the podium. It was while he was working odd jobs in European restaurants and kitchens that he recast Whitman's "I Hear America Singing" into the credo of "I, Too." Many of the Black writers of Hughes's generation traveled abroad in order to escape the stifling racism of American society. They felt more fully human in foreign territory, and it enabled them to think more clearly about the situation at home. Hughes's life experiences are interesting in their own right, but I am citing them because they figure into his practice and illuminate his project, reminding us of what he introduced into our canon, his contribution to a more inclusive American thinking.

Hughes was cosmopolitan in his sensibility but egalitarian in his sympathy, and he brought this democratic ethos to his cross-section portrayals of African American life. In 1926, he published his first book of poems, *The Weary Blues*, and his manifesto, "The Negro Artist and the Racial Mountain," which became two of the cornerstones of the Harlem Renaissance. He took what he needed from his primary poetic precursors, Walt Whitman, Carl Sandburg, and Paul Laurence Dunbar, and matched this to his sensitivity to oral Black forms, a cultural treasure house that he traced back to African rather than European sources. Hughes attacked the idea of Black middle-class deracialization: "But this is the mountain standing in the way of any true Negro art in America—this urge within the race toward whiteness, the desire to pour racial individuality into the mold of American standardization, and to be as little Negro and as much American as possible." There are two other elements here that are significant for Hughes's future work: his concentration on what he calls "the low-down folks, the so-called common element," and his formal turn to blues and jazz as a model for how to create an African American art that is both long established and state-of-the-art.

Hughes was both a poet and a fiction writer; he believed the two arts go hand in hand. When I started reading him in college—he was just becoming required reading by then—I didn't yet see the consequences of Hughes's formal decisions, how he had used his self-education to center the lives and bring out the dignity of people who had mostly been excluded from our literature. I was turned off by the title of his second book, *Fine Clothes to the Jew* (1927), and was later relieved to discover that Hughes regretted the prejudicial title, which he felt was misunderstood, and wished that he had called the book *Brass Spittoons*, after his poem of that name. This was a poem I could identify with because it brought back the memory of working as a busboy in a Chicago restaurant, a degrading experience, though I didn't have to deal with the racism that Hughes had routinely encountered on the job.

It wasn't until I took a class with the literary critic and scholar Charles T. Davis that I began to see why some of Hughes's decisions were so meaningful. Hughes was influenced by the collage-like methods of Eliot and Pound, but unlike them he did not believe that modern writing needed to be "difficult" in order to capture the complexity of modern civilization. After all, he named the main character in his fiction Jesse B. Semple (aka Simple), an uneducated Harlem man-about-town, a folk philosopher on a barstool who drinks because he's lonesome and offhandedly says things like "I'm lonesome inside myself" ("Conversation on the Corner"). So, too, Hughes determined that his own poetry was about "workers, roustabouts, and singers, and job hunters on Lenox Avenue in New York, or Seventh Street in Washington or South State in Chicago—people up today and down tomorrow, working this week and fired the next, beaten and baffled, but determined not to be wholly beaten, buying furniture on the installment plan, filling the house with roomers to help pay the rent, hoping to get a new suit for Easter—and pawning that suit before the Fourth of July."

Hughes always had his admirers, but he was also routinely attacked from both sides of the racial divide. He faced resistance from white critics for his uncompromising idea of a self-defining Black art, but he also took heat from the African American press for his early portraits of the Black proletariat, which did not try to uplift the race by portraying wholesome characters. There is always internal social pressure on writers to put on a good face for the outside world, to show the group in a positive light, but Hughes did not back down or waver in his commitment to dramatize the uninhibited life of African Americans in situ, actual people on the move.

Hughes wrote "Harlem" in the late 1940s. The Great Depression was over, the Great War had been won, and yet what had changed for Black Americans? Hughes had a knack for formulating what every African American implicitly understood—that the American dream, our national ethos, the fantasy that anyone could achieve anything, the fiction of upward mobility, seemed a mockery in a racist Jim Crow America. And yet there is also a hint of optimism in Hughes's opening question: "What happens to a dream deferred?" The word *deferred* suggests something that is put off, postponed; it doesn't indicate something that can never be realized. I don't mean to underestimate Hughes's political radicalism—he stood on the far left side of the Harlem Renaissance and would soon be hauled up to testify before Senator Joseph McCarthy's House Un-American Activities Committee to answer questions about the Communist Party and communist influences on his work. And yet he did not entirely subvert the ideal of the American dream, he opened it up. After all, he might have asked, "What happens to a dream *destroyed*?" There is a reckoning implied in Hughes's careful phrasing. The poem holds America accountable, but also suggests that the country can be redeemed—perhaps, or else.

I have been puzzling over the odd, compelling phrasing of Hughes's question. There are no people in the sentence—"What happens to a dream deferred?" It's as if they have been eliminated, such is their subjugation. The word *deferred* is itself delayed, a verb that acts as an adjective. One of the mysteries of poetry is how the exact formulation matters, the rhythmic precision. If Hughes had said, "What happens to a dream that is deferred?" or "What happens to a deferred dream?," we probably wouldn't be talking about the poem.

It's uncommon to find a poem that consists primarily of questions. Indeed, Hughes's opening is so powerful that it's possible to overlook the fact that he indents the rest of the poem for emphasis. It's a question-and-answer session, a call-and-response. Hughes poses the sequence of four additional or follow-up propositions in the form of an interrogative quartet. Though they make up a stanzaic unit, the longest one in the poem, they also seem slightly disjointed, not exactly continuous. All four of the questions are similes. You feel the speaker trying to find the right image to summarize an agonizing racial deferment. There is an underlying logical formulation, as in a metaphysical poem:

> *Does it* dry up
> *like* a raisin in the sun?
> *Or fester like* a sore—
> And then run?
> *Does it stink like* rotten meat?
> *Or crust* and sugar over—
> *like* a syrupy sweet?

Hughes repeats the *d* and *r* sounds in *dream* and *deferred*, which recur in the wording "*Does it dry* up?" He also clinches the sound with two rhymes (*sun* and *run*, *meat* and *sweet*). There is an almost sickly repetition of the consonant *s*. The letter *r* reverberates from *deferred* through *fester* and *sore*; it runs from *run* to *rotten*. He is using the visceral image to great effect here: the shriveled grape, the oozing sore that becomes infected, the stench of tainted meat, or some remnant candy, now sickening in the open air. This imagery is enacted by the active verbs *dry up*, *fester*, *run*, *crust*, and *sugar over*, which suggest a kind of development, something coming to culmination, painfully overflowing, weeping out.

These bodily images, nutrition gone wrong, natural and animal decay, build to a speculation, a new couplet: "Maybe it just sags / like a heavy load." The dream deferred weighs on you, like something you have carried a long way, and for a long time. It's an image of burdensome work. Hughes is continuing to take an abstract ideal and give it body, a sense of crushing heaviness. This builds to a final question, which is both set off as a one-line stanza and italicized, thus maximizing the emphasis: "*Or does it explode?*" The word *load* has been carried across the divide of a stanza to rhyme with *explode*. Part of the compact power of this is that every one of the five syllables can be stressed: *Ór dóes ít éxplóde?* This question culminates the poem and resonates well beyond it because it implies an answer. It carries a veiled threat, the feeling that there is only so much that a people can take: you can't keep shattering their aspiration forever and think it won't have consequences. Hughes saw what happened to a dream deferred in the riots in Harlem in 1935 and 1943. And we have seen what happens, what will keep on happening until we right it; otherwise, it is going to explode—and not just in Harlem, but also in Los Angeles and Seattle, in Cleveland and Chicago, in Detroit and Kansas City, in Portland and Minneapolis–St. Paul.

"Harlem" stands alone as a lyric—that's how it is usually presented in anthologies—but as a young poet I was excited to discover that it's part of a much larger sequence. It appears as the first piece in the last section of Hughes's book-length suite *Montage of a Dream Deferred* (1951), which consists of more than ninety poems that picture Harlem life during the Jim Crow era. One of the primary subjects of the book is the dream or fantasy of American life versus the grim truth, the hard reality. *Montage* takes its title from film-editing. It creates a new composite and joins the idea of sequencing short shots to the art of jazz, as Hughes states at the outset: "this poem on contemporary Harlem, like be-bop, is marked by conflicting changes, sudden nuances, sharp and impudent interjections, broken rhythms, and passages sometimes in the manner of the jam session, sometimes the popular song, punctuated by the riffs, runs, breaks, and disc-tortions of the music of a community in transition."

Hughes was translating Federico García Lorca's *Gypsy Ballads* during the same period that he was writing *Montage*, and I hear something of Lorca's idiom here, a writerly poet ventriloquizing oral forms to dramatize the suffering of a community. But whereas Lorca's poems are narrative, Hughes's are purposefully nonlinear, crosscut, and syncopated, rhythmically modulated. They have an associative or dream logic, and in this way are closer to Lorca's sequence *Poet in New York*. Hughes realized that he had hit upon something anthemic in the phrase *a dream deferred*, and so he uses it for the title and dilates on it throughout the book. The title comes up in the poem "Deferred," where it is centered, segmented into three lines like a haiku, and italicized:

> *Montage*
> *of a dream*
> *deferred.*

By the time you get to the poem "Harlem," the phrase has already had a long adventure, which begins at the beginning with the first poem, "Dream Boogie," of the first section, "Boogie Segue to Bop." A jive young woman wakes up the book:

> Good morning, daddy!
> Ain't you heard
> The boogie-woogie rumble
> Of a dream deferred?

The title phrase starts off as something that underlies and drives the upbeat tempo of the boogie-woogie. "Listen closely: / You'll hear the feet / Beating out and beating out a—"; now the speaker breaks off and either interrupts herself or gets interrupted: "*You think / It's a happy beat?*" The boogie-woogie is a type of piano music for two hands, and here Hughes imitates the right hand responding to the left one. The poet is enacting a postponement, which he hears in the musical vocabulary, instructing us to listen closely to something frustrated and continually broken off, unsaid, growing. There's a fervent, perhaps even desperate Dionysian undercurrent to the rhythm. Over the course of the sequence, Hughes himself will self-consciously segue from a dance music, "boogie-woogie," to a performer's high art, "be-bop."

The formula comes up again in the poem "Tell Me" in the second section, "Dig and Be Dug," where it is now pinned and personalized to an unnamed speaker: "Why should it be *my* dream / deferred / overlong?" The book progresses through a series of "Riffs, smears, breaks," accruing stories, vignettes of poverty, the daily struggle of a group of people trying to survive, looking for "the Freedom Train." It is also cross-stitched with Hughes's personal memories. And one hears the transformations of a new night music, too, as in "Boogie: 1 A.M," where the first voice of the poem comes back, wiser to a wiser music:

> Good evening, daddy!
> I know you've heard
> The boogie-woogie rumble
> Of a dream deferred
> Trilling the treble

> And twining the bass
> Into midnight ruffles
> Of cat-gut lace.

You can hear Hughes hitting the consonants: "*Tr*illing the *tr*eble / And *tw*ining the bass." I like the scholar Steven Tracy's observation that "here the right-hand treble notes and the left-hand bass notes are united in performance, as the minds and souls or thoughts and feeling of blacks are meant to be united in a common cause: the recognition of the dream deferred, and the organization of a unified front to confront the problems of blacks in America." You can also hear that Hughes is taking his formula to a new place, letting it well up at the canonical hour, a midnight jam session.

Hughes riffs in such a way that sometimes the high phrasing of deferral gets pegged to something vernacular, as in the poem "Dime": "Montage of a dream deferred: // *Grandma acts like / She ain't heard.*" Granny can't scrape together ten cents but carries herself otherwise with dignity. There's a moment in the portraiture that brings up Jewish shopkeepers in Harlem, but what at first might seem cringeworthy or antisemitic—there are some growls about pawnshops closing on Yom Kippur—ultimately turns into an image of people, likewise, also struggling to survive, also punished: "Sometimes I think / Jews must have heard / the music of a / dream deferred" ("Likewise"). Hughes keeps enlarging his sympathies and turning the words in ways that enable us to hear them afresh, changing the line breaks, pressing the rhymes (*heard / deferred*), and varying the diction, sometimes taking it down a register, sometimes lifting it up.

"Harlem" kicks off the last section of the book, which is named after Lenox Avenue, now called Malcolm X Boulevard, one of the primary north-south routes through Harlem but also one of the most important thoroughfares in Black culture. In Hughes's day, Lenox Avenue was a street of commingling and colliding cultures, a place where African Americans crossed with people of color from a wide range of different places, from Georgia, Florida, and Louisiana, as part of the Great Migration, but also from Puerto Rico and Cuba, Haiti and Jamaica. You used it to cross upper Manhattan, but also to savor the complex of the New World, a stopping point for jazz joints and corner food shops, a place to listen and eat.

All this seems relevant to the poem because "Harlem" is immediately followed by a lyric called "Good Morning," where a speaker meditates on the changes to the place where he was born, people coming up to Harlem, "dusky sash across Manhattan," arriving by train in the middle of Manhattan: I've seen them come, he says, floating out of Penn Station, where the trains are always late: "The gates open— / Yet there're bars / at each gate. // What happens / to a dream deferred?" Hughes breaks his characteristic line here to give special emphasis to the first part of the phrasing—*What happens*—so that it acts as both statement and question. People come with a dream of freedom, but what they discover are many gates, and all of them seem like prison bars.

Hughes scholars have pointed out that in earlier drafts of *Montage* the short lyric "Harlem" was actually embedded in the poem "Good Morning" where the question of what happens to a dream deferred is voiced by puzzled and stunned migrants:

> I've seen them come,
>
> > > Wondering, wide-eyed, dreaming and dark.
> > > What happens to a dream deferred?
> > Does it dry up like a raisin in the sun?
> > Or fester like a sore—and then run?
> > Does it stink like rotten meat?
> > Or crust, and sugar over—
> > like a syrupy sweet?
> > Maybe it just sags
> > like a heavy load.
> > Or does it explode?
> Pouring out of Penn Station
> a new nation—
> but the trains are late.

When Hughes broke off "Harlem" as a single poem, he also divided it into meaningful stanzaic units, separate rooms. Reading it as part of "Good Morning," we can see that Hughes's question—"Or does it explode"—has an additional connotation. The word *explode* refers to social protest and rebellion, but also to a population swell, a discharge of new immigrants to New York. In the end, Hughes severed this lyric into two parts and then joined them in sequence. The underlying question of Black life in Harlem—"What happens to a dream deferred?"—may not be entirely divorced from Emma Lazarus's rousing declaration about impoverished immigrants coming to America: "Give me your tired, your poor."

Throughout *Montage*, the first voice of the poem keeps popping back with more and more pressing excitement: "Daddy, ain't you heard?" The phrasing of "a dream deferred" resonates in the next poem, too, "Same in Blues," where it now migrates successively through a refrain. The dreams of individuals get kicked around as people get kicked down the ladder of the American dream. Hughes progresses through four iterations:

> *There's a certain*
> *amount of traveling*
> *in a dream deferred.*
>
> . . . .
>
> *A certain*
> *amount of nothing*
> *in a dream deferred.*
>
> . . . .
>
> *A certain*
> *amount of impotence*
> *in a dream deferred.*
>
> . . . .
>
> *There's liable*
> *to be confusion*
> *in a dream deferred.*

As in a ballad by Yeats, the repetitions also point to the differences, and so one feels the pressure on the words and concepts of "a certain amount" of *traveling, nothing, impotence*, and *confusion*. Hughes keeps finding ways to blood his abstraction, to work through the individual and collective consequences of a seemingly endless suspension of freedom. "There's liable to be confusion," he riffs, "when a dream gets kicked around."

That's why the last poem in the book, "Island," turns the phrasing one final time. The island is Manhattan, and it mixes colors—black, white, gold, brown—and cooks them into a "Chocolate-custard / Pie of a town." Hughes follows this culinary racial image with his signature phrase, now a stand-alone two-line stanza: "Dream within a dream, / Our dream deferred." Now, Hughes creates a sort of labyrinthine image, one dream inside another one—say, a Harlem dream tucked inside of an American dream—and introduces the first-person plural for the first and last time, "*Our* dream deferred." He has waited until the last moment to include himself in the larger collective. He ends the poem where it began with a voice we've heard before—"Good morning, daddy! // Ain't you heard?" I love the final flash of this female speaker, jaunty but also urgent, whose voice has a slang eloquence and sounds a wake-up call. Hughes has given us a "Harlem of the bitter dream," but also a jazz Harlem, a changing music for a changing community, a changed world.

"What happens to a dream deferred?" That question was formulated in the late 1940s by a poet thinking about his people, his place, and his country, but it has never really been answered, never adequately responded to by the society at large. Langston Hughes understood that African American poetry is an integral part of African American life, but I believe he also understood and modeled something else, too—indeed, his practice reminds us that all of American poetry is part of American life. The two are connected, like a dream within a dream. One can't be sundered from the other. Ain't you heard? Langston Hughes reminds us that American art is wedded to the quest for a fairer society, a more just world.

STERLING A. BROWN (1901–1989)

Southern Road

Swing dat hammer—hunh—
Steady, bo';
Swing dat hammer—hunh—
Steady, bo';
Ain't no rush, bebby,
Long ways to go.

Burner tore his—hunh—
Black heart away;
Burner tore his—hunh—
Black heart away;
Got me life, bebby,
An' a day.

Gal's on Fifth Street—hunh—
Son done gone;
Gal's on Fifth Street—hunh—
Son done gone;
Wife's in de ward, bebby,
Babe's not bo'n.

My ole man died—hunh—
Cussin' me;
My ole man died—hunh—
Cussin' me;
Ole lady rocks, bebby,
Huh misery.

Doubleshackled—hunh—
Guard behin';
Doubleshackled—hunh—
Guard behin';
Ball an' chain, bebby,
On my min'.

White man tells me—hunh—
Damn yo' soul;
White man tells me—hunh—
Damn yo' soul;
Got no need, bebby,
To be tole.

Chain gang nevah—hunh—
Let me go;
Chain gang nevah—hunh—
Let me go;
Po' los' boy, bebby,
Evahmo' . . .

1931

OCTOBER 1980. I can still see the four of us standing outside of State Hall, that concrete brutality where we had set up shop in the English department at Wayne State University. We were talking about poetry with the youthful hijinks that powered our conversations in those days. I was quoting the poem "MLA," which John Berryman had written for our friend and colleague Daniel Hughes, and it filled us with glee:

> Hey, out there!—assistant professors, full,
> associates,—instructors—others—any—
> I have a sing to shay.
> We are assembled here in the capital
> city for Dull—and one professor's wife is Mary—
> at Christmastide, hey!

Our chair hurried past on the way to a meeting, and I couldn't restrain myself: "a chairman's not a chairman, son, forever, / and hurts with his appointments; ha." Luckily, he didn't hear me, and soon we drifted off to teach our freshman composition classes, overtired, underpaid, but buoyed by the comedy and the comradery.

The next day Alvin Aubert stopped by my office to continue the conversation. He liked the linguistic wackiness of Berryman's *77 Dream Songs*, he said, especially #35, which we were bandying about, but only up to a point—and that point was Berryman's wielding of minstrelsy, his Tambo and Bones routine, a misuse of Black dialect, which Al considered—I want to get his wording right—unfortunate and undignified. This was just a slapstick sideshow to the whole poem, the patter of end men in blackface, Al said, but it marred the main performance. Al was a gentle, well-mannered person, a latecomer to the academy who had grown up in the rural South, and his angle of approach sometimes surprised me. Now he fished a book out of his backpack that he wanted me to review for *Obsidian*, his journal of Black literature. It was Sterling A. Brown's *Collected Poems*. I took the book: one month, five thousand words, the spring issue. It wasn't exactly a request. I knew I was being given a sly corrective and witty schooling. I just didn't know how sly, how witty.

Sterling Brown's name wasn't entirely new to me—I knew from my folklore studies about his work in the 1930s for the Federal Writers' Project and his capacious sourcebooks for Black culture, which dismantled stereotypes and enlarged the canon: *The Negro in Washington* (1936), *The Negro in American Fiction* (1937), *Negro Poetry and Drama* (1937), and *The Negro Caravan* (1941), a comprehensive anthology that he coedited with Arthur P. Davis and Ulysses Lee. I had taken note of their statement that "white authors dealing with the American Negro have interpreted him in a way to justify his exploitation. Creative literature has often been a handmaiden to social policy." But I had never read Brown's poetry. My sole excuse is that most of the poets and critics of my generation had also missed out on his work until Michael S. Harper rescued it for the National Poetry Series. But Harper didn't pick a prizewinning book and leave it at that. He made the claim: "The publication of Sterling A. Brown's *Collected Poems* is an historical event, though he has never been a poet of fashion, this collection secures his place at the center of American letters."

Sterling Brown's poems had to wait a painfully long time to find an audience. His first book, *Southern Road* (1932), broke new ground—I now think of it as the key book of African American poetry in the 1930s—but it was the Depression, and he couldn't find a publisher for his next book, *No Hiding Place* (it would eventually appear in his *Collected Poems* in 1980). He had to wait more than forty years to print *The Last Ride of Wild Bill* (1975), which consists of eight idiomatic literary ballads rewritten in African American terms out of the central tall tale tradition of American literature. Over the decades, Brown found solace in saving the archive and documenting the record, but his own poetry languished. This was a shame because Brown was not, as he had often been portrayed, a minor satellite of the Harlem Renaissance, but a poet of comparable stature to Countee Cullen and Claude McKay, someone engaged in a different, parallel poetic revolution.

I was beginning to see why Aubert, who had grown up in Lutcher, Louisiana, and championed African American cultural life along the southern Mississippi River, had pivoted to Brown as a model presence. Influenced by the concept of the New Negro and energized by the writings of Alain Locke and W.E.B. Du Bois, Brown used his considerable verbal gifts not to portray the urban life of his contemporaries but to explore the social nature of the southern Black experience. As Langston Hughes experimented with jazz rhythms to render Harlem nightlife, so Brown turned to folk forms like the blues, spirituals, and work songs to create an accurate, unsentimental, yet dignified portrait of southern Black life in the twentieth century. In the deceptively simple forms of his chosen folk idiom, Brown's poems successfully brought an unknown African American world into the realm of recorded literature. He did so at a time when a group of white Southern Agrarians led by John Crowe Ransom and Allen Tate were putting together a nostalgic, reactionary defense of the lost Confederacy and the Old South, *I'll Take My Stand* (1930).

The operant formal influence on Brown's work was his reliance on both secular and sacred African American musical traditions. It was virtually unprecedented for Brown, who was born and raised in Washington, D.C., and educated at Williams College and Harvard University, to turn his considerable intellectual resources to rural southern culture. But then Brown always had a sense of "the connecting timbre," as the historian Sterling Stuckey puts it, "a feel for the reciprocity between past and present." Brown taught at Howard University for forty years and considered himself primarily a teacher, which he may have been, though his reach extended well beyond Howard. He was a raconteur who celebrated what he called "the extraordinary in ordinary lives" and took what he needed from Whitman and Emerson, from Edwin Arlington Robinson, Robert Frost, Edgar Lee Masters, Amy Lowell, and Carl Sandburg, to redefine a new American aesthetic of the local. "When Carl Sandburg said 'yes' to the American people," Brown recalled, "I wanted to say 'yes' to my people." To do so, he turned to James Weldon Johnson, Zora Neale Hurston, Langston Hughes, and other Black contemporaries, too. What was especially radical about his work was how he affirmed the value of vernacular traditions by writing in dialect at a time when it was associated not with vigorous living speech but with the mawkishness of the plantation and blackface minstrel traditions.

I realized how cleverly Aubert had set me up when I read Johnson's introduction to the first edition of *Southern Road*. Johnson had notoriously shredded the dialect tradition in the introduction to *God's Trombones* (1927), his marvelous recasting of African American sermons. Dialect was "an instrument with but two stops, humor and pathos," Johnson argued, and the Black poet needs "to find a form that will express the racial spirit by symbols from within rather than symbols from without, such as the mere mutilation of English spelling and pronunciation. He needs a form that is freer and larger than dialect." Johnson was recasting his own earlier verse, such as the section "Jingles & Croons" in *Fifty Years & Other Poems* (1917), and reconsidering the dialect poetry of Paul Laurence Dunbar, but he was also slamming the excesses of Tin Pan Alley and the pseudo-folk idiom of white poets, who stood in the shadow of the plantation. It was this contested area that Berryman, a committed supporter of civil rights, had self-mockingly but unwittingly stumbled into, for his own psychological reasons, without knowing the African American tradition or history. It was a costly racial mistake.

Over the years, Johnson had continued to target parodic traditions, which, he said, "had but slight relation, often no relation at all, to *actual* Negro life." Given this history of usage and critique, it was noteworthy when he reversed course to praise Brown "for adopting as his medium the common, racy, living speech of the Negro in certain phases of *real* life." What he discovered in Brown's poetry was both the denial and the dismantling of the cloying sentimentality and misuse of dialect tradition. *Southern Road* in effect rewrote and reformulated the nature of the Black vernacular as it had often been presented in American poetry. By turning to an oral folk tradition as opposed to a written literary one, Brown's poetry reevaluated the written tradition and privileged the external immediacy of Black life.

As he later put it in "A Son's Return: 'Oh, Didn't He Ramble'":

> I love Negro folk speech and I think it is rich and wonderful. It is not *dis* and *dat* and a split verb. But it is "Been down so long that down don't worry me," or it is what the spirituals had in one of the finest couplets in American literature: "I don't know what my mother wants to stay here for. This old world ain't been no friend to her."

By using his poetry as an instrument to redefine the character of African American speech and song, Brown was also redefining the character of rural southern Blacks, replacing geniality with fierce stoicism, ironic humor, and deep tragedy.

The poem "Southern Road" is a fictive work song. Brown wrote it himself in seven six-line stanzas that carefully mimic the sound and heavy rhythmic beat of a collective oral poem that has been passed along and refashioned over time. It also appeared in a section called "Poetry in the Folk Manner" in Langston Hughes and Arna Bontemps's *Book of Negro Folklore* (1958). Brown contributed essays on spirituals and the blues as folk poetry to this anthology, which also contains a section of collected work songs. There is a strong but subtle difference between a folk poem and a poem in the folk manner. Think, for example, of the difference between Wordsworth and Coleridge's lyrical ballads and the oral ballads that circulated in northern England in the late eighteenth century. The poets of the Harlem Renaissance era were also highly aware of the Irish renaissance precedent, the way that sophisticated writers like Yeats and John Millington Synge modeled their work on oral Gaelic forms.

It's instructive to compare "Southern Road" to a resilient work song like "Take This Hammer," which stands behind it as a battle-weary older brother worn down by hard labor:

TAKE THIS HAMMER

Take this hammer—huh!
And carry it to the captain—huh!
You tell him I'm gone—huh!
Tell him I'm gone—huh!

If he asks you—huh!
Was I runnin'—huh!
You tell him I was flyin'—huh!
You tell him I was flyin'—huh!

If he asks you—huh!
Was I laughin'—huh!
You tell him I was cryin'—huh!
You tell I was cryin'—huh!

c. 1870s

"Take This Hammer" is part of a group of songs called "hammer songs" that date to the Reconstruction era. These work songs, which have an enormous backdrop of suffering, were sung by African American convicts forced to labor on chain gangs and gigantic plantation-like prison farms, in mines, brickyards, and railroad camps in the American South. The work song is a utilitarian vehicle whose main function is to synchronize the efforts of workers who must move together in a unit. A leader provides a strong rhythmic cue with two or three bars that are then answered by the ejaculatory word or words of moving workers. The rhythmic interactions and continued interplay create a call-and-response pattern, making music a participatory activity. Often the words are created in an improvisatory mode called "signifying," which the folklorist Roger Abrahams characterizes as "a technique of indirect argument or persuasion" and "a language of implication." The singer creates a mask of address to the so-called captain, the white boss, and at the same time satirizes and undercuts that very voice, building morale by subversively talking back to power. By contrast, "Take This Hammer" is ruthlessly straightforward and direct—it is about shunting the iron shackles and escaping a chain gang. It is infused with hatred and sorrow, upending expectations—even the wished-for escape comes not with the vengeful or triumphant laughter that the white man expects, but rather with crying.

John and Alan Lomax's *Folk Song U.S.A.* (1947), which Brown especially appreciated, gives a memorable description of a work song going at full swing. It is worth paying attention to because the folklorists are delineating the collective rhythm and movement of an American art form in situ, something formulated out of a mean, tough prison life, and I'd like to claim it as part of the canon of our poetry:

> The hot southern sun shines down on the brown and glossy muscles of the work gang. The picks make whirling rainbow arcs around the shoulders of the singers. As the picks dig into the rock, the men give a deep, guttural grunt; their pent-up strength flows through the pick handle and they relax their bodies and prepare for the next blow.
>
> The song leader now begins—pick handle twirling in his palms, the pickhead flashing in the sun:
>
> *Take this hammo—Huh!*
>
> The men grunt as the picks bite in together. They join the leader on his line, trailing in, one in harmony, one talking the words, another grunting them out between clenched teeth, another throwing out a high, thin falsetto cry above the rest. On the final syllable, the picks are descending and again they bite a chip out of the rock and again there is a grunting exhalation of breath:
>
> *Carry it to my Captain—Huh!*
>
> The picks whirl up together in the sunlight and down again, they ring on the earth together, with maybe one or two bouncing a couple of times in a sort of syncopation. When the leader comes to the third—
>
> *Carry it to my Captain*
>
> he holds on to the word "captain" as long as he can, looks around at the boss and grins; his buddies chuckle and relax for a moment,

knowing he is giving them a little rest; then, "wham" the steel
bites at the rock and the whole gang roars out the final line, so
that the hill gives back the sound.

The way the group responds to the leader here—one voice slipping in har-
monically, another talking words, a third grunting them, a fourth lifting a
falsetto cry over the rest—is a polyrhythmic variation on the West Indian
and West African call-and-response pattern. The song takes possession of a
hard, imposed experience and challenges the nature of work itself by chang-
ing the framework of the workers. The singer supplies the beat and relieves
the tedium, transposing the space, creating a different relationship to time.
In *Black Culture and Black Consciousness*, the historian Lawrence W. Levine
argues:

> Secular work songs resembled the spirituals in that their end-
> less rhythmic and verbal repetitions could transport the singers
> beyond time, make them oblivious of their immediate surround-
> ings and create a state of what Wilfrid Mellers has referred to as
> "ritualistic hypnosis" which made it possible to persevere under
> the least favorable circumstances.

Mellers also notes that "the chant becomes a positive rhythmic ecstasy, rather
than a negative numbing of pain" (*Music in a New Found Land*). The expe-
rience is time-stopping and becomes a medium of transcendence.

"Southern Road" is shadowed by this thick background, but as a written
work of art it removes the work song from its immediate sociohistorical
context. The lyric loses its primary function—no one ever thought it was
going to be sung on the road—and thus becomes non-utilitarian, a different
kind of animal, which behaves in a different way. When an individual singer
such as Lead Belly puts a personal stamp on "Take This Hammer" (1940),
it also changes function, but, at least in Lead Belly's case, it is haunted by
memory and experience. For example, he summoned up his own time on a
prison farm in Angola, Louisiana, when he added *haah* at the end of each
line and included a stanza about refusing the paltry prison food, corn bread
and molasses, which, as he phrases it, "hurts my pride." As a collector and
writer rather than an informant, Brown compensates by asking the poem to

do independent symbolic work. He creates a speaker with a particular history and textualizes the feeling of an individual testifying to the community. He models the relationship between the singer and the group but his poem doesn't sing and so he supplies a storytelling value that is missing from the oral source. It has a lyric bluesy element.

Brown noted that the work song sometimes gets close to the blues. Here, if you change the lineation and drop the choral response, you have a slightly foreshortened but otherwise classic three-line blues stanza. Changing the lineation in this way also emphasizes the rhyme, which belongs to the blues and not the work song tradition.

> White man tells me damn yo' soul;
> White man tells me damn yo' soul;
> Got no need, bebby, to be tole.

This is apt because the work song contributed to the statement-and-response pattern of the blues, which retains elements of the field holler. Like the classical four-line ballad stanza, the blues form is a good vehicle for telling a story of any length, but it stages a different sort of drama through its repetitions. Here's a blues verse that Brown admired:

> I'm goin' down to de river, take my rockin' chair,
> Yes, down to de river, rock in my rockin' chair,
> If de blues overcome me, I'm gonna rock on away from here.

Brown imitates the blues form undisguised in his three-part sequence "New St. Louis Blues." The first stanza of part two, "Tornado Blues," shows how he works the form:

> Black wind come-a-speedin' down de river from de Kansas plains,
> Black wind come-a-speedin' down de river from de Kansas plains,
> Black wind come-a roarin' like a flock of giant aeroplanes—

The blues are more personalized than the work song since the call-and-response pattern remains, but the singer tells his or her own story. In *Blues People*, Amiri Baraka (LeRoi Jones) argues that the form resonates with a powerful individual ethos that would have been alien to African society and thus shows a high degree of American acculturation. Thus, the blues becomes a more characteristically American form of verbal art.

We hear the voice of an individual in "Southern Road." At the beginning of the poem that voice is almost neutral, even generalized, as if a speaker is trying to keep himself and his crew on an even keel—"Swing dat hammer— hunh— / Steady, bo'"—since he knows they have a heavy load to carry and a long way to go. In the next stanza, he refers to his crime metaphorically, in logging terms, suggesting "Burner tore his—hunh— / Black heart away"— and this lack of heart, some cold unnamed crime, led to his sentence: "Got me life, bebby, / An' a day." The last line here has a rueful, comic punch, as if to say that the sentence will get the better of him, lasting even beyond his death.

So, too, in the penultimate line of the second stanza, we discover the repetition of the word *bebby*, which recurs at precisely this point in every stanza, so that it becomes something the reader starts to listen for, a small refrain or staple point. The word takes on many valences over the course of the poem and suggests variously that someone is speaking to an intimate, exclaiming aloud, calming himself down, talking to himself or his crew—putting the reader in the position of a listener, almost a confidante.

The speaker becomes more personal in the third and fourth stanzas. He's got a woman working the street, a son who disappeared for good, a wife having a baby, and a father who died cursing him. He's not just a victim of white people alone; he participates in his own fate. Every time he states something, say, "Gal's on Fifth Street," the group punctuates and interrupts his story, creating a refrain, "hunh," before he continues, "Son done gone." The voice of the group recedes when the punch line drops: "Wife's in de ward, bebby, / Babe's not bo'n."

Brown once said that he modeled the speaker of "Southern Road" on the character of Calvin "Big Boy" Davis, a traveling guitar player who is also the speaker of "Odyssey of Big Boy," a poem that begins with a singer's call for community with a race's folk heroes:

> Lemme be wid Casey Jones,
> Lemme be wid Stagolee,
> Lemme be wid such like men

When Death takes hol' on me,
When Death takes hol' on me. . . .

Brown reported that he first learned about John Henry from Davis, who was an ex-coalminer. There are often verses attached to "Take This Hammer" about the legendary "steel-driving man," who boasted that no machine could ever break him down. His presence often overhangs and valorizes the song. For example, the folklorist Newman Ivey White published this variant in 1915:

This old hammer killed John Henry,
But it can't kill me.
Take this old hammer, take it to the Captain,
Tell him I'm gone, babe, tell him I'm gone.

Mississippi John Hurt featured a poignant version of these lines in "Spike Driver Blues" (1928), which gained recognition in Harry Smith's ground-breaking six-album compilation, *The Anthology of American Folk Music* (1952). Big Boy Davis also stands at the center of Brown's poem "When de Saints Go Ma'ching Home," where the spiritual becomes the vehicle for the singer to create his "chant of saints." This phrase, which recalls the Gregorian chant "The Litany of the Saints," is so resonant that Michael S. Harper and Robert B. Stepto borrowed it as the title for their gathering of African American literature, art, and scholarship: *Chant of Saints* (1979).

Brown captures the fierce undercurrent of pain in the blues. As he put it, "Irony, stoicism, and bitterness are deeply but not lingeringly expressed." One striking feature of "Southern Road" is the way the speaker moves through his own story. In the last four stanzas, he returns to the present. The tense is subtly managed, the verbs noticeable: "My ole man *died*—hunh— / Cussin' me; / Ole lady *rocks*, bebby, / Huh misery." The loaded word, *rocks*, propels him back. There are no verbs at all in the next stanza:

Doubleshackled—hunh—
Guard behin';
Doubleshackled—hunh—
Guard behin';

202 THE HEART OF AMERICAN POETRY

> Ball an' chain, bebby,
> On my min'.

This sense of an ongoing present enlarges into an allegory in the penultimate stanza. Race is explicitly referred to only twice in the poem, in the second stanza ("Burner tore his—hunh— / Black heart away") and now near the end of the poem:

> White man *tells* me—hunh—
> Damn yo' soul;
> White man *tells* me—hunh—
> Damn yo' soul;
> Got no need, bebby,
> *To be tole.*

"Southern Road" is a dramatic work song, but it is also an understated, angular protest poem like the original work song, and the white man here becomes a representative figure, a cruel guard who by swearing and eternally damning the prisoner implicates and condemns himself.

There is a tragic undertow to the close of this work song. The narrator knows in his bones that the chain gang will never release him:

> Chain gang nevah—hunh—
> Let me go;
> Chain gang nevah—hunh—
> Let me go;
> Po' los' boy, bebby,
> Evahmo' . . .

Heart-wrenching is the speaker, supposedly a hardened criminal, who refers to himself as a poor lost boy. The final ellipsis is heart-stopping because the agonizing work feels as if it will go on forever. The road is endless and a disconsolate person, who is part of a doomed group, needs poetry to keep going.

Sterling A. Brown gave a poetry reading in Detroit in November 1981. I pretended that I had known his work all along and got him to sign my book, which he did graciously, though he wasn't fooled. He had the spring issue of *Obsidian* under his arm and said, "For a long time I thought I was the model for Ralph Ellison's *Invisible Man*, but now I see that I was just off standing in the shadows." It was a wry, funny, poignant thing to say. There are some decisive turns in any education, moments when someone hands you a hammer, and the experience of reading and writing about Sterling A. Brown's *Collected Poems* was one of mine. Now when I reread "Southern Road," I think of all the people who stand behind it, some of them legendary like John Henry, others of them known, such as Big Boy Davis, but most of them anonymous, lost to the record, all those singers and workers who re-created and reclaimed a song to transcend their circumstance and turn suffering into art.

THEODORE ROETHKE (1908–1963)

Cuttings

Sticks-in-a-drowse droop over sugary loam,
Their intricate stem-fur dries;
But still the delicate slips keep coaxing up water;
The small cells bulge;

One nub of growth
Nudges a sand-crumb loose,
Pokes through a musty sheath
Its pale tendrilous horn.

Cuttings (later)

This urge, wrestle, resurrection of dry sticks,
Cut stems struggling to put down feet,
What saint strained so much,
Rose on such lopped limbs to a new life?

I can hear, underground, that sucking and sobbing,
In my veins, in my bones I feel it,—
The small waters seeping upward,
The tight grains parting at last.
When sprouts break out,
Slippery as fish,
I quail, lean to beginnings, sheath-wet.

1948

A SATURDAY MORNING in September 1979, a perfect fall day in the Midwest, football weather. I had recently moved to Detroit for my first teaching job, and I felt a sudden urge to get in the car and drive north on I-75 for a hundred miles, to sail past Warren and Flint into the Saginaw Valley—the towns are gritty, but the countryside is ancient, flat, and vast. "Michigan seems like a dream to me now," Simon & Garfunkel sang on the cassette, "I've gone to look for America." When I arrived in Saginaw, which had once been a magnet for German settlers in the lumber trade, I bought orchids and roses at a local floral shop, parked the car on the corner of Gratiot and Midland Roads, and walked through Oakwood Cemetery to section 86, lot 394, where Theodore Roethke (1908–1963) is buried next to his parents, Otto T. Roethke (1872–1923) and Helen Huebner Roethke (1881–1955). I stood in a light wind and felt "the dry scent of a dying garden in September" and placed my flowers on the nubby ground. I don't know how long I stayed there, out of respect, not praying, though every now and then the odd line popped into my head, such as "God, give me a near. I hear flowers" or "I've crawled from the mire, alert as a saint or a dog." I had meant to drive past the Roethke house on Gratiot Avenue afterward—it's just a couple of miles away—but I was unsettled and forgot and wheeled back onto the highway toward my new home.

Theodore Roethke pitted himself against oblivion—"I practice at walking the void," he said—and was not afraid of the strange, the uncanny, the mysterious. He grew up in the harsh soil and savage climate of central Michigan, where his family owned a twenty-five-acre set of greenhouses. His grandfather, Wilhelm, had been the Prussian chancellor's chief forester before immigrating to America and starting a floral company. His father and his uncle Charles, who lived next door, eventually built it into the largest complex of greenhouses in the state. Roethke wondered whether they did it out of love or some "obscure guilt" for coming from such warlike Germanic tribes. They were violent men with green thumbs. Something was off in the family wiring, and it was rumored that they had *einen nagel im kopf,* "a nail in the head," an expression for arrogant eccentricity. As a boy, Roethke roamed the property, near and far, especially a game sanctuary that the family maintained—"a wild area of cut-over second-growth timber"—and dwelled in the midst of rocks and plants, weeds and moss. There were flowers of all kinds, especially orchids and roses, his father's specialty. Subsequently, the world of the greenhouse came to stand for the lost country of childhood and, at the same time, to serve as the central symbol, both the heaven and hell, of his poetic universe.

The men in Roethke's family clashed over something or other, probably the fate of the business, and sold the greenhouses in 1922. Roethke was a young teenager when his father died of cancer a few months later, and the kingdom of his childhood collapsed. As his biographer Allan Seager points out, "what he lost when the dirt fell in his father's grave was going to take him the rest of his life to learn." Nothing more momentous ever happened to him, and his Oedipal love and fear of his father, which is encapsulated in his most well-known lyric, "My Papa's Waltz," was inextricably intertwined with his passionate, idiosyncratic feelings for nature. As he recalled in his late poem "Otto":

> In my mind's eye I see those fields of glass,
> As I looked out at them from the high house,
> Riding beneath the moon, hid from the moon,
> Then slowly breaking whiter in the dawn;
> When George the watchman's lantern dropped from sight
> The long pipes knocked: it was the end of night.
> I'd stand upon my bed, a sleepless child
> Watching the waking of my father's world.—
> O world so far away! O my lost world!

Roethke never recovered from childhood, but like a spunky, roaring, post-war American version of Rilke, who counseled the young poet Franz Xaver Kappus to "raise up the sunken feelings of this enormous past," he turned it into fertile soil for his art. It was this feeling for a vanished midwestern childhood as well as the poet's sense of forever being "the lost son"—to use the title of his second book—that first drew me into the world of Roethke's poetry in the early 1970s.

Roethke links the moderns he ingested, like D. H. Lawrence ("For Lawrence and I are going the same way: down: / A loosening into the dark") and Dylan Thomas ("This rare heedless fornicator of language") to the poets reading him, such as Ted Hughes, Sylvia Plath, Seamus Heaney, Robert

Bly, W. S. Merwin, and James Dickey, who considered him the greatest twentieth-century American poet. All these poets schooled themselves on Roethke's dark pastorals; they were especially influenced by the way that he traveled backward and tried to recover primordial experience. As he phrased it in a notebook entry: "A poem that is the shape of the psyche itself; in times of great stress, that's what I tried to write."

The deep-seated struggle to become a poet is one of the defining features of Roethke's life. He possessed what in a student essay he called "a driving sincerity" and all his life considered himself an initiate, "a perpetual beginner." He loved the catchy, strongly stressed rhythms of Mother Goose and other folk material, and he incorporated them into hilarious nonsense poems and innovatory long sequences. A childlike orality—"I sing a small sing"—with an undertow of need or longing is one of the hallmarks of his poetry: "Snail, snail, glister me forward, / Bird, soft-sigh me home, / Worm, be with me. / This is my hard time" ("The Lost Son"). He caressed the primitive sounds of words and believed that "repetition in word and phrase and in idea is the very essence of poetry."

Roethke was a huge, dancing bear of a man, a heavy drinker and "ring-tailed roarer." He had gargantuan emotional needs, disabling insecurities, and insatiable appetites. Sunk in what he called "a full-life crisis," he suffered from periodic bouts of mental illness. His sense of himself could be wobbly and he often overcompensated. As a young writer, he sought out mentors and made strong early alliances with Rolfe Humphries and Louise Bogan, with whom he had a tumultuous affair—"I hope that one or two immortal lyrics will come out of all this tumbling around," she said—that metamorphosed into a sweet lifelong attachment. He showed up unannounced at Stanley Kunitz's house in the Delaware Valley, mumbling compliments and clutching a copy of Kunitz's first book tucked under his left paw. They stayed up all night drinking and talking about poetry. "The image that never left," Kunitz later recalled, "was of a blond, smooth, shambling giant, irrevocably Teutonic, with a cold pudding of a face, somehow contradicted by the sullen downturn of the mouth and the pale furious eyes: a countenance ready to be touched by time, waiting to be transfigured, with a few subtle lines, into a tragic mask."

Roethke was devoted to poetry as a form of "memorable speech" and didn't so much read as devour the work of other poets—from John Donne and Sir John Davies to Emily Dickinson, W. H. Auden, and Léonie Adams. He was so absorbent that you can't always distinguish him from his models, which is why he used the nonsense poem "The Kitty-Cat Bird" to caution himself: "Be sure that whatever you are is you."

Roethke's gift for immersion helped to make him a compelling role model and teacher. He invested a mammoth amount of energy into teaching poetry, which he once said is like "lugging hunks of pork up the lower slopes of Parnassus." He did stints at Lafayette College and Pennsylvania State University, where he was also the tennis coach ("Roethke, Penn State Tennis Coach, Author of Book of Verses," the *New York Herald Tribune* announced in its "Sports Here and There" column in March 1941) before moving on to Bennington College and the University of Washington, where he spent the last fifteen years of his life. He taught students to revel in the sounds of words and conveyed his passion for every sort of verse form. He praised verbal immediacy and paid special attention to texture, rhythm, and energy, which he called "the soul of poetry." He said, "I am overwhelmed by the beautiful disorder of poetry, the eternal virginity of words."

Too young to study with him, I used to seek out testimonials by his former students, such as Carolyn Kizer, James Wright, Richard Hugo, Jack Gilbert, and Tess Gallagher. They remembered how he recited poems—he boomed and purred—and described his mercurial personality in class. Hugo said he was "arrogant, hostile, tender, aggressive, receptive." Kizer noted that though he could be high-handed toward everyone else he was "charmingly deferential" to the old people in her class, a rabbi and a sea captain, because "he said that they knew things the rest of us didn't know." Above all, as Wright put it, "A course with Roethke was a course in very, very detailed and strenuous critical reading." Roethke's disciples remembered him in the specific—his tripartite sense of dramatic structure (turn, counterturn, and stand), his idea that every line of a poem should be a poem—and the general: his impetuousness and impatience, his full-throated devotion to the art. Like Hart Crane, he liked to quote Rimbaud's idea of the "systematic derangement of all the senses," but, unlike his Romantic precursor, he invariably left off the word *systematic*. As an undergraduate, I studied with Glenn Leggett, the president of Grinnell College, who had taught with Roethke in Washington, and he regaled me with stories of his friend's intense competitiveness and vocational fire. "You don't want to play tennis with him,"

Leggett recalled, "though you do want to take his course in verse writing." He seemed to forget that Roethke had been dead for nearly ten years. "Gee," Leggett said, looking at one of my poems and channeling the growly sarcasm of the master, "maybe you should dump the participles, cut the adjectives, and tighten the rhythm." Then he blue-penciled the lines he thought were slack. I held up my poor potted plant. It was eviscerated.

I've been reading Roethke sympathetically all my life, but I've never been able to warm to his first book, *Open House* (1941), which took him ten years to write. It has a compact, witty, ironic manner alien to his natural abilities and Romantic inclinations. As a hardworking, highly susceptible young poet, he took his lead from T. S. Eliot and imitated the seventeenth-century metaphysical poets. Roethke himself later criticized the "chilly fastidiousness" and austere vision of his apprentice volume.

Roethke's breakthrough second book, *The Lost Son and Other Poems* (1948), freed him from the censors. It was as if he had suddenly discovered the American vein of Emerson and Thoreau, as if his work had gotten a transfusion from Whitman and Williams. His first book made a promise—"my secrets cry aloud" and "my heart keeps open house"—that his second fulfilled. He found his poetic when he discovered how to use free verse to make contact with the loamy soil of his childhood. The figure of the open house gives way to the memory, a poetic discovery, of the glass enclosure, a hothouse world that he called "a symbol for the whole of life, a womb, a heaven-on-earth."

The family greenhouse was for Roethke both sacred and abysmal ground, simultaneously a natural world and an artificial realm, a locale of generation and decay, order and chaos. It was wilderness brought home. The fourteen Greenhouse poems in *The Lost Son* explore the instinctual sources of life. The sequence begins with the pendant lyrics "Cuttings" and "Cuttings (*later*)," which read as a single poem separated into two parts. They are invariably considered together. Roethke admired Rilke's animal poems and tried to apply the same active, concretive method to plants. His language is thickly textured, noun clustered, as in Hopkins, and I hear "Inversnaid" in the background ("O let them be left, wildness and wet; / Long live the weeds and the wilderness yet"). Closer to home, I suspect that Williams's poem "Spring and All," which is about the difficult struggle of everything to be born and grow, stands behind this two-part sequence, though, as the son of a florist, Roethke brings a ground note of experience, a level of contact, to use one of Williams's favorite words, to his characterizations that gives them a more granular specificity. Roethke enclosed these poems in a letter to Williams in 1944 and the older poet recognized in them a fully mastered fresh sound, what he described as "a cello note, one of the lower strings, but near its upper register."

Roethke re-creates the experience of cutting a section of a living plant, replanting it, nurturing it along, inducing it to grow into independent life. It's cut off from its parent, like a person. Roethke had become almost physically allergic to abstraction, and now uses a visceral language to dramatize a small, momentous, dangerously fraught journey.

"Cuttings," which was first called "Propagation House," consists of one sentence stretched across two quatrains. The poet is trying to look at something stirring to life more acutely than it has been observed before, and so the act of seeing becomes part of the poem. Here, the speaker is personally removed, like a scientist or a filmmaker. Although the lyric is brief, you can closely trace its staging. If you wanted to shoot it in slow motion for a magazine like *Nature*, you would start by placing the camera at a certain distance. The tone is nerveless, the minidrama intense.

Hover from above:

       Sticks-in-a-drowse droop over sugary loam,

Now move in for a closer shot:

       Their intricate stem-fur dries;

Zoom all the way inside to see them absorbing water:

       But still the delicate slips keep coaxing up water;
       The small cells bulge;

Keep camera focused on something tiny peeking up tentatively from the soil:

       One nub of growth

Keep the camera steady to catch the minute nub making way for itself:

       Nudges a sand-crumb loose,

Shine the spotlight so that it finally becomes visible above ground:

> Pokes through a musty sheath
> Its pale tendrilous horn.

The poem "Cuttings (*later*)," which tracks the next stage of the journey, is more subjective, the verse irregular. The first stanza is a quatrain, which structurally continues the first poem, but the second stanza stretches out to seven lines. Bogan once sent Roethke a copy of Rilke's *Letters to a Young Poet* and advised him "to *look* at things until you don't know whether you are they or they are you," and that's the process enacted here. Another element enters the poem, something lightly, even humorously spiritual. The objectivity gives way, and you hear a distinctive voice trying to describe a stemming rebirth:

> This urge, wrestle, resurrection of dry sticks,
> Cut stems struggling to put down feet,

When I first read this, I was caught off guard by the first line because I kept expecting those first two active words—*urge, wrestle*—to act the way they usually do, as verbs, but they turn out to be nouns ("This urge, wrestle of dry sticks"). There is a progression, too, enacted through the increasing syllable count of the three words, the movement from *urge* to *wrestle* to *resurrection*. Roethke loved to key sound and so the *ur* of the word *urges* plants itself in the word *resurrection*, which has an unmistakable religious valence, though it's playfully attached to *dry sticks*. It's a tiny rising from the dead. There is no verb in these lines, which enact an infant *struggling*. I am reminded of one of Roethke's notebook entries from 1944: "I learned to struggle in the stem." There is something light-footed, too, in the way that Roethke now introduces a metaphor from the human body. The cut stems are both a plant trying to take root and a wobbly baby striving *to put down feet*.

The next question is both playful and serious: "What saint strained so much, / Rose on such lopped limbs to a new life?" If you were skeptical about the underlying meaning of *resurrection* when you initially read this, as I was, then this funny rhetorical question answers your doubt about the poet's elementary intention. Roethke has a way of being both comically self-deprecating and deadly serious at the same time. He is describing the rebirth of a plant, but he is also talking about the rebirth of a person, a self. When you leap the gap to the second and final stanza, the speaker aggressively enters the poem for the first time. You can catch him in the act of listening and speaking up:

> I can hear, underground, that sucking and sobbing,
> In my veins, in my bones I feel it,—
> The small waters seeping upward,
> The tight grains parting at last.

At first, the speaker seems as if he is putting his ear to the ground, listening to an infant-plant crying from underearth—this begins the hissing undercurrent of *s* sounds—but in the second line he feels the birth pangs inside his body. He mingles this image in the third line so that what he feels inside himself is the same water that the plant absorbs as it springs to life. By the fourth line, the plant and the speaker have merged so that the "tight grains" are parting from both the cuttings and the person.

There is an astonishing fusion in the poem's final three lines, as Roethke now weds together his imagery of the vegetal, the animal, and the human:

> When sprouts break out,
> Slippery as fish,
> I quail, lean to beginnings, sheath-wet.

Here, the tender sprouts suddenly break out; they emerge—smooth, moist, and clammy—like a fish, and the speaker quails because he is scared of what's happening, not just to the plant but to himself. He starts shaking as he moves backward toward his own *beginnings*. The precise noun, the newly coined word *sheath-wet*, recalls the "musty sheath" that first poked up in "Cuttings," though now it's become wet with slime and birth. Over the course of two short poems, a mere nineteen lines, Roethke has re-created a vulnerable experience of rebirth.

I wish I had space to linger over the entire sequence of Greenhouse poems, which explore the instinctual sources of life from the dank minimal world of roots in "Root Cellar" ("And what a congress of stinks!") to the open, flowing reality of young plants in "Transplanting" ("The whole flower extending outward, / Stretching and reaching") to the daredevil giddiness of "Child on Top of a Greenhouse" ("And everyone, everyone pointing up and shouting!"). Roethke was compulsively conscious of the agony of birth, the painful effort of things to emerge out of an underworld swarming with malevolent forces. There is a sense of "tugging all day at perverse life" in "Weed Puller," of plants acting like reptiles in "Orchids" ("So many devouring infants!"), of tearing the ground and disturbing the natural rhythms of the living planet in "Moss-Gathering" ("As if I had committed, against the whole scheme of life, a desecration"), of ferocious adult sexuality in "Big Wind," of one surviving tulip swaggering "over the dying, the newly dead" in "Flower Dump." These poems go underground to dark obsessive realms and then chart the struggle back up for light. Roethke was searching for "news of the root," the vigorous green force of life. He was determined to keep going further down, further back, to locate the primary of life, what Dylan Thomas characterized as "The force that through the green fuse drives the flower."

As I think about Roethke's contribution to the American project, I recall that the greenhouse was linked to two other discoveries that he made in the 1940s. Largely prompted by Kenneth Burke, our Coleridge, who later wrote an insightful essay about his friend's "vegetal radicalism," Roethke began to explore the poetic possibilities of the unconscious, returning to the murky realms of childhood and thus commencing what he called "the retrospective course" of a "hallucinatory dream." He also recognized that the organic process of plants could stand as a metaphor for free verse, each poem taking on its own sensuous form and intrinsic shape. This was an Emersonian notion of poetic form, a fundamental of Romantic expressiveness, and it enabled Roethke to become the figure that John Berryman dubbed "the Garden Master."

The garden has a long poetic history, and yet no one ever probed plant life quite the way Roethke did—no one got so far down in the dirt to write a spiritual autobiography. He seemed always to be thrusting himself into the past, courting childhood terrors, struggling to be born and born again, to climb out of the slime and make something more of himself. Sometimes he viewed human beings "as no more than a shape writhing from the old rock." He believed that this view came to him, at least in part, from his Michigan childhood. "Sometimes one gets the feeling that not even the animals have been here before," he said, "but the marsh, the mire, the Void, is always there, immediate and terrifying." This was where he schooled his spirit. We don't usually think of flower poems as terrifying, but there is nothing of the bright pastoral in Roethke's view of the green world. He goes down to the depths before he hits the heights. He looks at things until he loses himself and becomes them. Then he struggles to separate. There is mortal dread and mental anguish in his difficult descents, tentative reawakenings, and ecstatic fusions. That's why the Greenhouse poems have such harrowing force.

Theodore Roethke never forgot where he came from. He was an exemplar of the poetic extreme, the one who went to the edge, who modeled the commitment. When I consider the totality of his project, I also like to think about a September morning many years ago when I impulsively decided to drive to Saginaw to visit his gravesite. I was nervous and excited about beginning my first university job, and it seemed whimsical to take the day off when I had so much still to prepare. I realize now that I wasn't just paying my respects to one of my formative poets, but also summoning his example and presence. I was touching the soil and reminding myself of the cost, the calling, and the vision.

In the Waiting Room

In Worcester, Massachusetts,
I went with Aunt Consuelo
to keep her dentist's appointment
and sat and waited for her
in the dentist's waiting room.
It was winter. It got dark
early. The waiting room
was full of grown-up people,
arctics and overcoats,
lamps and magazines.
My aunt was inside
what seemed like a long time
and while I waited I read
the *National Geographic*
(I could read) and carefully
studied the photographs:
the inside of a volcano,
black, and full of ashes;
then it was spilling over
in rivulets of fire.
Osa and Martin Johnson
dressed in riding breeches,
laced boots, and pith helmets.
A dead man slung on a pole
—"Long Pig," the caption said.
Babies with pointed heads
wound round and round with string;
black, naked women with necks

wound round and round with wire
like the necks of light bulbs.
Their breasts were horrifying.
I read it right straight through.
I was too shy to stop.
And then I looked at the cover:
the yellow margins, the date.
Suddenly, from inside,
came an *oh!* of pain
—Aunt Consuelo's voice—
not very loud or long.
I wasn't at all surprised;
even then I knew she was
a foolish, timid woman.
I might have been embarrassed,
but wasn't. What took me
completely by surprise
was that it was *me*:
my voice, in my mouth.
Without thinking at all
I was my foolish aunt,
I—we—were falling, falling,
our eyes glued to the cover
of the *National Geographic*,
February, 1918.

I said to myself: three days
and you'll be seven years old.
I was saying it to stop
the sensation of falling off
the round, turning world.
into cold, blue-black space.
But I felt: you are an *I*,
you are an *Elizabeth*,
you are one of *them*.
Why should you be one, too?

I scarcely dared to look
to see what it was I was.
I gave a sidelong glance
—I couldn't look any higher—
at shadowy gray knees,
trousers and skirts and boots
and different pairs of hands
lying under the lamps.
I knew that nothing stranger
had ever happened, that nothing
stranger could ever happen.

Why should I be my aunt,
or me, or anyone?
What similarities—
boots, hands, the family voice
I felt in my throat, or even
the *National Geographic*
and those awful hanging breasts—
held us all together
or made us all just one?
How—I didn't know any
word for it—how "unlikely" . . .
How had I come to be here,
like them, and overhear
a cry of pain that could have
got loud and worse but hadn't?

The waiting room was bright
and too hot. It was sliding
beneath a big black wave,
another, and another.

Then I was back in it.
The War was on. Outside,
in Worcester, Massachusetts,

were night and slush and cold,
and it was still the fifth
of February, 1918.

                    1971

ELIZABETH BISHOP described the world with a scrupulous, exacting, variegated, almost offhanded virtuosity that is still startling. She had a keen eye and a painterly gift, and she looked at things in a way that incites you to look at them again—more closely and more truly. She was a precisionist. Randall Jarrell was characteristically observant and set the terms for discussion when he reviewed Bishop's first book and said, "All her poems have written underneath, *I have seen it.*" This is accurate, and yet it doesn't quite account for the near-visionary intensity of her poetry. Bishop observes everything with such minute and patient attention—objects, creatures, landscapes—that it all starts to seem more foreign and improbable. Reality becomes stranger. There was a strong element of anxiety and at times even desperation that gave her descriptive hold on the world so much of its tenacious force. "Surely there is an element of mortal panic and fear underlying all works of art?" she asked in her memoir of Marianne Moore, "Efforts of Affection." Surely there's more than an element of such mortal panic and fear—there's a deep oceanic undertow—in most of Bishop's characteristic poems.

Here is a key passage in Bishop's letter to Anne Stevenson about Charles Darwin, which reveals a great deal about her practice. It clarifies why Bishop is a subjective poet of vision as well as an objective one of eyesight.

> There is no "split." Dreams, works of art (some), glimpses of the always-more-successful surrealism of everyday life, unexpected moments of empathy (is it?), catch a peripheral vision of whatever it is one can never really see full-face but that seems enormously important. I can't believe we are wholly irrational—and I do admire Darwin! But reading Darwin, one admires the beautiful solid case being built up out of his endless heroic *observations*, almost unconscious or automatic—and then comes a sudden relaxation, a forgetful phrase, and one *feels* the strangeness of

his undertaking, sees the lonely young man, his eyes fixed on facts and minute details, sinking or sliding giddily off into the unknown. What one seems to want in art, in experiencing it, is the same thing that is necessary for its creation, a self-forgetful, perfectly useless concentration.

Bishop has been overpraised for her reticence and modesty and under-appreciated for her painstaking heroic observations that suddenly give way and swerve off into the unknown. Like Wordsworth, she's an odder, dreamier, and at times more introspective poet than most criticism would allow. She's also nervous about her own introspectiveness—she's afraid of falling through endless interior corridors—and tethers herself to the watery world, the wet and sandy shoreline. In her poem "Sandpiper," she must have seen herself reflected in the sandpiper who takes the roaring of the ocean for granted and recognizes that the world is going to tremble:

> The world is a mist. And then the world is
> minute and vast and clear. The tide
> is higher or lower. He couldn't tell you which.
> His beak is focussed; he is preoccupied,
>
> looking for something, something, something.
> Poor bird, he is obsessed!

Bishop was a homeless traveler, a nervous quester, a seeker who sometimes saw the world as a mist and sometimes as minute and vast and clear.

Elizabeth Bishop was born in Worcester, Massachusetts, in 1911. Her father, William Thomas Bishop, died of Bright's disease when she was eight months old; her mother, Gertrude May (Bulmer) Bishop, suffered a series of severe mental breakdowns and was permanently committed to an asylum when her daughter was five years old (see the chilling story "In the Village"). She never saw her mother again. At first she lived with her maternal grandparents, whom she adored, on a farm in Great Village, Nova Scotia. But her father's much more prosperous family was horrified by the poverty of her Canadian relatives and brought her back—unconsulted, against her will—to Worcester, where she lived in a large, gloomy, old colonial house. She felt she had been "kidnapped." She rarely spoke—"I felt myself aging, even dying," she recalled—and learned to conceal herself. Over a nine-month period, she developed eczema, asthma, and other illnesses, and so she was eventually shipped off to live with her mother's relatives in Revere, near Boston. There, she was nursed back to health by her devoted aunt Maude, but abused by her uncle George Shepherdson, a sadistic person. It was a sickly, unhappy childhood. Once she got to Vassar College, she tried not to return, though over the course of her life, she also tried to make sense of it.

A lonely child grows up to view the world as a lonely place. Bishop spent much of her life on the move and carried on what her friend James Merrill acutely called her "instinctive, modest, lifelong impersonations of an ordinary woman." She had a gift for revealing and concealing herself in her poems, for escape and transfiguration. She situated her four poetry collections geographically: *North and South* (1946), *Poems: North & South/ A Cold Spring* (1955), *Questions of Travel* (1965), *Geography III* (1976). She had many amorous outbursts and a few long-lasting love affairs, especially with Lota de Macedo Soares and Alice Methfessel, and her compulsively readable letters to Robert Lowell and other poets suggest that she had a gift for the lifeline friendship. But loneliness is woven into the fabric of her writing. She was descriptively lush but personally guarded and gave herself away only reluctantly. She did not view herself as a victim—"Please don't think I dote on it," she said with characteristic rectitude in a letter about her mother's mental illness—but naturally identified with misfits and outlanders. There is a long line of misallied and misshapen creatures in her work, from "The Man-Moth," which she wrote in 1936, to "Pink Dog" ("Oh, never have I seen a dog so bare!"), which she completed before her untimely death in 1979.

This brings me to the quietly intense and self-revealing dramatic lyric "In the Waiting Room," which tries to answer a question that usually goes unasked: What is the first time you realized that you had an actual, identifiable self? This question immediately puts you on shaky or tentative ground—is it desirable or even possible to recover and re-create such a singular moment in poetry or therapy or anywhere else? Is such a realization invented or recalled? Bishop fearlessly enters this fraught terrain in her deceptive, ambitious, and artful poem.

David Kalstone was the first critic to write about Bishop's immersion in her childhood experiences when she began her life with Lota de Macedo Soares in Brazil. In *Becoming a Poet*, he pointed out that "The Country Mouse," a reminiscence in which the visit to the dentist with her aunt Jenny is described on the last page, was written in 1961 but only published posthumously in *The Collected Prose* (1984). It is a prose draft of the experience that is more acutely rendered and fully realized in "In the Waiting Room." Bishop returned to the subject and reconceptualized the memory after a period of great upheaval in her life. It was the first poem she completed after the death of her longtime lover and companion, who had committed suicide in 1967. After nearly two decades in Brazil, Bishop had been moving around the United States for three years—"The trouble is, I really don't know where or how I want to live anymore," she confided to a friend—and had just settled in Boston and started teaching at Harvard. She surprised herself by completing "In the Waiting Room," which she published in *The New Yorker* in 1971. It is the lead poem in *Geography III*.

"In the Waiting Room" dramatizes an epiphany, a profound loss and realization of self, a painful memory of coming into self-consciousness. It enacts a child's realization that she truly has a self which simultaneously separates her from others even as it connects her to them. She reexperiences nothing less than some primary, original separation.

For "In the Waiting Room," Bishop turned to one of her favored meters, a three-beat line. The accents are so irregular and variously placed that it is practically an accentual poem. Bishop first got this meter, which she used in such poems as "The Burglar of Babylon," "Manuelzinho," and "The Moose," from Edmund Waller and W. B. Yeats, but the music of "In the Waiting Room" was most directly influenced by the Brazilian poet Carlos Drummond de Andrade, whose trimeter poem "Poema de Sete Faces" (Seven-Sided Poem) she translated into English. It was a meter she could pace, sometimes dialing it toward prose, sometimes pitching it toward song, nervously speeding it up or calmly slowing it down.

The extant drafts of "In the Waiting Room" in the Vassar College Library show that Bishop first conceived of her ninety-nine-line poem as a single stanzaic unit, an organic whole, one long push, but later divided it into five irregular stanzas for emphasis. This verse paragraphing gives it more breathing room and segmentation. She labored the tenses, which troubled her, and struggled with the punctuation, which she nailed, but the poem was remarkably composed from the beginning. The rhythm was there, and so was the emotional starting point, the surprised experience. She knew what she was about, the feeling of lostness she was after.

Bishop's lyric starts by establishing a firm sense of locale—a recognizable setting, a clear narrative coherence. It is winter in Worcester, Massachusetts; the protagonist is waiting for her aunt in the public space of the lobby at the dentist's office. It is a darkening winter day, and she is surrounded by other people, all strangers. The poem is spatially static. This mundane, generic space, neither outside nor inside, is an unlikely setting for a poem. In *A Lover's Discourse*, Roland Barthes claimed that "wherever there is waiting there is transference," and this particular waiting room becomes a transference situation, a place for psychological projection. It is notable that Bishop identifies both the city and the state where she was born, a place where she was unhealthy, a city she loathed and tried not to know. Whenever she writes about Worcester, a queasy sense of unhappiness shadows the poem.

Bishop declared that she *always* told the truth in her poems. She insisted that she was faithful to facts, literal reality. Like her role model Marianne Moore, she prided herself on meticulous descriptions and accountings. This was a way of authenticating her work, emphasizing the documentary record, but it was not quite accurate. In truth, she often made small changes and adjusted the facts. "In the Waiting Room" is an autobiographical poem, but a few of the details are changed. As she put it in a letter to Frank Bidart, "it is almost a true story." Bishop did not have an Aunt Consuelo, for example. Out of tact, she withheld the name of her actual relative, Aunt Florence, whom she considered "a foolish, timid woman."

Bishop also specifies the precise issue of *National Geographic* that she was reading (February 1918), but, as Jerome Mazzaro first pointed out, she "tampers with the actual contents." The February issue did feature an article on volcanoes, extravagantly titled "The Valley of Ten Thousand Smokes: An Account of the Discovery and Exploration of the Most Wonderful Volcanic Region in the World." It also featured the explorers Osa and Martin Johnson, who are dressed identically, androgynously. But there were no photographs of African babies or women. When asked about it, Bishop said her memory had conflated the February and March issues of the magazine. But what she called the "African things" were not to be found there either. What is key, however, is that for the first half of the twentieth century *National*

Geographic was one of the few places where one could see topless or half-naked women's bodies. Under cover of "science," the field of anthropology, sexuality was on display.

"In the Waiting Room" notably re-creates a scene of reading. The poem often blurs and inhabits two perspectives—the adult's observations and memories, the child's viewpoint. The language is flat and childlike. The first sentence rolls along naturally enough: "In Worcester, Massachusetts, / I went with Aunt Consuelo / to keep her dentist's appointment / and sat and waited for her / in the dentist's waiting room." But then there is a quiet change in the clipping of the sentences and the syncopation of the lines:

> It was winter. It got dark
> early.

The brief hesitation on the word *dark* is disquieting. You are almost unaware of how casually the language has drifted to the child's vocabulary: "The waiting room / was full of *grown-up people*." The narrator sounds like a soon-to-be-seven-year-old when she parenthetically boasts: "(*I could read*)."

This newly initiated reader is riveted by the photographs and fascinated by images of "nature": a volcano spilling over, two adventurers or hunters standing next to "a dead man slung on a pole," and, most shockingly, babies with pointed heads "wound round and round with string" and "black, naked women with necks / wound round and round with wire / like the necks of light bulbs." She is stunned to see the women so bound up and exposed, irremediably—horrifyingly—marked by gender. I would call her experience "uncanny," which, as Freud described it, "is the name for everything that ought to have remained hidden and secret and has become visible." She is glimpsing what was not intended to be seen—at least by her. It is likely that she was also embarrassed by her newly awakened sexual attraction to women's bodies. That would be one reason that she was "too shy to stop."

Turning away, the speaker looks at the cover of the magazine, fixing it in her mind—a marker of ordinary time, which she is about to leave. She is moving outside the yellow margins, as it were, outside the date, as she passes from external eyesight to internal vision. As in Wordsworth's *Prelude*, the word *Suddenly* marks the crisis point in the poem, delineating a threshold experience.

> Suddenly, from inside,
> came an *oh!* of pain
> —Aunt Consuelo's voice—
> not very loud or long.

There is a clever pun on the word *inside*: the voice is coming from inside the other room, apparently from Aunt Consuelo, but, also, surprisingly, from inside herself:

> What took me
> completely by surprise
> was that it was *me*:
> my voice, in my mouth.

The speaker is experiencing a greater degree of interiorization. Self is turning into something Other, that "I—we—were falling, falling." As she discovers that she is identical to her silly aunt, the protagonist is falling outside the recognizable boundaries even as she tries to fix the date of the magazine in her head. She tries to hold on to the familiar world by telling herself (and us) that she is almost seven years old. She is unsuccessfully trying to cling to what she already knows in order to keep from falling off the far edges of experience. She is free-floating now, losing her previous sense of gravity, responding to an enormous hole that is opening inside of her, in the narrative sequence of her life. She is intuiting that she is, in fact, a separate self, a named person, an *Elizabeth*, recognizable to others, simultaneously Other to herself, "one of *them*"—a female, a human being. In one sense, she is still inside the waiting room, but in another she has floated into space. Here, the poet carefully modulates the line breaks for emphasis:

> I knew that *nothing stranger*
> had ever happened, that *nothing*
> *stranger* could ever happen.

The real world is completely estranged; she is tumbling into an abyss.

The speaker is simultaneously meditating and commenting on what is happening to her; she is puzzling it out for herself, trying to come to grips with the knowledge of having a self that seems both knowable and unknowable. For a brief moment, the gap between language and actuality becomes the subject:

> How—I didn't know any
> word for it—how "unlikely" . . .

The modest and understated word *unlikely*, a characteristic Bishop word, is literally accurate even as it suggests the inability of language to capture the intensity of experience. How *unlikely*, the poem reminds us, it is to be anyone at all. What a strange and specific constellation of factors comes together in the shaping of an identity. The thought trails off in an ellipsis. There is no precise answer to the question, "How had I come to be here, / like them, and overhear / a cry of pain that could have / got loud and worse but hadn't?" Bishop is a trustworthy witness here because she does not overstate that cry of pain.

The next stanza, a mere quatrain, prolongs the experience for a final moment. This is the most lyrical instant in the poem precisely because it decisively interrupts the narrative momentum. It creates a hole in the story line through a sense of time stretched out. Notice the passive voice, simple repetition, and syntactic parallelism, as well as the compulsive stutter over the letter *b*:

> The waiting room *was bright*
> and too hot. It *was sliding*
> *b*eneath a *b*ig *b*lack wave,
> another, and another.

The room was both too hot and too bright. In such moments of pure duration, the philosopher Henri Bergson writes, "our perceptions and memories acquire an indefinable quality, comparable to heat or light" ("On the Intensity of Psychological States"). Such a moment is intensely physical and uncomfortable. It is as if the speaker recoils or needs to hide from the intensity of what she is "seeing" even as the room seems to be sliding into some primal darkness, an unindividuated place, a succession of waves. The lens is bright, the ground uncertain.

Then comes the conclusion of the poem. You can see the pulley working on the word *then*, which in the epiphanic mode marks a turn or return to a different level of time.

> *Then* I was back in it.
> The War was on. Outside,
> in Worcester, Massachusetts,
> were night and slush and cold,
> and it was still the fifth
> of February, 1918.

Thus, she turns from the intense brightness and heat that she has just experienced to the dark coldness of the external world. She has been "out of it" and now she is "back in it." The short declarative sentence—"The War was on"—is a non sequitur. This observation, which also jumps out of "The Country Mouse," comes from an adult perspective. World War I was still going on, but the overtone is unmistakable that another kind of War was being waged, which is the interior struggle between isolated selfhood and collective identity, between naked and clothed bodies, between her childhood and adult selves.

The speaker of Bishop's poem is now back in the wintry world; she has been cast into the realm of linear time, which carries with it the hard knowledge of mortality, of the fact that you will die. The lineation—"The War was on. Outside"—brings together the War and the external world. The line break emphasizes the world *Outside*, Outsiderness. We're placed back in Worcester, Massachusetts: night, slush, cold. The date has stayed the same. In one sense, nothing has changed, but in another sense, for her everything has changed. She has lost and reconstituted herself. She returns to the outer dark where it is still February 5 with a sense of the utter strangeness of life itself, with what Yeats calls "a new knowledge of reality."

"When you write my epitaph," Bishop wrote to Lowell in 1974, "you must say I was the loneliest person who ever lived." That sense of existential isolation drives Bishop's work, which is outwardly reserved and inwardly anguished, carefully well made, and cool to the touch, but also deeply fevered and molten underneath. She was a poet of what she calls "a self-forgetful, perfectly useless concentration," but she was also a poet of soul-making.

ROBERT JOHNSON (1911–1938)

Cross Road Blues [Take 2]

I went to the crossroad
    fell down on my knees
I went to the crossroad
    fell down on my knees
Asked the Lord above "Have mercy
    save poor Bob, if you please"

Mmmmm, standin' at the crossroad
    I tried to flag a ride
Standin' at the crossroad
    I tried to flag a ride
Didn't nobody seem to know me
    everybody pass me by

Mmm, the sun goin' down, boy
    dark gon' catch me here
ooo ooee eeee
    boy, dark gon' catch me here
I haven't got my lovin' sweet woman that
    love and feel my care

You can run, you can run
    tell my friend-boy Willie Brown
You can run, you can run
    tell my friend-boy Willie Brown
Lord, that I'm standin' at the crossroad, babe
    I believe I'm sinkin' down

1937

228 THE HEART OF AMERICAN POETRY

FROM THE time he was twenty-one years old, Robert Johnson was a walking musician, a country blues singer and guitarist who played house parties and juke joints. He was a magpie who picked up and mastered the Mississippi Delta blues style from Willie Brown, Son House, and Charley Patton. He learned popular songs from the radio and listened hard to the phonograph records of Kokomo Arnold, Skip James, Leroy Carr, and especially Lonnie Johnson, whom he idolized to the point that he sometimes claimed that they were brothers. He had a wonderfully lonesome, high, tragic voice, an aching sound, a falsetto that could turn into a lost and broken howl, and a way of playing acoustic slide guitar so that it let off a series of precise percussive shocks. His versatile bottleneck playing was unexampled—he was a rounded rhythm section unto himself—and helped him display his uncanny voice. He was a vernacular African American artist working in the Jim Crow South during the Great Depression, and his lyrics are intensely dramatic, fateful, wary, and doom-ridden. Philip Larkin said that "poetry is emotional in nature and theatrical in operation," and that's how I think of Robert Johnson's twenty-nine songs, one apex of the blues tradition.

Johnson recorded "Cross Road Blues," which he had been performing for some four years, in an improvised studio in room 414 of the Gunter Hotel in San Antonio, Texas, on November 27, 1936. He was twenty-five years old and had just two more years to live. He cut two takes of the song while facing a corner of the room. He was not shy about performing, as is sometimes conjectured, and was not hiding his technique from observers; rather, he was corner loading, creating a reverb-like effect and more muscular sound by bouncing it off the walls. The first take was released by ARC/Vocalion as a 78 rpm record in May of the next year with "Ramblin' on My Mind" on the flip side. It took several decades for the second take to be released on *King of the Delta Blues Singers* (Columbia, 1961). Both takes were eventually released on the Columbia box set of *The Complete Recordings* (1990).

It was the second take, which is slower and tighter, that inspired a freewheeling cover by Cream in *Wheels of Fire* (1968). I belong to a generation of rock-and-roll kids who were mesmerized by Eric Clapton's explosive four-minute electric guitar solo on "Crossroads," which was recorded live at the San Francisco Fillmore Auditorium. The noise was so loud at the venue that night, Clapton admitted, that he played most of the solo on the wrong beat. He considered Johnson the most significant blues singer who had ever lived—"It was as if I had been prepared to receive Robert Johnson, almost like a religious experience," he declared—and later recorded fourteen of Johnson's other songs on the album *Me and Mr. Johnson* (2004). We also discovered the steep rock-and-roll evocation of Johnson through the Rolling Stones cover of Johnson's song "Stop Breaking Down," which was part of an entire album, *Exile on Main St.* (1972), infused with Johnson's bluesy spirit. Keith Richards said later that the first time he heard Johnson's guitar playing it was almost like listening to Bach. My friends and I were eager to compare the blues originals to the rock-and-roll remakes. Listening to "Crossroads" again, we realized that Clapton had imported a stanza from one of Johnson's other songs, "Traveling Riverside Blues," which contained the line "Lord, I'm goin' to Rosedale, gon' take my rider by my side." In the meantime, a few of the music fanatics I knew had gone down to Rosedale, Mississippi, to search for the legendary crossroad, which Johnson had never included in his song.

On the most literal level, the title of Johnson's song refers to the intersection of Highways 49 and 61 outside of Clarksdale, Mississippi. For southern bluesmen, Highway 61 was the major northward route out of Mississippi toward Memphis, and thus became known as the Blues Highway, but for Bob Dylan, who memorialized it in his album *Highway 61 Revisited* (1965), it ran the other way, from north to south, Duluth to New Orleans. "Highway 61, the main thoroughfare of the country blues, begins about where I came from," Dylan wrote in *Chronicles*: "I always felt like I'd started on it, always had been on it and could go anywhere from it, even down into the deep Delta country. It was the same road, full of the same contradictions, the same one-horse towns, the same spiritual ancestors." One might say then that this is the corridor where, metaphorically speaking, Black and white musicians meet as equals, where the blues intersects with the folk revival and rock-and-roll.

There were many reasons for an itinerant African American bluesman to be scared while he was trying to catch a ride at a crossroad at dusk in the racist South. There was the danger of stray rednecks and white vandals, of white policemen who could use vagrancy laws to target anyone they considered "out of place." There was the even greater horror of getting trapped in one of the all-white "sundown towns" in which if a Black man was found outside after dark he would be brutally beaten and jailed, physically thrown out of town, or even lynched. The threat of death was real; the highest number of lynchings occurred in Mississippi. To add to the existential dread, there was also something menacing and inchoate, something sinister and frightening that the speaker can't quite identify.

There's no mention of an infernal deal at the crossroad in "Cross Road Blues," or in any other of Johnson's songs for that matter, but the legend dies hard that the bluesman sold his soul to the devil in exchange for supernatural musical gifts. That was one way to explain his preternatural talent. In his youth, Johnson copped licks directly from Son House, who later in life vividly recalled how Johnson developed from a bad guitar player to a "master" in just two years. During that time, Johnson learned to play guitar from Ike Zimmerman, who liked to say that he taught himself the blues sitting on gravestones at midnight. In Beauregard, Mississippi, Johnson lived with Zimmerman like an adopted son, even though he had a wife he had secretly married ten miles away in Hazlehurst, and it seems likely that the two of them headed out to practice in the local cemetery, where it was quiet.

It is true that within the African American community, the blues have often been contrasted to the spirituals, a sacred form, and thus likened to devil's music. The *Oxford English Dictionary* states that the color blue was associated with the devil as early as the sixteenth century; hence the expression "blue devils." Johnson fuels the idea of a Faustian pact, for example, in "Me and the Devil Blues," which has a spooky fatalism. He draws this out when he sings the song with a slow extremity:

> Early this mornin'
>> when you knocked upon my door
> Early this mornin', ooh
>> when you knocked upon my door
> And I said, "Hello, Satan,
> I believe it's time to go."

In *Mystery Train*, Greil Marcus suggests that "the only memory in American art that speaks with the same eerie resignation is that moment when Ahab goes over to the devil-worshiping Parsees he kept stowed away in the hold of the *Pequod*." So, too, Johnson uses another infernal metaphor for his furious need to keep moving when he sings "Hellhound on My Trail," which has a kind of mad excitement and Orphic restlessness.

> And the days keeps on worryin' me
> there's a hellhound on my trail
> hellhound on my trail
> hellhound on my trail

When Johnson sings this, his voice sounds mortally panicked, infernally chased by a hellhound that is ruthlessly tracking him down and will never let him escape.

Some folklorists and ethnomusicologists have argued that Johnson's notion of the devil syncretizes the Christian Baptist figure of his childhood and the Haitian voodoo deity of Papa Legba, a spiritual gatekeeper, Lord of Travel and God of the Crossroads. To me, Johnson's characterization of the devil seems like an externalization of something demonic he felt inside of himself, some irrational element in his behavior that manifested in his refusal to settle down, his sexual restlessness, and his overriding musical ambition. He didn't entirely understand the forces driving him.

Johnson's song taps the motif of the crossroads, which has a powerful resonance in African American folklore. Sometimes it's portrayed as a site where one makes a difficult or life-changing decision, other times it serves as a border crossing or boundary line between the human and the supernatural, the world of spirits and gods. The motif links the Delta to West Africa. The scholar Craig Werner points out, "For many West African tribes, the crossroads were the place where the spirit world and the material world converged, where you went when you needed spiritual energy. For the Yoruba, the crossroads were a place of power and danger." The singer of Johnson's song feels the concentration of this power at the end of the song when he desperately calls out, "Lord, that I'm standin' at the crossroad, babe / I believe I'm sinkin' down." He doesn't seem to be calling out to the Lord, as he did earlier in the song, but using *Lord* as an exclamation, now past the possibility of such help. He is going lost.

"Cross Road Blues" modifies a classical twelve-bar country blues song. Johnson uses a G tuning, like most of the Mississippi bluesmen, and expands the verses to fourteen or fifteen bars. The blues is an oral form with roots in sub-Saharan African culture, in the music that enslaved Africans brought to the New World and transformed on plantations all over the Deep South. The blues adapts and personalizes the call-and-response pattern of the field holler and the work song. Instead of a leader and a group, the singer internalizes his or her own dialogue. Depending on how strongly one feels the caesura, the song is transcribed as either three or six lines per stanza. The singer repeats the first two sentences or phrases, occasionally with a slight emphatic variation, and then clinches the stanza with a different statement. It's a couplet stretched to three lines. For Johnson, the slide follows a line of verse and responds to his high-pitched vocals and shivering vibratos, heightening the tension.

The blues is an accentual poetry, which means that the singer counts only the number of stressed or accented syllables. This is the rhythm of nursery rhymes, of early Germanic and Old English poetry, such as *Piers Plowman* and *Beowulf*, of John Skelton's rough-and-tumble *Skeltonics*, which James VI called "tumbling verse," of Coleridge's "Christabel" and Gerard Manley Hopkins's poems in sprung rhythm. It has a strong, driving beat. In "Cross Road Blues," which has a baseline of four accents, the somewhat loose rhythm of the vocals plays out against the very regular accentual pattern of the music, and this creates a kind of syncopation that adds to the feeling of violent anxiety radiating throughout the song. Formally, the blues customarily rely on an AAa rhyme pattern. This means that the initial rhyme is identical, while the second one conjoins different words.

"Cross Road Blues" begins in the past tense. The first sentence establishes the premise and scene—"I went to the crossroad, / fell down on my knees"— and the second repeats and hammers it in—"I went to the crossroad / fell down on my knees." The first phrase, "I went TO the CROSSroad," is spread out over four musical accents. Johnson changes the accent and hyperextends the language to fill up the surplus musical space: "I WENT to the CROSS-roooAAdd" so that the word *crossroad* either slides the accent or gets extra accents. Then he quickens the second half of the line: "fell down ON my KNEES" (rest rest). The first half of the sentence is stretched, the second clipped, and this creates a rhythm of expansion and contraction, which feeds into the core angst developing in the song. The third statement then punches, develops, and turns the premise: "ASKED the Lord above 'Have

MERcy, / save poor BOB, if you PLEASE.'" You can hear the long pile of syllables and Johnson's virtuosity in jamming them to the beat or count. This line makes clear that this is a personal prayer—the speaker calls himself by his nickname "Bob"—and a plea for mercy.

In the second stanza, Johnson once more repeats the first sentence—"standin' at the crossroad / I tried to flag a ride"—which gives a sensation of time passing, of the speaker standing at the intersection trying to hitch a ride. Once more, the third sentence serves as punch line: "Didn't nobody SEEM to KNOW me / EVerybody pass me BY." Listening to the song, you can hear the contrast between the way that the word *nobody* is enunciated (*no-bod-y*) and the word *everybody* is abbreviated (*ev-body*). Johnson moves from the vertical, the realm of the transcendental, to the horizontal, the realm of the social. The speaker has now gotten up from his knees and turned from God to the road, where no one recognizes him and cars whistle by. There's a dissonant near rhyme in the words *ride* and *by*. *Ride* is also a slang term for a sexual partner, a lover. No one stops to pick him up, and so he can't pick anyone up, either.

There is a change from the past to the present tense in the third stanza. Structurally, the blues often turn like sonnets in this way. Listening to the song, you notice that the music speeds up as the story progresses. It's now dusk, a transitional time of day. We can overhear the speaker talking to himself in the first sentence: "Mmm, the sun goin' down, boy / dark gon' catch me here." Johnson emphasizes the speaker's anxiety and fear when he replaces the first half of the sentence, "Mmm, the sun goin' down," with an intense nonverbal cry, a wordless vocalization—"ooo ooee eeee"—followed by the repetition, "boy, dark gon' catch me here." This is the terror of being trapped at sunset in a sundown town, which very possibly could mean a death sentence. The worry and loneliness are palpable: "I haven't got my lovin' sweet woman that / love and feel my care." Once more Johnson skillfully jams the syllables to the four-beat count. The edgy slant rhyme of *here* and *care* is worthy of Emily Dickinson.

There is a sense of an ongoing present in the final stanza. When he initially recorded this song, Johnson may have been cut off by the producer because of time—the first take ends with a cry of lovelorn distress. In contrast, the second take sharply concludes. The implication is "you" (one) can run—he repeats the phrase three times—but you can't hide. It's almost as if he's sending some unseen listener off to find his male friend and mentor Willie Brown, whose name he rhymes with *down*. You can hear the explosive accents in "TELL my FRIEND-BOY Willie BROWN." The use of names helps give this song the sensation of something personal, even confessional, as if there is no gap in real life between the speaker and the maker. The last sentence—"Lord, that I'm standin' at the crossroad, babe / I believe I'm sinkin' down"—gives an intense feeling of being spiritually lost at the crossroad, forever unable to leave. I'm struck by the way he uses the word *believe* and combines the two addressees of the poem—"Lord," "babe"—at the beginning and end of the last lonely line, which suggests that he is doubly bereft—without God, without love. We usually think of the sun going down at nightfall, but here the speaker is sinking down with it, and the hard night comes on. The feeling of doom is overwhelming.

Robert Johnson's songs seems menacing and magnetized downward. His work is scarifying and beautiful. He is one of our great American troubadours of the open road and the fateful crossroad, of rambling and homesickness—the evil thought, the unrequited love, the tearful goodbye, the hunger to come back home. There is a deep plaintiveness in the way he sings the blues, in his lyrics of faith and faithlessness. "I *believe*," he sings in "Rambling on My Mind," the song on the flip side of "Cross Road Blues," "I *believe* my time ain't long":

> I believe
>   I believe that my time ain't long
> But I'm leavin' this mornin'
>   I believe I will go back home

Middle Passage

I

Jesús, Estrella, Esperanza, Mercy:

Sails flashing to the wind like weapons,
sharks following the moans the fever and the dying;
horror the corposant and compass rose.

Middle Passage:
    voyage through death
            to life upon these shores.

"10 April 1800—
Blacks rebellious. Crew uneasy. Our linguist says
their moaning is a prayer for death,
ours and their own. Some try to starve themselves.
Lost three this morning leaped with crazy laughter
to the waiting sharks, sang as they went under."

Desire, Adventure, Tartar, Ann:

Standing to America, bringing home
black gold, black ivory, black seed.

    Deep in the festering hold thy father lies,
    of his bones New England pews are made,
    those are altar lights that were his eyes.

Jesus Saviour Pilot Me
Over Life's Tempestuous Sea

We pray that Thou wilt grant, O Lord,
safe passage to our vessels bringing
heathen souls unto Thy chastening.

Jesus   Saviour

    "8 bells. I cannot sleep, for I am sick
    with fear, but writing eases fear a little
    since still my eyes can see these words take shape
    upon the page & so I write, as one
    would turn to exorcism. 4 days scudding,
    but now the sea is calm again. Misfortune
    follows in our wake like sharks (our grinning
    tutelary gods). Which one of us
    has killed an albatross? A plague among
    our blacks—Ophthalmia: blindness—& we
    have jettisoned the blind to no avail.
    It spreads, the terrifying sickness spreads.
    Its claws have scratched sight from the Capt.'s eyes
    & there is blindness in the fo'c'sle
    & we must sail 3 weeks before we come
    to port."

       What port awaits us, Davy Jones'
       or home? I've heard of slavers drifting, drifting,
       playthings of wind and storm and chance, their crews
       gone blind, the jungle hatred
       crawling up on deck.

Thou   Who   Walked   On   Galilee

    "Deponent further sayeth *The Bella J*
    left the Guinea Coast
    with cargo of five hundred blacks and odd
    for the barracoons of Florida:

"That there was hardly room 'tween-decks for half
the sweltering cattle stowed spoon-fashion there;
that some went mad of thirst and tore their flesh
and sucked the blood:

"That Crew and Captain lusted with the comeliest
of the savage girls kept naked in the cabins;
that there was one they called The Guinea Rose
and they cast lots and fought to lie with her:

"That when the Bo's'n piped all hands, the flames
spreading from starboard already were beyond
control, the negroes howling and their chains
entangled with the flames:

"That the burning blacks could not be reached,
that the Crew abandoned ship,
leaving their shrieking negresses behind,
that the Captain perished drunken with the wenches:

"Further Deponent sayeth not."

Pilot   Oh   Pilot   Me

II

Aye, lad, and I have seen those factories,
Gambia, Rio Pongo, Calabar;
have watched the artful mongos baiting traps
of war wherein the victor and the vanquished

Were caught as prizes for our barracoons.
Have seen the nigger kings whose vanity
and greed turned wild black hides of Fellatah,
Mandingo, Ibo, Kru to gold for us.

And there was one—King Anthracite we named him—
fetish face beneath French parasols
of brass and orange velvet, impudent mouth
whose cups were carven skulls of enemies:

He'd honor us with drum and feast and conjo
and palm-oil-glistening wenches deft in love,
and for tin crowns that shone with paste,
red calico and German-silver trinkets

Would have the drums talk war and send
his warriors to burn the sleeping villages
and kill the sick and old and lead the young
in coffles to our factories.

Twenty years a trader, twenty years,
for there was wealth aplenty to be harvested
from those black fields, and I'd be trading still
but for the fevers melting down my bones.

III

Shuttles in the rocking loom of history,
the dark ships move, the dark ships move,
their bright ironical names
like jests of kindness on a murderer's mouth;
plough through thrashing glister toward
fata morgana's lucent melting shore,
weave toward New World littorals that are
mirage and myth and actual shore.

Voyage through death,
            voyage whose chartings are unlove.

A charnel stench, effluvium of living death
spreads outward from the hold,

where the living and the dead, the horribly dying,
lie interlocked, lie foul with blood and excrement.

Deep in the festering hold thy father lies,
the corpse of mercy rots with him,
rats eat love's rotten gelid eyes.

But, oh, the living look at you
with human eyes whose suffering accuses you,
whose hatred reaches through the swill of dark
to strike you like a leper's claw.

You cannot stare that hatred down
or chain the fear that stalks the watches
and breathes on you its fetid scorching breath;
cannot kill the deep immortal human wish,
the timeless will.

"But for the storm that flung up barriers
of wind and wave, *The Amistad,* señores,
would have reached the port of Príncipe in two,
three days at most; but for the storm we should
have been prepared for what befell.
Swift as the puma's leap it came. There was
that interval of moonless calm filled only
with the water's and the rigging's usual sounds,
then sudden movement, blows and snarling cries
and they had fallen on us with machete
and marlinspike. It was as though the very
air, the night itself were striking us.
Exhausted by the rigors of the storm,
we were no match for them. Our men went down
before the murderous Africans. Our loyal
Celestino ran from below with gun
and lantern and I saw, before the cane-
knife's wounding flash, Cinquez,

that surly brute who calls himself a prince,
directing, urging on the ghastly work.
He hacked the poor mulatto down, and then
he turned on me. The decks were slippery
when daylight finally came. It sickens me
to think of what I saw, of how these apes
threw overboard the butchered bodies of
our men, true Christians all, like so much jetsam.
Enough, enough. The rest is quickly told:
Cinquez was forced to spare the two of us
you see to steer the ship to Africa,
and we like phantoms doomed to rove the sea
voyaged east by day and west by night,
deceiving them, hoping for rescue,
prisoners on our own vessel, till
at length we drifted to the shores of this
your land, America, where we were freed
from our unspeakable misery. Now we
demand, good sirs, the extradition of
Cinquez and his accomplices to La
Havana. And it distresses us to know
there are so many here who seem inclined
to justify the mutiny of these blacks.
We find it paradoxical indeed
that you whose wealth, whose tree of liberty
are rooted in the labor of your slaves
should suffer the august John Quincy Adams
to speak with so much passion of the right
of chattel slaves to kill their lawful masters
and with his Roman rhetoric weave a hero's
garland for Cinquez. I tell you that
we are determined to return to Cuba
with our slaves and there see justice done. Cinquez—
or let us say 'the Prince'—Cinquez shall die."

The deep immortal human wish,
the timeless will:

Cinquez its deathless primaveral image
life that transfigures many lives.

Voyage through death
 to life upon these shores.

1945, 1962

R OBERT HAYDEN wrote this devastating historical poem about
the slave trade, "Middle Passage," in the early 1940s when there
was virtually no interest in revisiting the dark truths of American history. It
is a landmark for American poetry, a breakthrough in subject matter com-
parable to "The Love Song of J. Alfred Prufrock" and "Sunday Morning." It
stands as a barrier-breaking poem—lyric, narrative, dramatic—that coolly
and forcefully leads us to confront one of the most fundamental horrors of
the American past.

As a young poet, Hayden was moved by Stephen Vincent Benét's long
poem *John Brown's Body* (1928) to write his own poems about American his-
tory, most especially the struggle of Black people to overcome slavery during
the Civil War and post–Civil War eras. His first unpublished collection, *The
Black Spear*, was triggered by a passage in Benét: "O, black-skinned epic,
epic with the long black spear, / I cannot sing you now, having too white a
heart." Hayden wanted to be the Black poet who sang of that black spear,
who corrected the misconceptions and destroyed the stereotypes surround-
ing African American history. He just had to figure out the right means.

Hayden put himself to school on the formal poetry of John Keats, W. B.
Yeats, Elinor Wylie, Countee Cullen, and W. H. Auden, his role model at
the University of Michigan, who taught him about the necessity of reshaping
the canon for the present day. He had also been reading the free-verse poets
of the Harlem Renaissance, Langston Hughes and Arna Bontemps. Going
to the archives at the Schomburg Center in New York and researching an
extended poem steeped in America's slave-trading past, Hayden gradually
realized that writing a poem with epic aspirations would demand a different
arsenal. He read ships' logs, notebooks, journals, memoirs by slave traders,
historical accounts. It is as if the variety and intensity of the material itself
pushed him into becoming a postmodernist, an innovator who adapted
the collage method of Eliot's *The Waste Land*, the documentary poetics of

Pound's *Cantos*, and the "mystical synthesis" and mythical history that drove Crane's search for an American identity in *The Bridge*. He was not only influenced by these epically scaled poems but also responding to them, and, in so doing, he was repurposing the resources of modernism. In his own quiet but firm way Hayden emerged from the archives and turned modernism, which has strong undercurrents of racism, into an African American mode, a poetics of color.

Hayden began "Middle Passage" in 1941 and originally planned it as the opening gambit of *The Black Spear*. He worked on it during the war years—World War II and the Holocaust hover invisibly in the background—and published it in *Phylon* in 1945. He continued to revise and whittle it—he cut forty-three lines and shaped the second section from an irregular collage into six quatrains—and republished it as the centerpiece of *A Ballad of Remembrance* (1962). After that he made a few minor changes when he reprinted it in *Selected Poems* (1966) and *Angle of Ascent* (1975). It took Hayden a great deal of time and painstaking effort to create and revise a poem that incorporates a wide range of voices. Too short to be an epic, it nonetheless has an epic mission. Hayden told an interviewer that at times the voice of the poet "seems to merge with voices from the past, voices not intended to be clearly identified," such as the voices of slave traders, hymn singers, unnamed diarists, "perhaps even of the dead." He called the style or method "cinematic" because of the way that "one scene ends and another begins without any obvious transitional elements."

"Middle Passage" is a poem in three parts that tracks a journey out of Africa. It is "a poem including history," to use Pound's definition of epic. The first section treats the inhuman brutality on various slave ships. The second section cuts to the reminiscences of a greedy and corrupt retired slave trader. The third section introduces Joseph Cinquez (Sengbe Pieh), who is now often referred to by the mononym Cinqué, the insurrectionary hero, and re-creates the mutiny aboard the *Amistad*. It also condenses the story of the winding, ultimately successful legal journey of the imprisoned Africans after the ship landed in America. The driving principle of the entire poem is the historical creation of a group of people, African Americans, and their abiding quest for liberty.

I immersed myself in Hayden's work in the late 1970s when I moved to Detroit, his hometown, for my first teaching job. To me, he has been a touchstone, a great poet of freedom, a figure who had written our first magnificent lyric about the Middle Passage and its tortures. That's why I was surprised to discover that he had been vilified in the 1960s by the Black Arts Movement, which demonized him for his white influences, his Western forms, his prioritizing of literary values, and his poetic eloquence. I realize that I am an outsider, but this argument seems both callous and wrongheaded about a poet who had so meaningfully documented Black oppression. "Middle Passage" is part of a long tradition of African American self-documentation, such as slave narratives and memoirs, field hollers, work songs, the blues, the insistent lyrics of the Harlem Renaissance, jazz songs like Billie Holiday's "Strange Fruit," written by Abel Meeropol, jazz compositions like Duke Ellington's orchestral piece "Black, Brown and Beige," and, more recently, Wynton Marsalis's *Blood in the Fields*, which won the Pulitzer Prize for Music in 1997. Hayden was part of a long lineage of poetry and music in quest of freedom and justice. He considered the need for freedom a constant beyond history, something timeless, but he also understood that the struggle for freedom takes place inside of history.

"Middle Passage" was Hayden's first experimental contribution, his epic bid. The poem begins in medias res ("in the middle of things") by listing the English and Spanish names of the slave ships. This is an epic strategy, like the catalogue of ships in book 2 of the *Iliad*. The first version of the poem began with a ten-line prologue, an elegy for precolonial Africa ("It was long, long after the burnished riding of those conquered kings"). However, Hayden chose to begin the revised version by launching in, thereby exploiting the cruel irony of the ships' Christian names: *Jesús, Estrella, Esperanza, Mercy.* Later in the poem he describes these ships with "bright ironical names / like jests of kindness in a murderer's mouth." The names are confessions and calls, but they are also pleas from their captives: *Jesus, Star, Hope, Mercy.*

Hayden follows the list of ships with a colon—think of a camera panning—and an indented tercet that reads like a lost stanza from Dante's *Inferno*. We are tossed into the journey.

> Sails flashing to the wind like weapons,
> sharks following the moans the fever and the dying;
> horror the corposant and compass rose.

244 THE HEART OF AMERICAN POETRY

His next move is to sound the name "Middle Passage" and equate it with an image and statement that is both literally and metaphorically true: "voyage through death / to life upon these shores." Hayden does not pause to explain that the First Passage was the trip that a European ship made to the west coast of Africa to trade goods for people. The Middle Passage was the second leg of the journey crossing the Atlantic from Africa to the Americas with a cargo of enslaved Africans, human beings kidnapped or captured in war. Instead, he thrusts us directly into the harsh reality. He does this by crosscutting the lyrical passages with documentary ones, such as the next dispassionate, matter-of-factly horrifying diary entry of a captain:

> "10 April 1800—
> Blacks rebellious. Crew uneasy. Our linguist says
> their moaning is a prayer for death,
> ours and their own. Some try to starve themselves.
> Lost three this morning leaped with crazy laughter
> to the waiting sharks, sang as they went under."

Thus, indirectly, we glimpse a vision of people so desperate to escape the bonds of slavery (does it really take a linguist to interpret their moaning?) that they try to starve themselves to death or even—madly, triumphantly—sacrifice themselves to the sea. Against this backdrop of suffering: the rolling on of ships (*Desire, Adventure*) driven by economic greed, turning people into "black gold, black ivory, black seed."

Immediately after this the poem refers to Ariel's famous song in *The Tempest*. Here is the Shakespearean text:

> Full fathom five thy father lies;
> Of his bones are coral made;
> Those are pearls that were his eyes:
> Nothing of him that doth fade,
> But doth suffer a sea-change
> Into something rich and strange. (1.2.395–400)

Hayden twice recasts and refashions Shakespeare's lines, giving them a sea change. First:

Deep in the festering hold thy father lies,
of his bones New England pews are made,
those are altar lights that were his eyes.

And then later:

Deep in the festering hold thy father lies,
the corpse of mercy rots with him,
rats eat love's rotten gelid eyes.

Derik Smith, Aldon L. Nielsen, and other critics have pointed out how in these reworkings Hayden "mutinies" against Shakespeare's figure of Prospero—he takes Ariel's lie and turns it into a shattering truth—and simultaneously upends Eliot's previous use of Ariel's speech in *The Waste Land*. Hayden adapts Eliot's theme, which he characterized as the "spiritual emptiness of an industrialized civilization," and shows that it has a much older and deeper root causality. In his revisionary text, it is the Black father who lies suffering "*Deep in the festering hold.*" The bones of an enslaved person are undergirding the pews—so says Hayden, rewriting the Puritan origins of New England churches. That the eyes of a slave have been transmogrified into altar lights casts an intense moral light on the blindness of white Christians. The horrific images keep festering in Hayden's imagination as he talks back to two of his main poetic precursors by laying bare what is missing in their work—the human exploitation of slave traders, those white European fathers.

Hayden's revisionary tactic also becomes evident in the way that he exposes Christian hypocrisy by quoting a Protestant hymn that Edward Hopper wrote especially for seafaring men ("Jesus, Savior, Pilot Me"), which the poet spaces out, capitalizing and emphasizing each individual word in Hopper's first two lines:

Jesus   Saviour   Pilot   Me
Over   Life's   Tempestuous   Sea

Hayden intercuts these allegorical lines with a prayer from one of the slavers, a pillar of the church: "We pray that Thou wilt grant, O Lord, / safe passage in our vessels bringing / heathen souls unto Thy chastening." Two beats later he employs a diary entry ("'Which one of us / has killed an albatross?'") to expose an unlucky omen and nod to Coleridge's poem "The Rime of the Ancient Mariner," where everyone but the mariner dies on the fated ship.

It took iron discipline for Hayden to chronicle the fears and stay within the viewpoint of the cruel slavers, to cite dispassionate ships' logs and legal briefs ("'Deponent further sayeth'") in order to narrate the story of people stolen and stored at the bottom of ships like "'sweltering cattle,'" to chronicle the misdeeds of rapists ("'That Crew and Captain lusted with the comeliest / of the savage girls kept naked in the cabins'"), and to document a fire that killed countless numbers of people ("'That the burning blacks could not be reached'"). He also shows, as if from inside, how enslaving people drove the slavers themselves crazy.

Part II of the poem changes to a dramatic monologue. Written in regular quatrains, the entire twenty-four-line section consists of a single aged speaker explaining to some unseen younger listener ("Aye, lad") just what he had experienced during twenty years as a slave trader in Africa. Hayden composed the story from various sources, such as Théodore Canot's *Adventures of an African Slaver* (1854), Richard Drake's *Revelations of a Slave Smuggler* (1860), and George Francis Dow's *Slave Ships and Slaving* (1927). What matters is how so much of "Middle Passage" is described through the slaver's voice, which creates both a feeling of poignancy and one of exclusion. It reminds us how history itself always seems to speak through its arbiters, its victors and not its victims. The composite speaker recalls nostalgically the places and countries on Africa's western coast—Gambia, the Pongo River, Calabar in Nigeria—that served as the centers of the slave trade. The catalogue of African tribes—Fellatah, Mandingo, Ibo, Kru—recalls the genealogical lists in oral and written poetry, such as Genesis 10. The speaker brings home the collusion of African leaders, such as the ruthless Ashanti king who sent "his warriors to burn the sleeping villages / and kill the sick and old and lead the young / in coffles to our factories." The speaker has not gained a deeper understanding of his own complicity; he is simply dying, and so he can no longer participate in trading human beings.

The camera suddenly pulls back, and part III begins with an overview of ships sailing across the rocky Atlantic: "Shuttles in the rocking loom of history, / the dark ships move, the dark ships move." The ships weaving across the sea are also weaving slavery into the fabric of history. It is loomed and threaded with cotton. Hayden describes how the dark ships "plough through thrashing glister toward / fata morgana's lucent melting shore," thereby alluding to Morgan le Fay, the enchantress of Arthurian legend, and characterizes them weaving "toward New World littorals that are / mirage and myth and actual shore." The image and sound chamber here seem close to Hart Crane, especially the "Ave Maria" section of *The Bridge*.

Hayden returns to his collage method to interweave the narrative with an allegorical refrain ("Voyage through death, / voyage whose chartings are unlove") and the worried voice of a slaver, whose speech is italicized: "*But, oh, the living look at you / with human eyes whose suffering accuses you.*" The anonymous white speaker recognizes or at least voices that one "*cannot kill the deep immortal human wish, / the timeless will.*" These lyrical lines will recur near the poem's conclusion, but this time they will be forcefully reclaimed by the voice of the poet-narrator.

All this prepares us for the longest single stretch of the poem, the narrative account in blank verse of the uprising aboard the *Amistad*, whose name ironically means "Friendship," a Spanish ship carrying fifty-three enslaved people from Havana to Principé, Cuba. Hayden gathered most of the details of the uprising from the second chapter of Muriel Rukeyser's biography of the nineteenth-century scientist Josiah Willard Gibbs, whose abolitionist father had helped the imprisoned Africans communicate once they had been arrested in the New World. Rukeyser lifted much of her account from John W. Barber's book *A History of the Amistad Captives* (1840), and some of the details find their way into Hayden's text.

Hayden tells the story of the mutiny, which took place on July 2, 1839, through the stilted lens of Montez, one of the two white slaveowners whose lives were spared in order to navigate the ship. This tactic forces the reader to glean what is happening—a heroic, bloody insurrection—through hostile eyes. Part of what's so striking about this passage is how the reader feels the inevitable righteousness of the rebellion, as if nature itself were moving through the Africans ("'It was as though the very / air, the night itself were striking us'"). This is how Hayden introduces the leader of the mutiny, Joseph Cinquez, whom Rukeyser characterizes as "a powerful young rice planter, a powerful leader." This figure, "'that surly brute who calls himself a prince,'" is close to an epic hero. In the first version of the poem, Hayden designated him "its superb Homeric image."

The rest of the section telescopes a formidable amount of information. It begins with the wayward movement of the ship over a two-month period—instead of steering the ship back to Africa, Montez and Ruiz managed to misdirect and reroute it so that it eventually washed ashore in Montauk, Long Island. The Africans were straightaway arrested and imprisoned in New Haven. This began a long legal journey that ended with the successful intervention of John Quincy Adams, the former president of the United States, whose "Roman rhetoric" won the case before the Supreme Court in 1841. Hayden lifted the phrase "timeless will" from Adams's eight-and-a-half-hour speech, which relied on a notion of justice gleaned from the Institutes of Justinian ("*The constant and perpetual will to secure to every one HIS OWN right*"). The thirty-seven Black defendants were then released to return to Africa. Here America suddenly lives up to an ideal. Hayden closes the section with the white trader's helpless vow that "'Cinquez— / or let us say "the Prince"—Cinquez shall die.'"

Robert Hayden once said that he viewed history "as a long, torturous, often bloody process of becoming, of psychic evolution," and that idea is enacted at the conclusion of "Middle Passage." First, he juxtaposes the empty threat against Cinquez with the reclamation of the lines "The deep immortal human wish / the timeless will," which he claims in his own name, and then equates with Cinquez's "deathless primaveral image / life that transfigures many lives." Hayden takes three words that break the chain of temporality—*immortal*, *timeless*, and *deathless*—and links them to the figure of Cinquez, who now stands as a "primaveral" or springtime image, a figure of new blossoming, new birth, "life that transfigures many lives." Hayden closes with a further breakthrough into hopefulness by closing with the refrain line: "Voyage through death / to life upon these shores." This statement, a fragment, now takes on fresh meaning since we know so much more of what had to be suffered and endured, especially the primordial crime, the abomination of slavery, for a new resilient group of people, no longer Africans, not yet Americans, to be born.

St. Roach

For that I never knew you, I only learned to dread you,
for that I never touched you, they told me you are filth,
they showed me by every action to despise your kind;
for that I saw my people making war on you,
I could not tell you apart, one from another,
for that in childhood I lived in places clear of you,
for that all the people I knew met you by
crushing you, stamping you to death, they poured boiling
        water on you, they flushed you down,
for that I could not tell one from another
only that you were dark, fast on your feet, and slender.
        Not like me.
For that I did not know your poems
And that I do not know any of your sayings
And that I cannot speak or read your language
And that I do not sing your songs
And that I do not teach our children
                to eat your food
                or know your poems
                or sing your songs
But that we say you are filthing our food
But that we know you not at all.

Yesterday I looked at one of you for the first time.
You were lighter than the others in color, that was
    neither good nor bad.
I was really looking for the first time.
You seemed troubled and witty.

Today I touched one of you for the first time.
You were startled, you ran, you fled away
Fast as a dancer, light, strange and lovely to the touch.
I reach, I touch, I begin to know you.

1976

I HEARD Muriel Rukeyser read her poems aloud twice—once in 1976, once in 1978. The first reading took place in a long narrow room on the top floor of the Walnut Street Theater in Philadelphia. She was presenting with Gerald Stern, who had recently hired me for my first job with Pennsylvania Poets in the Schools, and he invited me to tag along. I hadn't been to many poetry readings yet, and I was overexcited by the crowd. Rukeyser looked stately but not vigorous, and slightly tilted, I suppose, if you knew how to look—I didn't—since she had suffered a few small strokes over the past decade. She seemed grandly old to me—she was sixty-three— and had a face shaped like an oversized heart. I was carrying my copy of *Breaking Open* (1973) because I loved her poem "Despisals," which filters Martin Buber through Walt Whitman to establish a personal ethos. It's an "I and Thou" for the American poet of difference:

> Never to despise in myself what I have been taught
> to despise.   Not to despise the other.
> Not to despise the *it*.   To make this relation.
> with the it :   to know that I am it.

I recall two of the poems that Rukeyser read that night, "Waking This Morning," where she refers to herself as a violent woman trying "to be non-violent / one more day," and "St. Roach," which would soon appear in *The Gates* (1976), the last collection published in her lifetime. After she read each poem, Rukeyser would let the page fall carelessly to the floor, so that the drift grew, like a scattering of leaves.

Since college, I have been enthusiastic about the eighteenth-century mystic, the mad, religious polymath Christopher Smart, who had wrenched his piercing observations, extensive reading, and jubilant faith into one of the most startling and unlikely epics of English poetry, "Jubilate Agno," and so

I was excited when Galway Kinnell choreographed a group reading of the poem in New York City at the Church of the Transfiguration, otherwise known as the Little Church Around the Corner. There was a full house for the twenty poets who were joined by a choir from Holy Cross that would sing Benjamin Britten's setting "Rejoice in the Lamb." I remember the grand procession, all those poets who are gone now, the older ones I looked up to, which included Etheridge Knight, Allen Ginsberg, Grace Paley, Philip Levine, David Ignatow, Allen Grossman, Nancy Willard, Jane Cooper, Joel Oppenheimer, Harvey Shapiro, Thomas Lux, Vertamae Smart-Grosvenor, Paul Zweig, Stanley Plumly, and James Wright, who read the passage about Smart's cat Jeoffry, his one faithful companion. Together, these poets had a rumpled collective glow, as if a group of union representatives had ambled into a fifteenth-century Italian painting. Here they were—the wiry and the whimsical, the burly and the lion-headed, some with high pipes, others with low growls, all of whom had come to give loving voice to one of the great outsiders of English poetry. It takes all types of major and minor figures—I don't consider the categories meaningful—to make a national poetry.

Rukeyser was last to take the podium—she looked more fragile now but still vibrant and undiminished—and what happened next was upsetting, strange, and majestic. In one of Kinnell's last poems, "Jubilate," he described the experience of listening to her edgy soaring voice in full song and swelling light. It felt as if the podium were trying to lift itself:

> And now it became evident that our podium
> was not rising, it was Muriel who was sinking,
> toppling in fact, hauling down on herself
> the microphone and amplifier and all their wires,
> into a heap on the floor. From under this wreckage
> her suddenly re-clarioned voice was heard: "*Let Zadok*
> *worship with the Mole—before honour is humility!*"
> And as we disentangled her, she sat up and scanned about
> and said: "*She that looketh low shall learn!*"

Rukeyser had collapsed at the podium. There was a flurry of activity, everyone on stage lurched forward, Kinnell and Paley rushed to lift and hold her up in her jeopardy. Someone in the back wanted to call an ambulance, a doctor rushed forward, but Rukeyser was adamant: No ambulance! No doctor! She seemed to be suffering a stroke—she would die just two years later—but for now she wanted a seat so that she could finish reciting her passage. She was a performer, and one did not quit a performance:

> Eased into a chair at last,
> she smiled: "*Let Carpus rejoice with the Frog-Fish—*
> *a woman cannot die on her knees!*"

Muriel Rukeyser was a poet and social activist—in her case, as her friend William Meredith put it, you couldn't wedge a knife between her art and political commitments. She linked her personal experience to a larger social experiment, the community. "Breathe-in experience, breathe-out poetry," she wrote in the first line of the first poem of her first book, *Theory of Flight* (1935), and it was a mantra she followed the rest of her life. Rukeyser was a political troublemaker and had strong leftist commitments that drove much of her work, but she was also hard to pigeonhole because she was neither a proletarian poet nor a socialist realist. She brought a Romantic utopianism and modernist aesthetic to the sensibility of the *New Masses*. T. S. Eliot may have disliked the poetry of Percy Bysshe Shelley, but both figures shadow her work.

Rukeyser is a ragged modernist—her poems were often rambling at a time when American criticism was clenching around the well-wrought urn and the sacred object. She ostentatiously included politics in her work at the very moment when New Criticism was intent on divorcing poetry from history, and her reputation paid the price. She also brought a messy irrationality into poetry in a way that enraged poets who believed in tight form and rational control. It's almost breathtaking the way that her work routinely pissed off some critics, like Louise Bogan, who attacked book after book of hers in *The New Yorker*. I love Bogan's poetry, which Marianne Moore described as "compactness compacted," but it's precisely the opposite of Rukeyser's Whitmanian free-verse sprawl. It's as if Rukeyser's formal unruliness, her freewheeling unconscious associations, troubled Bogan's mind.

There were contemporaries who admired Rukeyser's poetry, but it would take another two generations for poets to start contending with her. We haven't had many American poets with such a deep moral compass, such a sharp historical sensibility, and such a committed social consciousness. She often hastened a poem because of her moral outrage, but she was determined to bring all of herself into her work in a way that hadn't been done before. She wouldn't split herself off into different roles and identities. "To live as a poet, woman, American, and Jew—this chalks in my position," she wrote in 1944: "If the four come together in one person, each strengthens the other." Three years later she wrote a nine-poem cycle for her yet unborn son that described pregnancy with an honesty and complexity that was unheard of at the time. She chalked in single mother to her position.

Rukeyser believed that American poetry, "the outcast art," had a crucial place in American culture. I agree with her that poetry has been an essential resource that we have often wasted in our country. "American poetry has been part of a culture in conflict," she declared in her prose book *The Life of Poetry*, which is as valuable today as when she wrote it in the late forties. She goes on to define two essential features of American life:

> We are a people tending toward democracy at the level of hope; on another level, the economy of the nation, the empire of business within the republic, both include in their basic premise the concept of perpetual warfare. It is the history of the idea of war that is beneath our other histories. . . . But around and under and above it is another reality. . . . This history is the history of possibility.

Rukeyser understood that warfare has been interwoven into our history, and she opposed it with a vision of democratic possibility. She said: "To be against war is not enough, it is hardly a beginning. . . . We are against war and the sources of war."

Rukeyser spent much of her life opposing war and trying to imagine peace. She was concerned with root causes and social imperatives. She didn't view peace as something that automatically comes to us, but as something to be constructed, like a work of art, and to be made, like love. Rukeyser was unusual as a political poet because she was careful to locate the enemy within as well as outside of herself. It's true, she argues, that we need to reconcile

254 THE HEART OF AMERICAN POETRY

ourselves with each other, but we also need to reconcile our conscious and unconscious minds, sleeping with waking, "ourselves with ourselves." There is a fraught psychological recognition in her work that we are all divided beings, that we need not only to unify with others but also to make peace with ourselves. This is where a late poem such as "Waking This Morning" comes in. It's hard for a violent person to be "non-violent," she suggests, when our days themselves are repeatedly filled with our country's violence.

In the preface to her first *Collected Poems* (1978), Rukeyser argued that there are "two kinds of reaching in poetry, one based on the document, the evidence itself; the other kind informed by the unverifiable fact, as in sex, dream, the parts of life in which we dive deep and sometimes—with strength of expression and skill and luck—reach that place where things are shared and we all recognize the secrets." These two divisions of expression, two types of reach or ambition, don't separate out so neatly in her work. For example, she was groundbreaking in the way she brought the documentary into American poetry in the 1930s, especially in her long poem "The Book of the Dead," which responds to the Hawk's Nest Tunnel disaster of 1931 in Gauley Bridge, West Virginia. The poem interlaces her own experience of driving through West Virginia with a record of testimonies and memorials from survivors, which are reportorial and gut-wrenching to read. And yet even here the overall poem borrows a symbology from the Egyptian Book of the Dead, a collection of spells and inscriptions based on ancient tombs and tomb paintings. These spells are "the unverifiable fact" and they give a dreamlike Jungian weight to the documentary evidence.

Part of Rukeyser's achievement was to bring the inner life to the outer one, to infuse the facts with a visionary utopian gleam. What's moving is the way she kept showing up over a forty-year period to right the record, writing about the Scottsboro trial in Alabama and the Union Carbide catastrophe in West Virginia, the Spanish Civil War and World War II, the racial divide and the civil rights era. She protested vociferously against the war in Vietnam. She surprised people by talking about the troubadours of Provence and Languedoc and then declared, much to the dismay of some high school English teachers, that the Beatles were poets. She was not apologetic for writing from the body and championing a womanist subject matter. When I was eighteen, I read her book *The Speed of Darkness* (1968) and its sexual frankness shocked me:

Whoever despises the clitoris despises the penis
Whoever despises the penis despises the cunt
Whoever despises the cunt despises the life of the child.

The Speed of Darkness provided many people with a model of personal
presence. A line in "The Poem as Mask" ("No more masks! No more mythol-
ogies!") provided the title for the first key feminist anthology of the early
seventies. A question and answer in "Käthe Kollwitz" ("What would happen
if one woman told the truth about her life? / The world would split open")
provided the title for the next one. Rukeyser linked feminist issues to human
rights. When I met her in the mid-seventies, she had recently come back
from South Korea where she had gone to protest the death sentence of the
dissident poet Kim Chi-ha, the basis for "The Gates." She was porous as a
storyteller ("The universe is made of stories, / not of atoms," she asserted in
section IX of "The Speed of Darkness") and registered the lives of other peo-
ple on her pulse. For her, it was all personal. She said, "the emotional obstacle
is the real one." She was talking about people when she said with impatience
in the poem "Islands": "O for God's sake / they are connected / underneath."

Rukeyser got the idea for "St. Roach" while she was stuck in a Washing-
ton, D.C., jail, where she had been locked up for an antiwar demonstration.
It was inspired by a close encounter with a real roach. Rukeyser's son recalls
that she was a fan of Don Marquis's humorous verses and short stories,
Archy and Mehitabel, which describe the adventures of a cockroach, who
had been a free-verse poet in another life, and an alley cat. There's a touch of
self-mockery here, a backdrop of comedy wedded to politics. We don't need
to shy away from the fact that there's also something disturbing about the
poem; it's designed that way. The frisson comes from designating sainthood
to the lowliest and most disgusting of urban insects. Rukeyser plays on the
fact that St. Roch is the patron saint of plague victims; he embraces invalids
and others who are shunned. Rukeyser was a secular Jew and yet I hear
Christian sourcing in this poem. For example, the prayer "Litany to Saint
Roch" lingers in the background: "Saint Roch, whose heart was burning
with charity, pray for us." Behind this, too, stands St. Francis's "Canticle of
the Creatures." Galway Kinnell used the same model for his marvelous poem
"St. Francis and the Sow," which he wrote about the same time as Rukeyser
wrote "St. Roach."

From the opening line, there is something odd and old-fashioned in Rukeyser's phrasing, "For that I never knew you." The phrase "for that" is an archaic wording for the conjunction "because," i.e.: "Because I never knew you, I only learned to dread you." Here, the poet is not just employing an outdated English idiom, she is also using the diction to elevate the roach and invoke an older, more archaic form of knowledge. Most of us who grew up in cities have a primitive dread of cockroaches. That's why "St. Roach" is such a decisive and unlikely praise poem. It is a response to Kafka's pained depiction of Gregor Samsa in *The Metamorphosis*.

Rukeyser's lyric proceeds by a series of anaphoric repetitions. In the history of poetry, the strategic device of anaphora (from the Greek: "a carrying up or back") serves as the organizing principle for most catalogues and lists, as in the Hebrew Bible. It is a joyous piling up of particulars, which is why it was so useful to Whitman, whose litanies are the basis for American free verse. Here, the free-verse rhythm is almost stately, the diction slightly elevated. The opening movement, a single sentence of eleven lines, establishes the primary pattern:

> *For that* I never knew you, I only learned to dread you,
> *for that* I never touched you, *they told me* you are filth,
> *they showed me* by every action to despise your kind;
> *for that* I saw my people making war on you,
> I could not tell you apart, one from another,
> *for that* in childhood I lived in places clear of you,
> *for that* all the people I knew met you by
> crushing you, stamping you to death, they poured boiling
>   water on you, they flushed you down,
> *for that* I could not tell one from another
> only that you were dark, fast on your feet, and slender.

Rukeyser purposely uses a biblical cadence to invoke the despised roach. Christopher Smart provided a clear precedent in many of the most arresting passages in "Jubilate Agno," which leads with the word "For," as in "For I am not without authority in my jeopardy" and "For they work me with their harping-irons, which is a barbarous instrument, because I am more unguarded than others," and

For I will consider my Cat Jeoffry.
For he is the servant of the Living God, duly and daily
    serving him.
For at the first glance of the glory of God in the East he
    worships in his way.

Rukeyser brings Smart's sense of jeopardy to her thinking about a common insect scapegoated by terrified human beings. The language points up something cruel and excessive in our war on these small, indistinguishable beings, who are repeatedly targeted: crushed, stamped, scalded with boiling water, flushed down the toilet. The summary of the cockroach as dark, fast, and thin brings the speaker to a realization: "Not like me." This punch, which is delivered as a short, indented sentence, structurally turns the poem. What happens next doesn't have precedent in Smart but comes from Rukeyser's own ethical stance toward the world.

At this point in the poem, we understand what we have suspected all along: that the roach is both itself and a representative figure. It stands for other people, all the unknown and despised, the Other. The way the poet manages this identification is by bringing the idea of cultural inheritance to the cockroach. Think of Vietnam or El Salvador or any other culture that the United States has ignorantly confronted with our foreign policy. There may be something outlandish about Rukeyser's catalogue as it applies to the cockroach, but something deep and even self-evident as it applies to other cultural heritages. Now the list presses forward with a series of conjunctions: *For that* is transformed into *And that* and finally into *But that*. Each line is a unit but there is no punctuation to stop the rush of knowledge, the shame of not knowing:

For that I did not know your poems
And that I do not know any of your sayings
And that I cannot speak or read your language
And that I do not sing your songs
And that I do not teach our children
        to eat your food
        or know your poems
        or sing your songs

> *But that* we say you are filthing our food
> *But that* we know you not at all.

The psychiatrist Robert Coles said that the poem "St. Roach" provides "a beautiful lesson in the psychology and sociology of prejudice." Rukeyser distances herself from inherent prejudices when she says: "Yesterday I looked at one of you for the first time." She invokes racial difference in order to dismiss it: "You were lighter than the others in color, that was / neither good nor bad." The next couplet intensifies the speaker's education in two simple declarative sentences:

> I was really looking for the first time.
> You seemed troubled and witty.

This characterization of the cockroach is what is usually called personification, the attribution of human qualities to nonhuman beings and things, but that does not adequately describe what is happening here. Rukeyser is not so much projecting her own feelings as trying to describe the life of another being, which she is observing, how it seems to her. There is a slight self-amusement as she reaches to describe the reality of an utterly foreign creature, someone whom she has just stumbled upon and who now interests her. The cockroach also stands in for a human figure, the otherness of another person. She is attributing human feelings to a being that both is and is not human.

I've appreciated the last stanza ever since I heard it more than four decades ago. It has a physical charge. The time frame of the poem changes from "Yesterday I looked" to "Today I touched." The speaker has learned that we need to understand things not just intellectually but also bodily, by touch. "Who touches this touches a man," Whitman declared, but who touches this poem also touches a woman and a cockroach:

> Today I touched one of you for the first time.
> You were startled, you ran, you fled away
> Fast as a dancer, light, strange and lovely to the touch.
> I reach, I touch, I begin to know you.

In standing up for a lesser creature, Rukeyser is also speaking on behalf of all those who are different, such as Jews and women and disabled people and refugees. Rukeyser was bisexual and I have no doubt that today she'd include everyone under the rubric of LGBTQIA+. The end of this poem is also just a beginning. The poem comes full circle. Rukeyser began with the statements "For that I never knew you" and "for that I never touched you," and now rectifies that ignorance. The last line progresses in three distinct parts: "I reach, I touch, I begin to know you." Focusing on touch and knowledge, on knowledge by touch, "St. Roach" becomes an unlikely quest and wisdom poem.

"St. Roach" cleverly inverts the Nazi and fascist symbolism of enemies as vermin. It eerily anticipates the use of the term "cockroaches" in the Rwandan genocide where the Hutu extremists justified exterminating the Tutsi people by labeling them *inyenzi* (cockroaches). It's possible to dehumanize people by taking away their individuality. It is easier to murder people who are considered subhuman.

It takes a certain sort of poet but also a certain type of person to treat a cockroach as an individual and to sanctify an insect. It's not an obvious move. It takes a holy foolishness, the kind of grave and comic risk you find in Christopher Smart and William Blake. Muriel Rukeyser was the sort of poet and person who extended her democratic vision to other creatures as well as to other people and stood up for the derided and detested. She wasn't squeamish or territorial, she welcomed the stranger. She also understood that she was living in what she called "the first century of world wars," a time of crisis and global conflict, an unprecedented era of killing, a nuclear world. But she kept her bearings and stood her ground. She contributed to the aggregate. Her work is a testimony to the document and the dream life, and she opened the gates for others to walk through with dignity.

Farewell in Welfare Island

It has to be from here,
right this instance,
my cry into the world.

Life was somewhere forgotten
and sought refuge in depths of tears
and sorrows
over this vast empire of solitude
and darkness.

Where is the voice of freedom,
freedom to laugh,
to move
without the heavy phantom of despair?

Where is the form of beauty
unshaken in its veil simple and pure?
Where is the warmth of heaven
pouring its dreams of love in broken spirits?

It has to be from here,
right this instance,
my cry into the world.
My cry that is no more mine,
but hers and his forever,
the comrades of my silence,
the phantoms of my grave.

It has to be from here,
forgotten but unshaken,
among comrades of silence
deep into Welfare Island
my farewell to the world.

> Goldwater Memorial Hospital
> Welfare Island, NYC
> Feb. 1953

I AM WALKING over to get Federico García Lorca at his dormitory on 114th Street and Amsterdam Avenue. He bows and twirls, as he likes to do, and we head toward Harlem so that I can introduce him to the Puerto Rican poet Julia de Burgos, who admires his songs and ballads. I don't speak Spanish and Lorca has been pretending to learn English to please his parents, but de Burgos is fluent in both languages, and I'm hoping that she'll translate for us. She spent a couple of years in Cuba, where Lorca is traveling after his stint in New York, and I'm sure we're going to bond over Walt Whitman and Pablo Neruda, whose work we all love. I must be nervous because I'm chattering away about her name, which means something like "Julia Who Belongs to Herself," and her Afro-Spanish heritage, and her first book, *Poemas exactos a mí misma* (Poems to Myself), which she never published. I have slipped a typescript of her "Poema a Federico" into my back pocket just in case I need to prop up the conversation: "Es Federico" ("It's Federico"). You've got to listen to a poet who cries out "¡Oidme!" ("Hear me!") and demands "¡Decidme!" ("Tell me!") and concludes "He dicho" ("I have spoken").

It has been sunny all day, but once we hit 123rd Street, where she had her first breakdown, it starts to rain and my daydream dissolves, like a shower on the Hudson River. It's 2022, not 1977, when I lived on the Upper West Side and had this fantasy, or 1943, when de Burgos still worked as a journalist for the Spanish-language weekly *Pueblos Hispanos*, or 1929, when Lorca spent the year at Columbia University, gathering material for his hallucinatory sequence *Poeta en Nueva York*. But, perhaps, as Ezra Pound said, "All poets are contemporaneous," and somewhere there's a metaphysical corner where time gets confused and we can still meet, where de Burgos hasn't yet died of alcoholism and Lorca hasn't been executed by the fascist militia, where it would be right to say that three poets stood in the shade and talked about the poetry of Spain and the Americas, about Rubén Darío and Gabriela Mistral, about Miguel Hernández and Alfonsina Storni, who had what the philosopher Miguel de Unamuno called "the tragic sense of life."

Julia de Burgos was a feminist, a social activist, a Puerto Rican *independentista*, and a committed internationalist in the first half of the twentieth century. She was also a pan-Caribbean poet of the Americas influenced by Whitman's inclusive free-verse catalogues, Neruda's passionate early love songs, which she memorized, and Storni's unabashed erotic poems. She was born in 1914 in the mountainous countryside around Carolina, Puerto Rico, the oldest of thirteen children, six of whom died from malnutrition, and her life was shadowed by poverty. As a young woman, she had to figure out how to fight for her own as well as her island's rights, its natural beauty, and political independence. She joined a strong nationalist movement in Puerto Rico that developed after the former Spanish colony became a United States territory in 1898. You might say that she was forced to become an American poet after the Jones Act imposed U.S. citizenship on Puerto Ricans in 1917 so that it could start drafting people into the war effort. Her project was a decolonizing one.

De Burgos worked at a milk station for the Puerto Rico Emergency Relief Administration, as a schoolteacher ("Carry yourself seriously but speak with a sweet voice. Humiliate no one"), as a writer for the radio program *School of the Air*, as the secretary general of the Daughters of Freedom, a branch of the Nationalist Party. She suppressed her first book and travelled around Puerto Rico reading from her second one, *Poema in vente surcos* (Poem in Twenty Furrows, 1938), which she followed with *Canción de la verdad sincilla* (Song of the Simple Truth, 1939) and *El mar y tú* (The Sea and You, which appeared posthumously in 1954). Her most beloved poem, "Rio Grande de Loíza," links her childhood river ("My wellspring, my river / since the maternal petal lifted me to the world") to the source of her art ("and my childhood was all a poem in the river, / and a river in the poem of my first dreams") and the grief of her island, its legacy of slavery and colonialism ("Great river. Great flood of tears. / The greatest of all our island's tears / save those greater that come from the eyes / of my soul for my enslaved people").

De Burgos was a freethinker who flouted the mores of a mostly conservative Roman Catholic society. At times she tried to conform but could never manage it. "I wanted to be like men wanted me to be," she declared in "I Was My Own Route," "But I was made of nows." She married at twenty, divorced at twenty-three. She had a romantic relationship with Juan Isidro Jimenes Grullón, the great love of her life, who was a Dominican political exile and intellectual from a prominent family, who never accepted her. Outspoken, bohemian, working-class, a self-identified *mulata*, a person who wanted equal rights for women and social justice for African descendents, de Burgos found herself at odds with the *Generación del Treinta* (Generation of 1930), a group of male intellectuals who rooted Puerto Rican identity in the land and shaped the nationalist agenda. They also condescended to poetry as an inferior genre. She left Puerto Rico at twenty-five and vowed never to return.

De Burgos lived happily in Cuba with Jimenes Grullón, but he lacked the courage to buck his family and she ended up in New York alone. Soon after, she married a Puerto Rican musician and lived with him for a while in Washington, D.C., but it was another mistake, and she returned to New York and divorced again. She was part of the bloodstream of Puerto Rican cultural life, but over time her life devolved into a string of failed affairs, jobs that kept evaporating, depression, alcoholism, a series of institutionalizations. Here is how she described her first breakdown:

> I was on the street with all of my belongings on my back, suffering from the symptoms of my illness, with no job, no sense of stability, and with my most prized, worldly possessions, my books and my verse, abandoned in a basement for lack of anywhere to store them. I found myself on the verge of banishing this earth in the most violent way.

From 1950 to 1953 de Burgos spent long stretches at Goldwater Memorial Hospital on Welfare Island, now Roosevelt Island. During all these years poems kept coming to her—love poems and anti–love poems, hymns to the countryside, to the river and the sea, and to the island of her childhood. Poems of proletarian solidarity ("Continue the strike, comrades: / We are no longer slaves!") jostle with lyrics of exile, fatefulness, and destiny, agony and absence, and perpetual insomnia.

It's hard to pinpoint the underlying anxiety in de Burgos's work—part Kierkegaard, part Wagner—an existential angst, a longing for infinity, and an operatic sense of the cosmic whole. She refers often to her soul, which cannot find repose and lives in what she calls "broken harmony." Much of her work was a mystic search for the inexpressible, something beyond the terrestrial realm, and she kept finding figures of liftoff—fireflies, birds, flying stars, a constellation of wings, an inclination to soar—to embody her transcendental quest and desire for fusion. She was a walker in the city, a poet of the night stroll, and Lorca's poems were always close at hand, a sustaining model. I hear his echo in many of her surreal flights, which have titles like "Weeping Blood on Roses" and "The Silence Was Left Speechless" and "The Sky Has Worn Its Dress of Horizons." There's an ars poetica of sorts at the heart of "Poem for Federico":

> Flying stars,
> lengthen your five fingers of light
> toward my desire tortured by the impossible.
>
> Fireflies . . . Fireflies . . .
> lend me your wings
> to attain the grave silence
> of Silence.
>
> (Tr. Jack Agüeros)

De Burgos was ever searching for a language of the beyond, a wording beyond language itself. She also started writing poems that explicitly say goodbye, though sometimes, as she puts it, "The miserable star of the earth / says goodbye to us." She wooed and refused death; she wrote two fantasias called "Poem for a Death That Could Be Mine."

De Burgos nearly always composed in Spanish, but she wrote a pair of poems in English in the last months of her life, when she was hospitalized on Welfare Island: "Farewell in Welfare Island" and its companion piece, "The Sun in Welfare Island." The decision was a self-conscious and even symbolic one. The use of English for a final plea only underscores her isolation, her distance from home, from the island of Puerto Rico and from the Spanish language itself, her true home. De Burgos's choice reminds me of the way that James Joyce described his situation as an Irish writer. Here are Stephen Dedalus's thoughts during his discussion with the dean of studies in *Portrait of the Artist as a Young Man*:

> The language in which we are speaking is his before it is mine. How different are the words *home, Christ, ale, master,* on his lips and on mine! I cannot speak or write these words without unrest of spirit. His language, so familiar and so foreign, will always be for me an acquired speech. I have not made or accepted its words. My voice holds them at bay. My soul frets in the shadow of his language.

Rereading de Burgos's poem in light of this speech, one starts hearing certain words with a different emphasis, like *welfare, empire, freedom,* and *comrades.*

Her title "Farewell in Welfare Island" sometimes gets translated into Spanish as "Adiós en Welfare Island" and then back into English as "Farewell from Welfare Island." The small idiomatic change to *from* is understandable—personally, I wish she had been able to say "Farewell *to* Welfare Island"—but the choice of *in* was purposeful and suggests greater confinement. The poet is enclosed, surrounded, even imprisoned. So, too, Welfare Island was the literal name of the notorious strip of land in the East River filled with hospitals and asylums, but Puerto Rican readers have often heard its overtones and connected it, somewhat painfully, to Puerto Rico itself. I once read an infuriating newspaper piece about the Puerto Rican economy called "Trouble on Welfare Island."

"Farewell in Welfare Island" is carefully structured to seem like a lyric cry. It has the feeling of a last poem, a final goodbye. The rhythm is organic, and the lineation draws attention to the phrasing. The stanzas operate as paragraphs, each one an intact unit. The voice is urgent, intense, insistent:

> It has to be from here,
> right this instance,
> my cry into the world.

The speaker locates herself here, in Welfare Island. There is no time to lose. She uses the word *instance*, which suggests an example or single occurrence, rather than the more idiomatic word *instant*, which means immediately. In Spanish, the word *instante* means moment, but the effect in English gives this statement a sense of being slightly off—it increases the isolation. Alienated from herself, she is sending her small cry into the large world. This is a lonely poem, a plea created in illness and shadowed by death, something personal made in an impersonal setting.

De Burgos was inclined to allegorize, her life becomes "Life." Formally, her poem works through a series of analogs and repetitions. This rhetorical strategy of parallelism is something she learned from Walt Whitman. The riffing off phrases is something she might have picked up from Langston Hughes. She repeats and interweaves motifs in an almost jazzlike way, like "It has to be from here" and "my cry into the world." Something she learned from Neruda and Lorca was how to take a word with political connotations and use it metaphysically. That's what happens when she refers to "this vast *empire* of solitude / and darkness." This also seems like a fairly accurate description of a series of hospital buildings situated on an island at night. It was not lost on her that the long-standing nickname for New York is "the Empire State."

The poem intensifies by repetition. Listen to how the poet picks up the phrasing, repeating "*Where is*" three times. She doubles the word *freedom* and underscores "*to* laugh" with "*to* move." This next stanza also has rich overtones and has been taken as a battle cry for Puerto Rican independence. Thus, "the heavy phantom" becomes the shadow of imperial power.

> *Where is* the voice of *freedom,*
> *freedom to laugh,*
> *to move*
> without the heavy phantom of despair?
>
> *Where is* the form of beauty
> unshaken in its veil simple and pure?
> *Where is* the warmth of heaven
> pouring its dreams of love in broken spirits?

There are moments when this poem has a nervousness that reminds me of James Schuyler's "The Payne Whitney Poems." It, too, has an undercurrent of tamped-down glee over a cunning pun. De Burgos was an alcoholic, dying of cirrhosis of the liver, and so the play on "pouring its dreams" and "broken spirits" seems intentional. Her spirit was broken and so she felt lost, defeated, but she had also succumbed to alcohol, sometimes called "spirits." She knew that Apollinaire made this same pun in a high-spirited way in his book *Alcools*, though here de Burgos's grim merriment feels more disconsolate.

There is something drastic and even desperate in the repetition: "It has to be from here, / right this instance, / my cry into the world." But now the poet purposefully enlarges the claim beyond herself. I hear a political undercurrent in the language:

> My cry that is no more mine,
> but hers and his forever,
> the comrades of my silence,
> the phantoms of my grave.

De Burgos is linking her suffering to the permanent suffering of others, those companions in battle, fellow soldiers who have also fallen on silence. She echoes the end of *The Heights of Macchu Picchu* (1947) where Neruda finds solidarity with the anonymous laborers who built the ancient city that he is gazing down upon. There is evident parallel in de Burgos's phrasing: "the comrades of my silence, / the phantoms of my grave." The word *phantom* has migrated from being linked to despair to being connected to the tomb. It now seems ghostly, pluralized, and refers to various unnamed figures of haunting who surround her. The shadow of the lost cause surrounds all of this.

And yet the last stanza takes a resolute turn—the speaker stiffens her spine. We expect her to say, "It has to be from here, / right this instance," just as she has done twice before, but now she changes it up:

> It has to be from here,
> forgotten but unshaken,
> among comrades of silence
> deep into Welfare Island
> my farewell to the world.

There is new determination in the second line, "forgotten but unshaken," and a sociality in the move to "*among* comrades of silence." These comrades are all the people in the struggle, especially the ones who are locked up here with her in Welfare Island—the unheard, the mute, the lost. The small words matter because at the end of the poem "farewell *in* Welfare Island" becomes "deep *into* Welfare Island / my farewell *to* the world." This farewell cry has been carefully crafted as a goodbye testament. It is grand, grave, and final.

It is also gestural. Julia de Burgos was just thirty-nine years old when she died in July 1953. She was near the end of her life when she wrote "Farewell in Welfare Island," though two months later she added a sequel, "The Sun in Welfare Island." Here, she refers again to her unshakable solitude. She notes how the sun shines in despair at her "sorrowful heart" and concludes with the declaration that "all of me is loneliness / in a rebellious heart." The word *rebellious* speaks to something undefeated in her spirit.

Some poets take on iconic status as figures of resistance and solidarity. Like Langston Hughes, Julia de Burgos has this symbolic presence in her community. But unlike Hughes, she hasn't been assimilated into a refreshed American canon. She is missing from anthologies of American poetry—our literary experts haven't heard of her—but there's a United States postal stamp with her name on it and public schools are named after her in Puerto Rico, Philadelphia, Chicago, and New York. If you know where to look you find her looming up far ahead of the Nuyorican movement. Sometimes I hike over to a stretch of East 106th Street between Lexington and Third to take a gander at Manny Vega's glass mosaic mural *Remembering Julia.* This is where she collapsed for the last time. People are bustling across what is now Julia de Burgos Boulevard. I go down the block to the Julia de Burgos Latino Cultural Center to view Elizam Escobar's mural *Despedida en Welfare Island*, which has the poem inscribed at the two sides. Now when I head downtown to Poets House, I can also stop to read "Farewell from Welfare Island" painted on the side of an ascending glass spiral overlooking the river. It's part of a memorial for victims of Hurricane Maria in Puerto Rico. It would be a good place to bring Lorca when he returns to New York.

GWENDOLYN BROOKS (1917–2000)

A Bronzeville Mother Loiters in Mississippi. Meanwhile, a Mississippi Mother Burns Bacon

From the first it had been like a
Ballad. It had the beat inevitable. It had the blood.
A wildness cut up, and tied in little bunches,
Like the four-line stanzas of the ballads she had never quite
Understood—the ballads they had set her to, in school.

Herself: the milk-white maid, the "maid mild"
Of the ballad. Pursued
By the Dark Villain. Rescued by the Fine Prince.
The Happiness-Ever-After.
That was worth anything.
It was good to be a "maid mild."
That made the breath go fast.

Her bacon burned. She
Hastened to hide it in the step-on can, and
Drew more strips from the meat case. The eggs and sour-milk biscuits
Did well. She set out a jar
Of her new quince preserve.

. . . But there was something about the matter of the Dark Villain.
He should have been older, perhaps.
The hacking down of a villain was more fun to think about
When his menace possessed undisputed breadth, undisputed height,
And a harsh kind of vice,
And best of all, when his history was cluttered
With the bones of many eaten knights and princesses.

The fun was disturbed, then all but nullified
When the Dark Villain was a blackish child
Of fourteen, with eyes still too young to be dirty,
And a mouth too young to have lost every reminder
Of its infant softness.

That boy must have been surprised! For
These were grown-ups. Grown-ups were supposed to be wise.
And the Fine Prince—and that other—so tall, so broad, so
Grown! Perhaps the boy had never guessed
That the trouble with grown-ups was that under the magnificent
shell of adulthood, just under,
Waited the baby full of tantrums.
It occurred to her that there may have been something
Ridiculous to the picture of the Fine Prince
Rushing (rich with the breadth and height and
Mature solidness whose lack, in the Dark Villain, was impressing her,
Confronting her more and more as this first day after the trial
And acquittal wore on) rushing
With his heavy companion to hack down (unhorsed)
That little foe.
So much had happened, she could not remember now what that
foe had done
Against her, or if anything had been done.
The one thing in the world that she did know and knew
With terrifying clarity was that her composition
Had disintegrated. That, although the pattern prevailed,
The breaks were everywhere. That she could think
Of no thread capable of the necessary
Sew-work.

She made the babies sit in their places at the table.
Then, before calling Him, she hurried
To the mirror with her comb and lipstick. It was necessary
To be more beautiful than ever.
The beautiful wife.

For sometimes she fancied he looked at her as though
Measuring her. As if he considered, Had she been worth It?
Had *she* been worth the blood, the cramped cries, the little stuttering
    bravado,
The gradual dulling of those Negro eyes,
The sudden, overwhelming *little-boyness* in that barn?
Whatever she might feel or half-feel, the lipstick necessity was something
    apart. He must never conclude
That she had not been worth It.

He sat down, the Fine Prince, and
Began buttering a biscuit. He looked at his hands.
He twisted in his chair, he scratched his nose.
He glanced again, almost secretly, at his hands.
More papers were in from the North, he mumbled. More meddling
    headlines.
With their pepper-words, "bestiality," and "barbarism," and
"Shocking."
The half-sneers he had mastered for the trial worked across
His sweet and pretty face.

What he'd like to do, he explained, was kill them all.
The time lost. The unwanted fame.
Still, it had been fun to show those intruders
A thing or two. To show that snappy-eyed mother,
That sassy, Northern, brown-black—

Nothing could stop Mississippi.
He knew that. Big Fella
Knew that.
And, what was so good, Mississippi knew that.
Nothing and nothing could stop Mississippi.
They could send in their petitions, and scar
Their newspapers with bleeding headlines. Their governors
Could appeal to Washington. . . .

"What I want," the older baby said, "is 'lasses on my jam."
Whereupon the younger baby
Picked up the molasses pitcher and threw
The molasses in his brother's face. Instantly
The Fine Prince leaned across the table and slapped
The small and smiling criminal.

She did not speak. When the Hand
Came down and away, and she could look at her child,
At her baby-child,
She could think only of blood.
Surely her baby's cheek
Had disappeared, and in its place, surely,
Hung a heaviness, a lengthening red, a red that had no end.
She shook her head. It was not true, of course.
It was not true at all. The
Child's face was as always, the
Color of the paste in her paste-jar.

She left the table, to the tune of the children's lamentations, which were
    shriller
Than ever. She
Looked out of a window. She said not a word. *That*
Was one of the new Somethings—
The fear,
Tying her as with iron.

Suddenly she felt his hands upon her. He had followed her
To the window. The children were whimpering now.
Such bits of tots. And she, their mother,
Could not protect them. She looked at her shoulders, still
Gripped in the claim of his hands. She tried, but could not resist the idea
That a red ooze was seeping, spreading darkly, thickly, slowly,
Over her white shoulders, her own shoulders,
And over all of Earth and Mars.

He whispered something to her, did the Fine Prince, something
About love, something about love and night and intention.

She had no hoof-beat of the horse and saw no flash of the shining
    steel.

He pulled her face around to meet
His, and there it was, close close,
For the first time in all those days and nights.
His mouth, wet and red,
So very, very, very red,
Closed over hers.

Then a sickness heaved within her. The courtroom Coca-Cola,
The courtroom beer and hate and sweat and drone,
Pushed like a wall against her. She wanted to bear it.
But his mouth would not go away and neither would the
Decapitated exclamation points in that Other Woman's eyes.

She did not scream.
She stood there.
But a hatred for him burst into glorious flower,
And its perfume enclasped them—big,
Bigger than all magnolias.

The last bleak news of the ballad.
The rest of the rugged music.
The last quatrain.

                                        1960

WHEN I was growing up on the north side of Chicago, the
subject of poetry didn't come up much, but whenever it did
someone would start declaiming "Hog Butcher for the World" and "City
of the Big Shoulders." Carl Sandburg seemed like everyone's idea of a Chi-

cago poet, which is why as soon as I started writing poetry, I proclaimed my scorn for his aw-shucks manner and blue-collar affectations. But when I was a sophomore at Grinnell College, one of my friends, the poet Irma McClaurin, who was from the south side of Chicago, told me that her favorite poet was Gwendolyn Brooks, who was influenced by Sandburg, and so maybe I should go easier on his midwestern populism. I didn't understand yet that Sandburg's Whitmanian stance and egalitarian ethos, what Sterling A. Brown called his "common-man mythology," is more ethically sound than the politics of my modernist heroes, Eliot and Pound, greater poets who turned out to be contemptuous of democracy. I was catching up and decided that I should find out about a different sort of democratic poet from the other side of my hometown. I immersed myself in Brooks's work, which situates itself in Bronzeville, the Black metropolis, the historic center of African American culture in the city since the Great Migration. Chicago has always been a hyper-segregated city and I was getting educated.

Brooks called herself an "organic Chicagoan." From the outset, she peopled her poems with a multitude of characters, all sorts of folks who make up a neighborhood, part of the entirety. In her first four individual collections, *A Street in Bronzeville* (1945), *Annie Allen* (1949), *The Bean Eaters* (1960), and *In the Mecca* (1968), she gave voice to people who hadn't appeared much in poetry before. As she put it in her autobiography, *Report from Part One*: "If you wanted a poem you only had to look out of a window. There was material always, walking or running, fighting or screaming or singing." This is modest and revealing, and it speaks to Brooks's ambition to work both sides of the street, to encompass various viewpoints, reputable and disreputable, and to describe what happened in kitchenettes, taverns, and beauty shops, the front yard and the back one, vacant lots, shadowy alleys, and bustling street corners. She catches people on the move, in the thick of it.

Brooks was an American poet with a community principle and a modernist aesthetic. She said that she wanted "to vivify the commonplace," which sounds Wordsworthian, and she described her poems as "folksy narratives," which is comically understated, though it does point to a primary value in her work, a fierce commitment to telling stories about ordinary people. Like Langston Hughes and Robert Frost, two of her main models, she loved to redeploy and even rethink the nature of traditional forms, such as the blues, the sonnet, and the ballad. I think of her as a local poet in the same way that James Joyce was a local fiction writer. Joyce wrote from exile, Brooks stayed put, but both used literary tools at their disposal to work their home turfs.

Brooks's career was bifurcated by the Black Arts Movement, which was propelled by the Second Black Writers' Conference at Fisk University in 1967. She was radicalized by younger poets and awakened to a new consciousness about the social role of poetry in the Black community. She made new personal alliances and began to publish with Dudley Randall's Broadside Press, which was nobly committed to African American literature. I don't underestimate the importance that the movement had for her, but her work doesn't divide so neatly into two parts. The evidence suggests otherwise.

Take the politically charged issue of traditional Anglo-European or Western forms, which Brooks notoriously renounced. Many of her earlier poems don't just employ those forms, they also deconstruct and repurpose them in cunning ways, such as her invention of a hybrid form, "the sonnet-ballad" ("Oh mother, mother, where is happiness?"), and her use of the mock-epic ("The Anniad"). Strictly speaking, her poem "The Last Quatrain of the Ballad of Emmett Till," a coda to "A Bronzeville Mother," turns out to be neither a quatrain nor a ballad. Instead, it stages a confrontation between the generic or communal expectation of the form and the individual's resistance to it. So, too, many of her free-verse lyrics, which appear spontaneous, are shadowed by the ghost of lost forms. Think of the aggressive soundings, the alliterative echo chamber, in her most famous poem, "We Real Cool" (1960). Brooks liked to rhyme and then to disrupt rhyme, to echo and clang intermittently. Sometimes she intercut long free-verse stanzas with hidden couplets, other times she established a pattern and then ruptured it. She created vessels so that she could break them.

One of the most powerful examples of Brooks's method is her free-verse poem "A Bronzeville Mother Loiters in Mississippi. Meanwhile, a Mississippi Mother Burns Bacon," which appeared in *The Bean Eaters*, a book she initially intended to call *Bronzeville Men and Women*. This poem suggests that Brooks's ideology was well inscribed into her practice by the fifties. Her pen, she said, was already "dipped in blood, *stabbed* in, writhing blood." Brooks wrote this blood-soaked poem in response to the kidnapping and murder of Emmett Till, a fourteen-year-old from Chicago who visited his cousins in the tiny town of Money, Mississippi, in the summer of 1955. He was a fun-loving kid who made the mistake of going to buy bubble gum in a small store, Bryant's Grocery and Meat Market, where he said something possibly flirtatious, certainly innocuous, to Carolyn Bryant, the white proprietor, who stormed off and later fabricated a story that he had made "ugly remarks" and somehow assaulted her. That night Roy Bryant, Carolyn's husband, and his half brother, J. W. Milam, got Emmett Till out of bed at gun point, brutally tortured and killed him, and then dumped his body in the Tallahatchie River with a seventy-pound cotton gin fan tied to his neck. He was found by a fisherman three days later. His mother, Mamie Till-Mobley, had his body shipped north for the funeral, and then made the courageous decision to keep the casket open during the funeral so that the world could see what white racists had done to her son. Bryant and Milam were acquitted by an all-white male jury and later confessed to the killing, for which they were never punished. The entire gruesome episode was a catalyst for the civil rights movement.

Brooks's own son was fourteen at the time, and like everyone else, she saw the photographs of Emmett Till's mangled body with his devastated mother standing beside him. She was frightened and found her own way to respond even as she placed her work in a lineage of poems about lynching, that notorious grotesquerie of American history, which has been so persistent that it has led to a subgenre of outraged elegiac responses by African American poets. The tradition of lynching poems probably began with Paul Laurence Dunbar's mock-romantic ballad "The Haunted Oak" (1900), which takes the point of view of the tree where a lynching takes place. Early twentieth-century poets such as Claude McKay and Leslie Pinckney Hill continued the tradition, followed by an imposing array of poets from the 1920s to the present, including Richard Wright ("Between the World and Me"), Robert Hayden ("Gabriel," "Figure," "Night, Death, Mississippi"), and Lucille Clifton ("jasper texas 1998"). Over the course of his life, Langston Hughes wrote nearly three dozen lyrics that speak and sing against the violence of lynching. Brooks's poem stands out because of its angle of approach, the way it wields a female perspective and takes a sideways cut at a sickening barbarism and racist spectacle.

The long, narrative title—"A Bronzeville Mother Loiters in Mississippi. Meanwhile, a Mississippi Mother Burns Bacon"—consists of two equally balanced full sentences. It takes place in the present tense. The first woman is an unnamed stand-in for Mamie Till-Mobley, though her identity overlaps with the poet, who is also a *mother* from *Bronzeville*. The mother *loiters* over her dead son's casket, she *loiters* after the trial, which she attended, and she *loiters* in the mind of the Mississippi mother preparing breakfast for her family. It's not a stretch to say that the word *loiters* is shadowed by the memory of loitering or vagrancy laws, which were used to target African Americans in the Jim Crow era. Meanwhile, the Mississippi mother, an unnamed stand-in for Carolyn Bryant, is so unnerved that she *burns bacon*. The burning food immediately suggests that something is going awry. The poem takes place in what was then a female domain—it has the politics of the kitchen. Over the course of the poem, we don't ever hear from the grief-stricken Bronzeville mother, and yet she always seems nearby, a painful shadow presence.

"A Bronzeville Mother" is written in a tight third-person center of consciousness. Brooks leaps across the racial divide to imagine the consciousness of Carolyn Bryant, an ignorant local beauty who started the horrifying chain of events. This decision reminds me of Robert Hayden's determination in "Middle Passage" to narrate most of his poem from the viewpoint of the white slavers, which indicates how history is always narrated from the perspective of its adjudicators, its victors and not its victims. Emmett Till was unquestionably a victim, but what sort of a victor was Carolyn Bryant?

Brooks was always conscientious about her medium. No matter what her subject matter, her poems are also in dialogue with the enterprise of poetry. Here, she creates a sort of meta-ballad or anti-ballad. I recall a radio interview where she told Studs Terkel that she loved the ballad form, but when he connected "A Bronzeville Mother" to the British popular ballad "Sir Patrick Spens," she demurred and said, "Well, the events in this poem are a little sturdier, I believe, than those in that beautiful ballad." The word *sturdier* is a gentle way to say that the underlying events are more horrifically real than the fictive scene in "Sir Patrick Spens." That's why this written lyric demanded an alternative narrative strategy, something that hadn't been scoured by oral tradition. As a result, "A Bronzeville Mother" is structured in irregular stanzas, which operate as verse paragraphs, and not in quatrains, like other ballads. And yet it opens abruptly, focuses on a crucial episode, and moves toward a tragic conclusion.

From the beginning, Brooks portrays Bryant as someone trying to understand her own romantic tale, like a figure in a story-poem. She's unnerved and inarticulate. The word *it*, which somehow summarizes her experience, is vague and encompassing. There's a strong enjambment at the end of the first line, and the poet hits hard on the word *Ballad*. She follows this up with a double declamation: "*It had the beat. . . . It had the blood.*" Jimmy Driftwood makes a similar move in his 1959 song "Tennessee Stud": "He had the nerve and he had the blood." In Brooks's first stanza, there is a drumbeat of repeated sounds at the beginning of words ("*b*een," "*B*allad," "*b*eat," "*b*lood," "*b*unches," "*b*allads," and "*b*allads") and the end of them ("h*ad*," "Ball*ad*," "h*ad*," "h*ad*," "bl*ood*," "tie*d*," and "Underst*ood*"). The middle *l*'s connect *ballad* and *blood*.

> From the first it had been like a
> Ballad. It had the beat inevitable. It had the blood.
> A wildness cut up, and tied in little bunches,
> Like the four-line stanzas of the ballads she had never quite
> Understood—the ballads they had set her to, in school.

Brooks understood ballads—the word is repeated three times for emphasis—as narrative songs, and she recognized how the literary ballad echoed the primordial spirit of the traditional folk form. By my count, she wrote eight titled ballads and some forty other poems shadowed by the ballad format. Whereas epics were heroic songs sung by men, ballads were often sung by women and therefore told different kinds of stories. Beginning with Lucy Terry's poem "Bars Fight" (1746), which was transmitted orally for more than a century, ballads also have a lineage in African American poetry, where they have often been overlaid with blues or spirituals. Here, Brooks points to the ballad's powerful driving music ("the beat inevitable"), violent subject matter ("the blood"), and compacted wildness ("the four-line stanzas"). At the end of the first stanza, she catches herself and acknowledges that ballad-knowledge was beyond Bryant. She presses down on the word *Understood*—and then immediately links it to *the ballads*, which the unsophisticated Bryant connects to school learning.

Bryant was notoriously silent during the media coverage of the murder and trial, and here Brooks gives her a voice, an interior monologue. The white woman imagines herself as a figure of purity, a character in a fairy tale who is pursued by one allegorical figure, "the Dark Villain," and rescued by another, "the Fine Prince." But the fantasy starts to unravel in the third stanza, "Her bacon burned." It picks up again in the middle of a thought (". . . But there was something about the matter of the Dark Villain") and then comes crashing down again by something much more terrible than a story littered with dead knights and noble princesses.

> The fun was disturbed, then all but nullified
> When the Dark Villain was a blackish child
> Of fourteen, with eyes still too young to be dirty,
> And a mouth too young to have lost every reminder
> Of its infant softness.

> That boy must have been surprised! For
> These were grown-ups. Grown-ups were supposed to be wise.

Brooks enacts the dawning consciousness of a woman slowly realizing something terrible about her husband and herself. The fairy tale of the prince rushing to protect her maidenhood becomes impossible to sustain. I'm interested in the language here. There are moments when Brooks uses phrases that seem to be beyond Bryant's capability, such as "all but nullified," even as she strains to understand her viewpoint. Brooks takes the diction down a notch when Bryant refers to the Dark Villain as "a blackish child." So, too, the poet underpins Bryant's language with Emmett Till's devastating surprise that "These were grown-ups." Far from being wise, these grown-ups are shockingly cruel. Brooks then carefully separates the two viewpoints, "Perhaps the boy had never guessed / That the trouble with grown-ups was that under the magnificent shell of adulthood, just under, / Waited the baby full of tantrums."

This is a poet's way of telling a story or implying one. It isn't until a parenthesis late in the sixth stanza that we realize that the poem is taking place on the first morning after the trial and acquittal. This is one reason it's so difficult for Bryant to think straight (her "composition / Had disintegrated" and "The breaks were everywhere"). She could not sew things back together. Brooks filters the action, such as it is, through Bryant's mind as we see her rush to clean up the babies, to make herself pretty, and to seem worthy for her husband. But the reality keeps hitting this Mississippi woman that her husband has murdered a child on her behalf ("The sudden, overwhelming *little-boyness* in that barn").

As readers, we register the experience from a refracted point of view as the husband, the so-called Fine Prince, sits down to breakfast. The camera closes in as he starts to butter a biscuit, looks at his hands, now a murderer's hands, twists in his chair, scratches his nose, glances again "almost secretly, at his hands," and checks the newspapers ("More meddling headlines. / With their pepper-words, 'bestiality,' and 'barbarism,' and / 'Shocking'"). There are a few stanzas in the middle where Brooks shifts viewpoints to take in Roy Bryant's perspective, and the language shifts, too, moving closer to the racist way that he speaks and feels. As the poem progresses, the male pronoun becomes increasingly upsetting. Hence, "What he'd like to do, he explained, was kill them all." For the first time within the poem, the Bronzeville mother is mentioned, but through his nasty, unrepentant point of view:

> Still, it had been fun to show those intruders
> A thing or two. To show that snappy-eyed mother,
> That sassy, Northern, brown-black—

The thought breaks off and Bryant takes refuge in thinking about his home state of Mississippi.

The historical backdrop is significant. In 1954, the Supreme Court decided the landmark civil rights case *Brown v. Board of Education*, ruling that the segregation of public schools was a violation of the Fourteenth Amendment and therefore unconstitutional. The white supremacist backlash in Mississippi was intense. Hence Bryant's confidence in his future acquittal. Now Brooks's diction has migrated fully to his way of speaking:

> Nothing could stop Mississippi.
> He knew that. Big fella
> Knew that.
> And, what was so good, Mississippi knew that.
> Nothing and nothing could stop Mississippi.
> They could send in their petitions, and scar
> Their newspapers with bleeding headlines. Their governors
> Could appeal to Washington. . . .

Everything within this poem happens inside the house, the domestic interior. There's a family sitting around the kitchen table (the babies fighting, the father slapping one of them). All along this locale has been steeped in blood, but now Carolyn Bryant starts to figure it out. When her husband smacks her child, i.e., "When the Hand / Came down" and she looks at her baby, "She could think only of blood." She realizes that she is too terrified to object: "*That* / Was one of the new Somethings— / The fear, / Tying her as with iron."

A cinematographer could film the scene: how she goes to the window and her husband follows. He puts his hands on her shoulders, the children are whimpering, and she understands that she can't protect them. The next image is surreal:

> She tried, but could not resist the idea
> That a red ooze was seeping, spreading darkly, thickly, slowly,
> Over her white shoulders, her own shoulders,
> And over all of Earth and Mars.

The poet turns Roy Bryant into Mars, the god of war.

When Roy Bryant whispers something in his wife's ear—"something about love and night and intention"—and he kisses her, as always happens in a story, she sees and feels only blood, "His mouth, wet and red, / So very, very, very red, / Closed over hers." This leads her to a sudden, inescapable feeling of revulsion:

> Then a sickness heaved within her. The courtroom Coca-Cola,
> The courtroom beer and hate and sweat and drone,
> Pushed like a wall against her. She wanted to bear it.
> But his mouth would not go away and neither would the
> Decapitated exclamation points in that Other Woman's eyes.

> She did not scream.
> She stood there.
> But a hatred for him burst into glorious flower,
> And its perfume enclasped them—big,
> Bigger than all magnolias.

Here, the violent kiss propels her back into the courtroom as a kind of physical memory. She feels the sickening details. The specifics intermingle, hate situates itself between beer and sweat, and the boring drone of the lawyers becomes the soundtrack of her disgust. She can no longer escape the Bronzeville mother's terrible loss, which Brooks summarizes with an astonishing writerly image of "the / Decapitated exclamation points in that Other Woman's eyes." Bryant does not call out in protest, she does not "scream" in rage, but a hatred wells up in her that will never be extinguished, something more southern than the ever-present smell of magnolias. It took her all this while to recognize that her husband's actions were not chivalrous, but exceedingly cruel.

The final, three-line stanza is a coda. It's hard to imagine anyone but Brooks ending the story with this series of hard punches, a triple combination, this succession of increasingly clipped phrasing and shortening fragments.

> The last bleak news of the ballad.
> The rest of the rugged music.
> The last quatrain.

The repetition of the letters *b* and *l* threads the word *bleak* to the word *ballad*, the repetition of *r* connects "*the r*est" to "*the r*ugged." There is a syntactic parallel, which is reinforced by the lineation, in "*of the ballad*" and "*of the rugged music*." There is no full sentence. It's intentionally jarring to refer to these three fragments, a triplet, as a quatrain. This is the resounding end of the woman's story. The poem begins with a reference to itself as a ballad and so it ends with one, too. But the romantic fairy tale that has overlaid the ballad has fallen away, and we're left with the exposure of a white supremacist notion of chivalry, violence, and murder. Brooks's furious rewriting of the ballad convention is a rugged form of poetry.

Gwendolyn Brooks's technique, a "cut-up" of form and narrative, is akin to modern art and the metonymic style of social commentary in contemporary art. She breaks the narrative, the allegory, and the form, and yet the breakage, the overall assemblage, creates a power beyond the plain telling, the full illustration, the completed mythological comparison. When I first read "A Bronzeville Mother Loiters in Mississippi. Meanwhile, a Mississippi

Mother Burns Bacon," I thought that Brooks showed a remarkable, almost troubling sympathy for Carolyn Bryant. She granted her an interiority I've never believed that Bryant deserved. Later, when I started to teach the poem, I changed my mind and decided that it's an indictment of southern patriarchy, a piercing condemnation of a wife's complicity in her husband's gruesome crime. It exposed the dangerous politics of romantic fallacies, romance ballads. But now, when I return to the poem after all these years, I feel that both interpretations are simultaneously true, that Brooks shows sympathy for Carolyn Bryant even as she condemns her. So, too, it's an anti-ballad that is also a ballad, a ballad by other means. The magic of "A Bronzeville Mother Loiters in Mississippi. Meanwhile, a Mississippi Mother Burns Bacon" is also the magic of Brooks's practice. She could write poems that are both empathic and excoriating at the same time.

"More Light! More Light!"

for Heinrich Blücher and Hannah Arendt

Composed in the Tower before his execution
These moving verses, and being brought at that time
Painfully to the stake, submitted, declaring thus:
"I implore my God to witness that I have made no crime."

Nor was he forsaken of courage, but the death was horrible,
The sack of gunpowder failing to ignite.
His legs were blistered sticks on which the black sap
Bubbled and burst as he howled for the Kindly Light.

And that was but one, and by no means one of the worst;
Permitted at least his pitiful dignity;
And such as were by made prayers in the name of Christ,
That shall judge all men, for his soul's tranquillity.

We move now to outside a German wood.
Three men are there commanded to dig a hole
In which the two Jews are ordered to lie down
And be buried alive by the third, who is a Pole.

Not light from the shrine at Weimar beyond the hill
Nor light from heaven appeared. But he did refuse.
A Lüger settled back deeply in its glove.
He was ordered to change places with the Jews.

Much casual death had drained away their souls.
The thick dirt mounted toward the quivering chin.
When only the head was exposed the order came
To dig him out again and to get back in.

No light, no light in the blue Polish eye.
When he finished a riding boot packed down the earth.
The Lüger hovered lightly in its glove.
He was shot in the belly and in three hours bled to death.

No prayers or incense rose up in those hours
Which grew to be years, and every day came mute
Ghosts from the ovens, sifting through crisp air,
And settled upon his eyes in a black soot.

                                                    1967

ANTHONY HECHT had a daunting formality. He took a mea-
sured, classical approach to poetry that at face value could seem
emotionally cool and intellectually distanced. It was easy to misunderstand
his mannered approach to the lyric in the increasingly raucous world of
American poetry of the 1960s and after. I liked him immediately when I met
him in the early eighties, but his demeanor put me in mind of T. S. Eliot,
who by all accounts spoke with a dry, faintly concocted accent and always
dressed as if he were going to high church. As a Jewish American poet Hecht
was shadowed by a fear of exclusion, an anxiety he covered up with cunning
wit and cultivated gloss. He was an exceptional formal poet, like Richard
Wilbur and James Merrill, with whom he is often grouped, but he was also
a formalist with a difference.

   Hecht was more aware of his own affectations than I initially realized. In a
Paris Review interview in 1988, he told the poet J. D. McClatchy: "I suppose
my voice must sound affected in some way, though there is no 'natural' dic-
tion or pronunciation into which I might relapse. . . . Doubtless it's a mask
of some sort; a fear or shame of something, very likely of being Jewish, a
matter I am no longer in the least ashamed of, though once it was a painful

embarrassment." Hecht wasn't alone in the way he tried to cover up his origins and refashion himself as someone who belonged in sophisticated circles. There were very few Jews in the academy when he was starting out, and most of them tried to sound as if they had attended Oxford or Cambridge and took high tea with the dons. It was a mode of disguise.

The representation of Jews in the modern canon is a vexed one, and I'm not eager to repeat the whole painful story. Hecht was deeply influenced by Shakespeare, and yet he never forgot his first experience of reading *The Merchant of Venice* in grade school:

> It was mortifying, and in complicated ways. I was being asked to admire the work of the greatest master of the English language, and one universally revered, who was slandering all those of my race and religion. I was not even allowed to do this in private, but under the scrutiny and supervision of public instruction. And it took many class periods to get through the whole text. I can also remember the unseemly pleasure of my teacher in relishing all the slanders against the Jews in general and Shylock in particular. It was a wounding experience and the beginning of a kind of education for which I received no grades. And it has continued for the rest of my life.

To cite just two more telling examples: As a maker of elaborate sentences, Hecht owes an obvious debt to Henry James, but he was also aware that James once compared refugee Jews to worms that "wriggle away contentedly" as "denizens of the New York Ghetto" (*The American Scene*, 1907). Hecht schooled himself on Eliot's poetry and criticism, but he was cognizant of Eliot's comment that "reasons of race and religion make any large number of free-thinking Jews undesirable" (*After Strange Gods*, 1934). Eliot's prejudices were well-known but often excused, and the young poets of Hecht's generation were taught to imitate the ironic tone and well-crafted quatrains of Eliot's highly influential, openly antisemitic collection, *Poems* (1920). Its satiric hardness especially appealed to the New Critics. Hecht considered Eliot a poet of the highest order; he alluded to him often and said, "Almost every line of Eliot's poetry seems forged of the most durable steel." He felt personally wounded by Eliot's antisemitism, which troubled him more than

Ezra Pound's crude medieval slurs and virulent antisemitic outbursts. "Eliot's racism is deeper, haunting and more sinister," Hecht said.

History has a way of changing perspectives, forcing reassessments, reevaluations. American Jewish poets, even ones who were ambivalent about their origins, like Hecht, couldn't keep quiet about World War II and the Holocaust, and their interventions unnerved American poetry. Among other things, I am thinking of a succession of texts, such as Muriel Rukeyser's 1944 Petrarchan sonnet, which begins "To be a Jew in the twentieth century / Is to be offered a gift," and Karl Shapiro's early book *Poems of a Jew* (1950). The succession continues with Irving Feldman's harrowing long poem "The Pripet Marshes" (1965) and Charles Reznikoff's mid-seventies book *Holocaust*. I wish more people knew the war and postwar American poems of the Yiddish poets Kadya Molodowsky and Jacob Glatstein, or the work of the Eastern European Yiddish poets Abraham Sutzkever and David Fram, but Paul Celan's German-language Holocaust poems, especially "Todesfuge" ("Death Fugue"), forced poetry readers everywhere to contend with barbaric truths.

Hecht may have written with a quill pen and inkwell but that didn't change the fact that he was internalizing a history and inscribing a horror. One had no idea from his ornamental, lighthearted first book, *A Summoning of Stones* (1954), what he had already gone through, but it can be gleaned from his second book, *The Hard Hours* (1967), his greatest single collection. Here, just under the surface, are wounded experiences and barely concealed traumas. Some of these traumas go back to childhood ("A Hill," which suggests a lonely and unhappy early home life), some are revealed in psychoanalysis ("Behold the Lilies of the Field," which describes the flogging and flaying of a former emperor), and others evoke the Shoah with grimacing accuracy ("'It Out-Herods Herod, Pray You Avoid It,'" "Rites and Ceremonies").

Hecht's most harrowing poems are based on a bedrock of personal experience. In 1944, after graduating from Bard College, he was enlisted in the United States Army's 97th Infantry Division. His unit was sent into combat in Germany and Czechoslovakia, most notably in the battle of the Ruhr Pocket. For a descendent of Bavarian Jews, it was a strange way to return to his ancestral homeland. He despised the army, which he found dehumanizing, and disliked the officers, whom he deemed swaggering and incompetent. The experience was bitter. As a twenty-two-year-old private, he participated in the liberation of the Flossenbürg concentration camp on the Czech border. By the time his unit arrived to help free the camp, more than thirty thousand people had died there, and the SS personnel had fled. Prisoners were dying from typhus at the rate of five hundred a day. As he explained in a lengthy interview with Philip Hoy:

> Since I had the rudiments of French and German, I was appointed to interview such French prisoners as were well enough to speak, in the hope of securing evidence against those who ran the camp. . . . The place, the suffering, the prisoners' accounts were beyond comprehension. For years after I would wake shrieking.

Hecht also described an encounter with the Germans that left some of his battle-torn fellow soldiers "legless, armless, or dead." After the firing stopped, he said, he saw a group of German women leading small children by the hand and coming toward them, waving makeshift white flags of surrender back and forth:

> They had to descend the small incline that lay between their height and ours. When they were about half way, and about to climb the slope leading to our position, two of our machine guns opened up and slaughtered the whole group. . . . This was all due to the plain panic of soldiers newly exposed to combat, due also to guilt, to frustrated fury at the casualties we had suffered. In any case, what I saw that morning was, except for Flossenbürg, the greatest trauma of the war—and, believe me, I saw a lot of terrible things.

Hecht found the whole experience "inexpressibly horrible" and was forever changed by what he witnessed in a remote area of northeastern Bavaria.

After the war Hecht was stationed in Japan, then attended Kenyon College on the G.I. Bill, where he studied with John Crowe Ransom, whose classical learning, deft formalism, and ironic mode appealed to him, and William Empson, who initiated him into the pleasures of ambiguity. The young poet loved nothing better than the paradoxical statement and "the well-wrought urn." He was learning to armor himself, but when he started teaching at the University of Iowa his wartime experiences caught up to him, and he suffered from what used to be called "soldier's heart" and we now term post-traumatic stress disorder (PTSD). As he told Hoy:

> I had what in those primitive days was called a "nervous break-down," and which today would be styled a "post-traumatic shock syndrome." It was arrogant and foolish of me to have supposed that my war experiences could be smoothly expunged by a couple of weeks of heavy drinking. I returned to my parents' home in New York and entered psychoanalysis. Of course my analyst, a good and decent man, but an orthodox Freudian, was not prepared to believe that my troubles were due wholly, or even largely, to the war, so we went ambling back together, down the rocky garden path to my infancy.

This is revealing, poignant, and funny, and it helps to explain something of the strategies and defenses in *The Hard Hours* and subsequent books, where one finds dark personal reminiscences and satirical portraits intermingled with lovely lyrics about Italian gardens and devastated poems about genocide.

Hecht was teaching at Bard when he wrote "'More Light! More Light!'" in 1960, seven years before its publication. The poem is dedicated to his colleagues, the refugee intellectuals Heinrich Blücher and Hannah Arendt, both of whom had fled Nazism. To supplement his experience Hecht immersed himself in historical and philosophical reading as he tried to comprehend the totality of what was done and who was responsible. As he put it:

> In time I came to feel an awed reverence for what the Jews of Europe had undergone, a sense of marvel at the hideousness of what they had been forced to endure. I came to feel that it was important to be worthy of their sacrifices, to justify my survival in the face of their misery and extinction, and slowly I began to shed my shame at being Jewish.

In a general way, his thinking was informed by Arendt's *The Origins of Totalitarianism* (1951) and *The Human Condition* (1958). In a more specific way, "'More Light!,'" which joins distinct historical stories, relies on two previous texts. Hecht adapts the first narrative from John Foxe's Protestant history, *Actes and Monuments*, popularly known as *Foxe's Book of Martyrs* (1563, 1570), which describes the fate of three Oxford martyrs, the Anglican bishops Nicholas Ridley, Hugh Latimer, and Thomas Cranmer, who were burnt at the stake for heresy in 1555. He adapts the second from Eugen Kogon's *The Theory and Practice of Hell: The German Concentration Camps and the System Behind Them* (1950).

"'More Light!'" consists of eight quatrains, which rhyme on the second and fourth lines, as in a ballad or a hymn. It doesn't sing, like a ballad, but it does tell a tragic story. It is also a kind of anti-hymn because there is no God to appeal to for salvation. Hecht sometimes wrote a smooth iambic pentameter, but here he roughens the meter to suit the brutality of the subject matter. The poem evokes heroic quatrains without following them. The logic is remorseless, but the rhythm is slightly impeded. It doesn't amble along like Gray's "Elegy Written in a Country Churchyard" or Longfellow's "The Jewish Cemetery at Newport," but stumbles and changes pace, sentence by sentence, stanza by stanza.

The title is literary and alludes to Goethe's deathbed plea for "More Light!" (*Mehr Licht*). Goethe was calling for someone to open the shutters because his eyesight was dimming, but his words have taken on the power of legend as a desperate prayer for greater illumination, a last petition for enlightenment. Here, Hecht makes an unmistakably ironic allusion to Goethe's request, which he quotes twice. Light will not be coming. The lamp of Reason has gone out and the German Enlightenment has been blinded.

There is a steely, unshakable calm to this poem. The opening stanza consists of one fragmentary sentence sinuously moving across four lines. The poet puts special pressure on the first word, *Composed*, which suggests both *composition* (something created) and *composure* (self-possession). The poem purposefully elides a first-person speaker:

> Composed in the Tower before his execution
> These moving verses, and being brought at that time
> Painfully to the stake, submitted, declaring thus:
> "I implore my God to witness that I have made no crime."

Hecht loved W. H. Auden's poetry—he later wrote a book about it called *The Hidden Law*—and here he takes Auden's detached view of suffering in "Musée des Beaux Arts." There is a close syntactical resemblance between "About suffering they were never wrong, / The Old Masters" and "Composed in the Tower before his execution / These moving verses." The diction takes on the formality and even archness of an earlier period, thus migrating in the direction of the phantom poem composed in the Tower. This explains the phrasing of "being brought" and "declaring thus." The rhyme is exact and inevitable (*time / crime*). Hecht admired the formal logic in seventeenth-century poetry, especially Donne and Herbert, and he adapts it here to grim circumstance. Since none of the Oxford martyrs wrote poetry, Hecht had to import another example, perhaps something like Chidiock Tichborne's "Elegy" (1586), which was composed in the Tower of London. He combines this phantom poem with a statement of Latimer's on the night before his execution. Here, the unnamed figure implores God as a witness, but everything suggests that he will not be spared.

The first two quatrains comprise a unit and condense a terrible story. The second stanza consists of two sentences equally divided. One notes the logical phrasing (*Nor was he . . . but*) and lockstep rhyme (*ignite / Light*). Hecht borrows and condenses Foxe's story of Ridley's death:

> Nor was he forsaken of courage, but the death was horrible,
> The sack of gunpowder failing to ignite.
> His legs were blistered sticks on which the black sap
> Bubbled and burst as he howled for the Kindly Light.

The martyr cries for the "Kindly Light," a phrase Hecht lifted from an early nineteenth-century hymn, "Lead, Kindly Light" ("Lead, kindly light, amid the encircling gloom, / Lead Thou me on!"), based on the poem "The Pillar of the Cloud" by John Henry Newman, who later explained it as "the voice of one in darkness asking for help from our Lord." It was not lost on Hecht that he borrowed the words of a Catholic cardinal and placed them in the mouth of a Protestant martyr. Now the light is far from "Kindly" and God's salvation nowhere to be found.

The stories in this poem are riveting, but there is an underlying logic that places them in perspective and makes them operational. This explains the voicing, an unseen or omniscient narrator who sounds as if he is in a courtroom ("And that was but one, and by no means"). The language is removed, neither sympathetic nor unsympathetic, and mimics the diction of sixteenth-century clerics.

> And that was but one, and by no means one of the worst;
> Permitted at least his pitiful dignity;
> And such as were by made prayers in the name of Christ,
> That shall judge all men, for his soul's tranquillity.

In this one sentence, which includes a light, mildly stiff feminine rhyme (*dignity / tranquillity*), Hecht invokes an older worldview, a time when men were martyred for their Christian principles and died with their beliefs intact. The sound emphatically threads together the words *permitted, pitiful,* and *prayers*. But there is an allegorical element to this poem, and this story of martyrdom is just one of many stories that later become much worse. The second part of the poem seems nostalgic for a time when suffering still had meaning.

The documentary tone of the next line is nerveless: "We move now to outside a German wood." This is the voice of a newscaster reporting something in the present tense. The word *moving*, which was first attached to verses, has now migrated to something toneless ("We *move* now"). Hecht's poem has the authority of personal experience, but that experience is withheld—never mentioned, never spoken of in the singular. The speaker appears only as a generalized "we." At this turning point, "'More Light!'" becomes a Holocaust lyric. In a letter, Hecht explained and justified the tone not just here but in all his German war poems:

> Except for Wiesel's *Night*, I have read no "literary" works about the prison camps that seem anywhere nearly as effective as straight reportorial accounts, because the facts themselves are so monstrous and surreal they not only don't need, but cannot endure, the embellishment of metaphor or artistic design.

This explains Hecht's use of the documentary mode. He takes the horrifying individual story and lets it stand for the entirety. But it's not quite accurate to say the material "cannot endure" any supplemental artistry. If we take the next four stanzas as a narrative unit, for example, we can see how the gruesome story is infused with "artistic design."

> We move now to outside a German wood.
> Three men are there commanded to dig a hole
> In which the two Jews are ordered to lie down
> And be buried alive by the third, who is a Pole.
>
> Not light from the shrine at Weimar beyond the hill
> Nor light from heaven appeared. But he did refuse.
> A Lüger settled back deeply in its glove.
> He was ordered to change places with the Jews.
>
> Much casual death had drained away their souls.
> The thick dirt mounted toward the quivering chin.
> When only the head was exposed the order came
> To dig him out again and to get back in.
>
> No light, no light in the blue Polish eye.
> When he finished a riding boot packed down the earth.
> The Lüger hovered lightly in its glove.
> He was shot in the belly and in three hours bled to death.

This incident is a parable of the way that "casual death" drains the soul. Barbarism completely dehumanizes its victims. The story focuses on the two Jews, the Pole, and the German soldier, who is only identified metonymically as "a Lüger." Everyone is nameless, no one escapes the inhumanity. I have little interest in aestheticizing the subject matter, and yet it's hard not to notice the rhetorical use of *light*, a word that appears six times in the poem. Hecht finally repositions it as a pistol that "hovered *lightly* in its glove." Could Goethe's dream have devolved any further?

The acrid irony of the title only gradually comes into focus. Goethe's deathbed plea reverberates and echoes through a series of intense negations: "Not light . . . / Nor light" and "No light, no light." The Pole's refusal is a straightforward act of heroism. In narrating this event, Hecht specifically reports that a saving light does not come from Weimar, Goethe's home and thus the heart of the German Enlightenment, nor from heaven, which Cardinal Newman identified with the "Kindly Light." By referring to Weimar, Hecht is also calling attention to its proximity to Buchenwald, thereby identifying one of the cultural centers of Europe with historical atrocity. I am reminded of Walter Benjamin's observation, "There is no document of civilization that is not simultaneously a document of barbarism."

Hecht learned the grandeur of rhetorical negation from Shakespeare. He said that of all Shakespeare's plays the one that emotionally moved him the most was *King Lear*, which he called "the bleakest of the plays, the most unconsoling." He adapted the title *The Hard Hours* from *Lear* ("Is there any cause in nature that makes these hard hearts") and it stands behind all of his Holocaust poems, especially the conclusion of "Rites and Ceremonies," where he quotes Lear wandering on the heath: "'None does offend, / None, I say, / None.'" Hecht kept in mind Shakespeare's pun on *no* and *know*, negation and knowledge, and schooled himself on Lear's repeated refusals, the way he repeats "No, no, no, no!" and "Never, never, never, never, never." Lear comes to know "naught" and "nothing can be made out of nothing." Here, Hecht takes the Shakespearean pattern and marshals it for his own devastating consequence. There is a homing down and plainness of style. The literary embellishments, too, come to naught.

The poem moves from "'More Light! More Light!'" to "Nor was he forsaken" to "Not light . . . / Nor Light" to "No light, no light" and finishes, in the rhetorically insistent last stanza, with "No prayers or incense." In conclusion, Hecht both widens and narrows the camera view. First, he denies that any religious petition or magical incantation will come to save human beings from each other. He enlarges and allegorizes the hours into years and then notes the relentless dailiness of the horror. It's hard to think about line breaks when someone is delivering this kind of news, and yet it is enacted through the bracing cut from *mute* to *Ghosts*, and the eerie half rhyme on *mute* and *soot*. One feels the unsettling way that the poem settles into finality:

> No prayers or incense rose up in those hours
> Which grew to be years, and every day came mute
> Ghosts from the ovens, sifting through crisp air,
> And settled upon his eyes in a black soot.

The final image spotlights a permanent blindness. There is no escaping reality here—the indifference of nature, the cruel machinery of death that turned people into soot. Like *King Lear,* "'More Light! More Light!'" is bleak and unconsoling. It denies transcendence or the solace of faith. It refuses to let us look away or distract ourselves. As readers, we, too, are made to watch. No one sleeps better after reading it, but no one forgets what happened, either. The only redemption comes in the fact of "These moving verses." The lyric encounter becomes a challenge, an ethical act of testimony and witness.

Anthony Hecht was a poet of transfigured dread. He combined personal experience with deep reading to come to a moral reckoning and historical understanding. His formalism was a psychological necessity, a way of trying to distance and contain something that was psychologically threatening and perhaps uncontainable. Like that of many classically oriented poets, from Samuel Johnson to Louise Bogan, his literary mode was a way of holding off an overwhelming fear of breakdown and madness. We don't typically think of writing poetry as a form of courage, but Hecht's iron resolve to face the demonic, not just in himself but also in history, strikes me as courageous and humane.

DENISE LEVERTOV (1923–1997)

O Taste and See

The world is
not with us enough.
O Taste and See

the subway Bible poster said,
meaning The Lord, meaning
if anything all that lives
to the imagination's tongue,

grief, mercy, language,
tangerine, weather, to
breathe them, bite,
savor, chew, swallow, transform

into our flesh our
deaths, crossing the street, plum, quince,
living in the orchard and being

hungry, and plucking
the fruit.

1964

As a young poet, I pored over Denise Levertov's essay "Some Notes on Organic Form" (1965) as if it were a Talmudic text. I had been reading Levertov's poems in the American idiom, she clearly had been galvanized by William Carlos Williams and Robert Creeley, but I noticed a spiritual vocabulary and religious reference in her books *The Jacob's*

Ladder (1961) and *O Taste and See* (1964) that gave them a different torque, something I would later identify as Rilkean. There was a mystic element in her work that was difficult to pinpoint. She embraced Williams's motto "no ideas but in things," even as she searched for something beyond concrete reality, what she termed "Marvelous Truth" ("Matins"). She had a concept of the poet as both seer and maker. Now she was formulating a credo: "For me, back of the idea of organic form is the concept that there is a form in all things (and in experience) which the poet can discover and reveal."

It's hard to explain the intensity of the poetry conversation in those days, the excitement of reading magazines that were home-style and worldly, like *Origin* and *Kayak*, the letters, tracts, and position papers around "open field poetics" and "naked poetry." I was schooling myself on the distinction Coleridge made between "mechanic," or predetermined, form and "organic form," which is innate and "develops itself from within," like a living organism, such as a plant, something that evolves spontaneously and effectuates "its own secret growth." Levertov, who was steeped in the natural world since girlhood, liked the idea of art derived from nature, and understood how metaphors of natural form fueled American ideas of originality. She recurred to Emerson's credo in "The Poet" (1844): "For it is not metres, but a metre-making argument, that makes a poem,—a thought so passionate and alive, that, like the spirit of a plant or an animal, it has an architecture of its own, and adorns nature with a new thing." She quoted his aphorism—"Ask the fact for the form"—and studied the modernist preceptors who extended his axioms, Williams ("The Poem as a Field of Action," 1948) and Olson ("Projective Verse," 1950).

At the time I was considering "Some Notes on Organic Form" I was also combing through Robert Duncan's essay "Toward an Open Universe" (1966), which was a fortunate find because the two essays fit together like hand and glove. It was apparent that the two of them sparked off each other. They referred to many of the same precursor texts and injected an esoteric or theological element into the conversation. To me, this seemed both anachronistic and forward looking, as if Gerard Manley Hopkins had wandered into an argument about the nature of form in contemporary American poetry.

Levertov made clear that she spoke for herself. Poetry was part of her own quest—she was presenting "notes," her ideas were in progress—but she also invoked Hopkins's arcane vocabulary, his terms "inscape" and "instress," to describe the underlying order in things. She ventures: "A partial definition, then, of organic poetry might be that it is a method of apperception, i.e., of recognizing what we perceive, and is based on an intuition of an order, a form beyond forms, in which forms partake, and of which man's creative works are analogies, resemblances, natural allegories." Levertov hedges a bit (a *partial* definition, *might be*), but she also posits some ideal, vaguely eternal realm. She takes the Olson/Creeley formula, "Form is never more than an extension of content," and refashions it with religious wording: "Form is never more than a *revelation* of content." The subject was ostensibly modernist form, but it has an air of what Levertov later described as "do-it-yourself theology."

Denise Levertov was born in 1923 and raised in the semirural area of Ilford, Essex, a landscape she describes beautifully in her Wordsworthian poem "A Map of the Western Part of the County of Essex in England." Her mother, Beatrice Spooner-Jones, was a Welsh schoolteacher, an amateur painter and naturalist, an otherworldly person. Levertov deemed her "a virtual innocent." Her father, Paul Levertoff, was an Orthodox Russian Jew who had converted to Christianity and become an Anglican priest. He had an ecstatic streak and a scholarly temperament. He described himself as a Hebrew-Christian—he wrote the first modern Hebrew book about Jesus, *Ben ha-Adam* (1904)—and preached what he considered a form of Messianic Judaism, the unity of two ancient religions. From a Jewish perspective, Messianic Judaism is a strain of Jewish thought that has nothing to do with Christianity and introducing the notion of Jesus as Messiah is not "unifying" two religions but claiming Christianity's victory over Judaism—Levertoff was a Christian. The Jewish community considered him a traitor, the Christian fellowship had no idea what to do with him, but he discerned religious harmony where others saw conflict. He translated parts of the Zohar, studied the Kabbalah, and created a Hebrew-Christian liturgy.

Levertov was proud of the two mystical strains in her Russian and Welsh heritages. Tracking back in her work, I discovered "Illustrious Ancestors" (*Overland to the Highlands*, 1958), which refers to "The Rav / of Northern White Russia," her father's relative Shneur Zalman of Liadi, the first rabbi of Chabad, a Hasidic Jew who was reputed to understand the language of birds, and Angell Jones of Mold, her mother's relative, a Methodist preacher and tailor "whose meditations / were sewn into coats and britches." It was as if a mystical ancestry had been baked into her cells.

Levertov had an involved religious journey. She considered herself spiritually displaced, "by nature, heritage and as an artist, forever a stranger and pilgrim." She named language "her Jerusalem." She called the poet, when writing, "a priest," the poem "a temple." She started out as a skeptic who did not share her parents' fervencies, though her religious sensibility was formed early, and she later converted to a brand of Catholicism, Liberation theology, which married a love of God to an earthly quest for social justice. She called it her "slow movement from agnosticism to Christian faith, a movement incorporating much of doubt and questioning as well as of affirmation." In "A Sense of Pilgrimage," she suggests that "Illustrious Ancestors" reveals the "definite and peculiar destiny" that she shared with her older sister, Olga, who was troubled by mental illness and died in middle age (see the "Olga Poems").

Levertov never had a formal education. She was homeschooled by her mother and influenced by her father, who was emotionally remote but intellectually zealous. She was an avid reader who learned to prize the countryside, to pay attention to the mystery of ordinary things, to compare religions ("The Hasidim were a lot like the Franciscans," she said), and to stand against injustice. Her background made her an outsider. There's a hint of pride in her description of herself: "Among Jews a Goy, among Gentiles (secular or Christian) a Jew or at least a half Jew (which was good or bad according to their degree of anti-Semitism), among Anglo-Saxons a Celt, in Wales a Londoner who not only did not speak Welsh but was not imbued with Welsh attitudes; among school children a strange exception whom they did not know whether to envy or mistrust—all of these anomalies predicted my later experience."

Levertov set out to become a ballerina—she always carried herself like a dancer—but soon changed course and fixed on poetry. She worked as a civilian nurse during World War II and her granular experience of caring for war veterans fueled her later ferocious opposition to the Vietnam War and, eventually, to all wars. Her first book, *The Double Image* (1946), established her as a British Neo-Romantic with a textured sense of the island landscape, with a humanitarian streak and a melancholy tone. But then her life changed. You might say that first she married Mitchell Goodman, a writer and political activist, a secular American Jew—my sense from her biographies is that it was a good match but not a great love affair—and then she moved with him to the United States, and then she fell in love with and had a lifelong love affair with American poetry. They had a son and led a peripatetic life. She became an American citizen in 1955 and an American poet with her second book, *Here and Now* (1956). Kenneth Rexroth greeted it in *Poetry* magazine: "In my opinion Denise Levertov is incomparably the best poet of what is getting to be known as the new avant-garde."

Over a ten-year span, Levertov worked hard to remake herself as a poet of the New World—a poetic daughter of Williams, a sister to the Black Mountain poets. She has something in common with Charles Tomlinson, a British contemporary who was also influenced by Williams and the Objectivist poets, like George Oppen and Louis Zukofsky, but she is more improvisatory and rough-edged than Tomlinson, less Apollonian, more Romantic. So, too, her work is more jazzlike and spontaneous than her Anglo-American contemporary Thom Gunn, who was also influenced by Williams and Duncan but often worked in prescribed forms and crosshatched the Elizabethan lyric with gay life in California. But there is also something intangible driving Levertov's work, whose earthiness was inscribed with transcendental wistfulness and longing. She had internalized her father's fusion of Jewish and Christian sources, his keen attention to the mystic glory of the quotidian, which often seemed to her lit from within. Muriel Rukeyser once said that Levertov's poems were "hymns lying over the basis of that deep scholarship."

Levertov is most moving as a poet of numinous presence. In the mid- to late sixties, she was starting to connect her poetics to her leftist political activism and engagement, which fuse in a book like *The Sorrow Dance* (1967). There was a stridency that entered her poetry in the 1970s in such books as *Relearning the Alphabet* (1970) and *To Stay Alive* (1971) that didn't always fit comfortably with her focus on what she called "the eternal questions." But that intransigence was also part of her temperament and quest. She had a lifelong admiration for Duncan, an avowed spiritualist, but their relationship strained to the breaking point over her determined fusion of poetry and politics. You can almost read the volume of their letters as an epistolary novel—a drama of infatuation and disagreement, enchantment and disenchantment, friendship and difficulty, a wary reconciliation. Much of it hinges on the serious subject of the proper subject matter for poetry.

"O Taste and See," the title poem of Levertov's sixth book, is an explor-
atory lyric, compact and expansive. The poem consists of one short declar-
ative sentence and one longer winding one. Sixteen lines, five stanzas, a
dynamic of perception and discovery. Like Williams, she is a poet of the
taut line and the cunning line break—each line modifies and changes the
meaning of the one that came before it. Levertov lifts her title from Psalm
34: "This poor man cried, and the Lord heard him, and saved him out of all
his troubles. . . . O taste and see that the Lord is good" (King James Bible).
This is an injunction by the psalmist to experience the world for yourself and
know God's bounty. The poet lops off the part about the Lord and works
through the consequences of that initial precept for herself.

The lyric begins with a swipe at Wordsworth, who declared: "The world
is too much with us; late and soon, / Getting and spending, we lay waste
our powers." In a defining sonnet, Wordsworth compacted the idea of "the
world" to mean worldliness, industrial labor divorced from nature, but
Levertov redefines the terms and opts for immersion rather than removal.
She wants us to throw ourselves into the fray. She syncopates the lines, iso-
lating the phrases to create a minidrama of consciousness. Look at the first
stanza:

> The world is
> not with us enough.
> O Taste and See

The first line stands alone as an existential assertion, a statement about being:
"The world *is*." But then it spills over into a rhetorical refutation of Words-
worth's argument, and you hear it a little differently: "The world is / *not with
us* enough." The speaker follows this short sentence with a religious com-
mand: "O Taste and See," which is spotlighted as the title of the poem. The
speaker uses the first-person plural—it's almost imperceptible at first—and
has a design upon us. This poem carries its own sacramental instruction to
incorporate the world into ourselves.

There is a note of sly merriment here, too, because the poet deliberately
does not enclose this statement in quotation marks, and so it coils a sur-
prise as we drop from one stanza to the next. We're taking things down a
notch. O taste and see

> the subway Bible poster said,
> meaning The Lord, meaning
> if anything all that lives
> to the imagination's tongue

The statement is being lifted from a poster on the subway, one of those evangelical tracts that most of us shy away from. It's a work of unintended pop art. There's a clever chiasmus that also repeats the same word at the front and the end of the line, which was one of the favored rhetorical devices of John Donne: "*meaning* The Lord, *meaning*." The comma changes the timing. She interjects an element of doubt into the line break, "meaning / *if anything*," but then enlarges that into "all that lives" and associates that into an original phrasing, something that only she could have come up with: "imagination's tongue." We can comprehend the world only through a creative act of imagination, she suggests, but that imagination is incarnated in taste, in savoring the world. Taste first, she implies, and then you will see. The world exists.

One might expect to follow a call of this sort with an inventory of earthly riches, but Levertov rapidly upends that idea with a catalogue that is quirkier and more unlikely than a roll call of fruits in the garden. She chooses words with a more complex valence and segments the list into two parts.

> grief, mercy, language,
> tangerine, weather, to

The first line presses together and progresses from *grief*, a deep emotional response to loss, to *mercy*, the human capacity for compassion, and *language*, a structured system of communication, the poet's toolbox. These three nouns are also large and abstract—they all have resonance for the secular but religiously minded poet—and the next line counters with something weirdly specific, *tangerine*, and places that in the context of *weather*. We are playfully inferring something about fruit in the garden. This funny line—"tangerine, weather, to"—holds and then drops, so that the syntax joins the words "to / breathe them" and continues with a sensuous mouthful of verbs: "bite, / savor, chew, swallow, transform."

Levertov is associating rapidly, and here she characterizes the work of the "imagination's tongue," which is asking us to take our time and eat the world. The word *transform* stands out and suggests another kind of action. It is taking the food—grief, tangerine—and ingesting it, turning it into something else. You have to slow the poem down to catch its exact logic. The world is something that we transform

> into *our* flesh *our*
> deaths, crossing the street, plum, quince,

When you read this, you hover over the second *our* and then plunge down into the unexpectedly heavy word *deaths*—Rilke counseled each of us to have a death of our own. But then the action picks up, we seem to have come out of the subway into the fresh air: "crossing the street." The lineation is packed so that the line reads "deaths, crossing the street, plum, quince." And now the poem does move into an orchard, which feels like the Garden of Eden:

> living in the orchard and being
>
> hungry, and plucking
> the fruit.

The line for Levertov is a precise unit, and she purposefully segments "living in the orchard and *being*," so that we hear an echo of the opening line, "The world *is*." But then she crosses a gap of blank space to link the words *being* and *hungry*. She circles back to the first command, "O Taste," and gives it new meaning and resonance. For now, being in the world suggests that we are living in the orchard as in some original state, and having an appetite, or appetites, and "plucking / the fruit." The implication that we must live like Eve in the garden is unmistakable here. We should celebrate and eat the apple—the tangerine, the plum, the quince—and experience the world. We are incarnating paradise, here and now, in this fallen world, which is not with us enough. The bountiful sweetness of earth is a furthering of divine goodness. O taste and see!

I remember opening a large new tabloid in 1972 called *The American Poetry Review* and discovering Levertov's essay "The Poet in the World," which crystalized my thinking about her practice. It begins with an image of the poet in labor and ends with a figure of mindfulness. She quotes the section in Rilke's novel *The Notebooks of Malte Laurids Brigge*, "For the sake of a single verse": "Verses are not, as people imagine, simply feelings (we have those soon enough); they are experiences." She answers the question of poetry's relationship to politics by arguing that the poet is a participant in life, not a mere observer, and that we are living in *"a state of emergency,"* which is certainly still true now. She calls for a "fruitful reciprocity between poem and action" and takes up the meaning of Williams's credo, which she links to E. M. Forster's famous imperative in *Howards End*: "Only connect! That was the whole of her sermon." To quote her more fully:

> "No ideas but in things," said William Carlos Williams. This does not mean "no ideas." It means that "language [and here I quote Wordsworth] is not the dress but the incarnation of thoughts." "No ideas but in things," means, essentially, "Only connect." And it is therefore not only a craft-statement, not only an aesthetic statement (though it is these things also, and importantly), but a moral statement. *Only connect. No ideas but in things.* The words reverberate through the poet's life, through *my* life, and I hope through your lives.

Denise Levertov was a poet of thoughtful feeling, who worked her way toward a poetics of immediacy and incarnation. She was a political activist who insisted that she was not a mystic, though the mystical strain in her work seems everywhere apparent. She was ever eager to connect, to root down and look upwards. She was a passionate Jewish Christian who brought a dancing joy and fervor to an openly sacramental postmodern American poetry.

FRANK O'HARA (1926–1966)

The Day Lady Died

It is 12:20 in New York a Friday
three days after Bastille day, yes
it is 1959 and I go get a shoeshine
because I will get off the 4:19 in Easthampton
at 7:15 and then go straight to dinner
and I don't know the people who will feed me

I walk up the muggy street beginning to sun
and have a hamburger and a malted and buy
an ugly NEW WORLD WRITING to see what the poets
in Ghana are doing these days
                                    I go on to the bank
and Miss Stillwagon (first name Linda I once heard)
doesn't even look up my balance for once in her life
and in the GOLDEN GRIFFIN I get a little Verlaine
for Patsy with drawings by Bonnard although I do
think of Hesiod, trans. Richmond Lattimore or
Brendan Behan's new play or *Le Balcon* or *Les Nègres*
of Genet, but I don't, I stick with Verlaine
after practically going to sleep with quandariness

and for Mike I just stroll into the PARK LANE
Liquor Store and ask for a bottle of Strega and
then I go back where I came from to 6th Avenue
and the tobacconist in the Ziegfeld Theatre and
casually ask for a carton of Gauloises and a carton
of Picayunes, and a NEW YORK POST with her face on it

and I am sweating a lot by now and thinking of
leaning on the john door in the 5 SPOT
while she whispered a song along the keyboard
to Mal Waldron and everyone and I stopped breathing

1964

F RANK O'HARA'S poems are ever fresh. His work is sunburst and
street-savvy, off-the-cuff, in a hurry. He was a poet on the move, a
walker in the city, a flaneur. An art critic who specialized in abstract expres-
sionism and pop art, a curator at the Museum of Modern Art, one of the five
pillars of what would be named the New York School of poets—along with
John Ashbery, Kenneth Koch, James Schuyler, and Barbara Guest—he left
an indelible imprint on the cultural world of New York City. As a poet who
moved among painters and internalized the progressive spirit in art—Jasper
Johns compared him to the Greek god Hermes "carrying messages among
poets and painters"—he was our Apollinaire. O'Hara, too, took a stand
with the moderns and delivered a good-natured verdict on what the French
poet called "the long quarrel between tradition and invention, / Order and
Adventure" ("The Pretty Redhead").

O'Hara's insouciant poems crush the expectations of how poetry is sup-
posed to sound. Wordsworth took the diction of poetry down a peg to the
commonplace, then Frost and Williams lowered it even further, attuning it to
American speech patterns, sentence sounds—Frost in blank verse, Williams
in a new measure. And then the New York poets came along and crashed
the party altogether. Their poems are comfortable with popular culture in
ways that a lot of the coterie is not. The Beats did something similar, though
they were so rankled by consumer culture's materialism that you feel the
burn of hostility. O'Hara took things in a different, slyer direction. You drop
into a world when you read, say, "Having a Coke with You" or "Ave Maria"
("Mothers of America / let your kids go to the movies!"), or "Music," which
begins with the speaker having a liver sausage sandwich in the Mayflower
Shoppe near a gilded bronze equestrian statue of General Sherman in Cen-
tral Park, or "Poem" ["Lana Turner has collapsed!"]. A surprising number of
these high-octane adventures in the dailiness of life are called simply "Poem,"
as if to make a point—this, too, is poetry. There is an unusual democracy of

language and subject matter, a campy revel in everyday juxtapositions. Here is the beginning of "Today":

> Oh! kangaroos, sequins, chocolate sodas!
> You really are beautiful! Pearls,
> harmonicas, jujubes, aspirins! all
> the stuff they've always talked about
>
> still makes a poem a surprise!

There's visible pleasure in all the shiny stuff crammed into the opening of this poem, and a gleeful startle in the phrasing, too, the exclamatory voice, the joyous recognition that everything they've ever talked about still makes a poem—and, what's more, it still makes a poem a surprise. "These things are with us every day," O'Hara affirms, and "They / do have meaning."

O'Hara liked to upend the Romantic and modernist expectations, to astonish with the commonplace of it all and, even more, to be astonished. He also liked to demystify the idea of a poet. As he said in his playful manifesto "Personism," "I don't believe in god, so I don't have to make elaborately sounded structures. I hate Vachel Lindsay, always have; I don't even like rhythm, assonance, all that stuff. You just go on your nerve. If someone's chasing you down the street with a knife you just run, you don't turn around and shout, 'Give it up! I was a track star for Mineola Prep.'" This is droll and irreverent, but it also captures the quirky dynamism of O'Hara's work. He said that "after all, only Whitman and Crane and Williams, of the American poets, are better than the movies." He liked excitement and experimentation, crosscutting and cinematic presence, and his artful brashness was in the American grain. Like the American moderns he admired, he was a singer of the present tense, pitching himself forward, tuned to the immediacies, to the moment.

O'Hara was that appreciable American phenomenon—the homemade cosmopolitan, who didn't have any problem wedding the highs and lows of culture. The poets of the New York School had a strong French connection, and O'Hara was especially energized by the linguistic stylings of Arthur Rimbaud, Stéphane Mallarmé, and Pierre Reverdy. He also loved the Russian poets Boris Pasternak and Vladimir Mayakovsky, who keep turning up in his work. It was fitting when Don Draper, the handsome advertising executive in the show *Mad Men*, suddenly started reading O'Hara's poem "Mayakovsky" at the end of the second season. You can hear one of the stanzas in voic-eover: "Now I am quietly waiting for / the catastrophe of my personality / to seem beautiful again, / and interesting, and modern." There is something doomed and beautiful about this passage, which articulates the existential dilemma of an executive trapped in a gray flannel suit, but it also tells us something crucial about the emotional underpinnings of a mid-century American poet, who is speaking in the guise of one of the tragic suicides of modern poetry. It is as if he inhabits Mayakovsky's ghost to ward off his fate. Part of the distractedness of O'Hara's work is the way in which he keeps putting aside his knowledge of death.

John Ashbery pointed out that it was from Mayakovsky that O'Hara "picked up what James Schuyler has called 'the intimate yell.'" O'Hara dedicated his early hallucinatory poem "Second Avenue" to Mayakovsky, and then linked him to the painter Willem de Kooning. As he explained: "Where Mayakovsky and de Kooning come in, is that they both have done works as big as cities where the life in the work is autonomous (not about actual city life) and yet similar." This reveals O'Hara's ambition to rival city life, to capture its zeal without treating it as a destination subject. The method of a futurist Russian poetry has been joined to an abstract American art. At times it feels as if O'Hara is talking to you while you're walking together on a noisy street, say Second Avenue at rush hour. It's a bit surreal and frenetic, the intimate yell.

Thinking about O'Hara's project, I want to linger for a moment over his poem "A True Account of Talking to the Sun on Fire Island," which is inspired by Mayakovsky's "An Extraordinary Adventure Which Befell Vladimir Mayakovsky in a Summer Cottage." The sun in O'Hara's poem makes the comparison: "'When I woke up Mayakovsky he was / a lot more prompt' the Sun said / petulantly. 'Most people are up / already waiting to see if I'm going / to put in an appearance.'" Here, O'Hara distinguishes between the Russian poet, who took time off from his epic commitments to gossip with the sun, and the American one, who darts around the city and heads to Fire Island for a break from the tumult. The sun advises O'Hara—in other words, the poet advises himself in the voice of the sun—to "always embrace things, people earth / sky stars, as I do, freely and with / the appropriate sense of space. That / is your inclination." This is Whitmanian. Both Mayakovsky and Apollinaire loved Whitman. It's striking how the bedrock American poet was channeled back to O'Hara through the funny lens of two urbane moderns from other countries, who dropped punctuation from their poems and ventured into uncharted territory, talking to the sun or comparing it to a pretty redhead.

O'Hara was eager to present himself as an action poet—it was as if he was afraid of ever stopping. You can feel the dynamic in his two books of witty impromptus, *Meditations in an Emergency* (1957) and *Lunch Poems* (1964). He was a fast walker, his poems don't linger, but they do rove around, and they don't head anywhere in a straight line. He didn't like predetermined structures. In the mid-century aesthetic battle between open and closed forms, O'Hara took the side of openness, though without the battle-cry polemics of a poetic theorist like Charles Olson. He liked the momentum of "Projective Verse" but ignored the project in it—the prophetic stance irritated him. Instead, he wrote flirtatious gay love poems, campy odes to pop icons, conversational poems, and hymns to the city that were only partly about the city. He was alert and wrote: "It's not that I'm curious. On the contrary, I am bored but it's my duty to be attentive, I am needed by things as the sky must be above the earth" ("Meditations in an Emergency"). This is a playful American spin on the Rilkean notion of being needed by things. Thinking about Edwin Denby's dance criticism, he stated unequivocally, "attention equals Life."

O'Hara was a poet of lived experience. He liked to mingle with Manhattan crowds and timed his poems to the pace of the metropolis at different hours, sometimes rapid and carefree, other times quieter. Some of them he wrote at parties after work, some of them he scrawled on napkins at the Cedar Tavern, where the abstract expressionists hung out, many of them he dashed off on his lunch hour in midtown. There are a lot of casual poems that read like jottings or diary entries, but even his throwaways have charisma. Allen Ginsberg noted that he had "a common ear / for our deep gossip" ("City Midnight Junk Strains"). O'Hara's poetry is not confessional—in fact, he disliked Robert Lowell's work and mocked the whole idea of the confessional poem—and yet his personality shines so vividly that you feel as if he's still there. He's an extravagantly gay poet, but he's also an all-purpose seducer. You hear him talking and feel like ambling over with a drink. Maybe you'll start smoking again, just for the hell of it. It's hard not to believe that you're going to become friends. People tend to fall in love with O'Hara in the same irreparable way that they fall in love with Keats.

"The Day Lady Died" is one of those times that O'Hara was struck by lightning. He wrote the poem during his lunch hour on July 17, 1959, and read it that night at Mike Goldberg and Patsy Southgate's home in East Hampton. He says that he didn't know the people who would feed him that night, but that was something he said for effect—he was creating a slightly harried, alienated feeling—because he knew perfectly well that he and Joe LeSueur were taking the train out to their friends' house in the Hamptons for dinner. He published the poem the next year in Donald Allen's innovative anthology, *The New American Poetry, 1945–1960*, and then collected it in *Lunch Poems*.

Billie Holiday was nicknamed *Lady Day* by her music partner Lester Young, and there is a clever reversal of the phrase (a chiasmus!) in the title of O'Hara's poem, "The *Day Lady* Died," which forever marks a fateful day in the calendar. At first, the title is the only clue that this poem is an elegy for one of our greatest jazz singers, who died painfully early at the age of forty-four. It is a sideways elegy; it doesn't meditate on Billie Holiday's life and music. Instead, an immediate tension arises between the past tense of the title and the present tense of the poem itself. The title is retrospective, the poem ongoing.

"The Day Lady Died" has an engaging immediacy ("*It is* 12:20 in New York a Friday / three days after Bastille day, yes / *it is* 1959") and propulsive forward motion, a performing dailiness that carries it breezily along. O'Hara makes a point of saying that this is not Bastille Day; in other words, not a monumental day in the calendar, not a national holiday. O'Hara called his poetic genre "I do this I do that," a description that has caught on. Not many also observe that his jaunt is an update of the itinerary poem, like Gray's "Elegy Written in a Country Churchyard," or Wordsworth's "Descriptive Sketches," or, most pertinently, Apollinaire's "Zone," which tracks his urban rounds during a single day. The itinerary poem may wander around, but it is not haphazard.

"The Day Lady Died," which chronicles an otherwise ordinary day, is visibly aware of its own transience—yes, it takes place in 1959; yes, it moves in time from 12:20 to 4:19 to 7:15. It contains its own timetable. Three of the stanzas begin with movement: "I walk," "I go," "I just stroll." The poem charts its own activity so carefully that you could map it block by block as the speaker gets a shoeshine and walks up the muggy street for a quick lunch and picks up a copy of the paperback anthology *New World Writing*, featuring poets from Ghana. The dropped line ("I go on to the bank") creates a sense of impulsivity as he takes his trip around midtown. He finds it worth mentioning that the proper Miss Stillwagon doesn't even look up his balance "for once in her life," which seems like a bit of luck—maybe he's not so questionable to her, after all. Then on to the Griffin bookstore, where he perseverates over what to buy, then to the Park Lane liquor store and finally to the tobacconist in the Ziegfeld Theatre.

There are pauses but no rest stops in these twenty-nine lines; there are commas but no periods. It is all written in an onrushing ethnographic present tense. The speaker toggles between his all-American experience—he has a hamburger and a malted for lunch—and his more sophisticated tastes. You can tell how much he likes French culture as he zips around shopping for gifts. One of the oddities of O'Hara's walking poems is how often he refers to French culture while he is floating through Manhattan—it's as if he is always wondering what they are doing over there in Paris. He buys a copy of Paul Verlaine's poems with drawings by Pierre Bonnard, though he also considers two of Jean Genet's plays. It is all a bit diverted, even diverting. But while he is casually buying his European smokes, the speaker suddenly glances over at a local newspaper. His voice hits a radically different note at this moment when he spots Billie Holiday's face on the cover of a *New York Post* and abruptly realizes she is gone:

> and I am sweating a lot by now and thinking of
> leaning on the john door in the 5 SPOT
> while she whispered a song along the keyboard
> to Mal Waldron and everyone and I stopped breathing

O'Hara suddenly catapults back in memory as the poem turns for the first time to the continuous present: "and I am sweating . . . and thinking." He is marking the change from a temporal to a timeless experience. The speaker is transported back to the Five Spot, a bohemian hangout, and the night he heard Billie Holiday unexpectedly sing there. Holiday had lost her cabaret card in the late fifties, ostensibly because of narcotics, but much more likely due to the racist backlash against her performance of "Strange Fruit," Abel Meeropol's great protest poem. She paid dearly for her commitment, her art, and so could not sing legally at the Five Spot, though she sometimes dropped by to support her friend Mal Waldron, the house pianist. Every now and then, when the policeman agreeably looked the other way, she would get up to sing.

O'Hara aptly uses the word *whispered* to recall Holiday's late, whispery vocal style. He presses together the words *song* and *along* and thus slows down the movement of the line to capture something of her rhythmic method. Holiday learned something from the way that Louis Armstrong played his trumpet and sang, markedly slowing the phrase or holding back from it, hesitating, to create expectation, and then continuing with a little cache of fulfillment, making it seem completed, as if everything had been said. She had a way of slurring a word, sashaying a phrase. She would start, elongate, drop the volume a pitch, then hit it with a lilt. O'Hara captures the prolonged way she held certain vowels by noting how she whispered "a song *along* the keyboard." Her voice is moving with the piano music. He is trying to pin down the sudden, unexpected nature of his experience. He was standing near the toilet door and had a side view as he leaned into one of the transformative artistic experiences of his life. There's a marvelous enjambment in the penultimate line. It's as if you're standing on the edge of a cliff—"while she whispered a song along the keyboard"—and then go tumbling over—"to Mal Waldron."

Everything that happened on the day of Billie Holiday's death now takes on a retrospective shine, engraved in memory. What initially seemed so everyday turns out to be an elegy. Everything is memorialized on that day, held in place by its hidden significance. There is a dazzling rightness to the last phrase ("and everyone and I stopped breathing") that enacts a moment when art ruptures the surface of ordinary life and stops time. The poem itself breaks off and stops breathing. It is a moment of return, of transcendence recalled, that also reverberates with the hard knowledge of Billie Holiday's tragic death.

"The Day Lady Died" has travelled a long distance in a short time. Frank O'Hara was a poet of the present tense, but he also had a tense sense of time passing. We don't typically think of him as an elegiac poet, and yet his greatest single poem is a jazz elegy, a song for one of the necessary American artists, a timely improvisation that lifts us beyond time. It is heart-stopping. You just go on your nerve. Sometimes when I finish rereading the last lines I go back and read the poem again from the beginning in order to retrace the itinerary. As I rewalk the route, I feel as if this time I'm going to prepare myself for the ending, which seems both unexpected and inevitable. And yet each time I reread "The Day Lady Died" I get lured back into the trap, the shock—the catastrophe of death, the life of art. It takes my breath away.

ALLEN GINSBERG (1926–1997)

America

America I've given you all and now I'm nothing.
America two dollars and twentyseven cents January 17, 1956.
I can't stand my own mind.
America when will we end the human war?
Go fuck yourself with your atom bomb.
I don't feel good don't bother me.
I won't write my poem till I'm in my right mind.
America when will you be angelic?
When will you take off your clothes?
When will you look at yourself through the grave?
When will you be worthy of your million Trotskyites?
America why are your libraries full of tears?
America when will you send your eggs to India?
I'm sick of your insane demands.
When can I go into the supermarket and buy what I need with
    my good looks?
America after all it is you and I who are perfect not the next world.
Your machinery is too much for me.
You made me want to be a saint.
There must be some other way to settle this argument.
Burroughs is in Tangiers I don't think he'll come back it's sinister.
Are you being sinister or is this some form of practical joke?
I'm trying to come to the point.
I refuse to give up my obsession.
America stop pushing I know what I'm doing.
America the plum blossoms are falling.
I haven't read the newspapers for months, everyday somebody goes
    on trial for murder.
America I feel sentimental about the Wobblies.

America I used to be a communist when I was a kid I'm not sorry.
I smoke marijuana every chance I get.
I sit in my house for days on end and stare at the roses in the closet.
When I go to Chinatown I get drunk and never get laid.
My mind is made up there's going to be trouble.
You should have seen me reading Marx.
My psychoanalyst thinks I'm perfectly right.
I won't say the Lord's Prayer.
I have mystical visions and cosmic vibrations.
America I still haven't told you what you did to Uncle Max after he
   came over from Russia.
I'm addressing you.
Are you going to let your emotional life be run by Time Magazine?
I'm obsessed by Time Magazine.
I read it every week.
Its cover stares at me every time I slink past the corner candystore.
I read it in the basement of the Berkeley Public Library.
It's always telling me about responsibility. Businessmen are serious.
   Movie producers are serious. Everybody's serious but me.
It occurs to me that I am America.
I am talking to myself again.

Asia is rising against me.
I haven't got a chinaman's chance.
I'd better consider my national resources.
My national resources consist of two joints of marijuana millions of
   genitals an unpublishable private literature that jetplanes 1400 miles
   an hour and twentyfive-thousand mental institutions.
I say nothing about my prisons nor the millions of underprivileged who
   live in my flowerpots under the light of five hundred suns.
I have abolished the whorehouses of France, Tangiers is the next to go.
My ambition is to be President despite the fact that I'm a Catholic.

America how can I write a holy litany in your silly mood?
I will continue like Henry Ford my strophes are as individual as his
   automobiles more so they're all different sexes.
America I will sell you strophes $2500 apiece $500 down on your old strophe

America free Tom Mooney
America save the Spanish Loyalists
America Sacco & Vanzetti must not die
America I am the Scottsboro boys.
America when I was seven momma took me to Communist Cell meetings
　　they sold us garbanzos a handful per ticket a ticket costs a nickel and
　　the speeches were free everybody was angelic and sentimental about
　　the workers it was all so sincere you have no idea what a good thing
　　the party was in 1835 Scott Nearing was a grand old man a real mensch
　　Mother Bloor the Silk-strikers' Ewig-Weibliche made me cry I once saw
　　the Yiddish orator Israel Amter plain. Everybody must have been a spy.
America you don't really want to go to war.
America its them bad Russians.
Them Russians them Russians and them Chinamen. And them Russians.
The Russia wants to eat us alive. The Russia's power mad. She wants to
　　take our cars from out our garages.
Her wants to grab Chicago. Her needs a Red *Reader's Digest*. Her
　　wants our auto plants in Siberia. Him big bureaucracy running our
　　fillingstations.
That no good. Ugh. Him make Indians learn read. Him need big black
　　niggers. Hah. Her make us all work sixteen hours a day. Help.
America this is quite serious.
America this is the impression I get from looking in the television set.
America is this correct?
I'd better get right down to the job.
It's true I don't want to join the Army or turn lathes in precision parts
　　factories, I'm nearsighted and psychopathic anyway.
America I'm putting my queer shoulder to the wheel.

Berkeley, January 17, 1956

ALLEN GINSBERG was one of the holy eccentrics of poetry—a
gay, leftist, Jewish Buddhist, a spiritual seeker who fashioned
himself after two of the self-inventors, William Blake and Walt Whitman,
who were Romantic visionaries, prophetic guides. As an American outlier,
a Jersey boy, Ginsberg had to figure things out for himself and forge a path

through the morass of the thirties, forties, and fifties, the historical surround
of the Depression and World War II, the politics of the Cold War era, a mid-
century materialist popular culture. He had to figure himself out, too, and
deal with his own fearful desires and budding ambitions, irrational feelings
and conflicted loyalties. He was a good student—his high school classmates
called him "the Professor"—but it wasn't easy to fit in; he tried and realized
that he needed to break the mold and construct a lineage. When I met him
in the early 1980s, he was already a public figure, the most famous poet of
his generation, indeed, the most famous poet on the planet, and yet I still
felt as if I could detect in him the fervently literary kid from Newark, the
eager left-wing teenager who wanted to be president of the debating society
at Paterson Central High School. He had once intended to become a labor
lawyer. It's useful to recall the environment of his childhood—where he
came from, how he grew up.

Irwin Allen Ginsberg was born on June 3, 1926, at Beth Israel Hospital
and grew up in a secular Jewish family radically committed to social justice.
As agnostics and atheists, they were not observant Jews—he did not have
a bar mitzvah, for example—but they had Jewish values. His father, Louis,
was a clever but somewhat stiff formal poet, a high school teacher, and a
socialist; his mother, Naomi, a Russian émigré, was a stalwart communist.
They were so politically oriented that they named his older brother Eugene
after the Socialist Party candidate for president, Eugene V. Debs. Ginsberg
was devoted to both his parents; he rebelled against the attachments, and yet
he also had difficulty breaking from them—his father, who introduced him
to poetry, his mother, whose madness shaped his life.

Ginsberg was fragile and many times in his own emotional danger and
mental trouble. "Howl," the most influential poem in the second half of
the twentieth century, is dedicated to Carl Solomon, whom he met when
they were both in the New York State Psychiatric Institute. "The unworldly
love hypostatized as comradeship through thick and thin with Carl Solo-
mon rose out of primordial filial loyalty to my mother, then in distress,"
he wrote in 1986. "Kaddish," his radiant memorial dedicated to his mother
("Strange now to think of you, gone without corsets & eyes, while I walk on
/ the sunny pavement in Greenwich Village"), is a meditation that sweeps
through her tormented biography. Part of its motive was to compensate
for the kaddish that was never said at her funeral—there weren't enough

men there to comprise a minyan, or quorum. The poem is an anguished, guilt-ridden, and heart-wrenching testimonial written in a new American syncretism, as if Williams Carlos Williams had been steeped in the Psalms. Ginsberg knew what it was like to be an outsider and was ever sympathetic to the lost and marginal, the mentally anguished, the outcast—his mother, himself.

The Beat movement was launched when Ginsberg read "Howl" at a gallery in San Francisco in 1955. It was a poetic bombshell. Michael McClure later said that everyone immediately recognized that "a barrier had been broken, that a human voice and body had been hurled against the harsh wall of America and its supporting armies and navies and academies and institutions and ownership systems and power-support bases." Like *The Waste Land*, the poem had a tremendous generational reach. It seemed to diagnose and summarize an era, but it was also intensely personal, a confessional. It has a Whitmanian incantatory pulse and pays tribute to his wide band of acquaintances and friends—hipster angels, dharmic bums, the ones he felt were sacrificed to Moloch, the ancient Canaanite god that he deemed the ruthless god of capitalism, all those "who walked all night with their shoes full of blood on the snowbank docks waiting for a door in the East River to open to a room full of steam-heat and opium." "Howl" is the title poem of Ginsberg's first and most famous book, and so it tends to take up all the oxygen, but this whole book has an infernal comic radiance, and the light shines through each one of these unlikely poems, especially in the first section: "Footnote to Howl," "A Supermarket in California," "Sunflower Sutra," "In the Baggage Room at Greyhound," and "America."

Ginsberg wrote "America," a boisterous, funny, furious, and politically engaged poem, at a time when he was broke but America was booming. He was at the forefront of a nascent counterculture, young and colorful at a moment when most of the country seemed middle-aged and bland, a leftist in a socially conservative Cold War era. Joseph McCarthy had been discredited, but politicians were still weirdly paranoid about communism. These were the Eisenhower years—Robert Lowell deemed them "the tranquilized Fifties"—and Ginsberg wanted to crash them. He had friends with a shared purpose—*Howl* is dedicated to four soulmates: Jack Kerouac, "new Buddha of American prose," William S. Burroughs, Neal Cassady, and Lucien Carr—but he also felt like an alien in his own country. In the late sixties,

Richard Howard pinpointed the feeling when he titled his book about mid-twentieth-century American poetry *Alone with America*, which I read at the same time as Richard Hofstadter's treatise *Anti-intellectualism in American Life*.

Ginsberg locates his poem historically at an exact place (Berkeley, California) and moment in time (January 17, 1956). He doesn't pretend to disguise his speaker and performs as himself, addressing America directly—as a nation, a multiplicity of citizens, and a community idea and historical ideal. The poem is an apostrophe to America, and Ginsberg exploits the essential oddness of the apostrophic mode, of speaking to a nonhuman entity as if it is really a person. As Anne Bradstreet addresses a book she has written ("The Author to Her Book") and Hart Crane speaks to a hybrid cable-stayed/suspension bridge ("To Brooklyn Bridge"), so Ginsberg talks directly to his country. Sometimes he treats that country as a confidant ("You made me want to be a saint"), sometimes as a political monster ("Go fuck yourself with your atom bomb"). The address veers wildly between fury and comedy, intimacy and rage. Much of it has the feeling of an edgy family gathering that at any moment might go off the rails, but somehow never does. Tempting as it might be, he never storms off.

"America" has an air of the offhanded impromptu, but it is not mere stream of consciousness, as is sometimes thought, and it is not a diary, though it has a diaristic manner. Like the Romantic poets, Ginsberg valued spontaneity, and, like them, he sometimes pretended not to revise his poems. He liked to refer to Blake's maxim: "First thoughts are best in art, second thoughts in other matters." In Ginsberg's early work he professed not to rescript his poems, though the manuscripts indicate that he reworked them considerably. Later in life, he took his prescription to heart. Personally, I think he did himself a disservice by continually repeating the mantra "First thought, best thought," which was coined by his Buddhist teacher Chögyam Trungpa. It encouraged fearlessness but underestimated artistry. There is an improvisatory quality to his best poems, but they are far too considered to be labeled automatic writing.

Ginsberg kept a journal all his life, which included many early drafts of his finished poems, among them "America," begun in 1954. It originally opened with a long Whitmanian call for inspiration: "I'll sing of America and Time / for as I lie in my bed alone one night / I ruminated with my secret soul / in ancient rhetoric." And it concluded on a more furious and bitter note: "Dark America! toward whom I close my eyes for prophecy, / and bend my speaking heart! / Betrayed! Betrayed!" When he revised the poem, Ginsberg capitalized the first letter of each line, thus giving it a tiny bit more liftoff, formalizing each line as a unit of meaning. Most interestingly, he transformed the first-draft prophetic melodrama by making fun of it, which allowed him to be prophetic and parody himself at the same time.

So, too, as the writer Jonah Raskin discovered, when Ginsberg first published the poem in *Black Mountain Review* (#7, 1957), he added a second section, which begins "America how shall we cultivate the Cosmic Vibrations?" This picks up a line in the first stanza of the poem, "I have mystical visions and cosmic vibrations," but the change from "I" to "we" takes out the testimonial note and underlines the didacticism. Filled with generalizations and abstractions, this long-limbed, sonnet-length postscript drops any mention of "I" and "You," the central relationship that motors the poem, and Ginsberg wisely cut it when he republished the poem in *Howl and Other Poems*. It does have one charmed line, though, which I wish had found a place in the finished poem: "Man, listen to that band of angels swing!" This line rhymes with the seriocomic jazz combinations of "Footnote to Howl," such as "Holy the groaning saxophone! Holy the bop apocalypse! Holy the jazzbands marijuana hipsters peace peyote pipes & drums!"

"America" maintains a digressive manner, but formally it is a litany. Most of the lines are full sentences, though the poet sometimes extends the line inordinately so that it resembles prose. Ginsberg knew that the litany has its roots in religious practice, liturgical prayer. He was well aware of the difficulty of writing a sacred poem in a country dominated by the likes of *Time* magazine ("America how can I write a holy litany in your silly mood?"). Ginsberg treats the litany as a catalogue poem, a long syntactically repetitive work, like the book of Psalms. He liked to fool around, but he wasn't fooling when he turned to the English and American rhapsodists as models, to Christopher Smart ("Jubilate Agno"), William Blake (*America a Prophecy*), and Walt Whitman ("Crossing Brooklyn Ferry"), the great foolhardy lyricists of the prophetic mode.

Both Whitman and Ginsberg consistently relied on anaphora, the repetition of the same word or words at the beginning of lines and sentences, which creates a towering effect. The key to anaphora is that each line is a repetition with a difference. Robert Alter, a translator and scholar of the Hebrew Bible, calls it "a productive tension between sameness and difference, reiteration and development." Something is reiterated, something else added or subtracted. Our attention keeps shifting from the phrasing repeated to the phrasing newly introduced. What recurs is changed.

Whereas the anaphoric litany tends to be chantlike, Ginsberg is spiritually disenchanted and so repeatedly interrupts the rhythmic continuities. This is one way he undermines and destabilizes the Whitmanian praise poem for America, though he also tries to harness its energy and claim its amplitude. He may be extremely ironic about the Emersonian claim ("America is a poem in our eyes") and yet he is also writing a poem called "America."

"Art is the path of the creator to his work," Emerson stated in his essay "The Poet" (1844), and Ginsberg had to find his own rebellious path to that freshness, a personal encounter with a vast materialistic country. What can one person say to a nation? Ginsberg's exuberant poem begins with a sense of being depleted: "America I've given you all and now I'm nothing." He is fed up with capitalism and it is done with him. Now he is literally out of resources: "America two dollars and twentyseven cents January 17, 1956." Ginsberg comically confesses how little money he has in a country that values money above all. The country could not care less. He is self-mocking and tormented, being driven crazy by his own impotence ("I can't stand my own mind") before an inhuman machine ("America when will we end the human war?"). Sometimes he takes a Blakean tack ("America when will you be angelic?") or Beat attitude toward capitalism ("When can I go into the supermarket and buy what I need with my good looks?").

The premise of Ginsberg's poem is that a single human being is trying to talk to a mega-governmental abstraction: "Your machinery is too much for me." He brings it down to human scale and impatiently demands: "When will you take off your clothes?" Sometimes he tries to get on its nerves by bragging about being a tea head ("I smoke marijuana every chance I get"), other times he wants to shake the country by its lapels ("I'm addressing you") and give it a warning ("My mind is made up there's going to be trouble").

There's a strong leftist current running through the poem, a casually tossed-off history. The speaker feels attached to the followers of the ill-fated Leon Trotsky ("When will you be worthy of your million Troskyites?") and the members of the worldwide labor union IWW, the International Workers

of the World ("America I feel sentimental about the Wobblies"). He takes a
jab at anti-communists and confesses to reading Marx: "America I used to be
a communist when I was a kid I'm not sorry." He imagines that the country
might change if he confides the suffering of some of his relatives, like his
mother's younger brother Max Livergant, who paid the price for being a Jew
and a communist ("America I still haven't told you what you did to Uncle
Max after he came over from Russia"). It can be hard to tell if the poet is
addressing a friend or an enemy, someone he loves or hates, maybe both. At
a certain point he realizes that he is stalking himself: "It occurs to me that
I am America." But he worries about inhabiting an echo chamber: "I am
talking to myself again." Who's out there listening anyway?

Ginsberg introduces the second half of the poem by positing the notion of
a holy litany and joking about making and selling odes like Ford motorcars
("$2500 apiece $500 down on your old strophe"). But then he changes tone
and progresses in four unstopped lines from Tom Mooney to the Spanish
Loyalists to Sacco and Vanzetti to the Scottsboro boys. He may have been
making a genuine plea to "free Tom Mooney," who was still serving a life
sentence for a bombing he did not commit, but it was too late to "save" the
Spanish Loyalists, the destroyed Republican faction of the Spanish Civil
War. It was not too late, however, to save their dream of a just society. So,
too, there is something hopeless about his plea that "Sacco & Vanzetti must
not die," since the two Italian anarchists had been executed thirty years ear-
lier. "Two good men a long time gone," Woody Guthrie sang in 1935, "Left
me here to sing this song" ("Two Good Men"). Most powerfully, Ginsberg
declares, "I am the Scottsboro boys," meaning that he stands as one with the
nine African American teenagers falsely accused of raping two white women
on a train in Alabama in 1931. Ginsberg had left-wing causes at his finger-
tips—they were mother's milk to him—and he identifies with everyone
on the wrong side of power: the oppressed victims of racism and political
injustice, the dreamers, and utopians.

Ginsberg's politically charged childhood was very much alive in him, and
he liked to refer to his parents as "old-fashioned delicatessen philosophers."
He had a sweet, ironic, melancholy longing for the Old Left. The longest
digression takes place when he recalls how his mother schlepped him to
meetings. The language runs on, regresses, and gravitates toward the way a
seven-year-old speaks and remembers things:

America when I was seven momma took me to Communist Cell
meetings they sold us garbanzos a handful per ticket a ticket
costs a nickel and the speeches were free everybody was angelic
and sentimental about the workers it was all so sincere you have
no idea what a good thing the party was in 1835 Scott Nearing
was a grand old man a real mensch Mother Bloor the Silk-
strikers' Ewig-Weibliche made me cry I once saw the Yiddish
orator Israel Amter plain. Everybody must have been a spy.

Step back into the memories of a kid who grew up on arguments about
the fundamental injustices of capitalism, the working class and the means
of production, the crucial differences between anarchism, socialism, and
communism. I'm not sure why Ginsberg gets the date wrong here by one
hundred years—it is probably just a typo—but it should have been 1935,
because he affectionately brings up seeing the radical economist and pacifist
Scott Nearing, whom he calls "a real mensch," and Ella Reeve "Mother"
Bloor, the socialist feminist, whom he tenderly describes as "the Silk-strikers'
Ewig-Weibliche" (the archetype of the eternal feminine) who made him cry,
and Israel Amter, a founding member of the American Communist Party.

Ginsberg captures the astonishing memory of meeting one's hero ("I once
saw the Yiddish orator Israel Amter plain") through an allusion to Robert
Browning's poem "Memorabilia": "Ah, did you once see Shelley plain, / And
did he stop and speak to you?" Whenever he gets too deluged by sincere feel-
ing, Ginsberg has a way of pulling back and ironizing the emotion, thereby
protecting himself, which is what happens when he declares that everyone
"must have been" spying on one another.

The affectionate memory of encountering these folks leads Ginsberg to
the simple, poignant observation and plea: "America you don't really want
to go to war." But then the tone swerves again—everyone notices the goofy,
obstinate, sarcastic political hijinks of the section where the speaker breaks
into the caveman-like grunts and parody lingo of "America its them bad
Russians." This palaver seems meant to be read aloud, and in the many
recordings of Ginsberg reading the poem, you can hear how he plays it for
laughs. This schtick also demonstrates how much he owes to transgressive
Jewish and Yiddish humor, to a stand-up comedian like Lenny Bruce, whose
profanities landed him in jail, and to the Borscht Belt comics like Shecky

324   THE HEART OF AMERICAN POETRY

Greene, Red Buttons, Groucho Marx, and Jackie Mason, who cut up and cracked jokes in the face of power. Shelley claimed that poets are "the unacknowledged legislators of the world," but the Catskill comics, who headlined in what were nicknamed the Jewish Alps, may be the "unacknowledged legislators" of this poem. For Ginsberg, the mockery has a serious intent to expose the stupidity of the Cold War, the underlying racism of American society, and the ignorance fueled by mass culture: "America this is the impression I get from looking in the television set. / America is this correct?" Ginsberg slyly alters the word *at* to the word *in*—you are not going to find depth in a television set.

The poem turns in the final three lines. The tone is playful but also serious as the speaker focuses and comes to the point: "I'd better get right down to the job." There is an element of parody in his sudden American pragmatism, but there is something genuine about it, too. He is funny and self-knowing about his own impracticality. He may be an unlikely citizen—"It's true I don't want to join the Army or turn lathes in precision parts factories, I'm nearsighted and psychopathic anyway"—but he is a citizen nonetheless, who is figuring out and envisioning his own way to participate.

I love the famous final line of the poem: "America I'm putting my queer shoulder to the wheel." Ginsberg takes a common expression ("put your shoulder to the wheel") and completely upends it by inserting the word *queer*. He knew the history of a word that once meant "strange" or "odd" but by the 1950s had become a derisive term for homosexuals. In 1953, he had worked on the manuscript of William Burroughs's early short novel *Queer* (written 1951–53, published 1985), an extension of *Junkie* (1953), and the association with gay subjectivity was near at hand. Instead of hiding from his queerness, Ginsberg embraces it. By addressing America and inserting a single word, Ginsberg has taken a cliché and turned it into a line that is wry, memorable, and progressive. He is whimsical, determined, maybe even a little optimistic. In the end, he, too, is going to do his part to make a better America. It may not be what Emerson had in mind, but somehow Allen Ginsberg had found his patriotic gesture and staked his claim. America is a poem in his eyes. It is therefore a poem in our eyes, too.

JOHN ASHBERY (1927–2017)

Soonest Mended

Barely tolerated, living on the margin
In our technological society, we were always having to be rescued
On the brink of destruction, like heroines in *Orlando Furioso*
Before it was time to start all over again.
There would be thunder in the bushes, a rustling of coils,
And Angelica, in the Ingres painting, was considering
The colorful but small monster near her toe, as though wondering
   whether forgetting
The whole thing might not, in the end, be the only solution.
And then there always came a time when
Happy Hooligan in his rusted green automobile
Came plowing down the course, just to make sure everything was O.K.,
Only by that time we were in another chapter and confused
About how to receive this latest piece of information.
Was it information? Weren't we rather acting this out
For someone else's benefit, thoughts in a mind
With room enough and to spare for our little problems (so they began
   to seem),
Our daily quandary about food and the rent and bills to be paid?
To reduce all this to a small variant,
To step free at last, minuscule on the gigantic plateau—
This was our ambition: to be small and clear and free.
Alas, the summer's energy wanes quickly,
A moment and it is gone. And no longer
May we make the necessary arrangements, simple as they are.
Our star was brighter perhaps when it had water in it.
Now there is no question even of that, but only
Of holding on to the hard earth so as not to get thrown off,

With an occasional dream, a vision: a robin flies across
The upper corner of the window, you brush your hair away
And cannot quite see, or a wound will flash
Against the sweet faces of the others, something like:
This is what you wanted to hear, so why
Did you think of listening to something else? We are all talkers
It is true, but underneath the talk lies
The moving and not wanting to be moved, the loose
Meaning, untidy and simple like a threshing floor.

These then were some hazards of the course,
Yet though we knew the course *was* hazards and nothing else
It was still a shock when, almost a quarter of a century later,
The clarity of the rules dawned on you for the first time.
They were the players, and we who had struggled at the game
Were merely spectators, though subject to its vicissitudes
And moving with it out of the tearful stadium, borne on shoulders, at last.
Night after night this message returns, repeated
In the flickering bulbs of the sky, raised past us, taken away from us,
Yet ours over and over until the end that is past truth,
The being of our sentences, in the climate that fostered them,
Not ours to own, like a book, but to be with, and sometimes
To be without, alone and desperate.
But the fantasy makes it ours, a kind of fence-sitting
Raised to the level of an esthetic ideal. These were moments, years,
Solid with reality, faces, namable events, kisses, heroic acts,
But like the friendly beginning of a geometrical progression
Not too reassuring, as though meaning could be cast aside some day
When it had been outgrown. Better, you said, to stay cowering
Like this in the early lessons, since the promise of learning
Is a delusion, and I agreed, adding that
Tomorrow would alter the sense of what had already been learned,
That the learning process is extended in this way, so that from this
    standpoint
None of us ever graduates from college,
For time is an emulsion, and probably thinking not to grow up

Is the brightest kind of maturity for us, right now at any rate.
And you see, both of us were right, though nothing
Has somehow come to nothing; the avatars
Of our conforming to the rules and living
Around the home have made—well, in a sense, "good citizens" of us,
Brushing the teeth and all that, and learning to accept
The charity of the hard moments as they are doled out,
For this is action, this not being sure, this careless
Preparing, sowing the seeds crooked in the furrow,
Making ready to forget, and always coming back
To the mooring of starting out, that day so long ago.

1969

"HE'S ALWAYS distracting you from the subject," Donald Barthelme said to me once, "which is too sad to face directly." We were walking under a canopy of live oaks on North Boulevard in Houston, his hometown—I had just come to teach in the creative writing program that he helped to build—and we were talking about the American poets he most admired, like Gertrude Stein and John Ashbery. He didn't see much of a boundary between poetry and prose, between, say, Stein's triad of psychological portraits, *Three Lives*, and her collection of Cubist poems, *Tender Buttons*. His favorite book of Ashbery's was *Three Poems* (1972), which consists of three long, baffling, adventurous prose poems. It was Ashbery's favorite book of his own, too. He sounded just like Barthelme when he said, "The pathos and liveliness of ordinary human communication is poetry to me."

Barthelme favored writers who favored invention and pastiche, who worked obliquely and kept their feelings to themselves, fending off anyone who got too nosy or inquisitive. He thought that Ashbery's angle of approach was funny and tormented. Barthelme and Ashbery shared a taste for the surrealists, the Dadaists, the collagists; they liked abstract expressionism minus the heroism. They took the ironist's position. As the author of *Unspeakable Practices, Unnatural Acts* (1968) and *City Life* (1970), Barthelme struck most people as a quintessential New Yorker, a born insider, but when I got to know him I realized that this wasn't true at all, that he approached the city from the outside, with the wariness of a provincial who had come

328 THE HEART OF AMERICAN POETRY

to take a good look around and decided to stay—Grace Paley called him "a reporter and a poet." After teaching his poetry for a while I realized that this was true of Ashbery, too, who had grown up on a farm in far upstate New York and escaped to the great metropolises, Paris and New York.

There are all sorts of John Ashbery poems—he was an entire school of different poets—but one kind, possibly the one I value most, invariably diverts readers from the subject because it's too sad to face directly. He was a magician who defended against too much feeling, which sometimes threatened to overwhelm him, and so he surprised you with his tricks. He simply would not be hemmed in, and he took you to places you'd never been before.

It can be difficult to read John Ashbery's work in a disinterested way. Now he's a fixture of the canon, but when I was coming up in the 1970s his work elicited such intense responses that it seemed impossible to encounter it without entering a literary war zone. There were too many noisy disciples and vehement detractors. Some critics were certain that he was ruining American poetry; others felt that he was saving it. If you took a position on a certain book—say, his second collection, *The Tennis Court Oath* (1962), which I found offputting because of its extreme disjointedness, or *The Double Dream of Spring* (1970), his mid-career classic, which I found captivating because of its melancholy lyricism—then you were immediately put into one camp or another. Lines were drawn, allies solidified, enemies made. In the meantime, Ashbery recommended "fence-sitting / Raised to the level of an esthetic ideal," and carried on undeterred, trying on different modes—sometimes going on disjunctive sprees, as in *Hotel Lautréamont* (1992), other times following Wallace Stevens and Marianne Moore into a territory of reflective consciousness, as in *Self-Portrait in a Convex Mirror* (1975) and *Houseboat Days* (1977). He liked the drama of thinking, but his poetry is so emotionally cool and intellectually various—he veered between Rimbaud and Elizabeth Bishop, Parmigianino and Andy Warhol—that it's nearly impossible to pin down, which was precisely the point. If you asked for a key to his work, the poet Richard Howard observed, then he'd present you with a new set of locks. Ashbery confirmed my own hunch when he said, "A lot of people throw up their hands and say that I am writing poetry that isn't poetry at all. I don't think of myself as being a destroyer of poetry and I think I am continuing, in my own way, from a body of poetic tradition."

I admire people who seem to have read everything in order, but I was never one of them. My own sense of Ashbery's work is influenced by the fact that I was immersed in Wordsworth's *Prelude* at the time when I was puzzling over the method of *The Double Dream of Spring* and *Self-Portrait in a Convex Mirror*, which established him as a poet of meditative self-consciousness. In particular, I was focused on what Wordsworth called "spots of time," those spiritual cells and epiphanic moments, which he deemed "the hiding-places of my power." These solitary moments of crisis, "fleeting moods / Of shadowy exultation" and "unknown modes of being," break the narrative flow of the autobiography and rupture temporality. They take place in darkness; they are terrifying and hard to recall; they have an "awful Power" and visionary authority. Ashbery captures the fleeting feeling of them in "The Task" when he states, "For these are moments only, moments of insight." The more I read Ashbery's humorously self-reflexive meditations the more I came to think of him as a poet who recognizes the epiphany as a kind of terminal point, a shutting down of consciousness. Or perhaps he didn't want to feel disappointment or regret over not having certain luminous moments or piercing experiences.

I don't want to nail down what is intentionally unfixed in Ashbery's work, but one way to read his self-defining long poems ("Self-Portrait in a Convex Mirror," or "Grand Galop" and "A Wave," or the book-length *Flow Chart*) is as a continual avoidance or postponement of spots of time, a way of engaging consciousness to repeatedly hold off the concluding insight. As he defines it in "Self-Portrait":

> The locking into place is "death itself,"
> As Berg said of a phrase in Mahler's Ninth;
> Or, to quote Imogen in *Cymbeline*, "There cannot
> Be a pinch in death more sharp than this," for,
> Though only exercise or tactic, it carries
> The momentum of a conviction that had been building.

Ashbery's poems establish a pattern of opening up and closing down, of disclosure and concealment. They reveal, they re-veil. They embrace what he calls "the charity of the hard moments," they welcome and embrace change. They are flowcharts that repeatedly push back the locking into place that is "death itself." This is the reason Ashbery can be so rewarding and frustrating at the same time. He is a poet of perpetual deferrals.

"Soonest Mended" is one of the key lyrics in *The Double Dream of Spring*, Ashbery called it "a kind of signature poem." He loved Elizabeth Bishop's poem "Over 2,000 Illustrations and a Complete Concordance," which he considered her masterpiece, and said that it was the inspiration for "Soonest Mended." He admired and imitated the way that Bishop's lyric "plies continually between the steel-engraved vignettes of a gazetteer and the distressingly unclassifiable events of a real voyage." Bishop fused description and consciousness in a way that Ashbery found various and "indescribable," and his poem, like hers, leaves one feeling "ravished and unsatisfied." Ashbery also paired "Soonest Mended" with Thomas Traherne's seventeenth-century poem "Poverty" for an anthology called *Preferences* (1974), which suggests a bedrock memory of deprivation alluded to, if not quite described, in Ashbery's text. Traherne remembers growing up impoverished, "alone and desolate," and grieves that "all my wealth should be / Confined in such a little room, / Yet hope for more I scarcely durst presume." Presumably, Ashbery also mourns that "such a scanty store / Should be my all." His poem refers to growing up and maturing as a thwarted or disappointed quest romance.

The title, "Soonest Mended," lops off the head of a two-part proverb—"Least said, soonest mended"—and thereby enacts the meaning of the didactic statement. The title says even less than the proverb, which suggests that the less you say the less likely you are to get into trouble. This bit of conventional wisdom can be invoked in different familial or social contexts. It may be one way to keep you out of danger, another way of warning you to keep your mouth shut. One unexpected result might be a poetic of discretion and indirection. As a poem, "Soonest Mended" defies its proverbial advice; it doesn't really say less. In fact, it goes on for two long stanzas that total seventy-one lines, but it does keep avoiding what it approaches. One fifteenth-century version of the proverb was "Lyttle sayde, soone amended." Or as Ashbery once put it in a lecture: "Poetry bloweth where it listeth. It should never be thought of as a practical solution to life's mess."

There are some poets whose lines stab you with blunt force, others whose sentences meander off in different directions and take a while to knife you, so that you don't quite realize you've been cut until you get home and discover that you're bleeding. This is the difference between, say, Robert Lowell and

John Ashbery. The comparison seems apt because Ashbery called "Soonest Mended" "a one-size-fits-all confessional poem which is about my youth and maturity but also about anybody else's." In the breakthrough poems of *Life Studies*, the 1959 collection in which Lowell embraced a radically auto-biographical lyric, the poet tried to give the impression that the reader was getting "the *real* Robert Lowell." This was an enabling fiction that many readers and critics believed to be literally true. It was M. L. Rosenthal's review of this book that led to the moniker "Confessional Poetry" for the poetry of utmost personal disclosure. Ashbery took a different tactic—he mocked the idea of confessionalism and pretended that the reader was not getting "the *real* John Ashbery" but some generalized or distanced confession, as if we all had the same childhood and adolescent memories. "Some of it is not really about me," he said: "it's what Gertrude Stein called 'everybody's autobiography.'"

Like Stein, Ashbery poses as a representative American. She established the precedent when she stated, "I used to be fond of saying that America, which was supposed to be a land of success, was a land of failure." Ashbery's strategy: to present a speaker who does not refer to himself as "I" but as "we." The style is elusive, the thinking nonlinear. The cue to the feeling is in the first phrasing, "Barely tolerated, living on the margin." The poem is shadowed by Ashbery's memories of being an artistic gay kid growing up on a farm in the tiny village of Sodus, New York. He detested farm life and said that he was attracted to boys before he knew there was such a thing as homosexuality. But the speaker generalizes this situation into the idea that others, too, that indeterminate "we," which some readers understand as gay lovers or queer poets of the 1950s, were only just allowed—different, periph-eral, disenfranchised.

Barely tolerated, living on the margin
In our technological society, we were always having to be rescued
On the brink of destruction, like heroines in *Orlando Furioso*
Before it was time to start all over again.
There would be thunder in the bushes, a rustling of coils,
And Angelica, in the Ingres painting, was considering
The colorful but small monster near her toe, as though wondering
    whether forgetting
The whole thing might not, in the end, be the only solution.

To understand this passage of somewhat outlandish, feminized allusions—
we're being compared to heroines—you don't really need to have read
Ludovico Ariosto's sixteenth-century mock epic of chivalry, *Orlando Furioso*,
a romance (featuring a young lover named Angelica) that Vivaldi turned into
an opera, or to have viewed Ingres's nineteenth-century painting *Angelica
saved by Ruggiero* based on the poem, but these references do indicate the
way that Ashbery filters experience through the lens of other texts. Such fil-
tering seems to be the only way he can confront growing up on the margins,
feeling jeopardized, looking for a kind of rescue that would never arrive,
turning from one piece of culture to the next:

> And then there always came a time when
> Happy Hooligan in his rusted green automobile
> Came plowing down the course, just to make sure everything
>   was O.K.,
> Only by that time we were in another chapter and confused
> About how to receive this latest piece of information.
> *Was* it information?

Happy Hooligan, a popular comic book character from Ashbery's child-
hood, comes charging into memory, driving into the poem, and popping
out of his car to reassure him, or us, though personally I had not heard of
Happy Hooligan since the comic strip ended in 1932, when Ashbery was
only five years old. It's a little too late for a redemptive hero, like Ruggiero
or Happy Hooligan. It's as if life is a chapter book and we turn the pages as
we get older. The answer to the question posed is that it *was* information,
but what kind?

> Weren't we rather acting this out
> For someone else's benefit, thoughts in a mind
> With room enough and to spare for our little problems (so they began
>   to seem),
> Our daily quandary about food and the rent and bills to be paid?

The question raises another question, another doubt. One possible expla-
nation gives way to another, but all the explanations are incomplete. The

question also evokes the memory of poverty, the quotidian grind. It's about both daily life in the 1930s, the time of Ashbery's Depression-era childhood, and "the daily quandary" for the rest of us, too, at least those of us who grew up always looking around for the rich overlords of the system.

Then comes a tiny instance of Stevensian sublimity, of imaginative liberation. It's a moment of trying not to be noticed and of noticing, of standing outside on the lawn at night and gazing up at the stars:

> To reduce all this to a small variant,
> To step free at last, minuscule on the gigantic plateau—
> This was our ambition: to be small and clear and free.

The moment of plenitude can't last: "Alas, the summer's energy wanes quickly, / A moment and it is gone." A spot of time can no longer serve: the necessary arrangements, ordinary acts, "simple as they are," but also poems or paintings or comic books, don't come to rescue us.

In the next movement of the poem, the speaker associates his way into the recognition, if there is one, that it is time to hold on and get on with it.

> Our star was brighter perhaps when it had water in it.
> Now there is no question even of that, but only
> Of holding on to the hard earth so as not to get thrown off,
> With an occasional dream, a vision: a robin flies across
> The upper corner of the window, you brush your hair away
> And cannot quite see, or a wound will flash
> Against the sweet faces of the others, something like:
> This is what you wanted to hear, so why
> Did you think of listening to something else? We are all talkers
> It is true, but underneath the talk lies
> The moving and not wanting to be moved, the loose
> Meaning, untidy and simple like a threshing floor.

To the speaker, the star seems brighter when it is refracted in water and insight looms up as "an occasional dream, a vision." That robin flying across "The upper corner of the window" is a figure of transcendence, fleeting and barely glimpsed.

The speaker realizes that despite the reticence recommended by the title, we all participate in a lot of social chatter, though one wonders where it gets us because underlying it is an unresolved, unfulfilled longing and need. There is a remarkable progression and enjambment in the lines "We are all talkers / It is true, but underneath the talk lies / The moving and not wanting to be moved." Ashbery plays on what is true and false here, punning on the word *lies*, which suggests both untruth and resting and reclining in a certain state. The ambivalence shows. He also puns on the words *moving* and *moved*. The speaker is moving on, leaving one place for another, and trying not to be moved by it all. The meaning is also "loose" and therefore hard to describe easily, messy but also simple. I come away from the poem recognizing how hard it is to escape from the forlorn feelings of childhood, those long-lasting inarticulate wounds.

"Soonest Mended" is a poem in two parts. Ashbery wrote it in his early forties and the second section suggests that it is a middle-aged reckoning, a time of coming to terms. At first it seemed that life was filled with obstacles, but then it starts to occur to us that the journey consists of nothing but obstacles:

> These then were some hazards of the course,
> Yet though we knew the course *was* hazards and nothing else
> It was still a shock when, almost a quarter of a century later,
> The clarity of the rules dawned on you for the first time.
> *They* were the players, and we who had struggled at the game
> Were merely spectators, though subject to its vicissitudes
> And moving with it out of the tearful stadium, borne on shoulders,
>   at last.

There is a shuttling of pronouns between "we" and "you" and "they," an individual recognition posited as a general truth of adulthood, the hindsight that all along one was playing at a game that was someone else's game with someone else's rules. In fact, you weren't really a player at all, but a mere spectator, someone subject to a series of unwelcome changes, rules you didn't understand, filing out of "the tearful stadium" with the rest of the crowd. Ashbery was an unathletic kid, which can make you an outsider in high school, and the projection of crying onto the stadium pairs with the idea that it is the spectators, not the heroic athlete, who are carried out of the stadium in a sort of unlikely triumph. I suspect a purposefully vague but genuine memory of hurt behind all this.

Now the poem changes tense to an ongoing present, a recurring nightly recognition and acknowledgment. The next sentence is flickering and refractory.

> Night after night this message returns, repeated
> In the flickering bulbs of the sky, raised past us, taken away from us,
> Yet ours over and over until the end that is past truth,
> The being of our sentences, in the climate that fostered them,
> Not ours to own, like a book, but to be with, and sometimes
> To be without, alone and desperate.

Part of the effect here is an elusiveness that is driven by some underlying but hard-to-determine logic ("Yet ours," "Not ours," "but to be"). The language seems Stevensian and reminiscent of "Of Mere Being" ("The palm at the end of the mind, / Beyond the last thought") and "The Poems of Our Climate," especially the lines "There would still remain the never-resting mind, / So that one would want to escape, come back / To what had been so long composed." Ashbery is less direct than Stevens, but the references to "the end that is past truth," which seems like death itself, a finality beyond our constructions, "The being of our sentences," and "Not ours to own, like a book" all indicate the restlessness of an isolated imagination confronting an intractable reality, which we can approach only with uncertainty.

This leads to the conclusion: "But the fantasy makes it ours, a kind of fence-sitting / Raised to the level of an esthetic ideal." I am inclined to think of what Ashbery calls "fence-sitting," a lack of decisiveness, as a postmodern version of the Romantic Aeolian harp. It is the result of a personal temperament applied to an aesthetic position. Coleridge sounds positively Ashberian when he states, "Full many a thought uncalled and undetained, / And many idle flitting phantasies, / Traverse my indolent and passive brain, / As wild and various as the random gales / That swell and flutter on this subject Lute!" ("The Eolian Harp").

The next section of the poem is like glimpsing people through the window of a passing train. You can see that they are out there, but you're going by them so quickly that it's hard to interpret what you're seeing. This seems to be Ashbery's way of summarizing something like his high school and college years. The "we" now breaks down into two people in conversation. This is the first time that an "I" reveals itself in the poem. The lines have a stately progression:

> These were moments, years,
> Solid with reality, faces, namable events, kisses, heroic acts,
> But like the friendly beginning of a geometrical progression
> Not too reassuring, as though meaning could be cast aside some day
> When it had been outgrown. Better, you said, to stay cowering
> Like this in the early lessons, since the promise of learning
> Is a delusion, and I agreed, adding that
> Tomorrow would alter the sense of what had already been learned,
> That the learning process is extended in this way, so that from this
>   standpoint
> None of us ever graduates from college,
> For time is an emulsion, and probably thinking not to grow up
> Is the brightest kind of maturity for us, right now at any rate.

There is a play here on the gap between learning from memory and experience and learning from books. What seems to be a "delusion" is that we grow up and escape, that our book learning somehow protects us from the hard lessons. There is an oblique reference to the quest as the "friendly beginning" or promise of some sort of logical progression that turns out to be far from "reassuring." Two positions are staked out and ultimately joined. We may not grow up, but we do keep accumulating knowledge, if not wisdom. We progress, sort of, and keep our childhood selves alive in us.

I have loved the swerves of the final sentence ever since I first encountered them in my early twenties. The movement begins with a reference to King Lear's precept, "Nothing will come of nothing," which Ashbery modifies with a characteristic "somehow," and ends with the memory of starting out on a day long ago. Now the "you" and "I" might well be lovers, two people learning to live together, "Brushing the teeth and all that," which enlarges into a generalized lesson for all of us included in the "we," who have been socialized into citizenship:

And you see, both of us were right, though nothing
Has somehow come to nothing; the avatars
Of our conforming to the rules and living
Around the home have made—well, in a sense, "good citizens" of us,
Brushing the teeth and all that, and learning to accept
The charity of the hard moments as they are doled out,
For this is action, this not being sure, this careless
Preparing, sowing the seeds crooked in the furrow,
Making ready to forget, and always coming back
To the mooring of starting out, that day so long ago.

What seems most Ashberian here is not just the rapidly shifting diction and gorgeous phrasing but the lesson itself, the idea that not being sure is a kind of "action," a process of remembering and forgetting, of being moored and unmoored. Things are prepared not purposefully but carelessly, the seeds are crooked and not straight, which suggests some future obdurate growth, the hard moments are charitable and ongoing, and we keep returning to the past in order to leave it. There's a tone of acceptance, of resignation and even excitement, of dwelling in uncertainties and doubts, which Keats considered a key feature of what he termed *negative capability*. Not choosing one path or the other, not irritably "reaching after fact and reason," as Keats puts it, becomes a moral stance and aesthetic position. It's even filled with a sense of rueful wonderment and mystery.

John Ashbery was a poet of what he called "mandarin avoidance." He admitted that "we are all confessional sometimes," but didn't make a big deal of it, and embraced Auden's adage that poetry "makes us well / Without confession of the ill." His poetry is oddly dexterous: it counsels us to get on with it, to keep moving. It has its own ethos of experiment and verbal adventure, of charity and self-forgiveness, the prerogative of the fence-sitter. I can't always decipher if he is putting everything in or leaving everything out. "On and on into the gathering darkness—is there no remedy for this?" Ashbery asked in *Three Poems*. There is not. We are always on the brink of destruction. But attention can be paid, art created.

I didn't know Ashbery well, though we overlapped at poetry gatherings over the years and once we took a long walk around Houston together before a reading. We didn't follow a route but just ambled through the streets willy-nilly until we ended up in front of the Rothko Chapel. I mentioned the small funeral that I had recently attended for Donald Barthelme there. It felt as if the large dark paintings had stood in attendance, like figures in mourning. Ashbery looked at me with a somewhat pained expression; he had been losing friends at an alarming rate. "I can't tell if Barthelme's work is funny or sad," he said. "Sometimes it feels like the same thing."

Autumn Begins in Martins Ferry, Ohio

In the Shreve High football stadium,
I think of Polacks nursing long beers in Tiltonsville,
And gray faces of Negroes in the blast furnace at Benwood,
And the ruptured night watchman of Wheeling Steel,
Dreaming of heroes.

All the proud fathers are ashamed to go home,
Their women cluck like starved pullets,
Dying for love.

Therefore,
Their sons grow suicidally beautiful
At the beginning of October,
And gallop terribly against each other's bodies.

1963

JAMES WRIGHT was a homegrown, handmade, self-invented American poet and intellectual. He grew up during the Great Depression in Martins Ferry, Ohio, a small, blighted, industrial town on the Ohio River across from Wheeling, West Virginia, where both of his parents, who had dropped out of school, worked hard physical jobs for their entire lives. His father, Dudley Wright, was employed as a die-cutter at Hazel-Atlas Glass for fifty years. His mother, Jessie Wright, worked the giant ironing presses or "mangles" at the White Swan Laundry. The blue-collar town attracted waves of immigrants from different European countries, and he grew up with a sympathy for an ethnically disparate, perennially held-down working class.

Wright got out of Martins Ferry as soon as he could. He enlisted in the U.S. Army and served in occupied Japan, attended Kenyon College on the G.I. Bill, spent a year in Vienna on a Fulbright scholarship, got a PhD at the University of Washington, where he studied with Stanley Kunitz and Theodore Roethke, and became a university teacher. And yet Martins Ferry never got out of him. He found it hard to recover from his rough origins and invariably returned to it in his poems, almost always with a feeling of personal doom and desolation. In a letter, he said that he "abominated the Ohio Valley" and described it as

> that unspeakable rat-hole where I grew up . . . the slag heaps and the black trees, and the stool-washed river and the chemicals from the factories of Wheeling Steel, Blaw Knox, the Hanna Coal Co. which . . . are the only images of childhood I can ever have.

Wright had a persistent nightmare, his biographer Jonathan Blunk reports, that his degrees would be taken away from him, and he would need to go back to working in a factory in Martins Ferry.

For Wright, poetry was a means of salvation. He knew reams of literature by heart and astonished people with his prodigious memory. A Charles Dickens scholar, he declaimed long passages from the novels; he recited poems by Hardy and Yeats; he intoned lyrics by Horace and Goethe and then gave on-the-spot translations. But he also had trouble fighting the undertow of the past; it was as if a polluted river kept dragging him back under, and he battled alcoholism all his life. He also struggled with the right style for his intensities—the necessary form, the accurate shape of experience. The testimonial opening of "At the Executed Murderer's Grave" is the culmination of his early work:

> My name is James A. Wright, and I was born
> Twenty-five miles from this infected grave,
> In Martins Ferry, Ohio, where one slave
> To Hazel-Atlas Glass became my father.
> He tried to teach me kindness. I return
> Only in memory now, aloof, unhurried,
> To dead Ohio, where I might lie buried,
> Had I not run away before my time.

By the time he came to write "Autumn Begins in Martins Ferry, Ohio," Wright was remaking himself as a poet of plain style, always searching for what he called "the pure clear word," which he pulled out of his ribcage. He was one of our fevered poets of the distressed and desolate, people on the margins, folks who had gotten a raw deal in life. His subject matter was always painful. He never wavered in his dedication to the social pariah, but his style was undergoing a dramatic sea change. Wright had published two skillful books, *The Green Wall* (1957) and *Saint Judas* (1959), in the mode of Edwin Arlington Robinson and Robert Frost, but now he felt "trapped" by the traditional technique that he had labored so long to master. He had come to a dead end. "*The Green Wall* might very easily have been written by any normally educated Englishman of, say, the eighteenth century," he confessed. This is not accurate, objectively speaking, but the statement conveys the revulsion that he had developed against his old style. It had become a straitjacket. "My book was dead," he said with comic but miserable overexaggeration: "It could have been written by a dead man, if they have Corona-Corona typewriters in the grave. For all I know, it *was* written by a dead man."

In his despair, Wright resolved to stop writing poetry; he was leaving the playing field. But when the first issue of a new magazine, *The Fifties*, arrived in his mailbox at the University of Minnesota, he found an unexpected opening, a way forward. It was 1958. The magazine was edited by Robert Bly and his friend Bill Duffy, who had decided to disturb the old-fashioned politesse of mid-century American poetry. They particularly disliked the stodgy formalism of a new anthology, *New Poets of England and America* (1957), which was edited by Donald Hall, Robert Pack, and Louis Simpson, and they sent a copy of their energetic polemic to each one of that anthology's contributors. *The Fifties* hit a nerve with Wright, who immediately started corresponding with Bly. Soon he was visiting Bly and Duffy at their farms in rural Minnesota, changing his style, breaking the back of the pentameter that had been his self-defining metric. He sought something riskier, more image-centered and emotive. He would always regard himself primarily as a craftsman, a self-designated Horatian, but the craft now demanded a different type of clarity.

Wright was never as polemical as Bly, who made the case in "A Wrong Turning in American Poetry" (1963) that American poets after Pound and Eliot had exalted the conscious mind at the expense of the unconscious

mind. Eliot's phrase *objective correlative* is "astoundingly passionless," Bly
said.

> The only movement in American poetry which concentrated on
> the image was Imagism, in 1911–13. But "Imagism" was largely
> "Picturism." An image and a picture differ in that the image,
> being the natural speech of the imagination, cannot be drawn
> from or inserted back into the real world. It is an animal native
> to the imagination.

Wright didn't have Bly's grudge against Anglo-American modernism, but
he shared Bly's commitment to a more passionate, irrational, nondiscursive,
image-centered poetry, which they modeled on poets they translated. This
included the socially engaged Spanish and Latin American surrealists, Lorca,
Miguel Hernández, Pablo Neruda, and César Vallejo, as well as the Austrian
modernist Georg Trakl, a poet of "patience and bravery," who combined a
precise imaging of the natural world with a startled expressionist feeling.
Those translations not only opened up Bly's and Wright's own work; they
brought about a large psychic leap in American poetry itself.

Wright invented a new kind of lyric in his breakthrough volumes, *The
Branch Will Not Break* (1963) and *Shall We Gather at the River* (1968), which
closely track with Bly's first two books, *Silence in the Snowy Fields* (1962) and
The Light Around the Body (1967). These books are simultaneously inward
bound and politically committed. They eschew discursive logic, an overly
analytic mode of thinking, even as they attack the machinery of capitalism,
the Vietnam War, and the military industrial complex. There is something
of the same revolutionary feeling and political despair in the cool radiances
of W. S. Merwin, especially in *The Moving Target* (1963) and *The Lice* (1967),
and the emotional subjectivities of Galway Kinnell, particularly in *Body Rags*
(1968) and *The Book of Nightmares* (1971).

As soon as you opened *The Branch Will Not Break*, you became aware
that something unusual was afoot. The first poem had an extravagantly long
title, "As I Step Over a Puddle at the End of Winter, I Think of an Ancient
Chinese Governor"; the second one declared a departure from a hardened
formality, "Goodbye to the Poetry of Calcium": "Mother of roots, you have
not seeded / The tall ashes of loneliness / For me. Therefore, / Now I go."

The tone was prayerful, but it was hard to decipher the muse here, "Mother of roots," and the underlying logic that led to "Therefore." Wright's poems were plainspoken and yet had mysterious depths, muddy pools of feeling, dark wells of silence. They protected secrets. They moved through a solemn procession of images, many of them related to silent things, and often concluded with a statement or resolve. My generation of poets came of age on his Minnesota pastorals, such as "Lying in a Hammock at William Duffy's Farm in Pine Island, Minnesota," which ends with a shocking, Rilkean declaration, "I have wasted my life," and "A Blessing," which concludes with the radiant epiphany that if he stepped out of his body, he would break into blossom. There is a vulnerability in Wright's work, an untouchable spot, something hard and diamond-like that he tries to protect by burrowing deep into himself or heading out into the pasture. The natural world was salve and salvation, a redemptive of human suffering.

I recall how I was blindsided by "Autumn Begins in Martins Ferry, Ohio" when I first read it standing in the aisle of Stuart Brent's bookstore in downtown Chicago. It was the fall of 1968, and I was home visiting my family. At eighteen, I was just trying out the idea of becoming a poet, even though I had never met one, and I was playing Division III freshman football at a small college in the Midwest. It never occurred to me that you could bring those realities together—writing poetry, catching passes—and I felt my worlds collide. I was confronting two differing or alternate American masculinities, and it was a head-on clash. I closed the book and dusted myself off—it was a clean hit—but my head was still ringing, and the ground had shifted a little under my feet.

Wright wrote "Autumn Begins in Martins Ferry, Ohio" in 1960, and it still has the power to knock over an unsuspecting reader. There is a stately formal quality to the title, which radiates the feeling of a fall processional. But this is Belmont County, not Buckingham Palace, and so the annual ritual marks the beginning of the high school football season. All over America people are filing into stadiums for an annual autumn rite, something dangerous and defining that has the hallowed status of a secular religion, a very intense communal occasion and seasonal activity—Friday night football.

"Autumn Begins in Martins Ferry, Ohio" consists of three irregular free-verse stanzas that come to twelve lines, a truncated sonnet. Each stanza is one sentence long, a single intact section. The title creates a ritual or lyric feeling, but that is immediately countered by the first line, which locates us in a very particular, noticeably unpoetic place: a football stadium.

Thinking about sports in poetry, I would like to pause over the fact, historically speaking, that for every twenty-five poems about baseball, there are probably only one or two about football. Baseball has an older American provenance, it has the slower rhythms of the pastoral, and it is much more firmly rooted in the mythology of America. "I like your interest in sports—ball, chiefest of all—base-ball particularly," Walt Whitman reportedly told Horace Traubel: "base-ball is our game: the American game: I connect it with our national character." By contrast, American football is a rough-and-tumble twentieth-century game that grew out of the industrial Midwest. It's no accident that professional football started in Canton, Ohio, about one hundred miles down the road from Martins Ferry. "It's pretty simple," my high school football coach used to say, drawing up a play on the blackboard: "Football is a game of hitting and getting hit." He was from a hardscrabble mining town in the Allegheny Mountains.

James Wright, who was physically built like a lineman, never played high school football, but, as he told the poet Dave Smith, he did play "a lot of football with a sort of semipro team," which would have been an even tougher and more unruly game. As a former player, I can state with confidence that football itself, which is a highly aggressive, very masculinist game, sheds a harsh light on our national character. Football, too, is what Whitman, referring to baseball, called "the hurrah game of the republic," but, like boxing, it tells a much more primal and physically brutal story about us. That is one reason football seems so much more resistant to the lyric poem. But this is the challenge that Wright deliberately sets for himself.

"Autumn Begins in Martins Ferry, Ohio" is situated in the present tense. It took me a couple of readings to focus on the slightly odd locution: "In the Shreve High football stadium, / I think." We don't normally go to a football game so that we can think about the people around us, which suggests that the speaker is at one remove from the rest of the crowd. Wright attended Charles R. Shreve High School, which is why he blends in, but he also feels separate from everyone else there, an observer and a thinker. He is not at first interested in the action on the field—we don't learn anything about the teams—but he is very interested in the fans, especially the ones who aren't there, who never win at life. The narrator immediately moves outside the stadium and starts thinking about three classes of people. He knows all too well the nature of their hard, working-class jobs at the steel plant. First, he considers the "Polacks nursing long beers in Tiltonsville," then he narrows his view to the "gray faces of Negroes in the blast furnaces at Benwood," and finally, he considers the lone "ruptured night watchman of Wheeling Steel." These three groups of people are an amalgam: Polish immigrants lingering in a bar after work, African Americans whose tired faces are lit by blast furnaces in a mill, and a night watchman, presumably injured on the job, who patrols the plant at night. The first sentence and the first stanza close with the picture of working men fantasizing a way out, "Dreaming of heroes."

The poem, which is developing a critique of heroism, takes a psychological jump in the second stanza:

> All the proud fathers are ashamed to go home,
> Their women cluck like starved pullets,
> Dying for love.

The unnamed men are now grouped and summarized as "All the proud fathers," who have been so knocked down by life that they are "ashamed" to return home. This sense of shame is so deep that it leaves them feeling fearful and diminished, without self-esteem, even emasculated.

At Bly's instigation, Wright had been reading Carl Jung, whose archetypal idea of the shadow seems relevant here. Jung wrote: "The shadow personifies everything that the subject refuses to acknowledge about himself and yet is always thrusting itself upon him directly or indirectly" (*The Archetypes and the Collective Unconscious*). In Jungian terms, the shame of these men is a shadow that they are developing and projecting onto their sons, who are going to do what sons have always done, which is to try to become what their fathers want them to be—men—but men as their fathers imagine manhood. These proud men don't want to go home, because they bring their failures with them. At home, they find unhappy wives, women whom they have neglected, who are a complete mess, people who have been reduced to some animal status and need, figures so desperate for affection that they act like starving chickens. Pullets cannot reproduce if they do not eat anything. This three-line stanza compresses so much forlorn and loveless life that it makes me want to block out the light and turn away from the poem.

But the final stanza takes an unexpected logical leap. It's as if a Shake-spearean sonnet had gone off the rails and now turns back to formal logic. All our attention momentarily focuses on a single explosive word, which comprises an entire line: *Therefore*. This one word—the best use of *Therefore* in all of American poetry—suggests what I should have known all along but did not see coming and somehow missed on first reading, which is that the poet has been making an argument now coming to conclusion. And this is also the moment when the speaker suddenly turns to the violent action on the field. What has happened in the space between two stanzas is what Bly describes as "a long floating leap from the conscious to the unconscious and back again, a leap from the known part of the mind to the unknown part and back to the known."

This is the quatrain of conclusion, the final pathos:

> Therefore,
> Their sons grow suicidally beautiful
> At the beginning of October,
> And gallop terribly against each other's bodies.

All along the poem has placed us in the space of a quintessential American ritual, which we now realize has a human sacrifice at the center of it. The implication is that the sons are sacrificing themselves on behalf of their unful-filled fathers. This type of stylized violence is what happens when emotions have no other outlet, no other play. Wright describes the movement of the players on the field as "suicidally beautiful," an oxymoron one might use to describe tribal warriors. It speaks to their spirit of self-sacrifice and expressive physical grace. It sounds like something lifted from the story of the funeral games in book 23 of the *Iliad*. Wright also establishes this as a ceremonial tak-ing place every year at the beginning of October. Now we understand high school football in a fresh way as a primitive rite in which young players—I was once one of them—are like horses who "gallop terribly against each oth-er's bodies." The word *terribly* conjures a frightful physical violence. This final image of primal animal combat is thunderously accurate, bruising, and true.

James Wright savored, turned, and pressurized a local language, a tongue he called "my Ohioan," into an instrument of eloquence and compassion. He made a type of family, a mystic relation and brotherhood, out of the outcast and the powerless, people on the fringe, who have been shunted aside. The nameless poor, the common lot, had been washed out of Anglo-American modernism, but he brought them back with dignity and determination; he placed their suffering at the heart of his work. There is a primal loneliness in his poetry, a desolating isolation, but there is also a sense of stepping lightly through the ruins and coming out on the other side. He found a healing consolation and compensatory power in the natural world, which enabled him to turn back to the human one with pained curiosity and sympathy. He remembered home—in some ways, he was helpless to forget it—and validated working-class experiences in poems that are ruthless and beautiful. Therefore, he elevated our regard for ourselves and our desperate fathers, our forlorn mothers.

To Cipriano, in the Wind

Where did your words go,
Cipriano, spoken to me 38 years
ago in the back of Peerless Cleaners,
where raised on a little wooden platform
you bowed to the hissing press
and under the glaring bulb the scars
across your shoulders—"a gift
of my country"—gleamed like old wood.
"*Dignidad*," you said into my boy's
wide eyes, "without is no riches."
And Ferrente, the dapper Sicilian
coatmaker, laughed. What could
a pants presser know of dignity?
That was the winter of '41, it
would take my brother off to war,
where you had come from, it would
bring great snowfalls, graying
in the streets, and the news of death
racing through the halls of my school.
I was growing. Soon I would be
your height, and you'd tell me
eye to eye, "Some day the world
is ours, some day you will see."
And your eyes burned in your fine
white face until I thought you
would burn. That was the winter
of '41, Bataan would fall
to the Japanese and Sam Baghosian

would make the long march
with bayonet wounds in both legs,
and somehow in spite of burning acids
splashed across his chest and the acids
of his own anger rising toward his heart
he would return to us and eat
the stale bread of victory. Cipriano,
do you remember what followed
the worst snow? It rained all night
and in the dawn the streets gleamed,
and within a week wild phlox leaped
in the open fields. I told you
our word for it, "Spring," and you said,
"Spring, spring, it always come after."
Soon the Germans rolled East
into Russia and my cousins died. I
walked alone in the warm spring winds
of evening and said, "Dignity." I said
your words, Cipriano, into the winds.
I said, "Someday this will all be ours."
Come back, Cipriano Mera, step
out of the wind and dressed in the robe
of your pain tell me again that this
world will be ours. Enter my dreams
or my life, Cipriano, come back
out of the wind.

1979

PHILIP LEVINE was a poet of the night shift, a product of the
industrial heartland, a Romantic anarchist who repeatedly pro-
claimed Whitman's line "Vivas to those who have failed." His life's work was
a long assault on isolation, a struggle against the enclosures of suffering, the
private, hermetic, sealed-off nature of our lives. Over time, he increasingly
asserted a Keatsian faith in the boundlessness of human possibility. His work
began in rage—it practically breaks apart from anger—but then ripened

toward elegy and culminated in celebration. All three moods—rage, elegy, celebration—are present in his poem "To Cipriano, in the Wind," which appeared in his tenth collection, *One for the Rose* (1981).

Levine grew up in a lower-middle-class Jewish family in Detroit in the 1930s, and the Depression shaped him. His mother was a widow working full-time to make ends meet—his father died in 1933 when he was five years old—and he and his two brothers, one a twin, worked their way through school in a series of low-paying jobs. He toiled in an ice factory and a bottling company, at Railroad Express, Cadillac, Chevy Gear and Axle, Wyandotte Chemical. This was the norm then—my parents came from the same milieu in Chicago—but Levine's soul-crushing jobs became the basis for a lifetime work in poetry. He labored beside African Americans and immigrants of all kinds, especially Jews, Italians, and Poles, a quirky amalgam who sympathetically people his poems. He had a heightened sense of fascism—Father Coughlin praised Hitler and raged about Jewish bankers on the radio; his right-wing movement was called Social Justice—and a nervous alertness to politics. Levine attended what would become Wayne State University, worked full-time, and then left Detroit. He went to the Writers' Workshop at the University of Iowa, where he studied with John Berryman, and Stanford University, where he bristled under the tutelage of Yvor Winters, and then started a long teaching career at Fresno State University. He also taught for recurring one-semester stints at Tufts and New York University. But Levine never lost his ambition to become the poet of his hometown and vowed not to forget the gritty world he came from, the folks he worked with, the stubborn ones who dug in and wouldn't yield or give up. He made his early emblems the thistle and the fist.

Levine wrote with concentrated fury about what he called "the stupid jobs" of his youth, and his first books firmly established his working-class loyalties and themes. He primarily wrote about three cities: Detroit, Fresno, and Barcelona, all defined as landscapes of desolation, rugged cities of the enraged, the exhausted, and the exploited. He was determined to include a social class of people who have often been missing from poetry. His first book, *On the Edge* (1963), published when he was thirty-five years old, was a book of free-floating despair, forged by a slightly archaic formalism, alienated even from itself. His second book, *Not This Pig* (1968), exchanged despair for determination, digging in its heels. Levine was still writing in syllabics then and the urban furies reign in these tightly contained lyrics. A pig who refuses to squeal or break down on its way to be slaughtered at market becomes a tough metaphorical stand-in for his human counterpart, the worker who refuses to give up dignity.

In the 1960s, Levine abandoned his early formalism, the syllabic poetry he once called "the language of princes," and developed an increasingly narrative and supple free-verse style, a more open approach to the dramatic lyric. *They Feed They Lion* (1972) stands as his most eloquent book of industrial Detroit, evoking the world of grease shops and foundries, the city "pouring fire." The title poem celebrates the African American social insurrection, the Detroit riots of 1967. The oppressed speak through wildly destructive action. This is the peak point of his lyric of rage.

Levine's following two books, *1933* (1974) and *The Names of the Lost* (1976), marked a significant turning point in his work, as he became a poet absorbed by the deep past. A feeling of tenderness entered his work that had not been there before, a divergent mode of masculinity. The collection *1933* memorializes his father, eulogizes his older family members, and powerfully evokes "the blind night of Detroit," while *The Names of the Lost* explicitly links the people of his childhood, whom "no one remembers," with his doomed heroes from the Spanish Civil War, especially the anarchists Buenaventura Durruti and Francisco Ascaso. These martyred figures struggled against injustice and exploitation and kept alive a vision of the self that is freed from tyranny. He often reiterated their chant, "we shall inherit." As models they offered the American poet an escape from self-lacerating irony and paralysis. They gave him a politics, a vision of a new world. There is a plaintiveness in *7 Years from Somewhere* (1979) that turns into the challenged optimism of *One for the Rose* (1981).

This constellation of features brings us to "To Cipriano, in the Wind," which consists of one long stanza, a single stichic block of fifty-four lines. The sentences unroll across lines, generating narrative momentum and pressing the poem forward. Levine loved Yeats's three-beat, or trimeter, line, especially enacted in "Easter, 1916," and he mostly follows the triple-beat template. He often hits a strong beat on the first word or two after the enjambment and thus gives the line an extra spring.

The poem is addressed to Cipriano, a tutelary political and spiritual guide, first to the thirteen-year-old student-worker, then to the older poet. Who was he? In a memoir-essay called "The Spanish Civil War in Poetry," Levine recalls how he took a job delivering dry cleaning on foot in the summer of 1941. He often had to wait around and at first listened to a Bulgarian tailor, a long-winded communist theologian, whom he transforms into Ferrente, a dapper Sicilian, in the poem, but later turned his attention to a pants presser who worked in unpressed pleated trousers and a sleeveless undershirt in the intense heat. He had scars on his back as a result of his imprisonment for his loyalty to the Spanish anarchist cause. Levine later forgot his name and christened him Cipriano Mera, who commanded an anarchist militia unit in Barcelona in 1936. He also rechristened the name of the dry-cleaning establishment—there is no *Peerless Cleaners* in Michigan's "AQD Historic Dry-Cleaning List"—to get the full effect of the word *peerless*, which means incomparable, unsurpassed. This, too, heightens the allegorical character of the poem.

Levine observed how Cipriano worked with alarming suddenness, which he initially took to be theatrical, but soon understood differently: "Within some months I began to read in his movements not a disregard for work but rather the affirmation that all work was worth doing with elegance and precision, and that useful work granted a share of dignity to the worker." Cipriano spoke poor English with a heavy accent, but Levine could follow his argument about the unending struggle that every single person needs to wage for equality and independence. What struck him most forcefully was that despite all his defeats, Cipriano "was animated by an amazing optimism." He embodied the human spirit. In Levine's poem, Cipriano is now "in the wind," which is to say that he is missing, gone, possibly forever. His spirit is in the wind; it, too, seems absent from the world, but something to be called upon, perhaps retrievable.

Levine was obsessed with Spain and the Spanish Civil War, and he studied the poetry written by English leftists of the 1930s, especially W. H. Auden and Stephen Spender. He read closely the poems of the combatants Edwin Rolfe and John Cornford. However, his greater debt is to the politically committed Spanish and Latin American surrealists: Federico García Lorca ("What in my work had been a chaotic rant against American capitalism was in his a steady threnody circling around a center of riot"), Rafael Alberti, Miguel Hernández, Antonio Machado, Pablo Neruda, and César Vallejo, especially his elegy for the martyred worker-hero Pedro Rojas, who is a sort

of Spanish everyman, "With His Index Finger He Used to Write on the Air
. . ." "Long live the comrades," Vallejo declaims, "on the honor roll of the
air!" Levine fantasized a strong resemblance between Vallejo and Cipriano,
both physically ("spare, essential, shabbily dressed") and spiritually: "Like
Cipriano," he said, Vallejo "was intellectually ferocious: they were two seri-
ous men obsessed with the need for radical change." By this sleight of hand,
he turns his mentor into a brother of the greatest Peruvian modern poet. He
does something similar when he describes reading George Orwell's memoir
Homage to Catalonia, finding Cipriano's face in Orwell's descriptions of an
Italian militiaman: "It was the face of a man who would commit murder
and throw away his life for a friend—the kind of face you expect in an Anar-
chist." Levine keeps finding ways to connect personally through Cipriano to
the loyalist cause, the motivating anarchist dream, of the Spanish Civil War.

Levine is known for his use of the American vernacular, working in the
tradition of William Carlos Williams, and pitching his poems at the level
of speech. This last point is partly true—he does mine and import into his
poems the way people speak—but to my ear, most of his poems are launched
at a higher register than ordinary speech. They traffic back and forth between
the colloquial and something grander, more rhetorical. Levine loved Wil-
liams but owed an even greater debt to William Blake and John Keats, and
to Hart Crane and Dylan Thomas. He builds on Walt Whitman, and like
Whitman he takes the American quotidian and infuses it with something
operatic. He said that Whitman could have sponsored his poem "when in his
introduction to *Leaves of Grass* he advised the American poet to go among
powerful, uneducated people and take off his hat to no one."

Levine begins "To Cipriano" by asking not where Cipriano has gone, but
"Where did your words go, / Cipriano?" Cipriano is characterized by what
he said, like a poet. This sentence, which stretches across six lines, is not
posed as a genuine question—there is no question mark at the end of it—
but as a rhetorical statement. The scene is decidedly unromantic, the back
of a dry cleaner. Yet, there is slight but purposeful elevation here—Cipriano
was "raised on a little wooden platform" and "bowed," as if in prayer, "to the
hissing press." The speaker observes his scars, which Cipriano ironically calls
"'a gift / of my country,'" gleaming "like old wood," something dry that can
still burn. Cipriano's wartime experience provides backdrop to everything
he says. His optimism is far from naïve, but well paid for. So, too, the visible

354 THE HEART OF AMERICAN POETRY

light is heightened under "the glaring bulb." The intense light highlights the secret truth of this lyric, which poses as a realistic poem, a memory, but in actuality is a visionary political one.

Pause a moment over the fact that Cipriano uses a Spanish word, *Dignidad*, to define dignity. The dandyish tailor mocks him, but this is a setup, since Levine is learning what matters from his true teacher, Cipriano, who says: "'without is no riches.'" In English, we tend to define *dignity* as a personal trait of calm decorum, a form of self-respect. But as a Spanish political idea, it resonates much more deeply: as a democratic ideal, the respect and esteem that all human beings deserve. There is a long philosophical tradition running from Plato and Aristotle to Kant that recognizes the dignity of the individual as a political ideal of virtue and value related to the polis or city-state. Although the word does not appear in the U.S. Constitution, it has recently been viewed as the basis for human rights.

If you were a photojournalist filming this poem—Levine especially loved the war photography of Robert Capa—you'd make the camera pan back to give a documentary or historical overview: "That was the winter of '41." This has the quality of a photomontage or newsreel and gives you a feeling of epic sweep. It situates the individual in a larger historical context. The tense changes—"it / would"—and the poet thereafter intermingles what is happening in Detroit with what is happening overseas. He matches his fear for his older brother ("it / would take my brother off to war") to the outsize weather at home ("great snowfalls" and "the news of death"). The speaker is going to school and growing up, but he is getting his genuine education from Cipriano, who explains to him: "'Some day the world / is ours, some day you will see.'" Cipriano's slightly mangled tenses create their own form of poetry—they heighten the value of what he says. He speaks with overriding intensity here, as if searing his hopeful words into his young disciple so that they truly register: "And your eyes burned in your fine / white face until I thought you / would burn."

Notice the rhetorical repetition of "That was the winter / of '41," but now with a different line break and thus a different emphasis. Once more, we get a historical overview as Levine connects his budding knowledge of the Spanish Civil War to what is happening during World War II. He moves quickly and personalizes the Bataan Death March through the figure of Sam Baghosian, who makes the long march "with bayonet wounds in both legs."

I suspect that Levine is fictionalizing a fact here, taking the name of a person he knew or read about in Fresno, which was filled with Armenians who fought in World War II, and projecting back to Detroit. He probably took his memory of someone who did return to Detroit crippled from the war, someone he might have known through his older brother but whose name he didn't know or couldn't remember and christened him with a name that later resonated for him. What is true is the fear and rage he recollects at the memory of seeing such a devastated survivor, a shattered warrior. The fury wells up. He clenches the feeling by employing and enjambing an identical rhyme, the only one in the poem ("burning *acids* / splashed across his chest and the *acids* / of his own anger"). These acids would corrode Baghosian's heart when he returned to "eat / the stale bread of victory." This word *acids* brings back the opening of the third line in "They Feed They Lion": "Out of the acids of rage." Mark Twain said that "anger is an acid that can do more harm to the vessel in which it is stored than to anything on which it is poured."

As the speaker's anger threatens to overcome him, he turns once more to address Cipriano, but now more intimately. He asks him to recall how the snow turned to rain, the streets "gleamed," and the season changed from winter to spring. Now the student is teaching his mentor the English word *spring*, which Cipriano understands in a larger, more symbolic way. There are only two lines in the entire poem where the sentence and the lineation coincide, and this is one of them: "'Spring, spring, it always come after.'" That's why it comprises a subject rhyme with a subsequent line: "I said, 'Someday this will be ours.'" Spring suggests regeneration here and Cipriano echoes Shelley's rhetorical question at the end of "Ode to the West Wind": "O Wind, / If Winter comes, can Spring be far behind?"

War leaves a bitter taste, and so do the mounting personal losses: "Soon the Germans rolled East / into Russia and my cousins died." All this turns out to be a test of character for the speaker, who has enormous trouble holding on to a hopeful message, a spring that comes after. Hence, he remembers trying to console himself by repeating Cipriano's iconic word, *dignity*. He spoke into the winds, which had become a confusing plurality, a sort of whirlwind, and tried to reassure himself: "I said, 'Someday this will all be ours.'" We are six lines from the end and the poem structurally turns. The tense changes from the past to the present, and now the speaker is no longer a boy but a man. For the first time, he calls on Cipriano more formally by his full name, Cipriano Mera, emphasizing the conjunction of the pants presser in Detroit and the military figure of the Second Spanish Republic.

I love the way the rhetoric reaches a high, pleading, feverish pitch at the end of the poem:

> Come back, Cipriano Mera, step
> out of the wind and dressed in the robe
> of your pain tell me again that this
> world will be ours. Enter my dreams
> or my life, Cipriano, come back
> out of the wind.

Here, the speaker aggressively calls on Cipriano four times: *Come back*; *step / out*; *Enter my dreams / or my life*; *come back*. He breaks the neck of the modernist injunction to avoid mixing a concrete and an abstraction, and he pleads with Cipriano to return "dressed in the robe / of your pain." Levine intentionally defies the credo, established by Ezra Pound ("Don't use such an expression as 'dim lands of peace'"), and purposefully breaks the line on the word *robe*. Cipriano's scars have been transmuted into a "robe . . . of pain," a phrase that Neruda or Vallejo might have written. It is both an accurate description of the scars left on a prisoner of war, and an invocation of something larger, something allegorical, some cosmic Pain. I want to keep the final lines in mind in order to think about the changed and charged meaning of the wind here.

At the beginning of the poem, Levine addresses Cipriano, who seems to be in the wind because he has slipped away, like a fugitive. But by the end of the poem, he speaks to Cipriano in the wind for another reason altogether. He is seeking inspiration, which means in-breathing, and thereby also invoking the visionary tradition in poetry. He is calling on Cipriano to come back to him as a consoling presence, a prophetic voice. Think of the prophet Ezekiel, who held each of us responsible for our own actions, and beheld a whirlwind coming out of the north, a great cloud, and a fire unfolding itself (Ezekiel 1:4). Or think of how the wind operates with such liberating force in "Ode to the West Wind." As a Romantic poet and democratic anarchist, Shelley embraces the West Wind because it pushes aside the "dead leaves" and nurtures the "winged-seed." Listen to his invocation: "Wild Spirit, which art moving everywhere; / Destroyer and Preserver; hear, oh hear!" Levine invokes Cipriano as a visionary source of the wind itself, a destroyer and preserver, pushing things ahead when the world will be ours. Levine's politics were utopian. He has lost faith and calls on Cipriano Mera, his unlikely mentor, to return to reassure him that the dream of a just world is still vibrant and alive.

Philip Levine was a poet of joy as well as of suffering. He called on an otherwise unknown figure to remember a pledge, not to a flag, but to a future, a democratic ideal. When I think of Cipriano, the pants presser, and Cipriano Mera, a bricklayer by trade as well as a lieutenant colonel in the Spanish Republican Army, I think of something that Ralph Waldo Emerson once said: "I am Defeated all the time; yet to Victory I am born."

ADRIENNE RICH (1929–2012)

XIII (Dedications) [from "An Atlas of the Difficult World"]

I know you are reading this poem
late, before leaving your office
of the one intense yellow lamp-spot and the darkening window
in the lassitude of a building faded to quiet
long after rush-hour.   I know you are reading this poem
standing up in a bookstore far from the ocean
on a grey day of early spring, faint flakes driven
across the plains' enormous spaces around you.
I know you are reading this poem
in a room where too much has happened for you to bear
where the bedclothes lie in stagnant coils on the bed
and the open valise speaks of flight
but you cannot leave yet.   I know you are reading this poem
as the underground train loses momentum and before running
    up the stairs
toward a new kind of love
your life has never allowed.
I know you are reading this poem by the light
of the television screen where soundless images jerk and slide
while you wait for the newscast from the *intifada*.
I know you are reading this poem in a waiting-room
of eyes met and unmeeting, of identity with strangers.
I know you are reading this poem by fluorescent light
in the boredom and fatigue of the young who are counted out,
count themselves out, at too early an age.   I know
you are reading this poem through your failing sight, the thick
lens enlarging these letters beyond all meaning yet you read on
because even the alphabet is precious.

I know you are reading this poem as you pace beside the stove
warming milk, a crying child on your shoulder, a book in your hand
because life is short and you too are thirsty.
I know you are reading this poem which is not in your language
guessing at some words while others keep you reading
and I want to know which words they are.
I know you are reading this poem listening for something, torn between
    bitterness and hope
turning back once again to the task you cannot refuse.
I know you are reading this poem because there is nothing else left to read
there where you have landed, stripped as you are.

                                                    1990–1991

ADRIENNE RICH was a seeker. She had a restless, inquisitive imagination and a fierce determination to make poetry answerable to lived experience. From the time she was a small girl she had a bedrock confidence, a sense of mission and destiny—it was instilled in her by her over-exacting, imperious, learned, patriarchal father—that changed course and developed over time, but never faltered. She started adding dates to her poems in the mid-1950s, which nailed them to a historical moment. The individual poem was not a single event, an isolated capsule, but part of a continuum. Reading her work, it became increasingly difficult to think of writing or reading poetry as a disinterested activity, as something timeless or metaphysical, free from identity and history. Her thinking enables and even requires you, as a gendered reader, to situate yourself in relationship to her work.

Rich assaulted the modernist principle of "impersonality," which prevailed in her youth. She implicated herself in everything she wrote, staking out positions that energized her allies and infuriated her detractors. Her work is singular, but it's not confessional in the Lowellian sense of the term; it's not close to the sensibility of her contemporaries, Sylvia Plath and Anne Sexton, who were poets of exposure and performance. Aspects of Rich's biography are missing from her poetry. Instead, her work intimately traces an intellectual biography over the course of a lifetime, tracking the development of a poet's mind. For her, it wasn't just that the personal was political, to borrow her friend Robin Morgan's feminist slogan, but that everything was personal, everything political.

Rich conducted her education in public, she inscribed it on the page, and many readers, especially women, felt that she was tallying their lives. There was no mistaking her identity or identities, a leftist politics forged in the social turmoil of the 1960s and '70s. She positioned herself in her poems and essays as a daughter and a daughter-in-law, a wife and mother (she often stated that it was her experience of motherhood that radicalized her), a civil rights activist and fervent opponent of the Vietnam War, a writer of what used to be called the women's liberation movement, an inclusive feminist consciousness, a lesbian, a Jew, a woman warrior. She was aware that she had grown up in privileged circumstances, in a house on a hill in Baltimore, unaware of racial injustice, oblivious to the outsider status of Jews, even though she was one, and she labored to question and root prejudice out of herself—her work provides the record. There is a certain wariness in her poetry, a certain isolation—she's not the poet of the warm embrace and the friendly greeting, the fireside chat. But one also feels the excitement in her work, the incendiary thinking, the phenomenological rage, and exhilaration of what she called "awakening consciousness." She despised patriarchy, which she defined simply as "the domination of men," and redeployed what she called "the enemy's language" to change American poetry in the second half of the twentieth century.

Rich didn't take a straightforward aesthetic path; her route was messy and uneven. It was compelling to watch her probing her way into becoming a representative poet of the republic, an outspoken citizen-poet, like Muriel Rukeyser, who provided the model for a poetry of democratic fusions and principles. She also found a precursor in the Chilean poet Pablo Neruda, especially the democratic visionary of *Canto General*, which demonstrates the importance for American poetry of the ongoing multilingual and international conversation. More than anyone else, Rich created a legacy of woman's poetry; her essays on female poets, such as Anne Bradstreet and Emily Dickinson, enabled us to rethink the literary canon and unfix the categories. She is often considered a poet of social consciousness, which she undoubtedly was—she was eager to connect literature to politics—but this evaluation underestimates her lifelong work. To me, she is a poet of liberation. She quests for freedom in all its forms—the egalitarian imagination, the liberated self.

As a senior in college, I came into Rich's work with her sixth book, *The Will to Change* (1971). I had no idea that she had begun as a decorous formalist, someone on good terms with literary tradition who had tried to sound like Yeats and Auden. By the time I discovered her, she had already turned to social engagement—some of my political friends on the New Left loved her book *Leaflets* (1969), but they believed in causes, not poetry, and consequently I missed the Whitmanian impulse in that book, how she was rethinking the implications and imperatives of *Leaves of Grass*.

I took up *The Will to Change* because Rich had borrowed her title from Charles Olson's poem "The Kingfishers": "What does not change / is the will to change." I thought that she was under the impress of what Olson defined as "projective verse" or "composition by field," though it turned out that Rich was not a poet of the projective sensibility, like some of her contemporaries, such as her friend Denise Levertov, a theorist of organic composition. Instead, she was energized by the spontaneity of an engaged poetry sharpened by breath and sight: "What we see, we see / and seeing is changing" ("Planetarium"). She was experimenting with an altered punctuation and grammar in order to treat poetry as an agent of transformation. "The moment of change," she writes, "is the only poem." Later, I found her poem "Tear Gas" (1969), which explains: "The will to change begins in the body not in the mind." This turns out to be one of the premises of her felt poetic and politic.

The Will to Change was a discomfiting book. Rich was feeling her way into the revisionary sequence, improvisations on a theme, and figuring out a new idiom and language: "this is the oppressor's language // yet I need it to talk to you" ("The Burning of Paper Instead of Children"). In the seventies and eighties, she was reconceiving her poetic project and simultaneously teaching us how to read her. When I started out, she was on the cusp of a major change—"I had been looking for the Women's Liberation movement since the 1950s," she said later: "I came into it in 1970"—and the logic of that transformation was unfolding before our eyes. Rich was a serious maker, someone who was radically rethinking the history of poetry. It was exciting to see her developing the work in process, what Olson called "*the kinetics of the thing*," the serial and the sequence—the longer stretch, the linked chain, the book.

Rich was a rapid writer. I was troubled by the way she sometimes opposed the entire aesthetic enterprise, the history of eloquence. I couldn't relate to her most extreme statements, such as "The burning of a book arouses no sensation in me," though I see now she was overstating the case in order to tear up the script—at one point she quotes Antonin Artaud's saying *burn the texts*—and rethink the whole premise of the closed lyric and the male canon, which had come to seem to her a language of oppression. She was creating sequences, sectional poems that were themselves on the move, such as "The Burning of Paper Instead of Children," "The Blue Ghazals," "Letters: March 1969," "The Will to Change," and "Shooting Script Part I: 11/69–2/70," which brought a range of experimental cinematic techniques into the contemporary lyric. In those apprentice days, I sometimes asked myself: "Where would you set up the camera, how would you film that poem?" Rich was one of the few poets who provided a convincing answer.

Rich is a poet of the nonce form, i.e., the form invented for a single purpose or occasion. She was determined to reenvision her formal training and formulate a different poetic. The inherited forms wouldn't do. In the early seventies, she was often trying to talk to men in her poems, registering the impossibility of communication, the wrecked relationship, which was inflected and ruined by a dynamic of dominance and power, and simultaneously talking back to her poetic predecessors and fathers. Her poems aren't just about social causes and historical casualties; they also conduct a running conversation about the nature and efficacy of poetry.

To me, the breakthrough moment in *The Will to Change* comes at the end of Rich's revision and reworking of John Donne's "A Valediction Forbidding Mourning." The female speaker struggles to communicate with her emotionally remote husband. She is explaining, or trying futilely to explain, why she would never return to him. The poem is fractured, difficult to understand, even for the speaker, who cannot articulate her swirling desires. At the end of the poem, she abruptly declares:

> To do something very common, in my own way.

I love this last line—it stands apart and breaks free, a sudden ars poetica. It's like stumbling through a dense wood and unexpectedly coming into a wide clearing. Rich has now declared her purpose and destiny, "To do something very common," which suggests making something ordinary for the whole of a community. She is talking back to her poetic father John Donne and announcing her new commonality, the poetic of the open field, the public space, the Commons. But she would also do it "in my own way"—in other words, with her own idiom, her singular voice.

The phrasing was meaningful to Rich—she had found an operating principle—and she would carry it forward into one of her most revelatory collections, *The Dream of a Common Language: Poems 1974–1977*. It is a book of reconsideration and quest, of claiming a power and creating a female ancestry, of trying to break through the distances that separate women, of "limitless desire, / a whole new poetry beginning here" ("Transcendental Etude"). She was intent on thinking through the relationship between the writer and the reader and doing something personal for the invisible women's collective.

Given this history, it's interesting to consider the later modification of Rich's signature phrasing in the essay "Someone Is Writing a Poem" (1993):

> But most often someone writing a poem believes in, depends on, a delicate, vibrating range of difference, that an "I" can become a "we" without extinguishing others, that *a partly common language* exists in which strangers can bring their own heartbeat, memories, images. A language that itself has learned from the heartbeat, memories, images of strangers.

Rich was defining a poetry of personal accountability. Recognizing both kinship and difference, she was finding her way to a poetry of greater and greater inclusivity, which she explored in collections of large democratic expanse, the works of her maturity, such as *Your Native Land, Your Life* (1986), *An Atlas of the Difficult World* (1991), and *Dark Fields of the Republic* (1995).

Rich told Bill Moyers in an interview that her thirteen-part sequence "An Atlas of the Difficult World" "reflects on the condition of my country, which I wrote very consciously as a citizen poet, looking at the geography, the history, the people of my country." She was trying to fathom what it meant to love her country, the so-called *difficult world*, in a time of turmoil and crisis. The poem was conceived in grievance and fury over the Gulf War, but it travels well beyond that particular catastrophe of misplaced foreign policy and governmental revenge. In the different sections of this poem, Rich is sometimes walking in fog alongside the ocean, near her home in Northern California, sometimes driving the highways on the West Coast or returning to Vermont, recalling where she once lived. She thinks about "the wreckage, dreck and waste" of human lives, victims of domestic abuse, exploited immigrant workers. She ranges widely across the country, holding up a map, pointing out sites of historical calamity and resistance—a group of poems that were written by a Chinese immigrant detained on Angel Island in the early 1940s, a racial uprising in Detroit in the 1960s, a parade that turned into a massacre and lynching of an IWW worker in Centralia, Washington, in 1919—and matching the beauty of her surroundings to the hatred and racism that drive so much of our history. Rich's politically engaged poem confronts American oppressions, the gap between materialism and idealism, and tries to stage an ethical intervention. The idea was to provide a book of maps and charts, which sometimes morph into murals, through a challenging democratic morass. The poem is driven by three recurring formal questions, which have continued to haunt me as a poet, critic, and citizen:

> Where are we moored?   What
> are the bindings?   What be-
> hooves us?

"An Atlas of the Difficult World" is a spacious sequence that culminates in a thirty-seven-line stanza, a stichic poem, that is one of the high-water marks of Rich's work. We normally think of a dedication coming at the beginning rather than the end of a poem, but Rich reverses the pattern and employs it as an epilogue. She carefully places the title in parenthesis, "(Dedications)", and thus makes it seem like an afterthought. She also pluralizes and puns on the term *Dedications*, so that it takes on a variety of connotations. The poem becomes a type of commitment, a series of rites and actions, a set of names in tribute, a recurring act of devotion, and an ongoing ceremonial. It's not an accident that Rich concludes her atlas by reaching out across a yawning divide to bridge the chasm between the poet and the reader. She calls attention to her poem as something constructed and made for another person. The poet insists—she knows with certainty—that there is an audience for poetry, especially a poetry of testimony and witness. She treats the lyric as an intimate form of public art and reaches out to individuals at a moment of need.

Rich's epilogue is eager to make contact. The poem is a catalogue that lists and outlines twelve specific readers, one for every section, each a different type, all of them lonely and isolated, hungry for connection. The list may initially seem random, but it turns out to be carefully structured. The suffering of individual readers intensifies as we go along; there is a progression down the social ladder of privilege. The irregular extra space in certain lines emphasizes the distance between separated readers—it serves as a barrier to be crossed. She repeats the phrase "I know you are reading" twelve different times in the poem. As you reread the poem, you start to hear the phrasing differently so that sometimes the beat comes down on *I know*, sometimes on *I know you*, always on *I know you are reading*. The anaphoric repetition exudes a Whitmanian confidence that the poet can reach out and connect to every single person. "I wanted the poem to speak to people as individuals," Rich said, "but also as individuals multiplied over and over and over." The people are themselves, but they are also representative, allegories of themselves, the singular who stands for the entirety. Each one becomes archetypal. Rich calls it "an invisible collectivity" of "ordinary people trying to live their lives."

The speaker is intent on bringing these different isolates into a community. She reaches out to people who are lonely and struggling, disconnected, disenfranchised. She finds them wherever they happen to be and treats reading itself as a material act. Each one is pinpointed and placed in time. The gender of the people is indeterminate. Rich's empathy has stretched from the time when she could identify only with other women. In every case, the isolated reader could be identified as either a woman or a man.

The initial reader is an office worker stuck in an office late at night (the yellow lamp-spot and darkening window suggest an Edward Hopper painting), the second is someone standing up in a bookstore somewhere out there on the snowy plains. Rich is writing from her home in Santa Cruz, California, the far edge of the continent, and reaches out across the country to someone she knows can't or won't buy her book. The isolation of the lone individual stands out against the vast landscape. The third person has suffered from abuse, someone who has opened a suitcase but can't bear to leave yet. The fourth has escaped on an underground train and is poised to run upstairs "toward a new kind of love / your life has never allowed." The person is running toward a dangerous kind of love, presumably same-sex love, which has been socially proscribed.

Rich's potential readers aren't academic. She finds a reader, probably Palestinian, who has turned down the sound and is reading by the low light of a television screen, waiting for news about the *intifada*. The reference is to the First Intifada, a Palestinian uprising against the Israeli occupation that lasted from 1987 to 1993. Rich's political sympathy is evident. She jumpcuts to a reader in a waiting room, that bland space where people both do and do not look at each other, thrust together as strangers at some of the most excruciating moments of their lives. She then moves to a young person reading by a solitary light in a bedroom. There is an editorial moment when she speaks of the young "who are counted out, / count themselves out / at too early an age." She is a teacher and can't resist telling young people not to discount themselves.

Rich lists a person going blind who can scarcely make out the letters, a mother or father warming milk by the stove with an infant slung across one shoulder (this evokes her own challenging days of early motherhood) who seems desperately thirsty for something beyond domestic life. She finds a foreigner who can barely understand the words and wants to hear back from them ("and I want to know which words they are"). This recalls the woman at the very beginning of the "Atlas," the immigrant picking strawberries, and reimagines the lyric as a conversation between two people. Rich also finds someone else who is "listening for something" in the poem, someone "torn between / bitterness and hope," like the poet herself, who also faces a binding obligation, "the task you cannot refuse."

The final lines send out a life raft: "I know you are reading this poem because there is nothing else left to read / there where you have landed, stripped as you are." The last line is multilayered. Rich told Moyers: "And then in the last line, I thought of someone dying of AIDS. I thought of any person in an isolate situation for whom there was perhaps nothing but a book of poems to put her or him into a sense of relation with the world of other human beings, or perhaps someone in prison. But finally I was thinking of our society, stripped of so much of what was hoped for and promised and given nothing in exchange but material commodities, or the hope of obtaining material commodities. And for me, that is being truly stripped." Rich's lyric, a poem of dedications that illustrates her own single-minded dedication, carries with it an ideal of poetry as a dialogue between strangers, a refuge or shelter for loneliness, and a consolation in time of dire consequence and need. It exists like a flare sent up in the darkness, a flare that the speaker hopes, indeed, she *knows*, is going to find you.

Adrienne Rich wanted justice, and she wanted art, and she refused to separate them. She used her own tempestuous experience as a template and held her country to a high ideal. She registered the events of her time on her pulse, in her body, on her mind. I read her now as one of Emerson's representative figures updated for the second half of the twentieth century, an American poet of insight and self-determination, the utopian quest, someone who always wrote "not somewhere else, but here," and yet furiously dreamed of a better here and now, a more equitable world. I know that you are reading this essay on poetry "late, before leaving your office / of the one intense yellow lamp-spot and the darkening window."

Daddy

You do not do, you do not do
Any more, black shoe
In which I have lived like a foot
For thirty years, poor and white,
Barely daring to breathe or Achoo.

Daddy, I have had to kill you.
You died before I had time—
Marble-heavy, a bag full of God,
Ghastly statue with one gray toe
Big as a Frisco seal

And a head in the freakish Atlantic
Where it pours bean green over blue
In the waters off beautiful Nauset.
I used to pray to recover you.
Ach, du.

In the German tongue, in the Polish town
Scraped flat by the roller
Of wars, wars, wars.
But the name of the town is common.
My Polack friend

Says there are a dozen or two.
So I never could tell where you
Put your foot, your root,

I never could talk to you.
The tongue stuck in my jaw.

It stuck in a barb wire snare.
Ich, ich, ich, ich,
I could hardly speak.
I thought every German was you.
And the language obscene

An engine, an engine
Chuffing me off like a Jew.
A Jew to Dachau, Auschwitz, Belsen.
I began to talk like a Jew.
I think I may well be a Jew.

The snows of the Tyrol, the clear beer of Vienna
Are not very pure or true.
With my gipsy ancestress and my weird luck
And my Taroc pack and my Taroc pack
I may be a bit of a Jew.

I have always been scared of *you*,
With your Luftwaffe, your gobbledygoo.
And your neat mustache
And your Aryan eye, bright blue.
Panzer-man, panzer-man, O You—

Not God but a swastika
So black no sky could squeak through.
Every woman adores a Fascist,
The boot in the face, the brute
Brute heart of a brute like you.

You stand at the blackboard, daddy,
In the picture I have of you,

A cleft in your chin instead of your foot
But no less a devil for that, no not
Any less the black man who

Bit my pretty red heart in two.
I was ten when they buried you.
At twenty I tried to die
And get back, back, back to you.
I thought even the bones would do.

But they pulled me out of the sack,
And they stuck me together with glue.
And then I knew what to do.
I made a model of you,
A man in black with a Meinkampf look

And a love of the rack and the screw.
And I said I do, I do.
So daddy, I'm finally through.
The black telephone's off at the root,
The voices just can't worm through.

If I've killed one man, I've killed two—
The vampire who said he was you
And drank my blood for a year,
Seven years, if you want to know.
Daddy, you can lie back now.

There's a stake in your fat black heart
And the villagers never liked you.
They are dancing and stamping on you.
They always *knew* it was you.
Daddy, daddy, you bastard, I'm through.

1965

I RECALL the first shock and exultation of reading Sylvia Plath's posthumous book, *Ariel* (1965). I carried it around for months—it seemed impossible to read dispassionately—and especially focused on the poem "Daddy," which awed but also scared me. I had been reading Theodore Roethke's romping nonsense poems and originative sequences, which sometimes sound as if Mother Goose had gone haywire, and I wasn't totally unprepared for the lively and disconcerting rhythms, the nursery-rhyme quality and warp speed of Plath's poem. It wasn't hard to see why Plath had responded strongly to the childlike orality and undercurrents of need in Roethke's poetry. But I was unprepared for the Jewish swerve and Nazi imagery in "Daddy" and had no idea how to respond to a catchy Holocaust lyric, which Plath had casually referred to as "light verse." Along with "Lady Lazarus," its companion piece, "Daddy" is a distraught, completely unnerving piece of light verse.

Plath wrote her ferocious last poems in England in late 1962 and early 1963. "The blood jet is poetry," she declared, "There is no stopping it" ("Kindness"). Plath was poetically absorbent, and the figure of the blood jet is something she picked up from D. H. Lawrence's poem "Rabbit Snared in the Night," which she fastened on when she reread his *Complete Poems*. The notoriety of Plath's suicide has obscured how dedicated she was to her craft, how persistently she worked to shape experiences, even as she probed the depths—braving taboo subjects, courting a wildness that defies control. In an interview shortly before her death for a radio series called *The Poet Speaks*, she told the British Council's Peter Orr: "I believe that one should be able to control and manipulate experiences, even the most terrifying, like madness, being tortured, this sort of experience, and one should be able to manipulate these experiences with an informed and an intelligent mind." There is a dialectic in Plath's poems between the conscious struggle to contain and control experience and the unconscious longing to purge it, the desire and need for a liberating imagination.

Plath wrote "Daddy" on October 12, 1962. It was the first month of her separation from Ted Hughes, four months before her death. To be exact: it was the twenty-second anniversary of her father's leg amputation, the day after Hughes had moved out of Court Green, their thatched manor house in the village of North Tawton in Devon, England. Later, he discovered that his poem "Out" was sitting on her desk. "Out" is a three-part poem about Hughes's father's shell-shocked experience of trench warfare in the Great War. Here, the son describes his wordless father sitting in a chair "recovering / From the four-year mastication by gunfire and blood," and characterizes his childhood self as his father's "luckless double." Plath responded to this bitter, brooding English poem in an unexpectedly American way, changing the terms, and identifying Hughes with another silenced father, her own.

Plath was now on her own and as a besieged mother she needed domestic help with their two children, Frieda and Nicholas, a toddler and an infant. She was working in a state of controlled delirium. She had taken to dating her poems and so we know that "Daddy" was one of the twenty-five poems she wrote that month. The list includes some of her most prototypical lyrics, such as "Medusa," "Lesbos," "Fever 103°," "Cut," and "Lady Lazarus" ("Dying / Is an art, like everything else'). She wrote two poems on her thirtieth birthday, the ominous lyric "Poppies in October" and "Ariel," a stunning example of what Plath once called her "dawn poems in blood." She also wrote a fine-grained sequence of five bee poems, which chart a Dantean descent into the interior, the psyche, and a feverish quest for freedom and renewal: "Tomorrow I will be sweet God, I will set them free." Plath's original order for *Ariel* shows that she intended this liberation as the book's final gesture. It was going to end on the word *spring* ("The bees are flying. They taste the spring") and a hopeful note of renewal.

"Daddy" is a vengeful nursery rhyme, a nursery rhyme with a vengeance. Plath cannibalized her life to create a theatrical persona, a thin mask that lets you glimpse something of the face behind it, a brash alter ego. She pitched her voice to a higher frequency. Like Emily Dickinson, she stated herself as "the Representative of the Verse" and intended it not as her authentic self but as "a supposed person." Plath, too, constructed a purported, spectacular "I," even as she purposefully sowed confusion by using so much of her own autobiography in her work as she rushed headlong toward her thirtieth birthday.

Writing *Life Studies*, Robert Lowell, who had been her teacher at Boston University, said that he wanted readers to believe they were getting his true self. Plath loved this new development in his work, what she called "this intense breakthrough into very serious, very personal, emotional experience." The atmosphere at BU had been heady, and she had also been energized by the fearless personal exposures in the work of her classmate Anne

Sexton. Like Lowell and Sexton, Plath often led readers to believe they were getting an actual person, the portrait of her true self, though in her journals she mostly talked about escaping from the confines of that self by caring about something else, something more. She berated herself for her inability to inhabit other personas, especially for fiction-writing purposes. That's why the well-known label of "confessionalism" is so problematic to apply to her poems. Her work is both passionate and distant. It is confessional, and it is not.

In a reading of "Daddy" for BBC Radio, Plath explained that the poem "is spoken by a girl with an Electra complex. Her father died while she thought he was God. Her case is complicated by the fact that her father was also a Nazi and her mother very possibly part Jewish. In the daughter the two strains marry and paralyze each other—she has to act out the awful little allegory once before she is free of it." In 1959, Plath had written a combative elegy for her father, "Electra on Azalea Path" ("O pardon the one who knocks for pardon at / Your gate, father—your hound-bitch, daughter, friend"), which she revised into the surrealist elegy and antipatriarchal poem "The Colossus" ("I shall never get you put together entirely"). Now she doubled down on using a Jungian term to describe the psychosexual dynamic and complex in "Daddy." Whereas Freud believed exclusively in the Oedipus complex, Jung coined "the Electra complex" to characterize a girl's competition with her mother for her father's love and attention. The matter is agonizingly complicated if the father is also hateful and the mother a victim. The girl in the poem has therefore internalized an impossible dynamic, which she must act out a second time to liberate herself.

To be clear: Plath's father was proud of his heritage, he was pro-German, but he was not a Nazi. He was a pacifist who was alarmed by Hitler's rise to power and renounced his German citizenship in 1926. He felt victimized for his nationality. Her mother was not Jewish. This aspect of the poem, a power dynamic that has been internalized, is metaphorical. What is psychologically true is that Plath was haunted by her father's premature death. Otto Plath was a professor of biology and German at Boston University and a well-respected entomologist, the author of the monograph *Bumblebees and Their Ways* (1934), which is a secret influence on his daughter's later sequence about bees. The poem alludes to his birthplace in Grabowo (Grabow), Germany. At the age of fifty-five, he misdiagnosed himself with cancer, stubbornly refused treatment, and died from complications related to diabetes. His daughter was eight, not ten, and woodenly said, "I'll never speak to God again!"

Dr. Ruth Beuscher, who was Plath's psychotherapist at McLean Hospital—she is fictionalized as the life-affirming Dr. Nolan in *The Bell Jar*—has said that during their sessions it came out that Plath had never accepted her father's death. She maintained unconscious fantasies that he was still alive. Dr. Beuscher's diagnosis was that Plath had replaced her father with Hughes, and that when he left her "the desertion reactivated whatever Sylvia felt when the father deserted her." That reactivation might well have been the driving motive of the poem.

"Daddy" starts by crashing its title, an affectionate name for a father, and darkly turning a familiar nursery rhyme ("There was an old woman who lived in a shoe") into a psychological parable. Someone who calls her parent "Daddy" is not thinking like an adult but hurling herself back into childhood feelings. Formally, the poem unscrolls in rollicking five-line stanzas. There is something a little beyond reason, something emotionally excessive in punching past the symmetrical quatrain. In the background, I hear the wildly inventive mask of insanity that energizes the conventional "mad songs" of English poetry, like the sixteenth-century Tom o' Bedlam songs, or Yeats's "Crazy Jane Talks with the Bishop." As Heather Clark points out in her comprehensive biography of Plath, *Red Comet*, Plath also borrows the rhythm and tone from Sexton's early poem "My Friend, My Friend," which she had read in Boston in 1959, probably in a workshop:

> Who will forgive me for the things I do?
> With no special legend or God to refer to,
> With my calm white pedigree, my yankee kin,
> I think it would be better to be a Jew.

The speaker of "Daddy" seems determined to kill off a father who is already dead. Plath's friend, Clarissa Roche, reported that when Plath read her the poem the two of them started rolling on the floor with laughter, which reminds me of Max Brod's description of the uncontrollable laughter that erupted when Kafka read aloud parts of *The Trial* to a group of their friends. Part of the macabre fun of "Daddy," if you can call it that, is the way that Plath ricochets between tones. The speaker talks to her father in the present tense ("You do not do, you do not do / Any more") and characterizes him as a black shoe, in which his daughter has lived "like a foot" for her entire life, submissive and trapped. But now she is freeing herself.

Plath closes the first stanza with the comical word *Achoo*. Clark points out that Plath may be drawing on a half-recalled line from a limerick that she wrote as a child called "A-a-choo." There is an inside joke operating here, too, since Plath was partly responding to the odd phrasing in "Out," which recalls how "the dead man suddenly / Sits up and sneezes—Atishoo!" Hughes's poem is about how a son cannot connect to a father traumatized by war. From the beginning, Plath had her eye on the conflation of two men from different sides of a wartime divide—the German father, the English husband. As an advocate for the new poetry of extremity, Al Alvarez considered it a love poem.

Plath rhymes the deflationary onomatopoeia *Achoo* with the matter-of-fact statement in the next stanza: "Daddy, I have had to kill you." She is a phrasemaker and so she careens from "You died before I had time— / Marble-heavy, a bag full of God" to calling him a "Ghastly statue with one gray toe / Big as a Frisco seal // And a head in the freakish Atlantic." She undercuts the sincerity of "I used to pray to recover you" with a comical code switch to German: "Ach, du" (Ah, you). All this has a whiplash effect.

It is here that the poem turns to her father's German origins. Plath never had the opportunity to ask her father about his background—he emigrated from West Prussia in 1901 when he was sixteen years old—and she fills this absence, a lack of knowledge, with a series of obsessive associations. He came from a war-torn world, and she cannot locate his roots, her roots, because Grabowo was a common name for towns and villages all over an area that had become known as "the Polish Corridor." Step by step, the poem moves through short declarative sentences from "I could never talk to you" to "The tongue stuck in my jaw" to "It stuck in a barb wire snare" to "Ich, ich, ich, ich, / I could hardly speak." Otto Plath liked his daughter to speak to him in German and she recalls snaring on the very un-English sound of *Ich*. In her journals, Plath endlessly reprimanded herself for her inability to study and master German; the language defeated her and she felt excluded by the sight "of those dense, black, barbed wire letters." The daughter stammers in time—she is breaking her long silence—and before we know it, we have rolled up to "I thought every German was you. / And the language obscene." There is no comma after the word *obscene* and she sends herself rolling off—the word *chuffing* seems like something from a children's book about trains—to one concentration camp after another:

> An engine, an engine
> Chuffing me off like a Jew.
> A Jew to Dachau, Auschwitz, Belsen.
> I began to talk like a Jew.
> I think I may well be a Jew.
>
> The snows of the Tyrol, the clear beer of Vienna
> Are not very pure or true.
> With my gipsy ancestress and my weird luck
> And my Taroc pack and my Taroc pack
> I may be a bit of a Jew.

This is designed to be shocking. It purposely lacks perspective. Plath is reaching for an extreme of imagination to describe an extreme feeling, a girl who still believes that her father is almighty, someone who has complete power over her, like God. She feels victimized by him and so turns for an analogy to an end point of history, the image of victimized Jews being shipped off to concentration camps. She identifies with these victims, but perhaps not entirely: "I began to talk *like* a Jew," "I think I *may well be* a Jew," "I *may be a bit* of a Jew." There is a kernel of truth here since Plath speculated that she had a Jewish or partly Jewish relative on her mother's Austrian side of the family, which had changed its name from the common Jewish name Grünwald (Greenwood). Plath gave the vaguely Jewish name "Esther Greenwood" to the narrator and protagonist of *The Bell Jar*, who is not Jewish but finds herself identifying with Jews as victims.

   Plath's appropriation of Holocaust imagery has provoked extreme reactions and counterreactions. At first, I, too, was upset about the disproportions, but after reading the poem for fifty years, I now feel agnostic about Plath's metaphor. I still partly sympathize with the critic Leon Wieseltier's objection that "whatever her father did to her, it could not have been what the Germans did to the Jews." The metaphor of personal pain, no matter how genuine, seems incommensurate to the historical reality. And yet I recognize that Plath is intentionally overreaching. The girl who has been so psychologically wounded is fantasizing, and this desperate fantasy has tried to find a location in history, a correlative. It's a fiction, and not a particularly accurate one. Plath's idea of her "gipsy ancestress" and her "weird luck" and her magical Taroc pack seem like something she might have picked up from T. S. Eliot, say, Madame Sosostris's reading of tarot cards in *The Waste Land.* It's a mistake to invest too much realism into her claim to an imaginary Jewish ancestry and victimhood.

What is serious is her feeling. The tone is glib, but the fear is real and so the Plathean speaker keeps regressing back to her childhood complex, which seems inescapable: "I have always been scared of *you.*" The rhyming is childish: *you, gobbledygoo, blue, You.* She careens between her projection of him as "gobbledygoo" and someone from the German artillery, a "Panzer-man." As she describes her father's Germanic looks (the neat mustache and the Aryan blue eyes), she finds herself further identifying him as a Nazi, "Not God but a swastika." The speaker sexualizes violence in a troubling and even appalling way ("Every woman adores a Fascist") and recalls her father's rationality, a man who stands at a blackboard in a photograph but was nonetheless "a devil." She has thrown herself back in time to the fantastic evil that was somehow inflicted on her, which she pins to a suicide attempt: "I was ten when they buried you. / At twenty I tried to die / And get back, back, back to you." The poem emphasizes a ten-year cycle of death and rebirth and turns toward the present. The ten- and then twenty-year-old gets glued back together, and suddenly the woman knows what to do: "I made a model of you." She leaps forward to her marriage to a man who is just like her father: "And I said I do, I do."

This psychological identification of two men, two people she perceives as monsters, a father and a husband, has been driving the poem all along. Plath's stand-in continues to speak to the father, as in a child's voice, "So daddy, I'm finally through," but now we perceive that she is also talking as an adult about her husband: "If I've killed one man, I've killed two." Plath introduces the image of a vampire husband who drank her blood and devoured her not just for one but for the full seven years of their marriage. She sees him as cruel, sadistic, and authoritarian. Both men have damaged her heart, but now she is finally laying it all to rest. She is burying her father again, but this time knowingly, and with a vengeance: "Daddy, you can lie back now." The girl's Electra complex is finally being resolved.

> There's a stake in your fat black heart
> And the villagers never liked you.
> They are dancing and stamping on you.
> They always *knew* it was you.
> Daddy, daddy, you bastard, I'm through.

This progression—four simple declarative sentences in five lines—is primal, furious, aggressive. There is a bizarre comic silliness here too: "And the villagers never liked you." The difference from Lowell and Sexton is not merely that Plath mythologizes but also that she self-parodies, like Allen Ginsberg in "America." At the same time, the shamanistic female speaker imagines a lynch mob, the rite of villagers dancing and stamping out her father, an incarnation of the devil. It is an act of violent revenge. It is not difficult to see why Dr. Beuscher once said that Plath had what she called "an archaic attitude." There is great satisfaction, a wild triumphalism, in the last line, the final declaration. The exorcism is complete. The girl is finally done with her father, the woman is finished with her husband, and the poem is complete: "Daddy, daddy, you bastard, I'm through."

There is so much fury in the curse word *bastard* that it completely upends the nursery rhyme. It also crashes the genteel elegiac tradition. The speaker is not quietly laying the dead one to rest. Plath's rage, a kind of sacred wrath, destabilized the lexicon and altered the literary conversation not just about the elegy and the love poem, but also about mid-century poetry itself. She had taken perfect aim and hurled a rock through the window—American poetry, especially poetry by women, would never be the same again. Sylvia Plath had mined her personal experience and reached for the archetype, but she could not have known that she had created a tagline for second-wave American feminism. She would become its icon.

After all these years, I continue to be startled by the way that "Daddy" troubles and rewrites the unresolved relationship between a girl and her father. Plath understood how patterns of childhood are reproduced in adulthood, how defined gender roles repeat themselves and need to be upended, broken, and transformed. She was undeterred, funny, and furious. She changed herself, but she also changed American poetry when she turned a form of light verse into a chainsaw and cut her way to freedom.

["won't you celebrate with me"]

won't you celebrate with me
what i have shaped into
a kind of life? i had no model.
born in babylon
both nonwhite and woman
what did i see to be except myself?
i made it up
here on this bridge between
starshine and clay,
my one hand holding tight
my other hand; come celebrate
with me that everyday
something has tried to kill me
and has failed.

1993

L UCILLE CLIFTON believed in the radical hopefulness of con-
necting through poetry. She did not shy away from what she
termed "the terrible stories," either personal or communal, and faced
head-on the American traumas, especially the legacy of racism and slavery,
the original sins of our national history. She was proud of her Dahomey
ancestors—she wrote a memoir called *Generations* (1976)—and believed that
as an African American woman she had a crucial tale to contribute to the
larger human Story. In fact, *Story* was one of the few words she capitalized.
As a poet, she believed that her purpose was to speak not just for herself but
also for those who had not yet spoken, to tell the stories that they might
not have been able to tell themselves. At her poetry readings, she often

quoted an old preacher: "I come to comfort the afflicted and to afflict the comfortable."

Lucille Clifton, who was born Thelma Lucille Sayles, wrote poems from the time she was a small girl. She was not formally schooled in poetry and came to it with the perspective of an outsider, which may be one reason she decided early on in her work not to capitalize the pronoun *i*, or any other proper nouns for that matter. It was a move of insistent informality that she took from the playbook of E. E. Cummings and then retooled for her own ends. Altogether, her use of punctuation tended to be minimal. The absence of capitals is an egalitarian gesture that puts all nouns and pronouns on the same level. This was part of her arsenal as a poet of the American vernacular who created spells out of familiar words, plain speech. She liked the jazzy rhythm and the syncopated short line. She pressurized commonplace language into lyrics that are fast paced, cutting, and explosive.

Clifton was an extraordinary poet who positioned herself as *An Ordinary Woman* (1974), someone who came from poor folks in Buffalo, New York. Her mother, Thelma Moore Sayles, wrote poetry and worked in a laundry; her father, Samuel Sayles, worked in a steel mill and told her stories about their enslaved ancestors. He also sexually abused her (see "forgiving my father," "moonchild," "mercy," "my father hasn't come back / to apologize") and bullied her mother into burning her poems, which scalded Clifton (see "fury") and stiffened her resolve to become a poet and persist as a survivor, a voice for the victimized. She took her stand and declared, "i am on the dark side always" ("whose side are you on?"). Clifton's mother, who was epileptic, died at the age of forty-four when her daughter was just twenty-two. All her life, Clifton mourned the loss and vowed to complete the work that her mother had begun.

Lucille Sayles married Fred James Clifton in 1958, and the two of them had six children over the course of the 1960s. Much has been made of the fact that she started writing during the Black Arts Movement, less of the fact that she mostly missed out on it. She wrote as a daughter, a wife, a mother, a grandmother—a plainspoken woman, a truthteller. She was outraged by injustice, struggling for survival, determined to speak up for her family, the larger human family, and to assert her personhood as a woman of color. Because of her family responsibilities, she never had much time on her hands. She was only partly fooling when she explained that this is the reason that her poems are all so short. In her six-line poem "the poet," she characterized herself as "tap dancing for my life."

As a poet, Clifton embraced her sexuality and celebrated the Black female body. She was politically aware as well as historically conscious, and there is a streak of activist memorial in her poems of the Middle Passage and the southern auction block, the white terrorist church bombing in Birmingham, Alabama, that killed four Black girls, the assassination of the civil rights evangelist Medgar Evers, the murder of James Byrd, Jr., who was dragged along a highway in Jasper, Texas. She treats these atrocities as crimes against humanity, offenses against our very humanness. She balanced these poems of historical suffering with homages to African ancestors ("all my bones remember") and lyrics dedicated to racial heroes and martyrs (Jackie Robinson, Malcolm X), which are intertwined with invocations to spiritual exemplars, like the goddess Kali ("terrible hindu woman God / Kali. / who is black"), and the figure of Crazy Horse ("surely the heart of crazy horse must rise"), and even the original holy family, especially the Virgin Mother ("mary astonished by God").

Clifton also brooded about the character of the fallen angel Lucifer and determined to rethink the implications of his biblical story. Two sequences, "tree of life" and "brothers," reclaim the satanic figure as she identifies with Lucifer not as a Prince of Darkness but as a "son of the morning" (Isaiah 14:12), an illuminator who questions and criticizes God for His role in human history and indifference to human suffering. "I think I was struck by the idea of Lucifer being the Light-Bringer," she explained, "and Lucille means 'light.'" Clifton often took advantage of the meaning of her name. Tracking the many times that she makes the connection (Lucille = light), I began to see her as a poet of the compressed litany and regenerated religious ode. "call it our roots," she states in her poem "roots," "it is the light in us / it is the light of us / it is the light."

The light dawned on me that Clifton had combined the colloquial language of William Carlos Williams and Langston Hughes with the elevated language of the King James Bible when I read *Two-Headed Woman* (1980). The title suggests a woman with access to both the material and spiritual realms. The book begins with an invitation that combines biblical wording and imagery with an element of the circus spectacle: "in this garden / growing / following strict orders / following the Light / see the sensational /

382 THE HEART OF AMERICAN POETRY

two-headed woman." Tellingly, there are three memorial poems to Clifton's mother: "to thelma who worried because i couldn't cook," "poem on my fortieth birthday to my mother who died young," and "february 13, 1980." The book concludes with the sequence "the light that came to lucille clifton." She identifies these poems as testaments, explanations, and confessions, and they give her work a visionary feeling—part courtroom testimony, part Christian tent revival: "i / lucille clifton / hereby testify / that in that room / there was a light / and in that light / there was a voice / and in that voice / there was a sigh / and in that sigh / there was a world."

Clifton grew up in the church and there is more of the African American spiritual in her poetry than I had initially realized. As an adult, she was not a churchgoer, but she was steeped in scripture and eager to reconsider and rewrite the original biblical stories from an antipatriarchal African American perspective. Scholars have estimated that nearly one-third of Clifton's more than five hundred poems feature biblical characters or include biblical imagery. Clifton had her own brand of Christian spirituality, and one can chart an increasing turn to dreams and visions in her work. When, in one untitled poem, she wonders about the incandescent glow and the soft shuffle of strangers who people her light, they answer matter-of-factly: "lucille / we are / the Light."

Clifton was characteristically cavalier and down-to-earth about her contact with the other side, especially her conversations with her long-dead mother. In the mid- to late seventies, her mother began to speak to her through the Ouija board. Clifton then turned to automatic writing to transcribe her mother's messages. Eventually, as she told Akasha Gloria Hull, she no longer had to write down the communiqués because "writing and hearing were almost like the same thing." She also wrote a series of poems, "The Ones Who Talk," in which disembodied spirits speculate about "the fate and danger of the world of the Americas." Like Jack Spicer and James Merrill, who also wrote poems of spiritual dictation, Clifton self-consciously placed herself in the visionary tradition of William Blake and W. B. Yeats. It was as if she were destined to write a collection called *The Book of Light* (1992).

Clifton is a poet of distillation and compression, but her individual lyrics build into sequences and books, and thus create a sense of depth and expansion. She combines an incandescent language, a wording that seems lit from within, with the experiences of a Black woman writing through fifty years of an American century. Here the Blakean tradition takes a swerve and finds an outlet that Blake could not have foreseen. For example, an untitled poem about environmental awareness begins "being property once myself / i have a feeling for it."

Clifton's poem "study the masters" is clarifying. The title of this ars poetica seems to lead you in one direction—you think she is going to point to poetic exemplars, like Wordsworth or Dickinson—but then she surprises you in another direction. You take in the title and then suddenly plunge into the truth of the poem: "study the masters"

> like my aunt timmie.

Aunt Timmie was a laundress and her iron, "or one like hers," smoothed the sheets for "the master poet." Clifton makes clear that this is both a specific and an archetypal situation; Aunt Timmie is an individual who represents the aggregate. Aunt Timmie is the one we should be studying, not the one who sleeps on her handiwork like a conqueror. She has her dreams, too, which syncretize Native nation and African American traditions ("some cherokee, some masai and some / huge and particular as hope." The ending of this poem is edgy and purposeful:

> if you had heard her
> chanting as she ironed
> you would understand form and line
> and discipline and order and
> america.

Clifton homes in on issues of family, race, and class, of someone making art out of difficult circumstance. The word *chanting* is well chosen since chanting gives verse, as Northrop Frye puts it, "a hieratic quality, removing it from the language of common speech, and it thereby increases the exhilaration of poetry, bringing it nearer the sphere of the heroic." Aunt Timmie is timing her work song to her motion, and Clifton uses a vocabulary—*form, line, discipline, order*—that applies both to ironing sheets and to making poetry. This final sentence is also cleverly measured; the word *america* is of a different order than the other words in the catalogue, and thus drops on you with a shock: AMERICA. Aunt Timmie is teaching us something crucial about art and country. Clifton was vehement in stating that she didn't remember what other people wanted her to remember, and she didn't write the way that other people wanted her to write. That's why her small *i* has such large presence.

I remember reading Clifton's startling poem that begins "won't you cele-brate" when it appeared in *American Poetry Review*. It was the only untitled lyric in a group of eight, and it leaped off the page. Soon after it jumped out of *The Book of Light*. It is a short poem with a long reach—it became iconic in almost no time at all. The poem is written in a tight free-verse style and consists of fourteen clipped, mostly two- and three-beat lines. It does not present as a sonnet, but it is shadowed closely by the argumentative nature of the sonnet form. Rhetorically, it contains just two questions and answers. The questions are pointed, the answers resolute, definitive. This is a wisdom poem, a lyric gleaned from experience, and there is a powerful personal and social story behind it. Clifton doesn't tell us that story here—we surmise it from her other poems—but we feel its presence. This is a song of determi-nation, the song of someone who has come through, as D. H. Lawrence put it. The Turkish poet Nazim Hikmet said that poetry is an art "drenched with blood," and this is a poem that proves it.

Clifton's poem of self-definition is a dramatic lyric. It poses an inquiry that reverberates not just through American poetry but also through American life. She speaks as an African American woman, a person often considered a double outsider, and therefore can't take for granted that everyone is willing to come and join her self-proclaimed ceremonial. There is something a little edgy in the negative—she doesn't say, for example, "will you" but "won't you" (will you not) "celebrate with me?" What she is asking is this: Won't you come, whoever you are, and commemorate something unexpected with her? This is an invitation, but just what sort of invitation is it, and what are we being asked to celebrate?

It's worth slowing the poem down to figure out how it works. Take the first three lines:

> won't you celebrate with me
> what i have shaped into
> a kind of life? i had no model.

The first line has aphoristic power as a unit—"won't you celebrate with me"—and then spills over into "what i have shaped." The rhetorical and sonic parallelism between *won't you* and *what I* give the lines a rhythmic bounce. The word *what* is purposefully vague. The second line operates as an intact unit—"what i have shaped into"—that springs forward into "a kind of life." There is something approximate and slightly hesitant, maybe even a bit apologetic, about the way she asks you, asks each of us, if we will celebrate with her something that might seem unrecognizable, whatever it is, something she has shaped from very little, like a sculpture or a poem. It doesn't fit into a preexistent mold. She is asking you to honor something else altogether, something different, though she doesn't seem entirely sure that she knows precisely what it all adds up to, and thus she refers to it as "a *kind* of life."

Clifton answers her own question with a short, definitive phrase: "i had no model." This is a two-part line; the question and answer are joined together as a single unit. Clifton's declaration that she had to go it alone, that she had no precursors who were like her, is an old American story. I believe in her originality, but she's making a declaration of Emersonian self-reliance. She has learned on her own to take his primary motto to heart: "Trust thyself; every heart vibrates to that iron string."

The word *celebrate* has a special valence in American poetry. Clifton is quietly rewriting the most epochal opening in American poetry, which she had chosen as an epigraph to introduce her memoir *Generations*: "I celebrate myself, / And what I shall assume you shall assume, / For every atom belonging to me as good belongs to you." The Latin word *celebris* means crowded or populous—its secondary meaning is festive—and Whitman is asserting a democratic ideal of being one with the populace. He is filled with an American bravado new to world literature. Clifton aligns herself with Whitman's great claim, but she is also slyly suggesting that he is making a certain universalist presumption, which is that he can speak for all of us, that we can accept what he accepts, that one can stand for all. As an outsider, a newcomer with a starkly different pedigree, Clifton problematizes that idea. Is what she shall assume at all what you shall assume? So, too, Clifton is quite consciously following a precedent set by Langston Hughes in "I, Too," his conscientious recasting of "I Hear America Singing." Keeping Whitman and Hughes in mind as precursors, she taught a creative writing class at Saint

Mary's College called *I, Too, Sing America*. Thus, Clifton also sings America, and her untitled lyric is the same type of Whitmanian rejoinder, but from a womanist perspective.

Like Hughes, Clifton takes Whitman's long prophetic line and significantly contracts it. We inevitably feel such lineation as something drastically foreshortened, taken away. But Clifton is also adding something decisive to the American discourse by writing about herself as a Black woman with a fully developed consciousness. That's why her second question seems slightly more elevated and rhetorical. There's buzz in the sounding. The word *born* reverberates in the words *babylon* and *woman*. This sound also clangs through the first syllable of the word *"non*white." The letter *w* then threads the word *non*w*hite* to the word w*oman*. Clifton repeatedly presses down on the letter *b* and thus weaves together four words into a tale of emerging identity:

> *b*orn in *b*abylon
> *b*oth nonwhite and woman
> what did i see to *b*e except myself?

Clifton refers here to Psalm 137, which she knew from childhood but also heard recast during the protest movements of the 1960s and '70s. From the King James Bible:

> By the rivers of Babylon, there we sat down, yea, we wept, when
>   we remembered Zion.
> We hanged our harps upon the willows in the midst thereof.
> For there they that carried us away captive required of us a song;
>   and they that wasted us required of us mirth, saying, Sing us
>   one of the songs of Zion.
> How shall we sing the Lord's song in a strange land?

This beautiful and sorrowful song of exile is infused with longing, disbelief, and fury. It commemorates the feelings of Jews in response to the Babylonian conquest of Jerusalem in 586 B.C., but the legacy of dispossession and exile has spoken to many different peoples over the centuries. Frederick Douglass famously read it as a broadside against slavery in his 1852 oration "What to the Slave is the Fourth of July?" and thereby gave the psalm an American political weight and symbolism that it has never lost. "The rich inheritance of justice, liberty, prosperity, and independence bequeathed by your fathers, is shared by you, not by me," he told a white audience in Rochester, New York, near where Clifton grew up. So, too, the song "Rivers of Babylon" (1970) by the Jamaican group the Melodians, which recast Psalm 137 over a buoyant baseline, became an anthem for the Rastafarian movement. It stands behind Bob Marley and the Wailers' 1979 song "Babylon System" ("We refuse to be / What you wanted us to be").

Clifton was born in Depew, New York, in 1936, but by naming her birthplace Babylon she is responding to the exile she felt there, a legacy of bigotry, segregation, and racialism. She characterizes herself by her difference as both nonwhite *and* a woman, a double disadvantage, which she will defiantly turn into an affirmation of character and experience, of self-confidence. "I would like to be seen as a woman whose roots go back to Africa," she told an interviewer, "who tried to honor being human."

Here is her credo:

> i made it up
> here on this bridge between
> starshine and clay,
> my one hand holding tight
> my other hand;

I love the pride in this sentence, "i made it up," which is to say, I constructed a self. There is a pun on "made it," which suggests that she survived and succeeded, but also invokes *poesis*, a term derived from the ancient Greek word for poetry, which means "making." A poet is a maker, a poem a well-made thing. This speaker "made it up" at a particular time in a particular place, "*here* on *this bridge*." Clifton takes the physical reality of a bridge and reconstructs it as a metaphor, a liminal space, and thereby coins her most lyrical line. As a two-headed woman, she finds a place to stand "between / starshine and clay," and thereby situates herself in a space between sky and earth—the spiritual beauty of the transcendental, of gazing upward, and the reality of looking back down, of returning to natural soil. She then restates that she made herself up by digging in and standing tall, "my one hand holding tight

/ my other hand." She didn't reach out to others but to herself. The clasped hands stand metonymically for her stubborn determination and resolve.

Like a Miltonic sonnet, the poem turns after the semicolon in the middle of a line, four lines from the end. The question "won't you celebrate with me" has changed into something more direct and determined. There's an emphatic pause on the Whitmanian word *celebrate*:

> come celebrate
> with me that everyday
> something has tried to kill me
> and has failed.

Clifton asks us to celebrate her very survival, the way she has navigated dangerous waters. Each line here is tightly coiled. Reading it aloud, you notice the enjambments, the spring in the progressions, like a jazz piece. The lineation forces us to pause and then tumble forward—"come celebrate / with me that everyday / something has tried to kill me / and has failed." There's an internal slant rhyme between *me* and every*day*, a reverberation in phrasing from *with me* at the start of one line to *to kill me* at the close of the next one. The last line acts like a punch line, enacting what it is about.

Clifton doesn't specify the nature of that *something* which has tried to kill her, but the word gets pressure at the beginning of the line, and I take it to be multivalent. One of those things is obviously the way that African Americans, both women and men, have repeatedly been targeted in our country. She holds fast against all those people, those racial and social forces that have tried to kill her. She is also commemorating her private struggles—three bouts with cancer, a kidney transplant, the death of her husband and two of her children. All this serves as a deep backdrop to her invitation, her short and defining poem of survival. There is something triumphant and even winning in the last word: *failed*.

Lucille Clifton had an optimism that could not be vanquished. For all the rage and despair in her work, she ultimately viewed poetry as a way of reaching out to others, of not being alone in the world. I'm moved by the way that she repeatedly asks an unknown reader for companionship. She understood something fundamental about the work of American poetry, the spiritual work of poetry itself, and it's deeply gratifying to celebrate with her.

C. K. WILLIAMS (1936–2015)

My Mother's Lips

Until I asked her to please stop doing it and was astonished to find that
she not only could
but from the moment I asked her in fact would stop doing it, my mother,
all through my childhood,
when I was saying something to her, something important, would move
her lips as I was speaking
so that she seemed to be saying under her breath the very words I was
saying as I was saying them.

Or, even more disconcertingly—wildly so now that my puberty had
erupted—*before* I said them.
When I was smaller, I must just have assumed that she was omniscient.
Why not?
She knew everything else—when I was tired, or lying; she'd know if I was
ill before I did.
I may even have thought—how could it not have come into my mind?—
that she *caused* what I said.

All she was really doing of course was mouthing my words a split second
after I said them myself,
but it wasn't until my own children were learning to talk that I really
understood how,
and understood, too, the edge of anxiety in it, the wanting to bring you
along out of the silence,
the compulsion to lift you again from those blank caverns of namelessness
we encase.

That was long afterward, though: where I was now was just wanting to get
    her to stop,
and considering how I brooded and raged in those days, how quickly my
    teeth went on edge,
the restraint I approached her with seems remarkable, although her so
    unprotestingly,
readily taming a habit, by then three children and a dozen years old was as
    much so.

It's endearing to watch us again in that long-ago dusk, facing each other,
    my mother and me.
I've just grown to her height, or just past it: there are our lips moving
    together,
now the unison suddenly breaks, I have to go on by myself, no maestro,
    no score to follow.
I wonder what finally made me take umbrage enough, or heart enough,
    to confront her?

It's not important. My cocoon at that age was already unwinding: the
    threads ravel and snarl.
When I find one again, it's that two o'clock in the morning, a grim hotel
    on a square,
the impenetrable maze of an endless city, when, really alone for the first
    time in my life,
I found myself leaning from the window, incanting in a tearing whisper
    what I thought were poems.

I'd love to know what I raved that night to the night, what those innocent
    dithyrambs were,
or to feel what so ecstatically drew me out of myself and beyond . . .
    Nothing is there, though,
only the solemn piazza beneath me, the riot of dim, tiled roofs and
    impassable alleys,
my desolate bed behind me, and my voice, hoarse, and the sweet, alien air
    against me like a kiss.

1983

"IT STINKS. It stinks and it stinks and it stinks and it stinks."
I remember the moment, the spring of 1974, *American Poetry Review*, the newspaper format, which was still a novelty then, the print almost coming off in your hands, a poem called "Hog Heaven." "It stinks in the mansions and it stinks in the shacks and the carpeted offices, / in the beds and the classrooms and out in the fields where there's no one." It continued like that and did not let up for thirty-one lines; it was a desecration, an assault. It included everyone and everything: old people and money and Christ, too ("he knew how the slaves would be stacked into the holds and he took it"). Nothing was exempt from the poet's ruthless gaze and conviction: "The intellect stinks and the moral faculty . . . and the whole consciousness." Everything stinks: life, and death, and god, whose holy name was not capitalized. And yet imperceptibly the poem changed course, it repeated the lament so often that it became almost comical, or maybe not quite comical, but self-aware and funny and daring: "and every breath, daring to turn, daring to come back from the stop: the turn stinks / and the last breath, the real one, the one where everyone troops into your bed / and piles on—oh, that one stinks best!" I didn't expect this unobtrusive and suddenly joyful illustration of poetry as breath, as *verse*, which derives from the Latin word *versus*, "a line, row, line of verse, line of writing," which derives from the Proto-Indo-European root *wer-*, meaning "to turn, bend." It winds into an exuberant family scene, too. To my lasting astonishment, blasphemy becomes praise, and "Hog Heaven" turns into a song of breath and holiness, a lyric of marvels, a poem of poetry that circles back to its beginning, but now transformed: "each time the same stink, the amazement, the wonder to do this and it flares, / this, and it stinks, this: it stinks and it stinks and it stinks and it stinks."

C. K. Williams was a poet of audacious imagination, of girded anguish and celebration—the startling anecdote, the unexpected story line. He was also a poet of disquietude, of psychological exploration, the sorrows of a diligent, self-reflexive consciousness. His first two books, *Lies* (1969) and *I Am the Bitter Name* (1972), explored what he called "varieties of disjunctive consciousness." Influenced by the surrealism of the French dramatist Antonin Artaud and the Peruvian poet César Vallejo, this early work subverted logical connections and struggled to enact the movement of the mind as it swoops, hovers, and moves in multiple directions. He was unsparingly honest, violently self-divided ("I am going to rip myself down the middle into two pieces," he declared in "Halves"), and enraged by American politics. You could feel his disgust with the official lie, the government war machine, the flashpoints of history: Anne Frank, Cambodia, Kent State. It didn't quite add up. His fury turned inward, and his poems seemed as if they were breaking apart from frustration and rage. The same was true of Philip Levine's early work. This was the poetry of the stymied quest and the dead-end job.

"Hog Heaven" was the first poem I ever read in Williams's expansive mode. That issue of *APR* also included a poem called "Blades," which begins: "When I was about eight, I once stabbed somebody, another kid, a little girl." It went on with the memory, you couldn't put it down or stop reading, and yet it turned, too, it changed course: "I don't understand how we twist these things or how we get them straight again / but I relived that day I don't know how many times before I realized I had it all wrong. / The boy wasn't me at all, he was another kid: I was just there." Williams's breakthrough in thinking and writing, the enlargement of his work, became evident in his next book, *With Ignorance* (1977). Everything about it was oversized. I brought it home one night and devoured it for the story, like *Crime and Punishment*. Then I went back to the beginning and read it again. It was one of the grittiest books of poetry I had ever read and yet it had a kind of sanctity.

The decisive moment in C. K. Williams's writing life came when he decided to put things into his poems rather than to take them out, to become a poet of the inclusion. He extended his lineation even further than Walt Whitman's long free-verse lines. The test was to see how far he could push and shape that line before it faltered and became prose. By employing the line as the longest possible rhythmic unit, he forced himself to break the abbreviated rhetorical code and lyric shorthand that characterize so much of the poetry of any period. Like Allen Ginsberg, he dared to tell stories and create litanies in poems, but whereas Ginsberg focused on his dharmic angels, Williams turned the lens on more ordinary people, the ones he observed on the street and talked to in taverns. He took the commonplace to another limit. "If you put in enough hours in bars," he wrote in a poem called "Bob," "sooner or later you get to hear every imaginable kind of bullshit." What was striking about Williams's poems and what is still notable is how he guides you through the stories ("This is going to get a little nutty now, maybe because everything was a little nutty for me back then") with a self-scrutiny and forthrightness that make him utterly trustworthy—a self-conscious conscientious objector, a moralist.

Williams was a poet of the personal extreme who built on the psycho-dynamic models of Robert Lowell, Sylvia Plath, and Anne Sexton, though his mode was more ruminative and discursive than theirs, more societally oriented. One could tell that he was working through the texts of older contemporaries like Robert Bly in *The Teeth Mother Naked at Last* (1971) and Galway Kinnell in *The Book of Nightmares* (1973). But he trained his gaze on daily life in a way that is substantially different than other poets in the prophetic mode of the late sixties and early seventies. He was more person-ally hyperaware, more socially attuned, than the half generation above him. Williams was friends with the sociologist Erving Goffman, who paid close textual attention to the dramaturgy of daily life. Goffman was writing his book *Frame Analysis* (1974), which views ordinary life as a play and individ-uals as social actors, at the time that Williams was developing the strategies for *With Ignorance*, and there's an overlap in how scrupulously they look at things and wonder aloud: What's really going on here?

Williams created room to think in his poems and worked best in the long stretch. He observed people in confronting situations, commonly doing something outlandish, sometimes accidentally, sometimes on purpose, often breaking a collective norm, like exposing themselves in public or pissing in the middle of a roadway. There's an element of voyeurism in his work. He stood at the window and looked down into the street. Or he stopped on the sidewalk when he should have hurried by. He was watchful and caught him-self in the act of seeing something that he shouldn't be seeing. He noticed others seeing it, too. He remembered shameful behavior. He was willing to face hard truths about himself as well as about other people. He didn't just gaze out the window, he also looked in the mirror and pressed for a ver-dict of guilty. That's why his poems can be so discomfiting and fascinating to read. "Poetry confronts in the most clear-eyed way just those emotions which consciousness wishes to slide by," he declared in his essay "Poetry and Consciousness" (1987).

Williams was something of a mythicist. He knew how to tighten a grip and close in for the decisive shot, though he then pulled back the camera and took the overview. The story becomes representative, almost allegorical, the individual standing in for the group. Here, the long line especially suits him because it can be used to create an oracular feeling and extend the voice beyond speech. Osip Mandelstam once said that Anna Akhmatova developed her lyric with a glance at the psychological prose of nineteenth-century novels, and that's applicable to Williams, too. There is something of the novelistic method in his project; he is a poet of tormented Dostoyevskian psychology. He repeatedly interrupts his story to explore the motivation of the characters and the psychology of the situation. He airs his misgivings. His long lines are a way of telling a story and worrying its implications at the same time.

When Williams arranged his *Collected Poems* (2006), he took care to place a series of haiku-like lyrics that he derived from the Japanese poet Kobayashi Issa between his second and third books. He broke the otherwise lockstep chronology with *The Lark. The Thrush. The Starling* (1983). Williams was not characteristically very effective in the short form, but these lyrics are clear and precise, beautifully rendered. By studying and writing like Issa, Williams encouraged himself to narrow his focus and observe, not just the darting image, but the mind in the act of describing that image, of catching itself at work. Here's a good example of the timing and double take that he learned from the Japanese master:

> Listen carefully.
>
> I'm meditating.
> The only thing in my mind
> right now
> is the wind.
>
> No, wait . . . the autumn
> wind, that's right,
> the *autumn* wind!

"My Mother's Lips," the second poem in *Tar* (1983), is a prelude poem. It may not be ambitiously designed to trace the full growth of a poet's mind, as in Wordsworth, but it does try to pinpoint the first moment of poetic awareness. The development follows a Dantean arc from the *Inferno* of delusion to the *Paradiso* of love. The poet Allen Grossman believed that it was a commonplace that poets write poems for their mothers. He said, "My poetry is, in the most literal sense, the speech of my mother, or rather, the completion of the speech of my mother." Here, Williams vehemently opposes the idea that a son's work fulfills his mother's spoken or unspoken desires. When I met him in the mid-1970s, he was a psychological social worker who worked with troubled adolescents, and there is something decidedly therapized about his post-confessional lyric. He was suspicious of the fused relationship between mother and son and sought to rupture the pattern, to become an independent speaker and person. And he linked this separation to the beginning of his poetry.

The poem unfolds in seven long-limbed quatrains, the stanza of the ballad and the hymn, though here it is stretched nearly beyond recognition. Nonetheless, it is a basic four-square building block. The first stanza is a single snaking sentence. The poet creates dramatic suspense by using indefinite pronouns and objects. We don't confirm that the speaker is talking about his mother until the second half of the second line, and we don't find out what she was doing wrong, or even what she had stopped doing wrong, until the end of the third line.

> Until I asked *her* to please stop doing *it* and was astonished to find
>   that *she* not only could
> but from the moment I asked *her* in fact would stop doing *it*, my
>   mother, all through my childhood,
> when I was saying something to her, something important, would
>   move her lips as I was speaking
> so that she seemed to be saying under her breath the very words
>   I was saying as I was saying them.

This might seem like straightforward narration, but it's worth pausing over the way that Williams uses the subordinate clause to expand the timeline ("my mother, *all through my childhood*") and emphasize the significance ("when I was saying something to her, *something important*"). This brings out the oddity of the situation, the mother saying the son's words at the moment that he is saying them. It's unnerving to him—and becomes more so.

The second stanza continues: "*Or, even more disconcertingly.*" When I first read "My Mother's Lips" I didn't pay much attention to the unfolding of

time in the poem, but now when I reread it, I notice that the speaker moves
from childhood to adolescence and then immediately turns back to remi-
nisce and speculates about his earlier perspective:

> Or, even more disconcertingly—wildly so now that my puberty had
>   erupted—*before* I said them.
> When I was smaller, I must just have assumed that she was omniscient.
>   Why not?
> She knew everything else—when I was tired, or lying; she'd know if I
>   was ill before I did.
> I may even have thought—how could it not have come into my
>   mind?—that she *caused* what I said.

Williams is summing up an entire childhood relationship between mother
and son, an uncomfortable and wounding overidentification.

In the third stanza, the speaker leaps forward into the perspective of adult-
hood and then reads back his mother's motivation through his own lens as
a parent. Now, he speaks as both son and father. There's a quietly Ashberian
slippage of pronouns, too, so that the personal story becomes psychologi-
cally generalized:

> All *she* was really doing of course was mouthing *my* words a split second
>   after *I* said them myself,
> but it wasn't until my own children were learning to talk that *I* really
>   understood how,
> and understood, too, the edge of anxiety in it, the wanting to bring *you*
>   along out of the silence,
> the compulsion to lift *you* again from those blank caverns of nameless-
>   ness *we* encase.

I want to accentuate the change in linguistic register in the last line of
this stanza. This happens because the speaker's psychology has changed with
his new understanding. Less convictive of his mother's motivation, he now
recognizes that she was anxiously trying to lift him out of silence just as he
has tried to bring his children out of their silence. That's why the diction

of the poem lifts from the vernacular to the eloquent, which is phrased in "those blank caverns of namelessness we encase." This is a subtle change in discourse, a movement toward the high language of poetry.

It was from closely studying Wordsworth's *The Prelude* that I first began to observe how a narrative poet stage-manages the back-and-forth of time in a poem. You can see the pulleys working. Williams usually gets this out of the way in the first phrasing of the new stanza, hence:

> *That was long afterward, though: where I was now* was just wanting to get her to stop,
> and considering how I brooded and raged in those days, how quickly my teeth went on edge,
> the restraint I approached her with seems remarkable, although her so unprotestingly,
> readily taming a habit, by then three children and a dozen years old was as much so.

What strikes me about this is the complex double perspective, the way he dramatizes his own adolescent rage and marvels at his own restraint even as he realizes that it was not just his own diplomacy that got his mother to change her behavior but her own experience as a parent. He insinuates a family, too, a mother who has been doing this with three children for twelve years.

The speaker's memory of rage now takes on an unexpectedly nostalgic element as he hooks back to his adolescence. It begins with a sweet Proustian lens but then turns to something darker and more Freudian, a psychological breaking point. The stanza starts with an observation and ends with a question. As in a blazon, or, perhaps, the rejection of a blazon, which is, after all, a male form, a love poem that catalogues the physical features of the beloved, the focus closes in on the separate mouths of mother and son:

> It's endearing to watch us again in that long-ago dusk, facing each other, my mother and me.
> I've just grown to her height, or just past it: there are our lips moving together,

now the unison suddenly breaks, I have to go on by myself, no maestro,
    no score to follow.
I wonder what finally made me take umbrage enough, or heart enough,
    to confront her?

I'm still a bit surprised by the next move, an outright dismissal of the
question: "It's not important." The speaker emphasizes that he's trying to
describe something that has become more crucial to him than his adolescent
anger and perplexity. He does this by introducing a metaphor ("My cocoon
at that age was already unwinding") and using the image of the tangled
spiderweb ("the threads ravel and snarl") to describe the difficult passage of
time, of adolescence turning into adulthood. The employment of metaphor
indicates how the poem is turning before our eyes from a psychodrama into
an ars poetica:

When I find one again, it's that two o'clock in the morning, a grim
    hotel on a square,
the impenetrable maze of an endless city, when, really alone for the first
    time in my life,
I found myself leaning from the window, incanting in a tearing whisper
    what I thought were poems.

The speaker has jumped ahead to a crisis moment in his life. There's an
echo of Prufrock: "Of lonely men in shirt-sleeves, leaning out of windows."
What began as a poem about separating from one's mother turns into a
poem about first becoming or starting to become a poet. Once more the
phrasing hits a higher pitch, a different register: "*the impenetrable maze of
an endless city.*" He stands on a threshold at a hotel window in a foreign
city—the room behind him, the night in front of him. The window is a
crossover or liminal space. It creates what in *The Poetics of Space* the philos-
opher Gaston Bachelard describes as an "exterior dizziness" and serves as a
borderline surface between here and the beyond. The speaker underscores
that he is existentially alone.

Williams later wrote a prose piece for a series called "First Loves" describ-
ing the origin of "My Mother's Lips," which he attributed to his reading of
The Waste Land.

I've written a poem, "My Mother's Lips," about what happened
with that book: how I found myself improvising, declaiming,
orating, in a kind of ecstasy, ". . . what I thought were poems," my
own poems, from the window of a pension in Florence. Although
in "My Mother's Lips" I didn't mention that I'd been reading
Eliot, that was the first experience I had of the way another poet's
voice can so gratifyingly take yours and lead you to states of mind
and music you'd never have come to otherwise.

It might seem strange to say so but Eliot, who is unnamed but real, has at
first ventriloquized the speaker in the same way that his mother once took
over his words. But now we are talking about literary influence, about using
another poet's voice to discover your own. The poet-speaker longs to return
to that moment of origin, of first finding a way to break loose and speak for
himself in poetry. He is learning to trust language. The poem hits a higher
lyric register and the locutions become youthful, erotic, and Dionysian:
"I'd *love* to know what I *raved* that night to the night, what those *innocent
dithyrambs* were, / or to feel what so *ecstatically* drew me out of myself and
beyond." There can be no complete recovery of primary experience, but the
language of love has entered the poem in a new and different way.

There is a general proscription against using adjectives in modern poetry.
The idea that adjectives are slack filler and should be jettisoned tracks to
the Imagist movement at the beginning of the twentieth century. But the
evidence suggests that in many modern poems the adjective, like every other
type of speech, has been used with judicious, cutting power. When you focus
on the final rousing lines of "My Mother's Lips," you discover how much
work the adjectives are doing to create the empty feeling of a city, Florence,
in the middle of the night, which also describes the complex emotional state
of a speaker's loneliness and excitement, his blockage and liberation:

> Nothing is there, though,
> only the *solemn* piazza beneath me, the riot of *dim*, tiled roofs and
> *impassable* alleys,
> my *desolate* bed behind me, and my voice, *hoarse*, and the *sweet, alien*
> air against me like a kiss.

I love the final transformation of voicing in this poem, how the speaker takes possession of his own voice, as a person but also as a poet, and how he hears that voice, *a tearing whisper*, hoarse but insistent, declaiming his first desperate attempts at poetry. That's why the air is both *sweet* and *alien*, and why it touches him lightly with something akin to a kiss. The lips of the mother have been replaced by something else—virginal, obsessive—something closer to romantic love. The poet has revised the tools of speech, he has learned to trust expressiveness and elocution. He has grown into the redemptive of language.

The Russian poet Marina Tsvetaeva suggested that there are poets with history, that is, poets who develop over time, and poets without history, who arrive fully intact, completely formed from the beginning. According to this lexicon, C. K. Williams was a poet with history, a writer who grew into his story, whose interior consciousness was schooled by close observation, social awareness, and historical study. He had to fight his way into a novel mode. As a reader, you're not always aware of the changes in a writer's style as they are happening—that's something that you often discover afterwards. I wasn't alive when T. S. Eliot was writing *The Waste Land* or William Carlos Williams was scribbling the topsy-turvy lyrics of *Spring and All* or Marianne Moore was typing out *Observations*. I was an infant when Langston Hughes published *Montage of a Dream Deferred* and nine years old when Robert Lowell broke through with *Life Studies*. That's why I like to recall the morning nearly fifty years ago when I opened a democratic new tabloid and discovered a blasphemous type of praise poem, a voicing that hadn't been heard before in American poetry: "It stinks. It stinks and it stinks and it stinks and it stinks." That was an exciting beginning. But the even greater end point was the eloquence of love.

MICHAEL S. HARPER (1938–2016)

Dear John, Dear Coltrane

> *a love supreme, a love supreme*
> *a love supreme, a love supreme*

Sex fingers toes
in the marketplace
near your father's church
in Hamlet, North Carolina—
witness to this love
in this calm fallow
of these minds,
there is no substitute for pain:
genitals gone or going,
seed burned out,
you tuck the roots in the earth,
turn back, and move
by river through the swamps,
singing: *a love supreme, a love supreme*;
what does it all mean?
Loss, so great each black
woman expects your failure
in mute change, the seed gone.
You plod up into the electric city—
your song now crystal and
the blues. You pick up the horn
with some will and blow
into the freezing night:
a love supreme, a love supreme—

Dawn comes and you cook
up the thick sin 'tween
impotence and death, fuel
the tenor sax cannibal
heart, genitals, and sweat
that makes you clean—
a love supreme, a love supreme—

Why you so black?
cause I am
why you so funky?
cause I am
why you so black?
cause I am
why you so sweet?
cause I am
why you so black?
cause I am
a love supreme, a love supreme:

So sick
you couldn't play *Naima,*
so flat we ached
for song you'd concealed
with your own blood,
your diseased liver gave
out its purity,
the inflated heart
pumps out, the tenor kiss,
tenor love:
a love supreme, a love supreme—
a love supreme, a love supreme—

1970

MICHAEL S. HARPER wrote about family and friends, about iconic figures from his personal American pantheon, which spanned the centuries. It included a host of poets and musicians as well as historical figures—Roger Williams, John Brown, Martin Luther King, Jr., Jackie Robinson—all of them representative presences, exemplars who tried to wake us from the nightmares of American history. Ralph Ellison said that "while one can do nothing about choosing one's relatives, one can, as artist, choose one's ancestors," and that's precisely what Harper did. He looked for connection and elevation, inspiring heroes. He called his selected poems *Images of Kin*, thereby extending the idea of kinship, which for him consisted of bonding and recognition, a chosen family of lineage and ancestry. He believed in songlines and pathways, in the American continuum, in learning history from oral tradition and library archives—he argued that American poets needed to be better archivists—and he wove his personal story into a national tapestry. He despised injustice and countered it with his own idiosyncratic eloquence. Above all, he believed in poetry and music, modes of comparative humanity, and found solace in art.

Harper was determined to situate himself as both a Black and an American poet. He was capacious in his reading, his enthusiasms, and unapologetic about his love for John Keats and Robert Frost—his own work has a Keatsian intensity, a Frostian feeling for vernacular eloquence. He adopted two literary fathers, Sterling A. Brown and Robert Hayden, and celebrated their work with a relentless sense of mission at a time when they were often scorned and condescended to by the Black Arts Movement. More than anyone else, he helped bring them back into the family archive. He loved their work not just because they were consummate poets but also because they were moral historians. He appreciated the way that Brown had kept the folk spirit alive in African American poetry, the way he had built his own work on the dignity of folk forms, such as blues, work songs, spirituals, and folktales. Brown's commitment to the exceptional in the commonplace fueled Harper's project. So, too, Harper admired Hayden's perfect pitch as a poet, his succinctness and sincerity, his unearthing of crucial American sources, his essential humanity. In his poem "Healing Song," he characterized Hayden as "this creature of transcendence / a love-filled shadow, congealed and clarified."

404 THE HEART OF AMERICAN POETRY

Harper loved two art forms equally, jazz and poetry, and took consolation from both. Jazz came first and initiated him into poetry. He noted that he never would have become a poet if his family hadn't moved from Brooklyn to West Los Angeles when he was thirteen years old. He went to high school and college in L.A. The Angeleno poet Henri Coulette taught and encouraged him at California State University, Los Angeles, where he also took classes with Christopher Isherwood, who introduced him to another early influence and inspiration, W. H. Auden. Nurtured on the California jazz scene, Harper was surrounded by a group of highly talented musicians who shaped his sensibility, and he admitted that he would have liked to become a musician, but he never had the chops. It's not just that he took the rhythmic beat, the pulse of his poems, from jazz, but also that he got his emotional education from the music. He grew up on the big bands of Duke Ellington, Count Basie, Andy Kirk, Jimmie Lunceford, and Fletcher Henderson, and listened closely to jazz singers like Bessie Smith, Billie Holiday, and Mamie Smith. Most fundamentally, he witnessed the revolutionary change to be-bop.

Harper was friends with McCoy Tyner, who was Coltrane's pianist, and he often attended live performances of Coltrane's four-piece band in the 1950s and '60s. He nominated Coltrane as his Orpheus and wrote poems about him all his life. Coltrane's music sang to him, and so, too, did Coltrane's notion of the role of the artist, his rejection of minstrelsy in any form, his serious spiritual quest. Coltrane unabashedly transfigured pain into love and made love archetypal. That was the model.

Coltrane wasn't just a spiritual person; he was also a committed political one. Part of what Harper learned from him was how a major artist responded to racism and genocide, how he countered it with an awareness of Black identity and solidarity. With Harper in mind, it's worth listening again to Coltrane's composition "Alabama," a requiem for the four girls murdered in the Ku Klux Klan's terrorist bombing of the Sixteenth Street Baptist Church in Birmingham, Alabama, in 1963. It's also a response to Martin Luther King, Jr.'s eulogy. The way that Coltrane responded to Dr. King's rhetoric became the basis for Harper's later poem "Here Where Coltrane Is," which invokes a structure of feeling, the political and historical dimensions of Black art.

Harper wrote "Dear John, Dear Coltrane" in 1966, the year before Coltrane died. It's as if he intuited Coltrane's nearness to death. There's an element of magical thinking in his fear that he was signing a death warrant by creating an elegy in advance. He published the poem as the title piece in his first book, and it's been read as a retrospective ever since. He took the refrain line from Coltrane's album *A Love Supreme*, which was recorded in 1964 and released the next year. In one take, Coltrane led his regular quartet—pianist McCoy Tyner, bassist Jimmy Garrison, drummer Elvin Jones—through a suite in four parts. The title appears as a vocal chant in the first section, "Acknowledgment." Coltrane uses his tenor sax to play the opening four-note motif in all the keys, wringing dozens of changes out of it until it turns into words intoned by Coltrane and the other musicians. He is using his pre-ternatural musical dexterity to suggest that all musical paths lead to God. *A Love Supreme* has a spiritual grandeur that is rare in any era, but especially in modern times. It stands beside Rainer Maria Rilke's *Duino Elegies* and T. S. Eliot's *Four Quartets*, but is realized by four voices, four different musicians.

By the time Harper wrote his poem, the phrase "a love supreme" had already become a tagline, a sort of anthem or refrain, not just in Los Angeles but in Black and musical communities all over the country. Harper's poem weds the jazz lyric to the verse epistle. He takes a tradition inaugurated by Langston Hughes, who used the syncopated rhythms and repetitive phrases of 1920s jazz to address the struggles of African American life, and connects it to the philosophical letter poem, which has a much older provenance, dating back to Horace's *Epistles* (20–14 B.C.). The title of Harper's poem, "Dear John, Dear Coltrane," is a double take. The poem is a meditation on Coltrane's life that poses as a letter to the musician, and, like all verse epistles, it's meant to be overheard by the rest of us.

Unlike any letter I've ever read, the poem divides the addressee's name into two parts. It's as if the poet is both writing a love letter, "Dear John," and writing to someone he admires from a more formal distance, a symbolic figure, "Dear Coltrane." It's a proto-elegy. The title is the first indication of the importance of phrasing in the poem; indeed, as the title poem in Harper's first book, it points to the key lesson he learned from musicians. The phrasing itself seems to lead the artist somewhere he doesn't necessarily want to go. But that's precisely where he needs to go. Here, the title stammers and then jump-cuts to the italicized and indented refrain of the poem, which seems chanted in Coltrane's own voice. This is the inaugural movement of the poem and it's imperative to hear it four times:

a love supreme, a love supreme
a love supreme, a love supreme

Coltrane's music was addressed to God; Harper's poem is addressed to Coltrane. I think it has an erotic undercurrent ("I loved John Coltrane and I loved his music") and a religious overtone. There is a jolted jump, a serious downward turn, from the elevated refrain to the first brutal narrative section of the poem. The letter is structured as a collage. The first sentence unscrolls in a short Audenian mixture of two- and three-beat lines that culminate in a question:

> Sex fingers toes
> in the marketplace
> near your father's church
> in Hamlet, North Carolina—
> witness to this love
> in this calm fallow
> of these minds,
> there is no substitute for pain:
> genitals gone or going,
> seed burned out,
> you tuck the roots in the earth,
> turn back, and move
> by river through the swamps,
> singing: *a love supreme, a love supreme*;
> what does it all mean?

I never fully understood the harsh but cryptic first two lines until I read an interview in which Harper said that the first three words are the genitals, fingers, and toes of Sam Hose, who was brutally lynched, butchered, and burned alive by a white mob in Coweta, Georgia, in 1899. Harper seems to be taking the racist spectacle of a lynching, linking it back to the slave trade, and anachronistically relocating it near the church in the North Carolina town where Coltrane was born in 1926. The narrator thus proceeds to tell Coltrane's story—the tenor sax seems to be playing *A Love Supreme* while he is dying—inflected by a historical Black martyrdom.

It's striking how the intimate tone ("Dear John") jostles and even contends with the symbolic meaning ("Dear Coltrane"). It's almost as if Harper reaches back to Egyptian mythology, an African antecedent, for the story of the death and resurrection of Osiris, which licenses him to treat Coltrane as a scapegoat figure, a dying and reviving god, a king whose seed is buried so that it can be regenerated. The musician heads to the urban North, to "the electric city"—probably Philadelphia, where Coltrane started to make his true music, to transform the sorrow of the blues with a new passion and intensity: "You pick up the horn / with some will and blow / into the freezing night: / *a love supreme, a love supreme.*"

The first two stanzas are presented in an ongoing present tense: "Dawn comes and you cook / up the thick sin." Stanza two addresses Coltrane's heroin addiction, the space he inhabited "between impotence and death," the terrible need that fuels "the tenor sax cannibal." It condenses into seven lines Coltrane's long struggle to get clean and find independence. The section ends with the refrain line, the fourth time that Harper repeats *a love supreme.* He is imitating Coltrane and wringing the changes out of the phrase.

Coltrane grew up in a religious environment—his father preached, and both of his grandfathers were ministers—and became deeply religious as he overcame his addiction. That's why the third, italicized stanza cuts to the call-and-response of a Black Pentecostal church. Listen to it again and you feel almost as if you're participating in a service:

> *Why you so black?*
> *cause I am*
> *why you so funky?*
> *cause I am*
> *why you so black?*
> *cause I am*
> *why you so sweet?*
> *cause I am*
> *why you so black?*
> *cause I am*
> *a love supreme, a love supreme:*

This is the most idiomatic part of the poem (*"why you so funky?"*) and links the preacher to the parishioners, the musician to the community. The tone is lighter than elsewhere in the poem, but the meaning is serious, a pointed rhetorical catechism of Blackness. Every question culminates in the same determined, existential answer: "*cause I am.*" Yet the enjambment in the last two lines cleverly brings the interrogation to a large conclusion: "*cause I am / a love supreme, a love supreme.*" Harper views Coltrane, as he would someday view Hayden, as a figure of transcendence.

The church section ends with a colon, not a period, and turns the supreme love downward to Coltrane's earthly struggle with addiction. The last stanza moves as one sentence across twelve lines. The liftoff is remarkable. The speaker reenters the poem as a communal "we," a stand-in for the community, as in a ballad. The repetitions enact the intensities:

> *So sick*
> you couldn't play *Naima,*
> *so flat* we ached
> for song you'd concealed
> with *your own blood,*
> *your diseased liver* gave
> out its purity,
> *the* inflated heart
> pumps out, *the tenor kiss,*
> *tenor love*:
> *a love supreme, a love supreme—*
> *a love supreme, a love supreme—*

Harper inaugurates the last movement by recalling a time when Coltrane was too sick to play his signature ballad "Naima," and contrasts the musician's diseased body, his physical martyrdom, with the pure music that he attains, what "the inflated heart / pumps out." The two elements of the poem, the intimate address to "Dear John" and the symbolic address to "Dear Coltrane," come together and reach a high rhetorical pitch. The erotic charge and progression—"the tenor kiss, / tenor love"—reaches its culmination in the final transcendent repetition of the refrain: "*a love supreme, a love supreme— / a love supreme, a love supreme—.*"

"Dear John, Dear Coltrane" ends with a dash and not a period, as if to suggest that the poem is open-ended, the ending interrupted, indeterminate. This indicates that Coltrane's idea of a supreme love is ongoing and continuous, an unceasing legacy. But the strong repetitive chant at the end also takes us back to the beginning and brings the poem full circle. It has the ritual closure of a farewell letter and address. Harper found it difficult, maybe even impossible, to accept that he had written an elegy for John Coltrane even before Coltrane had died. Orpheus was gone, but he had left behind his music, which Michael S. Harper, his poetic protégé, would go on listening to and imitating, disheartened and enraged by social injustice but also continuing to seek transcendence, writing historical indictments but also love letters and elegies, homages and hymns.

LOUISE GLÜCK (1943–)

Retreating Wind

When I made you, I loved you.
Now I pity you.

I gave you all you needed:
bed of earth, blanket of blue air—

As I get further away from you
I see you more clearly.
Your souls should have been immense by now,
not what they are,
small talking things—

I gave you every gift,
blue of the spring morning,
time you didn't know how to use—
you wanted more, the one gift
reserved for another creation.

Whatever you hoped,
you will not find yourselves in the garden,
among the growing plants.
Your lives are not circular like theirs:

your lives are the bird's flight
which begins and ends in stillness—
which *begins* and *ends*, in form echoing
this arc from the white birch
to the apple tree.

1992

I WAS LYING in bed late at night, woeful, confused by another death, this one the death of a close friend—the losses had been mounting steadily, a bewildering number of losses, each one specific, difficult to accept, hard to overcome—and I must have dozed off because I heard a voice or thought I heard a voice saying: "At the end of my suffering there was a door." I listened for it again and realized that it had paused in the middle of a sentence:

> At the end of my suffering
> there was a door.

It was as if someone were speaking from the other side: "Hear me out: that which you call death / I remember." This was not possible, I understood that or almost did, I was still only half awake, but now I intentionally tried to recall what I had overheard: "It is terrible to survive / as consciousness / buried in the dark earth." Then it was over, I forced myself awake, it was too eerie and unnatural, and I realized that I was not hearing a friend speak but recalling a poem by Louise Glück, the title poem of *The Wild Iris*, which I had read and reread in 1992, the year it came out. The voice that came to me was the testimony of a wild iris or, more precisely, the voice of a poet brazenly speaking as a perennial, and it was so convincing that it startled me awake, as if she really did recollect the passage from another world and had come back to tell us what it was like, to give evidence, pay witness.

Glück herself has said that the image of the door at the end of suffering had been with her for a long time before she found a place for it. It was a strange gift at the beginning of a two-year dry spell, a long period of barrenness and unproductivity. And then a door opened, a barrier gave way, and *The Wild Iris* came to her, almost as dictation, and she wrote the entire book in eight weeks. It was a rebirth. "Whatever / returns from oblivion returns / to find a voice," she declared in a vein that was strange and familiar, hieratic, and beautiful, uncanny.

It's hard to explain the oracular authority of Louise Glück's work, the mesmerizing power of her voice. She embraces change from book to book; in fact, she seems to experience a fearsome drought between books, a period of disconnection and silence. Doubt itself—debilitating, all-encompassing—

is part of her process; she is listening and waiting for a new sound, a new mode of being. Her poetry has altered dramatically over time, it has become more spacious and inclusive of the world, and yet there is something ever identifiable in it, too, something that drives it, a certain tone of voice, a ruthlessness of insight, a way of drilling down and rethinking experience, her own experience, examined under a microscope, the lens of psychoanalysis.

In this poetry, nothing is taken for granted, nothing unexamined. I can't think of another poet who would begin a poem the way she does in "The Untrustworthy Speaker": "Don't listen to me; my heart's been broken. / I don't see anything objectively. // I know myself; I've learned to hear like a psychiatrist." As a thinker, she is investigative, oppositional—she resists the presumptions, the certainties—and goes for the jugular, convicting herself: "That's why I'm not to be trusted. / Because a wound to the heart / is also a wound to the mind." The speaker in Glück's poem is trustworthy because she draws attention to her own untrustworthiness, her subjectivity, her woundedness of spirit, emotionally, intellectually. We believe her. As a maker, Glück is undeterred: *Listen to me*, she advises in one poem; *Don't listen to me*, she asserts in another. She has no interest in charming the reader. Throughout her work, poetry is treated as sacred vocation, a primary mode of inquiry, uncompromising in its devotions, an unabating discipline and service to truth.

Glück has always used a spare, stripped-down vocabulary. She is a poet of the definite article, the precise noun, the cleansed word, and as a result her work is devoid of the linguistic fireworks that excite many other poets, a luxury eschewed. She is not a poet of the American idiomatic either, the line of William Carlos Williams, which celebrates the particulars of local speech. Rather, she prefers the plain word, the nerveless tone, the neutral sentence. Her language is Augustan. Two of her primary influences are George Oppen, whose intricate philosophical poems rely exclusively on little words (what he called "the small nouns"), and T. S. Eliot, who used an indeterminate language—not quite American, not quite British—to hit a surpassing register. Some of her early short poems read like mythic fragments spun off from *The Waste Land*.

Glück has said that she dislikes Rilke, though she is the most Rilkean of contemporary makers—that is, if you can imagine Rilke as an American poet who grew up on Long Island in a secular Jewish family and suffered from anorexia nervosa as a teenager (see "Dedication to Hunger"). Listening to Rilke, I sometimes hear her voice in his, quarreling with him and taking him to account for his attitude toward the primary feminine, his other-worldliness, the way he opposes daily life and the Great Work. Or maybe Rilke is beside the point because what I am really hearing is this quarrel inside of Glück's own work. She embraces and opposes what is most Rilkean in herself. She is a poet of refusals, an absolutist who distrusts absolutes. Her work is surrounded by a great solitude—loneliness is a given—and yet every poem of hers is a message in a bottle. She resists and craves connection. She confides in the reader one to one.

Glück's language is utterly clear but deeply mysterious. She often addresses an unnamed beloved in her poems, but she despises the ecstatic fusion of lovers—what in her most famous poem, "Mock Orange," she names "the low, humiliating / premise of union." She writes as the watchful lover, the sleepless thinker, the discontented storyteller. "How can I rest?" she wonders at the conclusion of "Mock Orange": "How can I be content / when there is still / that odor / in the world?" The speaker in Glück's poems is often impatient with other people, especially lovers, who seem unaware or oblivious to mortal peril—she has to shake them awake ("Don't you see?"). But she is also unsparing in her evaluation of herself. In the poem "Unwritten Law," for example, she recalls falling in love with "rather boyish men— / unformed, sullen," whom she did not see as "versions of the same thing," but then turns her whiplash intelligence on herself: "I, with my inflexible Platonism, / my fierce seeing of only one thing at a time: / I ruled against the indefinite article."

Glück's penchant for the definite article has often led her to probe and revise the original myths and tales. She is so distinctive as a poet that it's possible to overlook how often she relies on precursor texts. Sometimes she narrates these stories from the third person point of view, as in "The Triumph of Achilles," where she takes the position of the distanced storyteller ("In the story of Patroclus / no one survives, not even Achilles / who was nearly a god"). There is a strong precedent for this in Constantine Cavafy's work, especially in his poem "The Horses of Achilles," where he probes the story of Patroclus and Achilles to try to comprehend "the eternal disaster of death." Here, Glück also readjusts the lens, pulls back the camera, and looks down at the human character from above. Seamlessly, she shifts to the point of view of the gods:

> In his tent, Achilles
> grieved with his whole being
> and the gods saw
>
> he was a man already dead, a victim
> of the part that loved,
> the part that was mortal.

Glück returns to the story of Patroclus and Achilles ("the legends / cannot be trusted") in order to think about the primacy of mortal love, an original sin that compromises and distinguishes us, a fateful human flaw.

Glück's voice is so elemental that it's easy to overlook her turn from the third- to the first-person point of view, the way she relies on the dramatic monologue for effect and pitches her voice into other speakers. We tend to think of the dramatic monologue as a literary device, "the persona poem"— Robert Browning preferred the term "dramatic lyric"—but in Glück's case I think this designation mistakes the point. She longs to generalize her experience, to understand it through an archetypal lens, and so she presses these initial narratives exceedingly hard to wring out their significance. What in others might appear "literary," a mode of elevation, in her seems personal, urgent, and necessary. That's why she picks and chooses from the Greek myths, why she returns time and again to the story of Persephone, a girl whisked away to the underworld, and lifts characters from the *Iliad* and *Odyssey*. In *Meadowlands* (1996), for example, she intercuts poems from the point of view of Penelope, Telemachus, and Circe with personal parables and dramatic conversations from a failing marriage, so that it all seems part of the same story line, an extended family saga. The conversations with the husband are lifted out of context, purposefully decontextualized, but the conversations with herself are specified and nailed down, as in "Rainy Morning": "You don't love the world. / If you loved the world you'd have / images in your poems." Glück typically employs mythical stories as a way to substantiate experience and make it real, as if experience would otherwise remain floating in a void, inaccessible. She insinuates that what she is writing about is both temporal and timeless.

Glück has often turned to the garden in her poems, a green space both curated and wild, a field of conflicting forces. "Gardens always mean something else," Robert Harbison explains in *Eccentric Spaces*, his groundbreaking book on the garden as a form of art, and that's certainly true of Glück's portraits in the natural world, the way she enters a liminal space between house and country, the grounds nearby. I first picked up her extended garden motif in the initial section of *Descending Figure* (1980), which is titled after a five-part poem called "The Garden." It's as if the speaker is afraid of her own inwardness and forces herself into the exposed light, "into a field / without immunity." There:

> The garden admires you.
> For your sake it smears itself with green pigment,
> the ecstatic reds of the roses,
> so that you will come to it with your lovers.

Glück's garden is smeared with colors, but her observations seem very black and white to me. As a trope, the garden overflows with a surplus of meaning; it returns us to the story of the original garden in Genesis, the place of lovers. I hear echoes of Theodore Roethke's Greenhouse poems in her work—the primary of his Michigan pastorals, which stress the difficult struggle of everything to be born, to grow and thrive. Otherwise, Glück seems to skip over centuries of Western verse: the male history of the pastoral tradition, an ecological through line that runs from Theocritus to Frost, positing a green world that is ever renewed and renewable. Glück's botanical has an entirely different intention. Though she tends to de-emphasize her Jewish background, it seems to me that she often writes in the line of the Yahwist, or J writer, whom Harold Bloom notoriously supposed was a woman. This is the prophetic line not just of Hebrew but also of German poetry, of Hölderlin and Rilke, of Nelly Sachs and Paul Celan, to which she has given a contemporary American slant.

I find myself returning to *The Wild Iris* as a touchstone of Glück's work. She is avowedly antiromantic in her poems—she resists the allures and deceptions of romance—but she takes as a given the Romantic premise of organic form, the Coleridgean idea that each poem must find its own natural shape, like a growing plant. She literalizes this notion to an unprecedented degree in *The Wild Iris*, where many of the poems are spoken by beings, whether plant or human, who are desperate to find a form. The mode itself is elastic (for example, her son makes an appearance in the second poem: "Noah says / depressives hate the spring") and moves fluidly between the vegetal, the human, and the divine perspective. There is a ceremonial or religious dimension—the poems that address God are called "Matins" and "Vespers"—and the book returns repeatedly to the figure of the duo in the garden: "I couldn't do it again, / I can hardly bear to look at it," she confesses as she looks at a young couple planting a row of peas "as though / no one has ever done this before, / the great difficulties have never as yet / been faced and solved" ("The Garden").

"Retreating Wind" is the thirteenth poem in the sequence, and here Glück animates the voice of the Lord with confidence and conviction. It is as if her work had been an arduous preparation to speak without hesitation in the voice of the Creator. The Hebrew word *ruach* means "breath, wind, or spirit," and so the God who is speaking and retreating in Glück's poem is also withdrawing His breath, His spirit. In six irregular stanzas, twenty-three lines, God steps forth to speak to human beings, presumably Adam and Eve, who seem present but unspecified—the original couple, our stand-ins. It has been a while since God withdrew from the world. He has now returned to air His grievance and disappointment with His human creation.

God is not named in the poem but only designated by the title, and here Glück seems to follow the ancient prescription never to utter the name of the Holy One, blessed be He. But the use of the wind also calls to mind the long history of the visionary tradition in poetry. It has often been invoked as a sign of poetic destiny. "Human voices did not touch me, / it was the wind whose voice I heard," Anna Akhmatova writes in her poem "Willow," a love song to a silver tree from her childhood. Think of how Shelley calls out in "Ode to the West Wind": "Be thou, Spirit fierce, / My spirit! Be thou me, impetuous one!" D. H. Lawrence testifies: "Not I, not I, but the wind that blows through me" ("Song of a Man Who Has Come Through"). Glück's wind might be retreating, but she also hears it speaking and animates it; she understands its parental wording, its vatic call.

In Glück's poem, God speaks bluntly and uses plain language, declarative sentences; He uses her chosen idiom and does not hold back. From the beginning, He expresses supreme disappointment in His creatures: "When I made you, I loved you. / Now I pity you." This is unremitting. The first two-line stanza mirrors the original couple, a coupling, showing what they have made of themselves. The second repeats this pattern but carries it forward with a dash—it enacts God's retreating perspective. On first reading, I was taken aback by the audacity of the speaking voice and missed the artfulness of the maker behind it. In the second stanza, for example, you hear the phonic repetition of sounds (*b, bl*) and two-part balance of phrasing:

> I gave you all you needed:
> bed of earth, blanket of blue air—

One cannot film God speaking, but, if you could, you would see that the camera angle is complicated because God is both moving away from His human creation and at the same time viewing it more distinctly. That's because, as Milton describes in *Paradise Lost* (book 3, 56–59):

> Now had the Almighty Father from above,
> From the pure Empyrean where he sits
> High Thron'd above all highth, bent down his eye,
> His own works and their works at once to view:

Glück has always embraced the paradoxical statement. Now she has found her perfect speaker: "As I get further away from you / I see you more clearly." By invoking God's voice, Glück can speak freely of the human soul, which might have thrived in silence, but seems always compromised by speech: "Your souls should have been immense by now, / not what they are, / small talking things." Here, too, Glück breaks off with a dash, as if God is too disheartened to continue in this way. But He presses the case:

> I gave you every gift,
> blue of the spring morning,
> time you didn't know how to use—
> you wanted more, the one gift
> reserved for another creation.

Glück has found a way for God to summarize the whole of creation in two lines—"blue of the spring morning, / time you didn't know how to use." She also pins the move from the plural, "every gift," to the singular, "the one gift." God is speaking cryptically, but also making clear the one major difference between the human beings in the garden and the garden itself.

The poem concludes with a single authoritative sentence that crosses the ravine of two stanzas. I've always been interested in the way that Glück manages the high oracular or Rilkean mode. In his poem "Autumn Day," for example, Rilke writes: "Whoever has no house now, will never have one. / Whoever is alone will stay alone" ("Wer jetzt kein Haus hat, baut sich keines mehr. / Wer jetzt allein ist, wird es lange bleiben"). Though the German doesn't need to use "Whoever" but simply *Wer* (Who), the effect is the same. There is an overtone of steadfastness in the last word *bleiben*, which means to remain. Similarly, the God in Glück's poem contends: "Whatever you hoped, / you will not find yourselves in the garden." The combination of the inclusive pronoun—*whatever, whoever*—with the definite proscription gives this a definitive ring: "Whoever *has no* house now, *will never* have one"; "Whatever *you hoped*, / *you will not* find yourselves." This voice seems utterly certain, absolute in its refusal, unassailable in its negation.

You have to slow the poem down to see the distinction the poet is making between God's creations, plant and bird, nonlinear and linear time:

> Whatever you hoped,
> you will not find yourselves in the garden,
> among the growing plants.
> Your lives are not circular like theirs:
>
> your lives are the bird's flight
> which begins and ends in stillness—
> which *begins* and *ends*, in form echoing
> this arc from the white birch
> to the apple tree.

This two-part sentence enacts the expulsion. Adam and Eve will not find themselves in the garden with the plants because our lives are not "circular like theirs"—that is, renewable, like perennials. We are being compared to birds, traditional figures for the soul in poetry, which live in temporality. Glück repeats and italicizes the words *begins* and *ends* so they become unmistakable. She modulates from the bird's beginning and ending *in stillness* to the bird's beginning and ending *in form echoing*. The bird flits from one tree to another, creating an arc, a semicircle or trajectory, that does not bring it home. The presence of the apple tree seems particularly ironic here since it is the cause and site of the original banishment from the garden. God is disappointed in us, He considers us especially pitiable, because we are not immortal and renewable, but live and die in time. We are fallen into experience. It's chilling how God claims to be merely observing this fact about us rather than bringing it about—this is the traditional way of quarreling with God, accusing Him of eternal unfairness, as in Abraham (on Sodom) and Job, but it is excluded here.

No wonder the speaker in Glück's next poem, "The Garden," can scarcely bear to look at that young couple in the garden, who are in the first season of love. She looks at them in the same pained way that we look back at our younger selves, that earnest couple who had no idea what was in store for them, who thought they could ignore the "image of departure" and escape the sadness. Glück's speaker is wised up, disenchanted, knowing. The only compensation for lost innocence is cold consciousness.

God does not get the last word in *The Wild Iris*—that is reserved for the white lilies—but He does return in a pendant or sequel poem called "Retreating Light," where He appears much more sanguine and less judgmental, freer of his creation. "I was tired of telling stories," God says: "So I gave you the pencil and paper. / I gave you pens made of reeds / I had gathered myself, afternoons in the dense meadows. / I told you, write your own story." The Lord feels better because He gave people lives and tragedies, so He could see them "sitting there / *like* independent beings." That word *like* is a knife to the heart. The Creator enjoys seeing His creation sitting by the open window, daydreaming—like poets, like little gods "holding the pencils I gave you / until the summer morning disappears into writing." Glück presents this in the plural, but the suggestion is unmistakable that God withdraws and makes room for the individual maker, the storyteller excited by creation, the one who has taken up the tool and the vision, who is sometimes cold with terror but other times giddy with insight, who is filled with mortal agitation but also sees flashes of another life, eternal moments.

Louise Glück is a poet of the broken heart and the sundered mind, of darkness and splendor, of the individual testimony and the invented ceremonial, the shattered world, which she tries to put back together, to make whole. She is such a restless maker that no one poem sums up her achievement, and yet she is also so memorably herself that almost any poem accurately represents her sensibility, too. I find myself returning to the various testimonials scattered everywhere in her work, her mutability odes, songs of infernal longing and Orphic imagination, like "Lute Song," where she confesses:

> I made a harp of disaster
> to perpetuate the beauty of my last love.
> Yet my anguish, such as it is,
> remains the struggle for form
>
> and my dreams, if I speak openly,
> less the wish to be remembered
> than the wish to survive,
> which is, I believe, the deepest human wish.

When I reread these last lines, when I ponder the idea that the deepest human wish is the wish to survive, I also think back to a night twenty-five years ago when I half dreamt that a friend of mine was using the voice of a poem to reach me from the other side. It would be meaningful to think so. One interpretation of the J writer's term for blessing means "more life." How desperately we cling to the idea that something breaks through: "At the end of my suffering / there was a door."

Ancestral Graves, Kahuku

for Edward Hirsch

Driving off Kam Highway along the North Shore,
    past the sugar mill,
Rusting and silent, a haunt for crows
    and the quick mongoose,
Cattle egrets and papaya trees in the wet fields
    wheeling on their muddy gears;

We turn left, *makai* towards the sea,
    and by the old *76*,
Its orange globe a target for wind
    and the rust, and the bleeding light;
Down a chuckholed gravel road
    between state-built retirement homes
And the old village of miscellaneous shotguns
    overgrown with vines, yellow *hau* flowers,
And the lavish hearts and green embroidery of bougainvillaea
    stitching through their rotting screens.

At the golf course, built by Castle & Cooke
    by subscription, 60 some years ago,
We swing past Hole No. 7 and its dying grass
    worn by generations of the poor
And losing out to the traps and dunes
    pushing in from the sea.

It's a dirt road, finally,
  two troughs of packed earth
And a strip of bermuda all the way
  to the sandy point
Where, opposite the homely sentinels
  of three stripped and abandoned cars
Giving in to the rain and its brittle decay,
  a wire fence
Opens to the hard scrabble of a shallow beach
  and the collapsing stones
And the rotting stakes,
  o-kaimyō for the dead,
Of this plantation-tough
  cemetery-by-the-sea.

We get out, and I guide you,
  as an aunt did once for me,
Over the drying tufts and patchy carpeting
  of temple moss
Yellowing in the saline earth,
  pointing out,
As few have in any recent time,
  my family graves
And the mayonnaise jars empty of flowers,
  the broken saucers
Where rice cakes and mandarins were stacked,
  the weather-smoothed
Shards of unglazed pots for sand and incense
  and their chowders of ash.

The wind slaps through our clothes
  and kicks a sand-cloud
Up to our eyes, and I remember
  to tell you
How the *tsunami* in '46 took out
  over half the gravesites,

Tore through two generations,
     most of our dead
Gone in one night, bones and tombstones
     up and down the beach,
Those left, half-in, half-out of the broken cliff
     harrowed by the sea.

I remember to say that the land,
     what's left of it,
Still belongs to the growers,
     the same as built the golf course,
Who own, even in death,
     those they did in life,
And that the sea came then
     through a vicious tenderness
Like the Buddha's, reaching
     from his lotus-seat
And ushering all the lost and incapable
     from this heaven to its source.

I read a few names—
     this one's the priest,
His fancy stone scripted with ideograms
     carved almost plain by the wind now,
And this one, Yaeko, my grandfather's sister
     who bedded down one night
In the canefields and with a Scotsman
     and was beaten to death
For the crime—
     a hoe handle they say—
Struck by her own father,
     mythic and unabsolved.

Our shame is not her love,
     whether idyll or rape

Behind the green shrouds and whispering tassels
    of sugar cane,
Nor is it the poor gruel of their daily lives
    or the infrequent
Pantomime of worship they engaged in
    odd Saturdays;
It is its effacement, the rough calligraphy
    on rotting wood
Worn smooth and illegible,
    the past
Like a name whispered in a shallow grave
    just above tideline
That speaks to us in a quiet woe
    without forgiveness
As we move off, back toward our car,
    the grim constant
Muttering from the sea
    a cool sutra in our ears.

                                            1988

M ID-JUNE 1986. I was visiting the northeast coast of Maui—I
had just spent a few days interviewing W. S. Merwin for *The Paris Review*—and telephoned my friend Garrett Hongo, who was stuck in Columbia, Missouri, where he had moved for his first teaching job. We hadn't spent much time together yet—we've now been friends for forty years—but we connected immediately when we met in 1982 at a joint party for his first book, *Yellow Light*, and for his teacher Charles Wright's selected early poems, *Country Music*. I had gone to meet Wright, whom I have always admired as a poet of spiritual longing and luminosity, of landscape and yearning, but apparently so had everyone else and Hongo vowed to get in the face of the next person who showed up. I was on deck. I bought a hardcover copy of his debut, even though I already owned the paperback—it wasn't a sacrifice, I loved the watercolor on the cover by Wakako Yamauchi—and that appeased him. We started talking and ended up spending the day walking around Los Angeles together, declaring our principles, telling our stories—what linked

us to the past, what had incited and hurt us into poetry, the people and texts that lit the way. Garrett talked about some of the teachers that mattered to him, like Bert Meyers and Robert Hayden, and mentioned some of the texts that mentored him, too, like *The Book of Songs* and *The Consolation of Philosophy*, the preface to the second edition of *Lyrical Ballads*, *The Duino Elegies*, *Blues People*. I think now that we were trying to describe and characterize our emotional educations.

We were determined to bring the suffering of other people into our work, we wanted emotional presence and intellectual urgency, and our conversation ranged all over the place. Whenever we met, we added to our felt canon. Sometimes we tilted to the Japanese poets, like Bashō and Issa, whose work Garrett knew well, other times to the Eastern Europeans, especially the Polish poets, like Czesław Miłosz and Zbigniew Herbert, whom I had been studying, and often we returned to our touchstones and discoveries, like the imprisoned Turkish poet Nazim Hikmet, and the poet of the Spanish Civil War Miguel Hernández, and the Peruvian poet César Vallejo, whose commitment to *Poemas humanos* (Human Poems) instigated and inspired us. Some of these poets would later turn up in Hongo's sequence of seven poems, "The Wartime Letters of Hideo Kubota" (*Coral Road*, 2011), written from the point of view of a figure called Kubota, the name of Hongo's maternal grandfather—his name means "Wayside Field" or "Broken Dreams"—speaking from a Justice Department detention center during World War II. From the beginning, Garrett introduced me to poetries and histories I didn't know much about, parts of the past that had been suppressed, like the songs of Gold Mountain, the work of Chinese immigrants detained on Angel Island.

I had never expected to be on my own in a corner of the world so bewilderingly beautiful, but William and Paula Merwin had gone on a trip to the Far East and left me to mind the dogs and house-sit their three-acre property in the village of Ha'iku. I might have crowed a bit on the phone—Garrett had been born in Volcano on the Big Island and raised in Kahuku and Hau'ula on the North Shore of O'ahu, which his family left when he was six years old, turning him into a reluctant Angeleno—and I knew how much he cherished Hawai'i—a forfeited family source, his native land. I described the view—you could see the Pacific Ocean from the living room—and soon Hongo was on a plane to the fiftieth state. It would be just one of many returns. In a short while, we were on our way to Oʻahu and the territory of his early childhood.

Garrett Hongo is a poet of historical loss and personal recovery. He is a Yonsei, a fourth-generation Japanese American, whose work has been motivated by a search for origins and a desire to break a cultural legacy of silence and shame, which has been passed on like a virus—to right a series of wrongs, to reclaim a legacy and heritage. That's why so much of his work is populated by figures looming up from the past. I responded to the urban grit of *Yellow Light*, the way that "Los Angeles / seethes like a billboard under twilight" in so many of the poems, which are filled with people coming off late-night shifts and crying on crosstown buses, but I also sensed a longing for an olden world tracing back to Hawaiʻi and Japan. This becomes explicit in poems like "What For" and "Roots." Sometimes he's working from photograph ("The Hongo Store"), sometimes from document ("C & H Sugar Strike, Kahuku, 1923"), sometimes from story and speculation ("Kubota"). Much of his work struggles to answer the questions of "Stepchild": "Where are the histories / our tragedies, our books / of fact and fiction?" he wonders. "Where are the legends . . . Where are the myths, the tales?" While it was still a suppressed and unacknowledged fact, he wrote with desolating accuracy about the internment of Japanese Americans during World War II, one of the most shameful episodes of American history.

In his second book, *The River of Heaven* (1988), it became evident that Hongo's work swings between two worlds—Hawaiʻi and California, one a cast-off utopia, the other a failed dream. Like the Romantic poets, he has a gift for describing luxuriant and ruined landscapes. There are three poems of return at the beginning of *The River of Heaven*: "Nostalgic Catalogue," which is shot through with a feeling of what the Portuguese call *saudade*, a nostalgia for something vanished and a yearning for what might have been; "Village: Kahuku-mura" (*mura* is the Japanese word for "village"), a poem of pained memory and homecoming to a beautiful dereliction ("How did I know my own joy's beginning / would be relic in my own lifetime?"); and "Ancestral Graves, Kahuku," an itinerary poem—it describes a route through space. It has an element of documentary. Garrett has taken a drive that the two of us took to his ancestral graveyard and reconfigured it as a poem.

Like so much of Hongo's work, "Ancestral Graves, Kahuku" is a journey back in time. The driver, his companion, and the reader are all headed for a village cemetery, a fragile graveyard by the sea, that has special resonance for the poet. He is taking a friend, his interlocutor, to the place of his buried forebears, two generations of his mother's people, seeking connection, the link to a severed past. The Hawaiian phrase *ka huku* means "the projection" and refers to Kahuku Point, the northernmost tip of O'ahu. This is near where his grandfather Kubota had once set up a string of lanterns and gone torching or night fishing. Our destination is a watery funeral ground on the edge of the continent.

The itinerary poem is one of Hongo's favored modes, and you can see him driving through a landscape and describing what he sees in many of his other poems, like "Mendocino Rose" ("In California, north of the Golden Gate"), which was written in the aftermath of the death of his father. Hongo uses the itinerary for a poem of movement and pilgrimage. As a poet and thinker, he likes to syncretize traditions, and three of his greatest ancestral models—Dante, Bashō, and Wordsworth—all re-create the format of the itinerary poem. It turns out that many of the poets known for a sense of place are also poets of restlessness and travel, who venture out and return to sacred sites. Historically, the itinerary poem can be differentiated from the topographical lyric, which describes a landscape from a fixed standpoint. Two other itinerary lyrics and precursor poems come to mind. I hear an echo of Thomas Gray's "Elegy Written in a Country Churchyard," which also tallies up the loss of ordinary people, unknown commoners, people written out of history. Paul Valéry's "La Cimetière marin" ("The Cemetery by the Sea") uses the graveyard at Sète, where his father was buried, for a reflection on mortality, "impervious nothingness." These poems are pastoral elegies. Hongo's poem borrows from the tradition, it steps out of a long shadow and finds its own spot of sunlight near the abandoned cane fields. The American poet personalizes the pastoral elegy and pinpoints it to a beachside grave-yard, a jutting plot of grass and sand. Here, the grieving, and the grievance, start out far away and end close to home.

There is something very American about an itinerary poem that combines driving and walking and adjusts its pace accordingly. Like our culture, the poem is set in the present tense. At the beginning, we are slightly separated from the landscape, which we are speeding through, and its beauty works as a counterpoint to the speaker's unspoken longing and grief, which he holds at bay. The poem is highly cadenced and written in a flexible free verse. The lines accordion in and out, and the rhythm enacts the feeling of transit that drives the poem. The stanzas operate as turning points in the drive, stages in the journey. The syntax mirrors the turns in the road, which mirror the turns in the poet's thought, in his growing awareness and feeling.

"Ancestral Graves, Kahuku" is specifically placed. The driver is pointing out landmarks to his passenger, which also enables the poet to point them out and guide the reader. We begin en route, in medias res, leaving Kamehameha Highway: "Driving off Kam Highway along the North Shore." The speaker points to the sugar mill, which once dominated the landscape, though it's now abandoned, just another workplace gone to seed, overcome by birds who haunt the place, like souls of the dead. The details of this Hawaiian landscape matter to the speaker, the poet. He wants us to notice them, too—they're an integral part of the missed world. Hongo is a phrasemaker and as you read the poem you feel the extra punch of the indented lines. This rhythm has his personal stamp on it, but it's a jazz move he picked up and condensed from our friend Arthur Smith (*Elegy on Independence Day*, 1985), who learned and adapted it from Charles Wright (*The Southern Cross*, 1981), who learned and adapted it from Ezra Pound (*The Pisan Cantos*, 1948).

> Driving off Kam Highway along the North Shore,
> *past the sugar mill,*
> Rusting and silent, a haunt for crows
> *and the quick mongoose,*
> Cattle egrets and papaya trees in the wet fields
> *wheeling on their muddy gears;*

The image of the wet fields seems infected by machinery, the birds overseeing the turns in the highway. This sinuous sentence concludes with a semicolon; the poet and the driver turn at the same time: "We turn left, *makai* towards the sea." The word *makai* is a Hawaiian adverb for "seaward," and that's precisely where the two are headed. This is the second spot on the itinerary. If someday you decide to drive to the Kahuku cemetery by the sea, this poem maps the route for you, a sort of Wordsworthian GPS:

We turn left, *makai* towards the sea,
    and by the old *76,*
Its orange globe a target for wind
    and the rust, and the bleeding light;
Down a chuckholed gravel road
    between state-built retirement homes
And the old village of miscellaneous shotguns
    overgrown with vines, yellow *hau* flowers,
And the lavish hearts and green embroidery of bougainvillaea
    stitching through their rotting screens.

What's striking here is the memory and wastage of a place, and one can't help thinking about all those contract laborers who once lived in plantation housing and shotgun shacks. The poem provides a lavish catalogue of nature's revenge on cheap, now-abandoned housing. I had never seen a *hau* flower or sea hibiscus before, which changes color in the course of a single day. The fact that they are yellow suggests that we're there in the morning because the flowers start turning orange and red in the late afternoon. Garrett told me at the time that the plant is not native to Hawai'i, but was brought over with immigrants from Melanesia, Micronesia, and parts of Polynesia, and thus points to a story of migration. This was a luminous detail that he had picked up from his grandmother.

    The next stanza cleverly reapplies the imagery of golf.

At the golf course, built by Castle & Cooke
    by subscription, 60 some years ago,
We swing past Hole No. 7 and its dying grass
    worn by generations of the poor
And losing out to the traps and dunes
    pushing in from the sea.

Castle & Cooke was one of the Big Five, a group of companies that controlled the sugar industry and ran the economy of the islands, a massive agrobusiness and oligopoly. There's a reference to class and class structure here—the plantation built a golf course by pledge and membership with money gathered from "generations of the poor." The poor had paid to be displaced by entitled golfers. Now, the golf course, too, is a ruin of "traps and dunes."

The last stage of the journey turns us down a dirt road. The third stanza also consists of a single winding sentence that mimics the movement of the car winding down a narrow path. Everything is in a state of decay:

> It's a dirt road, finally,
>> two troughs of packed earth
> And a strip of bermuda all the way
>> to the sandy point
> Where, opposite the homely sentinels
>> of three stripped and abandoned cars
> Giving in to the rain and its brittle decay,
>> a wire fence
> Opens to the hard scrabble of a shallow beach
>> and the collapsing stones
> And the rotting stakes,
>> *o-kaimyō* for the dead,
> Of this plantation-tough
>> cemetery-by-the-sea.

The mode is naturalistic, it looks the way the speaker describes it, but it also describes an emotional state, the speaker's feeling for a place that is tough, lonely, and in a state of collapse. For example, those cars, which have been stripped to their bare bones, are figured as "homely sentinels," three relics standing guard over the ruins. Hongo refers to an "*o-kaimyō*," a posthumous name given to the dead in Japanese Buddhist funerary ceremonies, which introduces a Buddhist leitmotif into the poem, so that this naming seems part of its valedictory work, too.

We've arrived at a plantation-era Japanese graveyard at the north end of the Kahuku Golf Course. There are two other cemeteries in the area: one Catholic (Portuguese and Filipino), the other Chinese. We get out of the car. One person knows the history, the other does not, and this gives the speaker an imperative to guide his visitor, as he has been guided, to recollect the history and tell the story. I had never been in a Japanese cemetery before. The scene is still indelible to me—gutted cars pushed to the side of the road, cattle egrets rising languidly out of the turquoise waves. We've taken off our shoes to walk through the matted grass, "temple moss." Garrett is picking out family names. We're lingering over the graves, paying our respects to a few wooden markers washed clean by rain. I was struck by the way that mourners had once left jars of anthuriums and little plates of food, oranges and rice cakes, cups of saké for their loved ones, who were hungry and thirsty on the other side. At the time when Garrett and I visited, mourners still came here to pay respect and appease the dead.

It's windy and the wind triggers the speaker's recollection of a devastating natural event: "and I remember / to tell you / How the *tsunami* in '46 took out / over half the gravesites." The speaker is trying to keep his composure as he narrates how the *tsunami* wiped out the burial grounds, carrying away more than half the dead, leaving the others unnoticed, unremembered. The cemetery was "harrowed by the sea." The word *harrowed* is carefully chosen. This is agricultural country and there is a sense of the sea breaking up and smoothing the surface of the land. There is a current of distress. The archaic meaning of *harrowed* is plundered and sacked, as in a war, and that seems relevant here because it feels as if the past, too, has been obliterated.

The next stanza divides evenly into two six-line sections. There's a recurrent motif of the speaker reminding himself to include more of the story:

> I remember to say that the land,
>   what's left of it,
> Still belongs to the growers,
>   the same as built the golf course,
> Who own, even in death,
>   those they did in life,
> And that the sea came then
>   through a vicious tenderness
> Like the Buddha's, reaching
>   from his lotus-seat
> And ushering all the lost and incapable
>   from this heaven to its source.

There's a barely suppressed rage in this account of how the growers still own the land—or what remains of it. I love the oxymoronic phrase "vicious tenderness," which suggests that the sea is deliberately cruel and kind at the same time. So, too, the poet compares the action of the ocean with the hand of Buddha, who reaches out and rescues those who are buried, "all the lost and incapable," and carries them home. This is akin to Jesus's Harrowing of Hell, but here it is the Buddha who does it.

The penultimate stanza is a one-sentence unit, and it coils a tremendous surprise:

> I read a few names—
> this one's the priest,
> His fancy stone scripted with ideograms
> carved almost plain by the wind now,
> And this one, Yaeko, my grandfather's sister
> who bedded down one night
> In the canefields and with a Scotsman
> and was beaten to death
> For the crime—
> a hoe handle they say—
> Struck by her own father,
> mythic and unabsolved.

The traveler finds the grave of his great-aunt Yaeko, who suddenly emerges from the generalized melancholy and loss. Hongo tells her story, or part of it—there is an enormous unspoken backdrop and family history—and how she was murdered by her own father. That interjection—"a hoe handle they say"—lets us know that this is a story that has been whispered in the narrator's family for decades, though he is only now bringing it to light. There is fever in the final phrasing, "mythic and unabsolved." The word *mythic* suggests that the story, or shards of it, has taken on outsize status, something with more than personal or even historical significance, something foundational. The father who kills his own daughter out of rage is like a figure from a Greek myth—this is a primal crime, the story of a family devouring itself. The word *unabsolved* also indicates a crime that is not freed from blame, not settled or forgiven. Yaeko is remembered, a victim, and so is her father, a perpetrator, who is not named, but not forgiven, either.

The last stanza, one curving sentence, also makes clear that the other crime is silence, erasure. The speaker either doesn't know or isn't telling whether or not his great-aunt was actually having an escapade or a love affair or was taken by force, raped—in any case, he is not ashamed of her—but what strikes him is something worse than hints and insinuations. As you reread it, you feel the aggressive assertion, the increasing power of the rhetorical argument:

> Our shame *is not* her love,
>   whether idyll or rape
> Behind the green shrouds and whispering tassels
>   of sugar cane,
> *Nor is it* the poor gruel of their daily lives
>   *or* the infrequent
> Pantomime of worship they engaged in
>   odd Saturdays;
> *It is* its effacement, the rough calligraphy
>   on rotting wood
> Worn smooth and illegible,
>   the past
> Like a name whispered in a shallow grave
>   just above tideline
> *That speaks* to us in a quiet woe
>   without forgiveness
> As we move off, back toward our car,
>   the grim constant
> Muttering from the sea
>   a cool sutra in our ears.

This moving finale radiates with sadness, the sense of "quiet woe / without forgiveness." The itinerary has come to resolution, and the poem concludes with the two figures moving back to the car in silence, listening to the wind and water. There's an undercurrent here, an imperceptible dirge coming not just from the sea but also from the past, an inescapable undersong. Hongo hits a final Buddhist note with the sound of "a cool *sutra* in our ears." This reference to Buddhist scripture is more Japanese than Hawaiian, and it points to what has been buried in immigrant culture, what has been practiced in desultory fashion and now is almost entirely gone. It is both prayer and injunction.

Garrett Hongo's lifelong project is an act of reclamation. As you read through his work, both in poetry and prose, you can see him finding his way, claiming his heritage, or trying to, as he invents his own rituals and memorials, talking story, and trying to fill in the shoal of a family story line. "There is a little to tell and few enough to tell it to," he confesses in "Coral Road," which emerges from a family reunion: "All of us having survived that plantation sullenness / And two generations of labor in the sugar fields, / Having shed all memory of travail and the shame of upbringing / In the clapboard shotguns of ancestral poverty." Like Dante, he longs for a guide ("Where is the Virgil who might lead me through the shallow underworld of this history?"), but unlike his great precursor and model poet of exile, he cannot find a single epochal figure ready to hand and so, as an Emersonian American poet, he must invent the route to his work for himself.

I would add, however, that Hongo is an avowed Romantic—I consider him one of our most important practitioners of latter-day Romanticism—and this makes him the kind of American poet determined to make linkages, to create a continuity and tradition for himself. He broods over his familial isolation, the lack of a through line, but he does not revel in it. The idea of family is central, but not comprehensive, and that's one reason friendship is such an integral part of his project; it's crucial to his sensibility and enterprise ("Who else would even listen?"). He expands and extends the family to include the literary archive, the primary models, living and dead, the moral exemplars, those creative figures whom Michael Harper deems *Images of Kin*.

Keeping this in mind, I'd like to return for a moment to "The Wartime Letters of Hideo Kubota," which have not been fully understood or incorporated into the American canon. That's because there is now a certain wariness and misunderstanding about the very nature of the dramatic monologue. What in others might seem like literary performances, in Hongo's hands become pressing letters of address—a mode of sympathy, a way of projecting himself into the heart of what otherwise might seem like remote or historical experience. He takes everything personally. In these poems of the placed person, Hongo situates himself with a community of people—Buddhist ministers, Japanese language instructors, and others—who were forcefully detained and guarded in an abandoned Bureau of Indian Affairs boarding school in Leupp, Arizona, on the Navajo Indian reservation, which served as the Leupp Isolation Center. He takes his grandfather's persona in order to stand with other community leaders, so-called problem inmates, who were often persons of great rectitude and nobility.

It is in this isolated adobe stockade that Kubota begins to reach out to Hongo's poetic exemplars, artistic makers who wrote in times of grave crisis and suffering. It's an emotional delivery system, a creative way to access extreme experience. In the first poem, for example, Kubota writes to Miguel Hernández, who is now "in Heaven," but wrote his heartbreaking poem "Lullaby to an Onion" from a fascist prison cell in Republican Spain. What is especially startling about some of these poems is the way that Kubota fantasizes connection to poets in other parts of the world writing in real time. The letters are entirely intertextual. After he has been released, Kubota writes to Tadeusz Różewicz ("Kubota Returns to the Middle of Life"), who came back from World War II to write "In the Midst of Life," which stripped down and revolutionized Polish poetry (*"This is a man*, you said, *A man's life is important. / It is of the highest importance"*). In one of the most moving poems, he addresses Pablo Neruda, but in the mode of a love poem invented by Randall Jarrell in "A Man Meets a Woman in the Street." In the final poem of the sequence, Kubota returns to Kahuku Point and explains to Charles Olson that he, too, "has had to learn the simplest things last," thus quoting the poem "Maximus, to Himself."

> It is to you, Maximus, I address myself this morning, across oceans
> And the continent, with the sea stretching out from my feet.

What seems significant and representative is the way that in his work as a whole Hongo has carefully imagined another kind of family dispersed across the globe, poets and fiction writers, but also artists of all kinds—jazz saxophonists, fresco painters—all those who try to serve what Wordsworth called "the beauty that was felt."

This cross-cultural lineage deepens and expands Hongo's poetic of friendship and family. It is the emotional outcrop of his personal poems of ancestry. I wish I could guide you through the poems in *Coral Road* that return to the North Shore of Oʻahu, like "Pupukea Shell," a gas station that we drove past on Kam Highway, and "Cane Fire," which takes up "the stories and

photos from nearly a century ago," and "Kawela Studies," which memorial-
izes Hongo's landscape and literary studies and his vow at twenty to become
a poet, and "A Map of Kahuku in Oregon" ("I've been told so many bits and
pieces of story, / They don't add up"), and especially "Elegy, Kahuku," which
returns to the Kahuku Cemetery and tells a fuller story of his mother's clan
and places it in the context of the Japanese migration to Hawai'i. There's a
section of the poem where Hongo returns with his two boys to the cemetery
that we visited so many years ago. There is a photograph of the cemetery
on the cover of the book that captures something of its decaying beauty. He
knows more about the family now, and you can tell that he's adapted a set
of rituals and found a way to pay homage to his ancestors. This moment can
stand as an emblem for the other ritual moments, the reverent prayers, and
breakthroughs into feeling that define his lifelong project:

I've taken my sons there a few times now,
Taught them the bows and genuflections of worship,
The murmurs of a chant, homage to the Other Side
I brought back with me from Shōkoku-ji in Kyoto.
They seem to like it when I bow, clap hands and sing,
And louder sing than the wind, knees plunged in the pokey grasses
    and sands of eternity.

I placed a cup of rice wine and a plate of *pake* cake on the grave,
Strung a wreath of purple orchids on the worn headstone of Yakeo
    Kubota,
My grandfather's sister, the last time we were there.

                                        I chanted the Heart Sutra,
"Form is emptiness, Emptiness is Form," my sons holding their breaths,
Their postures of reverence like egrets posing in silver ponds near the sea.

JOY HARJO (1951–)

Rabbit Is Up to Tricks

In a world long before this one, there was enough for everyone,
Until somebody got out of line.
We heard it was Rabbit, fooling around with clay and the wind.
Everybody was tired of his tricks and no one would play with him;
He was lonely in this world.
So Rabbit thought to make a person.
And when he blew into the mouth of that crude figure to see
What would happen,
The clay man stood up.
Rabbit showed the clay man how to steal a chicken.
The clay man obeyed.
Then Rabbit showed him how to steal corn.
The clay man obeyed.
Then he showed him how to steal someone else's wife.
The clay man obeyed.
Rabbit felt important and powerful.
The clay man felt important and powerful.
And once that clay man started he could not stop.
Once he took that chicken he wanted all the chickens.
And once he took that corn he wanted all the corn.
And once he took that wife, he wanted all the wives.
He was insatiable.
Then he had a taste of gold and he wanted all the gold.
Then it was land and anything else he saw.
His wanting only made him want more.
Soon it was countries, and then it was trade.
The wanting infected the earth.
We lost track of the purpose and reason for life.

We began to forget our songs. We forgot our stories.
We could no longer see or hear our ancestors,
Or talk with each other across the kitchen table.
Forests were being mowed down all over the world.
And Rabbit had no place to play.
Rabbit's trick had backfired.
Rabbit tried to call the clay man back,
But when the clay man wouldn't listen
Rabbit realized he'd made a clay man with no ears.

2008

"THERE ARE also poems of grief for a people," she said, gently but firmly, and of course she was right—she had spent much of her life figuring out how to write them, and how to play them, too, as a jazz saxophonist, connecting her own story with the story of her Native nation, the Muscogee (Creek) tribe, which she characterized as "a stolen people in a stolen land" ("Autobiography"). I was visiting her poetry seminar at the University of Tennessee, and we were talking about the long history of lamentation in poetry, its oral roots and written branches, its elegiac rituals and ceremonies of mourning. It's not easy to find a written or singing language for grief, which can be disabling—raw, wild, inarticulate—and it takes a certain wiliness, a craft and angle of approach. Every poet needs to find a language, which serves as a lamp and a machete, to fight through the dark bramble. Harjo's strategy has been to tell stories in verse, sometimes highly compressed, sometimes long and winding, which ritually invoke and link her to roots and sources. She seeks continuity between what she calls her "past and future ancestors." Somewhat hopefully, she views each poem as a ceremonial object, which has the potential to make change.

The folklorist Henry Glassie said that "tradition is the creation of the future out of the past," an idea gleaned from Indigenous thinking. This ethno-poetic notion particularly applies to Harjo's work, which is filled with creation and re-creation stories, horse songs, deer dances and earth spirits, reimagined ceremonies. She calls the written text a "fixed orality," a somewhat wistful notion, which situates her work in relationship to verbal art and oral tradition—a tribal history, a mythical way of thinking. Now and then she brings the figure of Rabbit into play. Rabbit is the trickster figure of the Muscogee Nation and stories about him migrated with them from the Southeast when they were forcibly displaced to the south-central region of the country. This history isn't an abstraction. Harjo's work is everywhere shadowed by sorrow over the violent Removal and the Trail of Tears.

Harjo was born in Tulsa, Oklahoma, and tells stories about her grandmother Naomi Harjo, a painter who played saxophone in Indian Territory at the turn of the twentieth century, before Oklahoma was a state, and her ancestor Monahwee (Menawa), one of the principal leaders of the Red Stick War, the largest Indian uprising in history. He was allowed to visit his home in Okfuskee, near what is now Dadeville, Alabama, for only a single night before being forced into exile. No wonder he said, "for when I cross the great river, my desire is to never again see the face of a white man." Harjo's work is a trail of such storied memories. She is an activist American poet who writes in English, which she cleverly labels a "trade language," and recognizes that in some sense it is also what she calls "the enemy's language." This language therefore needs reconsideration, even reinvention.

Harjo's project has been to find resourceful ways of reminding us that there is ground under our feet, that we are part of the land, and the land is part of us. This land was in the keeping of people before us, her people, who were dislocated and destroyed, who have somehow survived with a story and a culture—in fact, a weave of cultures, hundreds of Native nations. Americans don't like to remember the horrifying truth that one people's manifest destiny was another's genocide. But the Native American poet cannot forget. Individually, poet by poet, but also collectively, tribe by tribe, poetry becomes a creative response to a devastating historical assault. Hence the title of Harjo's newly imagined, collectively edited anthology of Native nations poetry, *When the Light of the World Was Subdued, Our Songs Came Through* (2020). These poems comprise a dreaming path and song field.

As an emerging poet, Harjo didn't start out with a full arsenal of ancestral tales and Creek lore, but had to recover this material over time, to make it a personal idiom. She entered her past through the work of older contemporaries, who served as models and exemplars. I hear echoes of Native nations poets, such as N. Scott Momaday (Kiowa), Simon Ortiz (Acoma), and Leslie Marmon Silko (Laguna) in her early work, but also white ones, such as Meridel Le Sueur, Richard Hugo, and Adrienne Rich, as well as African

Americans, such as Ishmael Reed, June Jordan, and especially Audre Lorde, whose poems, she said, were like maps guiding her. So, too, she looked to poets from other countries whose written work had an Indigenous orality, such as Kofi Awoonor, who was Ghanaian, of the Ewe people, and Okot p'Bitek, who was Ugandan and whose masterpiece, *Song of Lawino* (1966), was written in Acholi, a tonal Luo language.

Harjo fused her literary influences to find an idiomatic of hopefulness and grief, something not just shaded by her own past but also inflected by tribal thinking. She turned her attention to a deeper homeland and this is where traditional stories figure in. Harjo has called up Rabbit in the way that Ortiz and Silko have summoned the figure of Coyote: a trickster who survives everything. She uses Rabbit to tell an unruly story and change the framework of a North American historical narrative, weaving an ancient character into a modern tapestry.

Rabbit is spiritually related to his outlandish cousin, Coyote, who roams around other Native nations, especially in the North American Plains, and goes where he will, even crossing over between life and death without trouble. Readers of Gary Snyder recognize how often he has recurred to the figure of old Coyote Man, an archetypal antihero and protector spirit, a preliterate source who goes back tens of thousands of years. As polymorphous human figures, Rabbit and Coyote can be baffling creatures, sometimes funny, sometimes fearsome, two rascals who walk the edges of the world and remind us that anything can happen at any time. As a folkloric type, this trickster appears in the guise of Raven in the Indigenous mythology of the Pacific northwest coast. He appears as the Great Hare in Algonquin mythology, and his name, Michabou, derives from the word for "Great Rabbit." Master Rabbit, as he is sometimes called, is cunning, disorderly, and agile, someone who uses his cleverness to outmaneuver anyone and everything. Sometimes he wins the day, other times he outwits himself. But always he returns, a god of guile and surprise.

As a consummate trickster, Rabbit appears in both Native American and African American traditions. There have been ill-tempered scholarly debates, complete with indexes of tale-types and transcriptions of oral sources, about the true origins of these stories. I don't underestimate the stakes for different fields of study, but it seems likely that the swap went both ways. The stories of Rabbit, or Chufi in the Muscogee language, go back thousands of years in the southeastern tribes (Cherokee, Alabama, Yuchi, Creek), possibly all the way to the Paleolithic, and some of these stories were assimilated by African Americans. At the same time, there are a significant number of folktales about Rabbit in West African folklore, which also stretch back thousands of years, and these versions became part of the storytelling inheritance of enslaved African Americas. Joel Chandler Harris notoriously bowdlerized this material in *Uncle Remus* (1881), which focuses on the antics of Br'er Rabbit ("Brother Rabbit").

The agonizing story of African American slavery is well documented, but there is a lesser-known history of slavery in the tribal territories—some tribes took war captives and held them as slaves, other Native peoples were captured and sold into slavery. Inevitably, folk stories also crossed between peoples and cultures. There is a body of explicitly African–Native American texts, such as "When Brer Rabbit Meets Coyote." "Here we are," John Horse, who was African Seminole, liked to say in the 1850s, "all living as in one house." Rabbit seems especially interesting as a trickster figure who syncretizes Native American and African American traditions.

Harjo embraces this expansive notion of the Creolization, rather than the purity, of culture. "In the rhythms of stomp dance," she says, "are the rhythms of blues and jazz, and of the land." The overlap between musical traditions self-consciously shadows her creation-story poem "Rabbit Invents the Saxophone," where she imagines the trickster climbing up to the stage at Congo Square in New Orleans. In *An American Sunrise* (2019), she follows this story of the ragged trickster with an untitled prose poem that crosscuts the turbulence of Creek history with Adolphe Sax's 1846 invention of the saxophone. "The saxophone is so human," she writes. "All that love we humans carry makes a sweet, deep sound and we fly a little."

Harjo's wrote "Rabbit Is Up to Tricks" in 2004 after George W. Bush had been reelected president—her dismay is evident. Four years later, she turned it into a song that she performed and published on her album, *Winding Through the Milky Way* (2008); the next year she used the poem to open her one-woman play *Wings of Night Sky, Wings of Morning Light*. The poem was subsequently printed in her book, *Conflict Resolution for Holy Beings* (2015), but I first came across it as an untitled poem rendered in italics in her memoir, *Crazy Brave* (2012), where she connects it to her birth and introduces it this way:

In some story realms the baby is born and the next day he or she is a giant who kills monsters. Mine was not that kind of story. I am born of brave people and we were in need of warriors. My father and I had lost the way. I was born puny and female and Indian in lands that were stolen. Many of the people were forgetting the songs and stories. Yet others hid out and carried the fire of the songs and stories so we could continue the culture.

This personal history suggests why the story of Rabbit might have become an integral part of her practice. She needed to find a way to turn herself from someone who had lost her way and forgotten the old tales into someone who remembered and passed them on in rejuvenated form. She recurs to legendary and mythological stories to locate and buoy herself, to reframe and recast her familial story in larger cultural terms. Storytelling becomes a ritual to help overcome a defeated history.

"Rabbit Is Up to Tricks" consists of one extended stanza, a single narrative unit. The lines are end-stopped. In some poems, the language races ahead of the thought—it communicatse before it is understood—but here the language is denotative and self-contained; it serves a clear storytelling purpose. The title puns on *tricks* and *trickster* and points to Rabbit's mischievous behavior. It suggests that he's up to his "old tricks" without exactly saying so. In fact, his usual sort of scheme will get away from him this time, since he is creating something that he can't contain or control.

The poem is a parable—a succinct, didactic story in verse—but it's not agitprop or poetic propaganda. In his introduction to the anthology *The Poet's Tongue* (1935), W. H. Auden redefines parabolic art by suggesting that "poetry is not concerned with telling people what to do, but with extending our knowledge of good and evil, perhaps making the necessity for action more urgent and its nature more clear, but only leading us to the point where it is possible for us to make a rational and moral choice." The era of the 1930s is relevant to the contemporary moment because it was also a time when poetry came under formidable pressure to respond to social injustice. Here, Harjo does this by inventing her own tale about Rabbit, a figure both old and new—familiar to many, foreign to others.

Harjo's poetic strategy is deceptive. She is something of a trickster herself and begins the poem in a formulaic way, like an old-time storyteller: "In a

world long before this one, there was enough for everyone." This points to
a sacred or timeless ancestral realm when people of Native nations lived in
fulfillment and harmony with their environment. But the collective story is
immediately unsettled and troubled in the second line. The language takes
a sharp turn toward the colloquial and the contemporary: "In a world long
before this one, there was enough for everyone, / *Until somebody got out of
line.*" The speaker situates herself as part of a group who heard some local
whispers: "We heard it was Rabbit, fooling around with clay and the wind."
This is a traditional pose, the modest storyteller who is not a spiritual spe-
cialist but a gossip, who reports in an idiom that shuttles between the con-
versational ("Everybody was tired of his tricks and no one would play with
him") and the legendary or mythological ("He was lonely in this world").
This last line especially resonates with me because my grandfather used to tell
us that God created the world because He was lonely and needed company.
It wasn't until I was much older that I discovered that it was unusual to think
of God as a poor lost soul.

Harjo's lyric reformulates a Muscogee creation myth of a sky god or earth-
diver who formed human beings out of the muddy ground. The story orig-
inates with a horticultural people:

So Rabbit thought to make a person.
And when he blew into the mouth of the crude figure to see
What would happen,
The clay man stood up.

The cosmology here is widespread. In Inca mythology, for example, the
supreme god Viracocha created human beings from clay on his second
attempt to form a living creature. The first one seems to have failed. Harjo
also knows and parodies Genesis 2:7: "And the Lord God formed man of the
dust of the ground, and breathed into his nostrils the breath of life; and man
became a living soul." There is a parallel with the traditional Jewish story of
the golem, who was created by the legendary rabbi Judah Loew of Prague
from clay or mud and magically breathed into life. But once the statue is
created it can't be restrained and becomes a monster. Mary Shelley's story of
Frankenstein comes to mind.

What localizes and distinguishes the story of Rabbit, however, is that he is both a god and a rogue. The poem establishes a simple call-and-response pattern as Rabbit teaches his obedient pupil some of his tricks for getting by. It's a lesson plan for minor criminals:

> Rabbit showed the clay man how to steal a chicken.
> The clay man obeyed.
> Then Rabbit showed him how to steal corn.
> The clay man obeyed.
> Then he showed him how to steal someone else's wife.
> The clay man obeyed.

At this point, the poem structurally turns, and the language becomes distanced and bureaucratic:

> Rabbit felt important and powerful.
> The clay man felt important and powerful.

Harjo's poem operates by the rhetorical principle of parallelism, a foundational strategy of modern free verse, but also one of the constitutive devices of oral and archaic poetries. Whitman's cataloguing method is one of Harjo's enduring models, but here the language isn't particularly lyrical and the semantic parallelism, a process of synthesis and accumulation, is so seamlessly employed that it nearly goes unnoticed:

> *And once* that clay man started he could not stop.
> *Once he took that chicken he wanted all the chickens.*
> *And once he took that corn he wanted all the corn.*
> *And once he took that wife, he wanted all the wives.*
> He was insatiable.

Harjo proceeds by pressing and enlarging the story. At first, Rabbit seems to be up to his usual funny, no-good tricks, but the trickster has created a creature he can't continue to manipulate and rein in. The Rabbit story no longer mimics a tale that you might tell children for their entertainment. It's a story for adults now, something with grave and devastating implications, a tale about primitive capitalistic greed and global imperialism. First, he wanted this, then he wanted that. It could be summarized this way: *And then he wanted.* Some form of the word *want* is repeated four times, twice as a verb, twice as a noun:

> Then he had a taste of gold and he *wanted* all the gold.
> Then it was land and anything else he saw.
> His *wanting* only made him *want* more.
> Soon it was countries, and then it was trade.
> The *wanting* infected the earth.

Harjo is using a traditional figure to simplify, condense, and convey in parabolic terms an overarching historical narrative. She doesn't want us to lose sight of the fact that U.S. global ambition, the insatiability of the clay man, affected her personally, which is presumably why she includes this poem in her memoir. She applies the next lines to her father and herself, her own family, her people:

> We lost track of the purpose and reason for life.
> We began to forget our songs. We forgot our stories.
> We could no longer see or hear our ancestors,
> Or talk with each other across the kitchen table.

These four lines are the emotional center of the poem. Here, Harjo deftly conveys what it means for a family to lose track of itself, to lose purpose and meaning. One feels a heavy shadow of addiction and loss. Harjo's familial history of disconnection and disinheritance also merges with an overarching tribal narrative. In her discouragement, she needed a lifeline and suggests that survival depended on those who "carried the fire of the songs and stories so we could continue the culture."

But that culture is up against a massive global force: "Forests were being mowed down all over the world. / And Rabbit had no place to play." Here, she takes the story of Rabbit's tricks and condenses it into the greatest failed trick of all, the creation of a man formed out of clay. That inhuman man seems to be a universal figure, but he also has a North American provenance. This does not refer to Adam in the Garden of Eden, but to the American Adam, who created what Leo Marx dubbed *The Machine in the Garden*

(1964) to refer to the industrialization of America, the capitalistic intrusion of technology on the natural world. It also began a history of imperialistic expansion and global reach, and thus became a story about the arrogance of the United States. Poor Rabbit, a character on the margins, a representative figure and symbol of tribal culture, had made a fateful error, one with far-reaching consequences, impossible to repair:

> Rabbit's trick had backfired.
> Rabbit tried to call the clay man back,
> But when the clay man wouldn't listen
> Rabbit realized he'd made a clay man with no ears.

After you've read or heard this story even one time, you never forget the mutilated American figure, the embodiment of our dominant culture, "a clay man with no ears."

Joy Harjo is a poet of displacement and relocation, of reckoning and con-sequence. It takes a lifetime, perhaps it even takes many different lifetimes, to make a single life's work in poetry. American literature is a complex tapes-try—we are all part of a web—and the oral texts and written scripts of Native nations are interwoven into its fabric. Our literary tradition faces in two directions, past and future. Poetry gives us an effective means of communi-cation, a way of connecting to each other through an embodied language and spirit. As a Muscogee poet, Harjo repeatedly reminds us that poetry is something to be passed on between people. Sometimes it is embodied in song and takes the shape of a story-poem, an unlikely parable for our times, our history. There are also poems of grief for a people, and they speak to us when we put on ears and listen.

ACKNOWLEDGMENTS & PERMISSIONS

THIS IS a book that I've been preparing to write for much of my life, and I'm grateful to Library of America for proposing it to coincide with its fortieth anniversary. That's a cause for celebration, and I'm glad to contribute to the American literary ideal. Special thanks to my friend Max Rudin, president and publisher, for the incitement. And warm gratitude to my editor, John Kulka, who scrupulously improved each one of these essays. Unbeknownst to me, John enlisted my friend and former colleague David Mikics to read the manuscript, and I'm grateful to both of them for their keen suggestions and close reading. I feel lucky to have Liz Darhansoff as my friend and agent. And special thanks as always to my dear friend André Bernard for his scrupulous editing of the manuscript. Each one of my prose books has benefited from his sharp blue pencil.

I was fortunate during the quarantine to be living with my great love, Lauren Watel, who encouraged my absorption in this book, and queried me about each one of the pieces. She is a superb, bracing, and astute reader. I took long walks every day and spoke on the phone to my sister, Arlene Hirsch, who is a keen listener and fine psychologist. I especially enjoyed her probing queries and quizzes.

Garrett Hongo was writing an extraordinary book about audio and music, *The Perfect Sound: A Memoir in Stereo*, at the same time that I was writing this book about poetry, and I've never had a more heartening experience trading pieces of writing back and forth. He emboldened me to write an intensely personal book about American poetry, to stake my claim, not to defer, and to write the book that I was destined to write. His encouragement and impress have sustained me throughout.

Special thanks for help with individual pieces to Alice Quinn and Dean Rogers (Elizabeth Bishop), T. R. Hummer and Ry Cooder (Robert Johnson), William Rukeyser (Muriel Rukeyser), Elizabeth Scanlon (Muriel Rukeyser, Julia de Burgos, Gwendolyn Brooks), Paula Deitz and Ron Koury (Anthony

Hecht), Meghan O'Rourke (John Ashbery), Kate Daniels (James Wright), Olena Kalytiak Davis (Sylvia Plath, Louise Glück), Wendy Lesser (Louise Glück), Boris Dralyuk (Michael S. Harper), Gerald Maa and Caroline Jean Bartunek (Garrett Hongo).

Warm gratitude to the editors of the publications where some of these essays first appeared, sometimes in different form:

The American Poetry Review: "An Appreciation of Gwendolyn Brooks," "An Appreciation of Muriel Rukeyser, 'St. Roach,'" and "An Appreciation of Julia de Burgos, 'Farewell in Welfare Island.'"

The Georgia Review: "Sacred Returns: Garrett Hongo's 'Ancestral Graves, Kahuku.'"

The Hudson Review: "Anthony Hecht, 'More Light! More Light!'"

Literary Imagination: "Poetic Transmission: Ezra Pound, 'The River-Merchant's Wife: a Letter' (1914–1918)—By Rihaku [Li Bai]."

Los Angeles Review of Books: "A Love Supreme: On Michael S. Harper's 'Dear John, Dear Coltrane.'"

Michigan Quarterly Review: "Theodore Roethke, 'Cuttings' and 'Cuttings (*later*)' (1948)," "On Robert Hayden's 'Middle Passage,'" and "On Philip Levine's 'To Cipriano, in the Wind.'"

The Threepenny Review: "On Louise Glück."

The Yale Review: "The Brink of Destruction: Revisiting John Ashbery's 'Soonest Mended.'"

This is an entirely new book, and all of these are original essays. Everything has been reconsidered, but I have written about some of these poets and poems before, and there is some drift and overlap with other earlier pieces.

Walt Whitman, "Out of the Cradle Endlessly Rocking": I consider the duende of this poem in the short chapter "Demon or Bird!" in my book *The Demon and the Angel* (2002).

William Carlos Williams, "Spring and All," Marianne Moore, "The Steeple-Jack," and Hart Crane, "To Brooklyn Bridge": Part of my consideration of the overall projects of Williams, Moore, and Crane is adapted from my essay "Helmet of

Fire: American Poetry in the 1920s" in a book edited by Jack Myers and David Wojahn, *A Profile of Twentieth-Century American Poetry* (1991).

Theodore Roethke, "Contact: Theodore Roethke's 'Cuttings' and 'Cuttings (*later*)' (1948)." Some of my consideration of Roethke's lifelong project is adapted from my introduction to his *Selected Poems* (2005).

Elizabeth Bishop, "In the Waiting Room": I first wrote about "In the Waiting Room" in a chapter on epiphanies in *How to Read a Poem and Fall in Love with Poetry* (1999).

Sterling A. Brown, "Southern Road": My review-essay about Brown's *Collected Poems*, "'Been Down So Long . . . ,'" appeared in *Obsidian* (Spring 1981). I also wrote about "Southern Road" in a section on work songs in *How to Read a Poem and Fall in Love with Poetry* (1999).

Robert Hayden, "Middle Passage": I first wrote about Robert Hayden's work in "Mean to Be Free," a review of his *Collected Poems* (*The Nation*, 1985).

Julia de Burgos, "Farewell in Welfare Island": I first wrote about Julia de Burgos for a column in *The Washington Post Book World*, which was reprinted in my book *Poet's Choice* (2006). I also wrote about her poem "To Julia de Burgos" in *100 Poems to Break Your Heart* (2021).

Anthony Hecht, "'More Light! More Light!'": I first wrote about Hecht's book *The Hard Hours* in the essay "Comedy and Hardship" in a collection edited by Sydney Lea, *The Burdens of Formality: Essays on the Poetry of Anthony Hecht* (1989). I wrote about his poem "The Book of Yolek" in *100 Poems to Break Your Heart* and carry over some of my thoughts about his treatment of the Holocaust in poetry.

Philip Levine, "To Cipriano, in the Wind": I am importing some of my thoughts about Philip Levine's larger body of work from my essay "The Visionary Poetics of Philip Levine and Charles Wright" in a book edited by Jay Parini, *The Columbia History of American Poetry* (1993).

Adrienne Rich, "XIII. (Dedications)" [from "An Atlas of the Difficult World"]: I also treat this poem in detail in *100 Poems to Break Your Heart*.

Permissions

Emily Dickinson, #479 ["Because I could not stop for Death"], *The Poems of Emily Dickinson: Reading Edition*, edited by Ralph W. Franklin, Cambridge, Mass.: The Belknap Press of Harvard University Press, Copyright © 1998, 1999 by the President and Fellows of Harvard College. Copyright © 1951, 1955 by the President and Fellows of Harvard College. Copyright © renewed 1979, 1983 by the President and Fellows of Harvard College. Copyright © 1914, 1918, 1919, 1924, 1929, 1930, 1932, 1935, 1937, 1942 by Martha Dickinson Bianchi. Copyright © 1952, 1957, 1958, 1963, 1965 by Mary L. Hampson. Reprinted by permission.

Robert Frost, "The Most of It," *The Poetry of Robert Frost*, edited by Edward Connery Lathem. Copyright © 1969 by Henry Holt and Company. Copyright © 1936 by Robert Frost, copyright © 1964 by Lesley Frost Ballantine. Reprinted by permission of Henry Holt and Company. All rights reserved.

Marianne Moore, "The Steeple-Jack," *The Collected Poems of Marianne Moore* by Marianne Moore. Copyright © 1935 by Marianne Moore, renewed 1963 by T. S. Eliot. Used with the permission of Scribner, a division of Simon & Schuster, Inc., and David M. Moore, Administrator of the Literary Estate of Marianne Moore. All rights reserved.

Hart Crane, "To Brooklyn Bridge," *The Complete Poems of Hart Crane* by Hart Crane, edited by Marc Simon. Copyright 1933, 1958, 1966 by Liveright Publishing Corporation. Copyright © 1986 by Marc Simon. Used by permission of Liveright Publishing Corporation.

Langston Hughes, "Harlem," *The Collected Poems of Langston Hughes* by Langston Hughes, edited by Arnold Rampersad with David Roessel, Associate Editor. Copyright © 1994 by the Estate of Langston Hughes. Used by permission of Alfred A. Knopf, an imprint of the Knopf Doubleday Publishing Group, a division of Penguin Random House LLC and of Harold Ober Associates. All rights reserved.

Sterling A. Brown, "Southern Road," *The Collected Poems of Sterling A. Brown*. Copyright © 1980 by Sterling A. Brown. Reprinted by permission of Jacqueline M. Combs.

Theodore Roethke, "Cuttings" and "Cuttings (*later*)," *Collected Poems* by Theodore Roethke. Copyright © 1948 by Theodore Roethke; copyright © 1966 and renewed 1994 by Beatrice Lushington. Used by permission of Doubleday, an imprint of the Knopf Doubleday Publishing Group, a division of Penguin Random House LLC. All rights reserved.